ORION'S LEGACY

ORION'S LEGACY

A CULTURAL HISTORY OF MAN AS HUNTER

CHARLES BERGMAN

A DUTTON BOOK

Again and always,
To Ian and Eric

DUTTON
Published by the Penguin Group
Penguin Books USA Inc., 375 Hudson Street, New York, New York 10014, U.S.A.
Penguin Books Ltd, 27 Wrights Lane, London W8 5TZ, England
Penguin Books Australia Ltd, Ringwood, Victoria, Australia
Penguin Books Canada Ltd, 10 Alcorn Avenue, Toronto, Ontario, Canada M4V 3B2
Penguin Books (N.Z.) Ltd, 182–190 Wairau Road, Auckland 10, New Zealand

Penguin Books Ltd, Registered Offices:
Harmondsworth, Middlesex, England

First published by Dutton, an imprint of Dutton Signet,
a division of Penguin Books USA Inc.
Distributed in Canada by McClelland & Stewart Inc.

First Printing, July, 1996
10   9   8   7   6   5   4   3   2   1

 REGISTERED TRADEMARK—MARCA REGISTRADA

LIBRARY OF CONGRESS CATALOGING-IN-PUBLICATION DATA:

Bergman, Charles.
    Orion's legacy : a cultural history of man as hunter / Charles Bergman.
        p.   cm.
    "A Dutton book."
    Includes bibliographical references (p.   ) and index.
    ISBN 0-525-93851-6 (acid-free paper)
    1 Masculinity (Psychology)   2. Men—Psychology.   3. Man—Animal nature.   4. Hunting—
History.   5. Hunting and gathering societies.   I. Title.
BF692.5.B47   1996   95-26502
155.3'32—dc20   CIP

Printed in the United States of America
Set in Times New Roman
Designed by Jesse Cohen

This book is printed on acid-free paper.

ACKNOWLEDGMENTS

For their help in conceiving, discussing, and reading the book in its various stages, I want to thank Sam Mitnick, Tim Schaffer, Marlene Blessing, Erin McKenna, Joan Barnowe, Lynne McGuire, Barbara Temple-Thurston, Susan Brown Carlton, and David Seal. For their superb help in the library, I want to thank Laura Lewis, Amy Reynolds, Susan MacDonald, Patty Koessler, and Sharon Chase. My special gratitude goes to Paul Menzel, Provost at Pacific Lutheran University, for all his support, both professional and personal. I want to express my deepest thanks to all the people in so many parts of the world who made the research of this book possible. Special thanks go to my agent, Beth Vesel, and my editor, Rosemary Ahern, for their ideas and their faith in this project. For their insight and depth, as well as their steady emotional support through all that writing a book entails, I want to thank the men on Tuesdays. And finally, thanks for everything to Carol Wright.

CONTENTS

1. Men on Ice   1

2. A Hunger Deeper Than Memory   28

3. The Hunter in Mind   67

4. The Metaphors of Male Desire   99

5. The Gentles Are at Their Game   132

6. The Shot and Danger of Desire   173

7. "That Master Creation . . . Independent Manhood"   204

8. The Long Hunt   242

9. That Stranger Man   289

Notes   319

Index   345

Questo mondo è una caccia, e cacciatrice la morte vincitrice.
(The whole world is a hunt, and death is the triumphant hunter.)
—V. Belli, *Madrigali*, Venice, 1599

1

MEN ON ICE

This is my song: a powerful song.
Unaija-unaija.
Since autumn I have lain here,
helpless and ill,
as if I were my own child. . . .

Do you know yourself?
How little of yourself you understand!
Stretched out feebly on my bench,
my only strength is memories.
Unaija-unaija.

Game! Big game,
chasing ahead of me!
Allow me to re-live that!
Let me forget my frailty,
by calling up the past!
Unaija-unaija.

I bring to mind that great white one,
the polar bear,
approaching with raised hind-quarters,
his nose in the snow—
convinced, as he rushed at me,
that of the two of us,
he was the only male. . . .
He thought he was the only male around!
But I too was a man!
Unaija-unaija.

—Orpingalik, "My Breath"[1]

All night long, whales are swimming through my sleep. I actually hear them, the soft exhalation from their breathing, as I wake frequently out of vivid dreams.

My tent is pitched directly over the sea. I am lying on ice over the sea, next to the floe edge, a fertile zone in Arctic waters where ice meets sea.

Behind my tent, a staggering sweep of white sea ice extends for about twenty miles and ends abruptly at a precipitous shoreline of mountains rising right out of the sea—rocky and barren and streaked with melting snow. The sense of vast distance and stark purity beggars vision. A swag of cirrus clouds slinks across the face of the mountains. Their snowy peaks rise above the clouds, and seem to float in the air, as if they're pale apparitions, levitating above the ice.

The steep shoreline off the extreme northwest corner of Baffin Island plunges into the depthless waters and strong currents of Baffin Bay, over which I'm camping with Inuit hunters. I'm lying on the sheeted ice above about three hundred fathoms of Arctic water.

It's spring in the high Arctic. I'm only a few hundred miles from the North Pole. The sun is shining inexorably, twenty-four hours a day. It doesn't set, it circles. The brightness is inescapable. Even at night, the sun shines through the flimsy fabric of my tent as if it were a very thin haze of cloud. I'm sleeping under a glowing dome of polyurethane clouds. The light is so pervasive, it seems to have invaded my skull. It keeps me awake in an eerie, lucid, sleepy way. I don't sleep. I drift back and forth through the night between sleep and waking, floating lightly on the ice beneath me in a vaguely hypnotic state. I float on my dreams, too, as if they're whales surfacing and diving. I hear the ice creaking at night. Camped near the floe edge, I hear the slosh of waves against the ice, and occasionally, through the night, I hear drifting pans of ice collide in the current. They thud and scrape, emitting infinitely slow, infinitely expressive moans in the night, like the great animals crying. Lying on my sleeping bag, directly on the ice, I rise and fall with the sea beneath me.

And I listen to the whales—narwhals. With their magical, improbable, miraculous tusks, narwhals are hanging about the floe edge through the night. Swimming under me. Rising beside me. I hear their gasps as they surface, blowing air. I rise and fall on the ice, listening to whales breathing through the brilliant night.

I have just arrived with Lamechi (pronounced "Lóm-e-key") Kadloo, a young man who grew up here, in the village of Pond Inlet. He's come to hunt narwhal with his relatives in this hunting camp on the floe edge. As the sea ice breaks up in spring, the narwhals of the high eastern Arctic return to the floe edge from their still-unknown wintering waters. The floe edge is a rich biological zone, and the narwhals fatten up here on cod and mollusks, before following the breaking ice into the deep-water fjords that cut into Baffin Island, where they calve and mate in the summer. Every spring, the Inuits, as these Eskimos call themselves, come to hunt the narwhal, one of the delicacies in their diet, in a traditional native subsistence hunt that may go back to when their Thule ancestors first arrived in the region, about one thousand years ago.

I'm here to begin a study of hunting, but feel like I'm moving amid heady and strangely lucid mysteries. And apart from the sense that here, on the floe edge, I'm in a place where life and land are intimately connected, I have an experience that first morning, when I wake, that defines for me the shape of my intentions, the scope of this study.

When I step from my tent in the morning, narwhals are surfacing just off the edge of the floe ice. I can't tell from the light what time it is, since it falls so steadily, so constantly. It feels almost timeless. So I check my watch. It's 9:05 A.M.

Lamechi is standing beside the ice edge with his uncle, Willy, and his two cousins, Elijah and Tony. Under thirty years old, Lamechi wears a teal green jacket with hot pink highlights, dark reflective aviator sunglasses that flash magenta in the low sun, and a black baseball cap with a golden Batman logo on it. He grew up in the Arctic, but he's traveled widely in Canada, the United States, and Europe. He has one of the warmest personalities I've ever encountered, relaxed and friendly and so attractive people are literally drawn to him. I am. A slow smile widens across his tanned face, and he points down the edge of the ice, about twenty-five yards. The soft sun makes the glittering, jagged edge of the floe look like a lemon ice.

There, less than five feet from the edge of the ice, three narwhals are swimming lazily. They blow a cloud of wet whale breath into the morning air, through which the sun shines, making the vaporous air glow as if the whales were breathing diamonds and crystals.

These whales are why the hunters are here.

Lamechi savors the scene, and then says softly to me, "Shall we go hunt now, while there is still light?"

It's a joke he repeats frequently, and I enjoy it every time he says it. For light is one thing we're in absolutely no danger of losing. I look at Lamechi. His long black hair hangs straight over his ears, flattened by his cap. His smile, and his joke, are irresistible. I smile back, and for a moment we grin at each other.

Willy, his uncle, doesn't bother with words or smiles. He's the quintessential hunter. Already he's swung into action. With his thin body, sharp features, and incisive gestures, he reminds me of a bird, a falcon. He's wearing a knit cap with earflaps that hang down, untied, and contribute vaguely to the general effect, a bit like wings. Willy drops to one knee, props his left elbow on his left knee, and aims his rifle. Elijah and Tony grab their rifles, too, and aim standing up.

Lamechi and I watch.

The hunters don't fire. The narwhals are floating low in the water, and the hunters wait, hoping for a better shot.

The narwhals are resting between dives. They have dark skin, full of swirls up close, rosettes. These are young whales. Narwhals typically get whiter with age. From our angle, they seem only dark shapes skulking in the water, more like oil-stained logs than fantastic, legendary creatures. They float indolently in the sea, about fifteen feet long, and from our angle, their unicornlike tusks are not visible. They are hidden under water. They drift, spin, and circle. The flat forehead of one of them comes into view, big, blunt, encephalic. The waves wash their sides, rippling from each of the whales in concentric rings of reflected sunlight. The whales, meanwhile, don't so much swim as languish beside the ice, broad-backed and brooding.

Then one of the whales begins that incomparable cetacean motion, arguably the most beautiful motion in all of nature—the dive. It's more physical and sensuous and evocative even than the orbiting of the stars and planets. Its back arches and lifts. Its body slips forward through the water, which sheets off its dark skin, darkly gleaming. The knuckling backbone (narwhals have no dorsal fin) rotates into the dive, and its tail flukes barely lift from the sea, smaller and more dainty than I expect for a whale. Inexpressibly smooth and slick, it's a motion instinct with animal grace and animal desire.

The first narwhal vanishes. The two others begin similar moves.

A shot. Then two others. Then several more. The reports of the rifle are dull thuds ringing in the frozen air, hollow smoky sounds that seem to hang around the rifles.

One of the whales seems to explode, itself. I'm not sure if it's wounded or just startled by the gun shots and bullets, some of which I can see ricochet off the water.

The whale no longer dives, but disappears in a thrash and splash of panic. There's a spray of water, and single droplets sparkle in the backlight of the sun. A tantalizing glimpse of the long romantic ivory tusk, vaguely like the lance of a medieval knight. A convulsion of head and tail, twisting upward and out of the water. Light on the belly. A fleeting, fleeing glimpse, and the whale is gone.

All the whales are gone.

In the crack of the rifle shots, my project opens before me. It isn't really the hunt, or hunting itself, that I'm here to study. It's not even the animals, as attractive and beautiful as they are. It's the hunter himself that I'm interested in. And in this study, I'm interested in the wild animals he chases as images through which he's defined himself as a man. Customarily, hunting is viewed as a natural activity that has shaped men and cultures. Without abandoning this notion, I want to reverse the perspective. What happens, what can we learn, if we view hunting as a cultural activity that takes place in nature? How can the hunt, how can inquiring of the hunter, lead us into the hearts and minds of men?

In this book, I follow real men as they hunt in the field, and watch as they invent the male landscape. I examine the vast literature of and about hunting, and ask how hunting has come to be one of the chief defining images of manhood and masculinity. And I ask, What is the relation between the two, the hunter in the field and the hunter in our heads? Between the hunter and the man? What can—and can't—the hunter tell us about men, and who they imagine themselves to be?

I am sexing the hunter. For the hunter has become a personification of Man—in his sense of self, his sense of desire, and his self-delusions.

The poem by the Eskimo Orpingalik, "My Breath," which I've placed at the beginning of this chapter, was collected in the early years of this century by the Danish explorer Knud Rasmussen, from the people of the high eastern Arctic. Rasmussen calls these poems "Songs of the Snow-Hut." This hunter says in a note that his powerful song is as important to him as breath itself. The song is almost a form of breathing. In it he states beautifully, movingly, the twin poles of my interest in hunting and manhood. What is the relation between self-knowledge in the male and self-creation in the hunter? How does the hunter give the male a way of knowing, a kind of knowledge—the knowledge that, as Orpingalik says, "I too was a man"? And what is the relationship of this knowing to self-understanding: What is the relationship in the male between doing and being, act and thought, outer and inner man?

Between the action of the hunt and the song of the hut?

The hunter brings us to the margins of nature and culture, and he is the figure who has taught us, for better or worse, how to move back and forth between them. Historically, it is the hunter who takes men, in his desire, to those psychic places where we encounter the creatures that begin to define us.

Where the whales swim through our sleep, and into our dreams.

Suddenly, Willy, too, has exploded. He's sprinting across the ice, to where the narwhals just were. To where they've vanished. The rest of us are still frozen in place, for the briefest of instants. Willy is the hunter among us, the most passionate hunter. He lives for the hunt. You could say he lives in the hunt, because that's when he seems most alive, most galvanized. In his instantaneous charge down the ice to chase after the submerging whales, he is most completely a hunter. We don't know if any of the narwhals are hit. Perhaps the bullets glanced off the water and missed. Or maybe, at least one of the whales is wounded. We have to wait, watching the sea for the whales to resurface, before we can know if the hunt is to be a success.

2

In that brief moment, while Willy is racing across the ice, I remain standing in my Sorels. I don't move. I feel frozen in place, a man on ice.

Many men now feel somehow on ice, waiting for a thaw. In middle-class American culture, the standard modes of being male are being challenged, and have been for almost the entire century. But in the last twenty or thirty years, as feminists have pointed more and more sharply at the role of gender in our lives—gender as a socially conditioned feature of our identities—men have grown more visibly defensive and confused. There is the sense that masculinity is being redefined. But men often have the sense that they are not controlling the terms. Even the defiance of some men, and the aggressive assertion of certain traditional notions of masculinity, belie an underlying anxiety about being "manned" and "unmanned."

The men's movement is the visible manifestation of male anxiety about manhood. For the entire summer of 1991, Robert Bly's book, *Iron John: A Book About Men*, written for the white middle-aged American male, topped the *New York Times* best-seller list. For all his prestige and prerogative, his power and his possessions, the white male seems a bit lost, a bit hapless, and if the truth be told, a bit hopeless—not exactly Dagwood Bumstead, but Homer Simpson or Al Bundy. The prizes of the patriarchy seem either to have passed him by, or he feels hollow inside, out of touch, his energies sapped by compromise and adaptation.

Many Americans, men and women, are turning to other, non-European cultures for wisdom and guidance. For men, that move has long been tied up with a return to an imagined primitivism. Jack London's tales are of men turning to predatory beasts, or of a domesticated dog named Buck returning to his predatory heritage as a leader of the pack, a wolf. Edgar Rice Burroughs gave us the image of Tarzan amid the apes, and suggested that men are, in truth, the disinherited kings of the jungle. Many men continue to long for that mythical birthright. We have a notion of the original man, a caveman, a jungle man, a man on the savannas. The original man, the real man.

The hunter.

In our century, the discoveries of anthropologists and archaeologists came together with the speculations of poets and philosophers to produce this image of the male as hunter. In this view, cultures like those of Arctic hunters and Australian bushmen are relics of our original lives as men close to nature, and reveal the early stages of our evolution.[2] In this view, man is the gender which, in his genes and his bones and his blood, was shaped by hunting. Literally, physically, biologically. Hunting is wrapped in the swirls of our DNA, and woven in the adaptations of culture. It is a natural and evolutionary pressure, the most important in all of humanity's evolutionary adaptations. José Ortega y Gasset is the great Spanish philosopher of this century, and he's also an avid hunter. He produced the most important piece of philosophy on hunting since Plato and Aristotle. He writes that hunting is a vacation from the "troublesome present," and through hunting men discover for themselves the natural man hidden beneath the harried businessman.

Ortega y Gasset, who will be quoted several times in the following chapters, writes that the hunt is a fact of nature, "the most obvious thing in the world—namely, that hunting is not an exclusively human occupation, but occurs through almost the entire zoological scale. Only a definition of hunting which is based on the complete extension of this immense fact, and covering equally the beast's predatory zeal and any good hunter's almost mystical agitation, will get to the root of this surprising phenomenon."

The hunter is the man who took us from nature into culture, and now he is the man who leads us back to nature. Or, in Laurens Van Der Post's lovely phrase, the hunter takes us back to our origins, "the first things."[3]

I come to the Arctic with these notions in mind. As a young boy growing up outside of Seattle, I often played Tarzan in the woods, literally swinging in the trees. More profoundly, I was deeply moved just before conceiving this study by the paintings on the walls of the cave of Lascaux, in France——an experience which distilled for me a deep engagement with the romantic notions of our early revolution and "primitive" origins. I knew I had to return, and did return to the caves of France and Spain, to take stock of the hunter in prehistory, and his relation to our own notions of manhood, and of prehistory as an undergird for the privileged place the hunter occupies in our minds and cultures.

And I've come to this spot in the high Arctic to begin. Without denying the integrity of the lives of hunters, I want to explore how the hunter came to such importance for us. His status in our imaginations predates the sciences of prehistory—in such figures, for example, as the prince as hunter or the English squire chasing hounds and foxes. The hunter's appearance has changed radically over the centuries. But by locating the hunter in prehistory, or in the "primitive," we've moved him outside of history. He transcends us, in some ways, as a pattern by which we are measured.

What if we locate this hunter, as a male, in history? The prehistoric hunter was nearly apotheosized, and became synonymous with certain notions of manhood, on almost no good evidence. He has been almost completely discredited now and discarded as a fruitful model of research into our origins, though the Paleolithic predator is still the subject of some scholarly debate. But in the popular imagination, the caveman with his first spear remains king.

Man, we like to think, is the erect predator. (The pun suggests how intertwined identity and sexuality are in men's thinking about hunting.)

The most powerful hunter does not live in the green forests of the Congo, with Tarzan. He does not live on the savannas of Africa, chasing big game. He does not live along the American frontier, or on the Arctic ice. The most powerful hunter is the one inside our heads, fixed as part of the male psyche.

I do not intend to suggest that hunting has not exerted a tangible, concrete, and physical influence in men's lives. The hunter is an incontrovertible fact, as every animal that has ever been shot learned. I simply want to see what the hunter in our heads has to say for himself. The idea of hunter is undeniably one of our great intellectual inheritances, one of our most influential emotional figures. I want to see what would happen if I were to view hunting, not as a fact of nature, but as a cultural phenomenon that takes place in nature. I want to treat the hunter as a metaphor that men have created, and then view that metaphor from the point of view of gender.

It's customary for men to imagine that they were created by hunting. I want to see what happens if we view hunting as something created by men. What if hunting is viewed, not as a male occupation, but a male preoccupation? Not as something men do, but something men enact? If the hunter, in his many and various historical incarnations, is one of the great myths of men's history, what do we learn about men from this great shaping fantasy?

To get an idea of what I mean by the way our lives and identities are shaped by the metaphors of hunters, and the way that language informs our consciousness, almost invisibly, consider the following list of phrases taken from our daily lives. These words are the tracks of the hunter. Even those who have never hunted have their days shot through—excuse the pun—with the hunt. It fills our newspapers and magazines and TV, permeating our lives and shaping our world. Here's a list of hunting language in our speech that illustrates the pervasive nature of the hunt:

> a buck (applied to men, as in young bucks)—a buck (a dollar, short for buckskin, unit of trade with American Indians on the frontier)—pass the buck (short for pass the buckhorn knife, another frontiersman metaphor)—

job hunt—witch hunt—fortune hunter—Nazi hunter—bounty hunter—
bargain hunter—headhunter (as in executive job placement, but also in a
baseball pitcher who aims at batters' heads)—manhunt—hunt club—
Easter egg hunt—back in the hunt—open season—closed season—fair
game—sure as shooting—shooting from the hip—straight shooter—long
shot—cheap shot—loaded for bear—bull's-eye—*bête noir*—square
shooter—cut to the chase—thrill of the chase—beat the bushes—beat
around the bush—lie low—take a stand—make a killing—move in for the
kill—kill or be killed—in the bag—bag a big one—dead meat—the heart
is a lonely hunter—hot on the trail—pick up the scent—track down—nose
out—hue and cry—full cry—run with the pack—leader of the pack—tryst
(a stand for medieval hunters)—play cat and mouse—gunning for—give
chase—chivvy (as in give chase)—whoop it up—catch as catch can—dog
you down—dogged—hounded (as by bill collectors)—on the wing
(when something is flushed)—winged (wounded)—flushed—roused (and
"aroused")—gamy—to be game—bait—vestige (meaning a "track" that's
left behind)—investigate (to track down)—go for the jugular—and,
finally, killer instinct.

This list might be extended, depending on how far we wished to pursue
the traces of the hunt in our language. You may also have noticed that I
left off many of the most interesting of our colloquialisms of the hunt—
the sexual hunt.

on the prowl (looking to pick someone up)—prick (long hunting associations here)—poaching (as in stealing someone's boy/girlfriend)—hit on
someone (especially a chick)—stag party—good catch (as in a husband)—
fall into my trap—my "love gun"—set my sights on you—poon hound—
go on the game (an English colloquialism, said of prostitution)—to snare.

If I included all the ways in which, in sexual matters, men refer to women
as prey animals, we could generate a whole erotic bestiary: bunnies, hares,
chicks, beaver, foxes, pussies. All these are prey for the libidinal hunter to
chase, harry, harass, and hound. Of course, they can also be bitches.

I think, though, that the way in which we can see the hunt enter our
imaginations in a way unique to late-twentieth-century America, and one
of the real reasons to try to understand the role of hunting in our lives, is
that we now speak of sexual predators and predatory criminals. Twenty
years ago, if a man bothered a woman, we might speak of him "hassling"
her. Now, we would speak of "harassment," with its hunting origins in a

dog which "harries," and hints at the deeply ingrained predatory notions we have of male sexuality.

Man the hunter. Woman the hunted.

When I speak of metaphor, I am not speaking of decorative language or "flowery speech." Metaphor is the simple process by which one thing—a man, say—is compared to another—a hunter. We don't have to get into the types of metaphor to recognize that this is a very important process, not merely of speech, but of thinking. Through comparison, people make sense of the unknown, comparing it to what they know. And by giving to such an abstract concept as "manhood" both face and feature, they make it more intelligible. In Shakespeare's language, metaphor is how we give to "airy nothing a local habitation and a name."[4]

Because it addresses and helps us understand the unknown, metaphor is a way of knowing. It actually produces knowledge—it gives us the point of view and the framework for understanding what we don't otherwise yet know. This is the Aristotelian view of metaphor. It gives us names for things—for ourselves, for others, for the mysterious world. So one of the important functions of metaphor is to provide us with the terms for both identity and relationship. A more postmodern way of putting this is that language is crucial to our thinking, and it is within language that we understand ourselves and our world. As the linguist Benjamin Whorf puts it, through the words we give to things, we build "the house of consciousness."[5]

Among the many things a man might call himself—plumber, lover, criminal, king, fool—he has chosen the "hunter." That is not to say that all men hunt, but that, regardless whether a man hunts or not, he is more or less a hunter in the way he thinks. And imagines himself.

As an activity in nature, the hunt might be thought of as a materialized metaphor. And as a metaphor in culture, the hunt is a psychological activity.

We are likely to imagine the hunter as a man in an orange vest and a baseball cap with the logo of his favorite NFL team on it. But what of those other hunters in history? The English country squire of the eighteenth century? Or Robin Hood, in the twelfth century? Or that other figure, the enamored god, chasing nymphs through the forests in his hunting tunic and his hunting sandals?

For the hunter is not simply a fellow with a pickup and a gun rack. The hunter is a mode of being in the world, or rather, he offers a number of ways of being to men.

If the hunt suggests that men follow a prewritten script of manliness, this study also has a powerful optimistic side. We can be the author of our language, hard as that often is, and we can be then the author of ourselves.

We can begin to rethink the metaphors that shape us. We are so surrounded by the hunt metaphor, so accustomed to it, so inclined to see the hunter as the human link between nature and culture, that the metaphor seems literal and even invisible to us.

If it is true that we come to consciousness in language, that our minds are shaped by the words and phrases we use, then it's fair to say that we are steeped in hunting. From Elvis's hound dog which "ain't never caught a rabbit" to Madonna's latest fabrication of herself as a "bitch" goddess in spiked leather collars, not so much an object as a target of men's lust, the hunt informs popular notions of erotic life. And from our first uniquely American national hero in literature, Leatherstocking, to the male anxieties of big-game hunters like Hemingway; from Daniel Boone to the thoughtful sense of southern white manhood at a crossroads in Faulkner; from the pursuit of the whale in Melville's great American novel, *Moby Dick*, to the crisis in masculinity as defined in hunter-authors like T. Roosevelt—the hunt is part of our historical identity.

America is a hunt culture.

The connections between the hunter, nature, and culture surround us in a kind of seamless, magic circle. I want to interrupt that circle, however, and see what we can learn about ourselves. The value of visiting another culture, like that of the Inuit hunters on the ice floe, is that, in its different values, it gives a new purchase from which to view our own hunting from the "outside." The outsider has the advantage of different perspectives.

It's that seamless circle of the hunt that ruptured just a little with the rifle shots at the narwhal. It's that sense of the inevitability of the hunter that I want to suspend, and see what we learn about men if manliness steps out from behind the costumes of the hunter.

3

"Do you think Willy sees the whale?" I ask Lamechi.

Lamechi is looking intently out to sea, watching Willy. We're standing on the very edge of the ice floe. Willy's in a small boat with Elijah and Tony, far off the floe edge and heading straight out to sea. Lamechi says nothing for a long time. Then he turns his head to me. His wraparound sunglasses flash magenta in the sunlight.

"Oh yes, oh yes." He smiles, repeating another of his favorite phrases slowly, savoring the moment. "Perhaps he may see the whale."

We've been standing on this ice all day now. We've been watching for the narwhal that Willy shot at earlier in the morning.

When Willy came racing back to us after the whales dived, he was absolutely convinced he'd wounded one of them. At exactly 9:35 A.M., after the three whales dove in a panic to escape the hunters, Willy shoved his small whale-hunting boat off the edge of the ice floe, into the sea, and clambered aboard. Elijah and Tony joined him. Together, they moved out among the drifting ice pans to watch for the whale to resurface. If he found it again, Willy would try to approach close enough in the boat to throw a harpoon at it. This is how contemporary Inuits hunt for narwhals: wound the whale with a rifle from the ice floe, and harpoon it by hand from a boat.

Willy's last name is Enoogoo. He has a patience and persistence as a hunter that distinguishes him even from his relatives. All day, I've watched him work the ice edge for that whale. I've watched him guide the boat as it moves among the large pieces of drifting ice—called pans—that have jammed up just off the ice edge. Occasionally, he and the others would land on one of the pans, pull the boat out, and stand up on the ice for a better view of the sea. It's a powerful image—Willy on a drifting piece of ice, the boat beside him, watching the blank and open sea.

In that image, he seems so small against the infinite sweep and scope of the ocean, so fragile standing on floating ice above this clear and depthless sea.

Then, apparently, he would spot a whale surfacing. Silently, he would get back into the boat with his relatives, and move farther out to sea. From where I'm standing, it's a slow and pantomimed game of Arctic tag.

Watching this, I feel suddenly and momentarily foregrounded, aware that I'm here on the edge, and Willy's out there hunting. I don't really know what's going on, but I'm trying to watch and understand. It's like listening to a foreign language that you only partially know, recognizing some words, but not sure you really get what's being said. I feel I'm peeking in on a narrative as it's being written. Nature is a text, and I'm suddenly aware of myself as a reader of this silent scene. And like all readers, I'm trying to understand its messages. What does it say? And where do I intersect with what these men are doing? What is its message for me? For *us*?

All through the day, I've been keeping a vigil for the narwhal. At 12:30, I think I glimpse one. Willy is heading toward it. The boat with the hunters moves toward the resting whale. It's quite small and gray on the water, but it must be the same whale. I can see the bullet wound, just behind the head, where Lamechi tells me they aim. There's a small hole from which has oozed a rosette of creamy-colored blubber, conspicuous against the whale's dark skin, like a macabre corsage. Long before Willy can get close enough to heave his harpoon, the whale dives again, and vanishes.

We watch through the afternoon, growing increasingly pessimistic, but enjoying the afternoon nonetheless. It's very difficult to keep watch, to keep focused, in the unremitting Arctic sun. Between the glare of the light and the slow motion of the ice pans as they drift past in the steady current, it's hard not to drift away into a sort of dreamy and pellucid reverie.

The warming sun carries the promise of impending summer, melting the ice floe right beneath our feet. I can actually see and hear summer coming as the ice melts. On the very edge of the floe, I can hear the ice melt. Through the afternoon, I can hear drops of water splashing into the sea. The ice we are standing on is melting away under our feet. This huge sheet of floe ice is melting, one drop at a time.

And the surface of the ice is turning to puddled blue ice-water all around us. The ice is softening. We sink into it in an eerie way. With the force of the current and the heat of the sun, occasionally chunks of ice break away from the edge and enter the drift of the sea. New pans are being spawned around us, and we have to retreat from the edge as it breaks around us.

I follow Lamechi's lead, since it's clearly dangerous on the edge of the ice. The two biggest dangers are falling off the ice into the sea and being stranded on a pan as it breaks from the edge. At one point, as we move back from the edge to take up a new position, I step through the soft ice and take a heart-racing plunge into the ice. My right foot sinks all the way up to my thigh. I almost choke on a momentary rush of fear. Lamechi laughs sympathetically.

"Our elders tell us a fact," he says to me as I pull myself out of my hole. "Our elders tell us that ice melts faster than it forms."

At 4:30 P.M., Willy seems to give up. He brings the boat back to the ice edge, pulls it all the way out of the water, and heads without a word back to the tents, where he begins to fix himself a meal. The hunt is over.

And then, just as suddenly and just as silently as he had returned to the ice, Willy sets down his plate, signals to Elijah and Tony, and walks back to the ice edge. He meets the two younger hunters next to the little boat. They jump in. Willy shoves off and leaps agilely from the ice into the boat. They chug once again out into the sea, which has grown calm and windless and glassy smooth. It's 5:09 P.M. when Willy climbs back into the boat to resume the hunt.

Pushing a small boat off the ice edge into that big cold sea seems extraordinarily brave to me. To be shoving off to chase a whale in that boat seems even braver. The boat is very small for three grown men—small enough to fit on a sled to be pulled out here, only about twelve feet. The boat's made of plastic, too, and its garish shade of industrial, postmodern green clashes absurdly with the delicate hues of Arctic blue and pale, turquoise-tinted white of ice and sky and sea. The contrast in colors intensifies the disproportion in scale between boat and sea, culture and nature. Everything makes the men seem diminutive and insignificant. As the men chug out to sea, getting smaller and smaller, I'm aware of how cold and how deep these Arctic waters are.

Soon, Willy, Elijah, and Tony are tiny silhouettes in their boat against the distant horizon, which reaches in a long reach and sweep of empty sea to Ellesmere Island, and not that far beyond, the North Pole.

And I turn to Lamechi once more. He too is watching Willy intently, silently now. And I ask again, "Do you think Willy has seen the same whale?"

This time, Lamechi grins. "Oh yes," he replies, "oh yes. Perhaps."

And before realizing what I'm saying, I almost blurt out, "But how?"

If Willy has seen that whale again, it's an amazing feat of vision and observation. He just keeps heading steadily farther out to sea, shrinking as we watch. Soon he's at least a mile off the ice edge. The whale he's chasing is less than fifteen feet in length, and floats low in the water, and is a very long way away. Plus, it's swimming in a sea that's dazzling with reflected sun, hard to look at steadily, blinding in its brightness. And there are also countless chunks of floating ice that both hide and impersonate a whale, like decoys for whale watchers.

Lamechi smiles broadly at me, like someone who knows something but isn't telling.

We just have to watch to see what's going to happen. The hunters are far out and heading farther. For all its starkness, there is an abundance of space and time on the floe edge. And an abundance, too, of life.

It's a gathering place for millions of seabirds. Common murres and kittiwakes nest on the huge cliffs of Bylot Island, a national reserve of Canada, just to the west offshore, and thousands of them fly and swim along the ice. Guillemots, looking like a cross between a pigeon and a penguin, all black and white, fish the waters. King eiders, with their spectacularly colorful green and black and orange plumage, beat their way past us, flying low in the air. And most impressive, the most beautiful seagulls in the world, ivory gulls, are common out here. They are exquisitely elegant and graceful birds, especially for those obstreperous and bullying birds, the gulls. Ivory gulls are almost dainty by comparison—their plumage is a deep, soft, almost waxen white, their bodies are small, their feet and beaks are black. Frequently they hover over my head, their wings outspread, and the blue sky filters through their translucent wings, and the blue ocean reflects off their snowy breasts, aquamarine birds.

If the Arctic is a barren place, it's a fecund barrenness.

I squint into the sunlight. The whole scene is blindingly beautiful.

Willy and Elijah and Tony keep plowing straight out. If Willy's seen the whale, it's at least two or three miles off the edge of the ice.

Even through my binoculars I can't see a narwhal. But they must be chasing one. Willy is standing in the bow of the boat, one leg on the gunwale, with a harpoon hoisted in his right hand.

"Oh yes," Lamechi says beside me. "Oh yes, they have seen the narwhal again."

"Do you think it's the same one Willy wounded this morning?" I ask.

"Oh yes. Willy can see the whale even at this distance on the water." Lamechi says this gently, reading my thoughts.

"But how?"

"It's because what you look for is not the whale," Lamechi says while I'm still looking for the whale.

"What you look for," Lamechi continues, "are the reflections of the light off the back of the whale. The light shines differently off the whale's back than it does off water. That's how Willy sees the whale."

Willy spotted the whale at two to three miles away, using his naked eyes.

I'm used to looking for wildlife. I love spotting animals, and I'm pretty good at it. And I know something of what Lamechi means about not looking for the animal itself. Looking for wildlife in the woods, for example, I'm only partly looking for an animal. What I really watch for is movement. It's become almost a reflex for me. Most bird-watchers understand this. So I understand that looking, seeing, is not quite what it seems.

But Willy's feat drives a powerful lesson home. These men have a particularly refined sensitivity, it seems, to the subtleties of light in a world of light, its shades and shimmers. They seem to me extraordinarily sensitive to their world in a way I suddenly envy. They are like photographic film, only not passive, as that implies, but receptive and open. Their sensitivity strikes me as a kind of knowledge and a way of being in the world. It is as if they are somehow shaped and shaded by the light.

In most Western hunting, the hunt is a kind of reckoning with the beast. If it seems poetic, it is nevertheless true, that in their hunt for the narwhal, these hunters discover something else: not the animal itself, but the light that shines from the body of the beast.

I recognize the blunt-headed whale, right in front of Willy's funny green boat, just as he's about to fling the harpoon. It is a mere glimmer on the horizon, a dark speck in the water. He heaves the harpoon. The whale dives. A brilliant fluorescent orange float flies out of the skiff and bobs across the water, with the boat chugging behind in pursuit.

But all this seems anticlimactic to me. The true climax of this narwhal hunt is not the contest at sea, as it would be in a Western story. It wasn't even the rifle shot in the morning, dramatic as that was. The true climax had gone unseen. It was when Willy sighted the whale, two to three miles off the ice, with his naked eyes. The climax of this hunt throws into highlight, if you will, the very different way in which men imagine hunting, and themselves as heroic hunters, in the West.

4

As in most cultures that hunt, hunting in the United States is overwhelmingly but not exclusively associated with men. It is largely a male activity, and a male language. It is an activity that, associated with the male gender, becomes in turn a mark or sign of maleness. It is gendered, and it engenders in men certain ways of being.

In the United States, men are much more likely to hunt than women. In its most recent national survey, the United States Fish and Wildlife Service calculates that there are some 14,063,000 people who hunted in 1991. It's a number that has been steadily declining over the last few years, down from 17.4 million in 1980. Of all hunters, only 3 percent were female; about 407,000 of all hunters were women.[6]

Man has named himself the hunter. I speak in gendered terms when I say "man." Men aren't born hunters. It's a name they give themselves. It's an identity they assume.

That's not to say that women don't hunt or that women don't figure importantly in the myths and history of hunting. One of the greatest of all the gods and goddesses in the Greek and Roman pantheon is the female huntress—Artemis in Greece, and Diana in Rome. Some Renaissance women were passionately devoted to the hunt, like Mary Queen of Scots, Queen Elizabeth I, and Diane de Poitiers. And in our own time, hunting among women seems to be on the increase—Jane Fonda has, apparently, taken up the sport.

When women hunt, they throw into high relief the male nature of hunting—whether as sport, recreation, or subsistence. When women hunt, they are inevitably making a powerful statement about gender.

In the Euro-American tradition, hunting is different from Inuits chasing a narwhal. There is a motif of male sensitivity in Western hunting, but the hunt's primary emphasis and justification has almost nothing to do with sensitivity. It's grounded in theories and anxieties about power.

Ancient and modern, power is built into the central definitions of the hunt. In examining hunting as subsistence activity, sport, and recreation, I will use the definitions of hunting of Ortega y Gasset and Plato and Aristotle. Despite their great differences as philosophers, they share similar definitions of hunting, and they advocate hunting for its values in promoting power and "virility" in men. They all view hunting as an "art of acquisition," in Aristotle's phrase. Plato says the hunt is the pursuit and capture of game, regardless what is done with the game after captured. Ortega y Gasset defines hunting as the attempt *"to take possession, dead or alive, of some other being that belongs to a species basically inferior to* [*the hunter's*] *own"* (italics in original).[7]

The philosophers' definitions may make the hunt look static. It is really dynamic, a contest for power—a physical or intellectual or even emotional contest in which power is negotiated. As in the photograph of a hunter with his gun and trophy, the hunt may seem to be merely the exhibition of power. But it is more, really, than the affirmation of power. In its most artful and subtle embodiments, the resolution of the power is actually in doubt through the unfolding narrative. The suspense in the outcome gives the hunt its psychological interest. In either chase or contest, pursuit or possession, we're not entirely sure until the very end who's the hunter and who's the hunted.

Hunting gives a story of how men (and sometimes women) acquire power. The "inferior species" that Ortega y Gasset talks about can be another kind of animal, a fantastic creature, another and lesser nation or kind of human, or the other sex. As Plato says, there is the hunting of animals, and there is, as we know, the "hunting of man." This is how hunting and war became so linked, so early, in men's minds. Aristotle connects hunting and warfare together as *political* ideas, because both are "arts of acquisition," properly employed against both animals and "such of mankind . . . designed for subjection. . . ."[8]

The hunter and the soldier share a twin birth in classical manhood.

This explains how hunting can be so broad in its metaphorical scope—always implicit in it for the West seems to be this infrahuman hunting of "inferior" humans. The ability to hunt them seems to *make* them inferior, and confirm their inferiority.

Hunting is not merely the exhibition of power, or the affirmation of power—one creature over another, or one "species" over another—whatever the notion of species might be. It is the creation of power and superiority. And out of that, an identity for the hunter and the hunted, both.

This is how hunting becomes a model for understanding "inferior" peoples, other races, and even women. Man the hunter is also manhunter.

This double action of hunting—internally, in making identity, and externally, in making relationships—I explore in the following chapters. Two crucial points here: one, hunting has metaphorical implications built into it from its earliest definitions; two, in the Western imagination, the hunt gives us a model for the acquisition of male identity through conflict with another, "an other," that's by definition inferior.

What's significant about this, to me, is how deeply ingrained in our cultural memories and personal imaginations this hunt is.

Consider the prototype of all hunters in the West, the bright and nimble hero of the winter sky, Orion. He's our original and perpetual hunter.

Like most people, I love the constellation of Orion, the most brilliant and beautiful constellation in the winter sky. He rolls up over the horizon, one knee raised, his sword carried on a slanted belt of white stars. In his left hand, he lifts a hero's lion skin, and in his right hand, he wields a threatening club. His body is defined by some of the most brilliant supergiant stars in the heavens—the reddish Betelgeuse and the blue-white, icy-looking winter star, Rigel.

He's one of the most familiar and easily recognized constellations, the hunter circling our heads. Orion is named for the first great hero of the Greeks, later largely displaced, but apotheosized in the heavens for his magnificence. He's still the pattern of the hero, and the patron of modern hunters.

The progenitor of a hunt culture. His has been a long career through the heavens.

The first heroes, the ones who mark the transition to history, are giants who eat flesh. Orion was a giant, and as he now strides through the skies, he once was able to stride across the seas and land. He made the land tremble. He was nocturnal in his depredations, and he despoiled whole islands of their wildlife, to make them safe for castles and kings. He was exquisitely beautiful, and while women and goddesses both loved him, he could not control his appetite.

He boasted he was the greatest hunter in the world. He challenged Apollo, the far shooter, to a contest with arrows at a porpoise at sea. And he was the consort of Artemis, the goddess of the hunt. She seems to have loved him. They hunted together through the island of Delos.

But he had a flaw in his character. He was the hero of excess, verbal and otherwise. With Artemis, the stories are confused, but he seems to have turned rapist.

He flies through the sky because Artemis either killed him herself, or had the goddess of the earth, Gaea, and her helpers kill him. And then he was given heroic honors and placed in the sky.

His appetite was carnal in both senses, for meat and for women.

Even in the heavens, where he seems so remote and pure, he chases Taurus, the constellation just ahead of him, with his uplifted club. But here, too, in the heavens, his appetite is ambiguous. For just inside Taurus's shoulder are the Pleiades sisters, whom the predatory Orion also seems to pursue.

This is Orion's legacy—the beauty of the superhero hunter, and the violence of his appetite, a carnal appetite.

The brutal nature of this bright celestial hunter contrasts vividly with the Inuit hunters.

The confrontation with the beast is a basic form of self-definition in the West. After Orion, the history of men is a pageantry of wild beasts. From Odysseus with the boar to Perseus and the Gorgon, from François I and his stags to Saint George with his dragon, the careers of men follow the creatures they pursue, and the confrontation with the beast sets the terms of their identity. Our history is a pursuit of the beast.

It is the career, not of men per se, but of the set of stories and myths associated with the male as hunter, that I trace in this book. In this way, it is not hunting as something that some men do that I am pursuing. I'm interested in how the hunter has become a pattern that all men, in some way, have to come to terms with. It is the myths of the hunter as underlying patterns for men that I'm describing.

By myth, I do not mean the popular notion of myth as a sort of "lie."

By myth, I mean the really important stories that a people or culture elevates to central importance. These stories gain wide currency, and last over time. Their value is not that they tell lies, but that they are fictions that define a culture's emotional and psychological truths. These stories become important because they coalesce important features of a people's historical and personal experience.

These stories typically identify the main features of a culture's historical experience, simplify that experience, clarify it and reflect it back to the people, and then are useful in teaching people how to understand experience. Out of this distilled reflection of its own experience, in centrally important stories, a people learns to make sense of itself and develop scenarios for action.

It is the job of every person to invent a plot for his or her life. Myth gives us stories and plots in which we can fit our own experience. We can't live our lives without some sense of meaning, and story is the most basic way we have of satisfying this deep need for emotional meaning in our lives. Story locates us in our own lives, and in the world. Story provides scenes and images that capture for us those two most crucial aspects of our emotional lives: identity and relationship.

The myth of the hunter, for example, links individual identity to a national history. More broadly, one of his primary cultural jobs is to show us how we move from nature to culture, from prehistory to history, and from history to destiny.

Plus, the narrative of the hunter is a journey that gives us one of our main structures for desire—the chase, the encounter, the passionate contest in the wilderness, the physical climax.

It's important to say, also, that as a group of stories, hunting defines a broad symbolic field. Stories and versions of myths can often contradict each other, or offer various permutations on the main theme. What's important, though, is that the stories all are working on the same issue—they define a central emotional issue for a culture, and provide ways of resolving issues that can't be resolved by logic and rationality.

Perhaps no story is more crucial than the hunter's in telling us who we are. Our reason for the importance of hunting stories in men's self-definition may well be that hunting extracts identity from the psychological interplay of desire and power. And now, as hunting becomes increasingly doubtful as a story for men, as old stories of manhood no longer suffice and satisfy, we are looking for new narratives that might give rise to new myths.[9]

What I suggest is that manhood may have less to do with testosterone than it does with names. Family names and family traditions. The myths of the hunter don't suggest that manly heroism is forever and immutable, though the hunter has a seemingly ageless tenacity. Why has this vision of manliness held on so long, and worn so many different outfits—a Greek tunic, hunter green, frontier buckskin, blaze orange and red flannel, Eddie Bauer Gore-Tex?

Orion is a pedigree, and his tradition is a male genealogy. He sets the terms within which men think who they are. It is a way of thinking. The hunter is more than a role model. He's more than a sportsman or a "game guy." He provides the thing we all desire more than anything else, and find most necessary in heart and gut. He's the image of our deepest longing—he gives an identity.

But he doesn't come without a price. The hunter is both the genius and the demon of masculinity. He gave men the fields of manhood—the landscapes of masculinity.

Like Orion, the hunter is a constellation of ideas, feelings, and attitudes. Even now, he's caught in a perpetual chase in the heavens, right behind Taurus and the Pleiades. They're just out of reach, bull and sisters, and he's locked in a chase he can't complete, desire unfulfilled. Orion is a pattern in the sky, and he remains one of the most important constellations by which we orient ourselves to the night, and to the entire universe. He continues to circle our heads, sending down old messages to us.

Under the phosphorescent glow of the beautiful stars of Orion the hunter, to what extent have we been named under a misappellation?

5

It's really a tooth, a tooth that's migrated from its mouth to its forehead. It looks like a horn, but it's really a tooth. *Monodon monoceros*—the narwhal. One-toothed, one-horned: that's what its Latin name means. It's got two names for the same thing, as if by repetition we might believe it better—twice a unicorn.

The truth of the narwhal's long, twisting tusk is as unlikely and magical to me as the legends it's connected with. I've always been drawn to the idea of a narwhal because it seems such a creature of fantasy. That's one of the big reasons that I've come to the floe edge with Lamechi and his relatives. I've imagined narwhals for so long.

And now Willy is chugging iceward with a narwhal strapped to his boat. Strapped to the belly of his boat. Though I'm watching him through binoculars, I can't actually see the whale anymore, once he has successfully captured it. For a short while, I wonder where it's gone, and then realize what's going on. I can see the small rounded flukes of the whale just above the leaded blue of the seawater. They're wrapped on either side of the crease of the bow, like a reversed mermaid. The body of the whale hangs under the boat, head and horn submerged and facing backward.

With the weight of the whale, the boat and its men look even tinier, more fragile. They're coming back with about two or three inches of freeboard to the boat. They look about ready to sink.

Once back to the ice, we all pitch in, and it's really quite exhilarating. The whale floats just off the ice, in transparently cold Arctic water, attached to its orange float. We put a long Inuit sled made of wood—a *kamutik*—off the edge and lever it under the whale. I walk out on the sled and grab the narwhal by its tusk while the others tie ropes around its body, and we haul it onto the *kamutik* and out of the sea.

Willy then drags the whale behind his snowmobile, still on the *kamutik*, away from the edge of the ice, behind the tents. There, rolled onto the ice, the whale lies fat and rubbery looking, its creamy belly a bit squished under its own weight, a dark deflated animal, like a large pneumatic tire with the air leaking out.

It's a she, and she's a small narwhal, three and a half meters long, about eleven feet. It's unusual for a female to have a tusk. I'm immediately impressed by her dark skin, blotched and mottled. More than that, it's her eyes and flippers and little rounded fins that surprise me. They're all so small, so incongruous for a fat whale. They give her a daintiness. I watch her eyes, sunken in her thick head, cloud over in a blue film.

We get the whale onto the ice at 6:50 in the evening. We first sighted this same whale at 9:05 in the morning.

Elijah begins the job of butchering the narwhal. As the shooter, Willy gets the tusk of ivory, which he will probably sell to an ivory carver. The tusk is two and a half feet long.

The tusk is what defines the romance of the narwhal. It looks like a weapon for jousting, and scientists speculate that it is a "secondary sexual" characteristic, useful for males in "sparring." When Renaissance Europeans discovered this creature, they brought their chivalric heritage to work on it. They thought maybe they'd found one of the great mythical creatures of the hunt, the unicorn. It just happened, they imagined, that the unicorn was not a horse, but a sea creature. Their credulity shouldn't detract from the wonder of *monoceros*. The tusk is no less a miracle on a whale that turns white than it might have been on a white horse.

In the legends and lore of the unicorn, only the purest of hunters could capture the creature. Men pursued the elusive creature through magical, mystical gardens—as the story is told in the great tapestries produced in Europe. One famous cycle of six tapestries of the unicorn hunt is on display in the Cloisters of the Metropolitan Museum, in New York, produced for the wedding of Anne of Brittany to Louis XII in 1499. Against a verdant background of flowers and streams, of elegant huntsmen and refined ladies, the unicorn is captured. It turns out that only a virgin is able to subdue the unicorn, and a tamed white unicorn rests his head, now with a lovely golden collar and chain, on the lap of the virgin.

It is a story woven of great chivalrous longing—great purity and great desire are rewarded in the realization of an impossible dream. The legend of the unicorn can give this great longing, this great and piercing desire, two faces—one mystical and spiritual, the other romantic and erotic. It can celebrate the virgin bride or the Virgin Mary.[10]

This fantastic creature is already a symbol of a vigorous imagination and a vigorous spiritual desire.

In the wide spaces of the Arctic, white as a blank page, it's hard not to find yourself writing your own words on the landscape. The sunlight falls so persistently and pervasively, it seems to turn everything white except people and a few animals. Living things come out of the whiteness like dark words on a white page. Creatures are the semantics of this landscape, and their relations are the syntax. I find it impossible, standing on the edges of the ice, looking at the narwhal, not to be aware of this deep and up-welling longing, this inner desire, somehow from depths inside us that rival the depthlessness of the clear seas I stand so precariously above.

I find myself longing to see how the hunter traces for us the outlines of this desire, this spiritual desire that also comes to us in the shapes of im-probable and beautiful creatures.

It's a tradition in the West, the spiritual hunt, that never had a strong hold on the imagination, despite the great poetic conception of the unicorn. Christianity finds the hunt largely uncongenial to its greatest and most no-ble longings, and uses the hunt mostly as a way to describe the harried, pure soul, tormented by the arrows of desire. But the hunt had its moments in Christian imagery, however tenuous and fragile.

As we've moved further into the postmedieval world, the hunt has re-flected an increased concern for political power and masculine vigor, but this spiritual dimension of the hunt, the relation of the hunt to cultivation of some inner strength, seems to have faded. Early in our century, the poet Rainer Maria Rilke used the unicorn as an image of the spiritual creature within that has largely atrophied and requires some new ministrations, some new cultivation.[11] It lives in "heart space, radiant and bare." It never existed, but can grow from love: "a pure beast arose." Rilke says that hunters fed the beast, not with grain, but "with the thought that it might be." And

> it grew a horn upon its brow. One horn.
> Afterward it approached a virgin, whitely—

Out of the hunt, turned inward, a new creature is nurtured and comes to being.

The poet Philip Booth describes the state that this unicorn hunt has come to "this late in the world," in a search for some new resurgence of spirit:

> How can it be
> this late in the world
> we also have come to hunt ourselves,
> ourselves in this creature,
> to hunt him in us. He lets us

close in: he allows us to see
that in him we are met, met with
a resurgent joy,

a joy in the world we walk back into. . . .[12]

The draw of wonder and reverie is great on the ice, and I frequently let myself follow in some sense the motions of ice and light and spirit, moving among the three. Living on the floe edge is living on a geographical and a psychological cusp that I love, that I find irresistible.

And then I am brought back with a jolt to the body of the whale. It is being butchered directly on the ice. Rather, it is being flensed. Its skin is being peeled off its body like an orange rind. The dark skin comes off in long rectangular strips, which are laid out beside the body of the whale, dark sheets with a thin layer of spongy, eggnog yellow. The narwhal looks naked, wrapped still in blubber and blood. It's the deconstruction of the beast.

Those thin layers of skin are the other prize, besides the tusk, of the whale.

If the tusk supports dreams, it's the skin which supports the flesh, and a more physical kind of longing. Lamechi explains to me: "Seal is the best thing when hunting. Get a seal, even in the awful winter cold, boil the meat, eat it. Drink the broth. Seal is so good, has warm blood, heats you all up out hunting. The warmth goes all over inside. Seal has kept us alive, mainly."

He pauses thoughtfully, then says, "But narwhal is good. Really good, too. We cache narwhal, for about four months, in the ground. Get a narwhal in summer. Chop up the *muktuk* [the skin] really fine. Bury it. In December, after the freeze, I go right away and dig it up. Gets a really good flavor. By spring, some people really long for narwhal."

He drops a tea bag on the ice and smiles at me.

I recognize a joke is coming.

"Labrador tea," he laughs, and I picture the tea bag melting into the current, and ending up on the shoreline of Labrador.

Elijah cuts a long, narrow strip of the *muktuk*. It's dark and looks leathery. He bites one end with his teeth, and with his knife slices a little piece to chew. He's wearing a black jacket with hot pink details, and his face glows as he chews. "That's the way, uh-huh, uh-huh, I like it, I like it," he sings.

He likes it raw. They all want me to try it, and I do. It's crunchy, from a thin layer of cartilage, I think, and the blubber is very rich, very fatty. An

acquired taste, I suspect. They all watch me. "Your first time for *muktuk*?"
Lamechi laughs.

Over the next week, I get to know Lamechi very well. We find walruses and bowhead whales together, hunt ringed seals and chase polar
bears. He takes me to his grandmother's summer camp, where she is enjoying a "time away." And we climb the great cliffs on Bylot Island. We share
a great deal of adventure. But we share more than that. We get to know
each other well, and share parts of ourselves with each other. Something
about this floe edge invites us to a kind of luminosity about our inner
selves.

I am as attracted to the light in Lamechi's spirit as everything else we
share. It's at this level that he seems to have something to share. It is this
inner wisdom, perhaps gleaned from personal struggles directly engaged,
that these hunters have to share with us. Not so much a truth, or even a
body of knowledge, but a direction. Lamechi is on a trajectory, in his life,
to bring him back to himself.

Lamechi tells me he's spent considerable time away from Pond Inlet.
He liked the cities, he wanted to make money. He worked on oil rigs in the
Arctic, out at sea. And he tried drugs. But something drew him home.
Partly, he says, it was the schedules, the desire to feel free. "I didn't like
having to wear a watch all the time on the oil rig," he tells me. "I want to be
free a little bit longer."

But he's looking for more than that.

He was born, he tells me, on a small chunk of rock off Baffin Island,
called Curry Island. At that time, the people still didn't really live in villages. They had their own places throughout the land, and the government
was just then rounding them up and trying to standardize their lives. By the
time Lamechi reached high school age, the government was trying to make
everyone go to school in Igaluit. That's several hundred miles to the south,
on Baffin Island.

Lamechi had the choice, and chose to stay in Pond Inlet.

"I cannot feel bad," he says in measured words, "for not getting my
diploma. I chose instead the education of a hunter."

He searches for the right words, as if they're precious, as if he wants to
get this just right.

"I took my education with my father. If I went to school, I would not
have many hunting experiences with my father. I would not have lived at
his camp for many years."

He speaks with a moving eloquence, in an unpretentious way, straight
from the heart.

I asked him what he learned from his father.

"The best person to learn from out hunting," he says, "is your father. Otherwise, you wouldn't know things and have many strange surprises. You have to watch the wind on the floe edge, for one. If it changes, you can get broken from the edge and blow away to sea very easily. Plus, my goal now," he says, "is to try to be more like my father. He was a very nice man, and I want to become a nice man also."

He's in the Pond Inlet theater troupe, and that takes him traveling as far as Europe. The actors write plays together, and perform them. In their performances, he now plays a shaman—one of the men who is in touch with the spirits. In this, he's connecting, not with his father, but his grandfather. He's on a personal spiritual quest.

"Can the shaman change into animals?" I ask him. I'm aware from my reading that there is a spiritual connection in Eskimo thought between animals and men. The two realms are not thought of as so entirely separate as they are in white culture, and this idea intrigues me very much. I've never met a shaman before.

"Oh yes," Lamechi answers. "Shaman in Inuit is called *ingankook*. He has special animals. He can even change into animals. My grandfather died of a curse that someone put on his ear."

For these Inuit, he tells me, there is a whole variety of spirit people, and some of them live under the ice. Lamechi tells me they're called *qallupiluit*, and you have to be careful because they'll steal children through the cracks, or "leads," that open up in the ice as it is jostled by waves and stressed by heat and cold.

"Some people claim to have seen the *qallupiluit*," Lamechi says. "People who are lost claim they have been taken away by these spirits. They're supposed to be squat, fat, and very hairy, and they smell like dead whales in summer. Plus, they make a sound like knocking under the ice. There's a children's story about them, called *A Promise Is a Promise*."[13]

It is not hard to imagine all sorts of creatures living under the ice. We have, after all, just captured in the narwhal one of the most improbable animals you could imagine.

I love talking with Lamechi. The hunters of the Arctic and subarctic have been the focus of anthropologists studying hunting for most of this century. Anthropologists focused on them as models of human origins, likening them to early ancestors, because they were a hunting culture. Hunting in the United States is steadily declining in popularity, and hunting as an evolutionary model no longer interests most anthropologists. And our own myths of the hunter may have themselves exhausted their usefulness, and in their model of violence may have done terrible damage.

Still, it seems to me that Lamechi as an actor in a troupe, performing as a shaman in the tradition of his grandfather, is as remarkable and meaningful as his sensitivities as a hunter.

When the butchering is done, I look at my watch. Lamechi isn't wearing one. It's 9:30 in the evening.

Lamechi wants to do something else. "Let's go to the cliffs," he says. "Murre eggs are very delicious."

If we go to the cliffs, we'll probably stay up all night. The light on the ice is constant, and it comes at us from every angle—sea and sky and ice. It fills us with energy, with an excess. I'm eager to go. The cliffs, with hundreds of thousands of birds on eggs, will be their own spectacle of excesses. Avian excesses, with huge numbers of birds—all this energy of fertility and continuous clamor of screaming birds coming and going all night long. It will be a night of sleepless, exhilarating abundance. I realize with a smile that the narwhal hunt is only the beginning.

We grab some food and load the snowmobile. Lamechi climbs on and looks at me over his left shoulder, flashing his slow, winning smile under his magenta glasses.

I climb on behind him, straddling his snowmobile, and hold on tight. The sun has spun completely around the sky since we arrived.

"Shall we go now," he asks, "while there's still light?"

2

A HUNGER DEEPER THAN MEMORY

The patterns of impulse and response inherent in nerves and protoplasm have thus a long prehuman history, pointing back through many stages of ascent from the earliest beginnings of life in the Paleozoic brine to the present chaos of international affairs; and from first to last, the question has not been "To be, or not to be?" but "To eat, or to be eaten?" of which desire and terror are the effects. . . .

—Joseph Campbell[1]

Man is in part a carnivore: the male of the species is genetically programmed to pursue, attack, and kill for food. To the extent that men do not do so they are not fully human.

—Paul Shepard[2]

Hunting, it is said, is the oldest male profession. At least, that's what the champions of hunting like to claim. But it's a doubtful claim, as it turns out, and it's a dubious distinction in any event—as dubious as the claim to fame of the world's oldest profession.

Together with sports and war, hunting is the most powerful metaphor we have for defining what it means to be male. The language of hunting permeates our conversations and our daily lives, defining both social relations and personal identity for men. This in itself is not particularly unique. Most Western cultures since Gilgamesh have used hunting in these ways. What's different about our use of hunting in this century is that we've underwritten its language with the pedigree of science. Through speculation on the daily activities of our prehistoric ancestors—Pleistocene to Paleolithic—hunting in the twentieth century has taken on an aura of scientific respectability. It has the imprimatur of archaeology and paleoanthropology. Even as hunting has declined in real popularity and prestige in the United States, it has been elevated to the status of a primary occupation for humans. Without any really good evidence, archaeologists and anthropologists made the hunter into the progenitor of the race and the shaper of men. All men, the argument goes, were shaped by the hunger that drove them to chase mammoths across the veld, to chip arrowheads from silica, and to mix ochers in the gloom of the caves for painting animals of the hunt on the dark walls. It was through hunting that we found the path from the woods to the city, from our animal appetites to our human glory. We grazed the trees of our past as vegetarians, but made a predatory leap onto the dusty but game-filled savannas of Africa—and into our humanity.

The future of men was glimpsed in the arcing trajectory of the first spear that a protohuman hunter heaved across the brown African veld.

The scientific basis for believing men were shaped by their hunting has been pretty thoroughly discredited. But it has not been dislodged. The prehistoric hunter has taken up residence in the landscape of myth, and the modern male still likes to trace his own genealogy back to the caves and campfires of a bone-wielding australopithecine. And the first step in seeing hunting as a cultural metaphor, the first step in seeing hunting as a myth used in history to shape men's views of themselves, is to remove the scientific underpinnings that have supported the prehistoric hunter as the model of the modern male.

You may not hunt, but if you're a modern man, you've probably pictured yourself as a sort of prehistoric hunter, a primal hero dueling with saber-toothed tigers and large woolly mammoths. The myth of the prehistoric male hunter is a modern imperative, and it has lodged the hunter in our psyches as the original father of us all, the primal patriarch. It sets a stereotype against which every man, consciously or unconsciously, has measured himself in his secret thoughts. The prehistoric hunter is the true source of our masculinity, and modern men are taught to trace their genealogies back to the caves and campfires of some bone-wielding, big-browed predator.

Hunting is our evolutionary legacy, in this view. Under our coats and ties, we each carry the prehistoric hunter in our bones and our blood, our passions and our psyche—it's a sweeping, staggering claim that one single activity created everything we recognize as human. Hunting assumed the mask and mantle of science, a universal and unchanged part of masculinity.

As the quotation from Paul Shepard at the opening of this chapter indicates, we imagine that evolution shaped our genetics, shaped our bodies, in ways dictated by hunting. We have been genetically hot-wired by hunting, the argument goes, with all the traits that seem to define the modern male—aggression, forethought and memory, the upright stance, the love of tools and technology. And it shaped our social lives, a kind of anthropology in the arrangement of social relations. And it shaped our spiritual and emotional lives. It has worked, in short, as both scientific model and archetypal myth. In his quotation at the head of this chapter, Joseph Campbell locates the predatory impulse at the origins of life itself, in the "Paleozoic brine." Hunting is registered on our nerve endings and in our impulses, our bodies and our brains. It is the single most important defining feature of men's lives, and in Campbell is infused with a kind of mythic if mistaken grandeur—"to eat, or to be eaten."

Hunting accounts for this deep hunger in the lives of men—a physical hunger that carries through our nerves into an emotional hunger. Desire is the hunger of the hunter.

But it's a hunger we can hardly see the face of, much less recognize clearly in the bones and pictures of our prehistoric predecessors. And what the projection of modern hunting backward onto these ancestors does, as a primary and determining activity for all human life, is create for us a memory of what is immemorial.

Our male desire is deep and powerful, and it shapes us more powerfully than we know. But men did not emerge as hunters from the Paleozoic brine, and I'd like to begin to rethink how it is that male identity and desire have come for us to be understood almost exclusively in terms of predation and hunting. And once we realize that the male as hunter is a cultural metaphor, a myth of the mainstream male, we will have cleared some space for rethinking what the male might be. We have room for expanding beyond the stereotypical bounds of masculinity.

Hunting runs deeply inside of us. It runs so deeply that we can't easily separate it from blood. Men like to imagine hunting is physically innate. Men like to be bonded by blood and grounded in blood—blood brothers, fellows of similar bloodlines. Hunters often picture themselves dipping their hands together in the blood of the slain animal. The appetites described by the human predator—located in prehistory and written into the male body—are deeply felt. The prehistoric hunter gives those impulses both a body and a rationale, a coherent shape and a justification. But for all his organizing power in giving men a forceful and coherent identity, the hunter also sticks a knot of darkness in men's longing. In the image of the prehistoric hunter we can often glimpse a grisly, demonic leer.

2

The common Darwinian wisdom has it that nature is a jungle, a contest between predator and prey. The common environmental wisdom has it that nature is, well, a national park. But I think nature is a labyrinth in which, when we enter, we're tracing the tracks of our own desire. When we walk in nature, we walk within ourselves.

I have that feeling strongly at this moment. After scuttling through a labyrinth of passageways in a damp darkness, I'm scrunched into the far end of a narrow cave. I squeeze through a small crack in the wall to a cramped little side closet to the cave. Except it's more like a side chapel, really, with a cupola beginning at eye level. In this dark recess, this *rincón*, was this part of the cave's true secret. When I look up into a mystic gloom, Paleolithic animals are swirling about my head.

They fill me with an inarticulate awe: sweet-faced, sway-bellied ponies, perhaps pregnant; big-jawed horses with their manes flying in an ecstasy of implied motion; the most beautiful long-necked female deers, engraved in lovingly delicate lines, their faces startled and their ears perked and alert, as if they just this moment were disturbed; and a bull with ominous horns lowered for the charge. They're painted in gorgeous colors on the rocks—yellows and reds, blacks and violets, oranges and a soft sienna.

They gallop around me in a heady vision of animal joy, so wonderful and so deeply felt, they make my heart leap inside my chest. It's easy to see why we find the origins of our dreams and desires in these prehistoric images.

I'm in a little-known prehistoric cave along the verdant northern coast of Spain. It's called La Pasiega, a narrow defile of tunnels, a seam really, in the rocky, scruffy mountains of Cantabria, small by the sizes of the caves in France. I'm in the epicenter of prehistoric art, the heart of the heart of the Upper Paleolithic. The intimacy of this cave, like others in Spain, gives the animal imagery a special charm, and increases the sense that I feel—that everyone I've talked to who's visited these staggeringly beautiful caves feels: it's the mystic sense that this art gives of evoking the deepest animal spirits inside us. You walk into the cave, and through its darkness and tunnels you simultaneously walk backward in time—geological time and human time. You crawl to some dawn time, forty thousand to twelve thousand years ago—the Paleolithic. If it's true that each individual relives the history of the race, you've stepped into that part of your own soul that contains the earliest experiences of the human race. A fissure in the rock leads into the dreams of your first yearnings.

There are actually two entrances to La Pasiega, and the second entrance leads to some of the most startling and puzzling images in the cave. It leads to a beautiful image of a bison that merges the hunt, sexuality, and the male—and illustrates why prehistoric cave art is conventionally viewed not simply as the art of hunters, but as the midwife of human symbolic thinking. We don't know if men or women painted the animals in the caves, or even what the social nature of the painting might have been—men alone, men and women gathered together, women alone. The idea of some ritual initiation of hunters and boys has always stirred the modern imagination. The assumption—almost completely unwarranted—has always been that male hunters painted the animals.

One sunny afternoon in the fall, I scoot through the narrow passageway from this second entrance to the cave, and in a short distance, the tunnel bulges into a mini-chamber. This space is dominated by a large rock in the shape of a throne, worn smooth from generations of Paleolithic spelunkers climbing on and sliding off. Perhaps some ritual, some ceremony, was conducted in the presence of the painted effigies, with the images of moody animals flickering out of the surrounding gloom.

On a flat panel, behind this rock throne, a prehistoric artist with some personality has painted a spirited, defiant bull in profile. The painter had an individual style, a sort of prehistoric Rubens, because his undulant baroque line is repeated nowhere else in Paleolithic art. The bull's back swells with a curved hump of muscle. His chest is massive, his shoulders thick, bulging. His head thrusts forward, covered by a jutting cowl of fur. A single horn flips up and forward from behind the tiny dot of his eye.

The scrolling and curving style of this bull gives him a sensuous power, heavy and thickset. He's full of male energy.

He appears to be wounded, as if he is the prototype of a bull in a Spanish bullring. From his back, what looks like a *pica* in a Spanish bullfight stands erect. It's really just a dark vertical line, but it looks for all the world as though this bull might have been stabbed by some daring early hunter. Or some powerful Paleolithic shaman.

The bull's obviously aggravated. He has strong narrow hips, and his tail's raised, as if ready to charge.

José Maria Ceballo, affectionately called Chema, is the *encargado*, or supervisor, of the archaeological caves of the province of Cantabria. He and I spend many afternoons in La Pasiega, as well as all the other caves in the region. He's incredibly social and funny, a loquacious, bearded man. He loves dirty jokes, which he's always telling me to test my Spanish, and he knocks down *manchados*—white wine "stained" with a splash of red—as he tells stories before lunch. He thinks it's the best way to see prehistoric art in the afternoon. The raised tail, he tells me, means the bull's "*macho*," Chema says. Sexually excited.

In a sort of triumphant gesture, Chema points to a distinct penis. *"¿Lo ves, Carlos?"* Do you see it?

The sexual and the venatic impulse come together in this prehistoric image.

But there's a bigger surprise in this bull, a more clever and interesting secret. I study him carefully. His face is drawn in tender black lines. His face looks more like a monkey's face than a bull's: small nose, delicate lips, jutting chin. His mouth almost has a smirk on it. Tiny monkey eye. He's more hominid than bovine.

Then I get it, the visual joke that these Paleolithic painters seemed so fond of playing. I gasp and laugh out loud. This is not a bull's face. This is the face of a man. And the bull's chin—the beard of a man. This is one of those beautiful images out of the Paleolithic in which the human and the animal intersect. They are quite literally merged. The hunter and the hunted are one.

The hunt, the male, and sexual arousal—they all merge together in the single image of this wounded bull.

I'm deep in the ardent Spanish earth, gazing at one of the first images of a male ever painted, a bearded male. It is the image of the prehistoric hunter that has entered our vocabulary. For modern commentators, you'd think that all these prehistoric men in furs did was hunt. He's the original "macho" male. And you can find him stalking the pages of modern philosophers, defining both identity and sexuality for men.

José Ortega y Gasset makes this bullish, aroused hunter limned on the wall of northern Spain into the quintessential male. For this twentieth-century Spanish existential philosopher, the hunter is the epitome of an authentic man, the man who has connected himself to his origins, the man living near the urgent impulses that give life meaning. In *Meditations on Hunting*, Ortega y Gasset writes that the urge to hunt derives from the Paleolithic hunter. He calls hunting a "deep and permanent yearning," a universal part of the human condition:

> When you are fed up with the troublesome present, with being "very twentieth century," you take your gun, whistle for your dog, go out to the mountain, and, without further ado, give yourself the pleasure during a few hours or a few days of being "Paleolithic." And men of all eras have been able to do the same, without any difference except in the weapon employed. It has always been at man's disposal to escape from the present to that pristine form of being a man, which, because it is the first form, has no historical suppositions. History begins with that form. Before it, there was only that which never changes: that which is permanent, Nature. "Natural" man is always there, under the changeable historical man. We call him and he comes—a little sleepy, benumbed, without his lost form of instinctive hunter, but, after all, still alive. "Natural" man is first "prehistoric" man—the hunter.[3]

Using contemporary views of archaeologists and artists, scientists and poets, Ortega y Gasset makes hunting into a grand drama that represents the
drama of life itself. As the "natural man" in prehistory, the hunter lurks under the tailored business suit, the essential truth of man's nature transcend-
ing history and historical epochs. The original and true man was—and is—a
hunter. This Paleolithic hunter resides, unchanged though forgotten, in each
modern man, under the stultifying veneer of civilization. Our essential self
is this prehistoric hunter, the first and most perfect man. This essentialism in
male nature is a crucial part of the modern use of the image of the prehistoric hunter.

Ortega y Gasset wants to wake this dormant natural man out of his
false dreams and his sloth. Because hunting exists outside of history, for
Ortega y Gasset, it is not the stuff of change and fashion. It is not something in men that we can alter, leave behind, or deny. Much better that we
embrace the hunter's energy, face his bloody facts of life. There are modes
and styles in hunting. But there is only this one truth in all hunting—the
pursuer and the pursued.

You don't have to go far to find this Paleolithic hunter shoved forward
as the idealized model of maleness. The men's movement in the United
States has used him to justify certain features of the male, particularly his
longing for power and sex.

For example, in *Fire in the Belly: On Being a Man*, Sam Keen suggests
that the first great version of maleness was the prehistoric hunter, and the
art of these caves was the "first manifesto of man." This manifesto of manhood, painted on the walls of prehistoric caves, testifies to men's twin obsessions of identity and sexuality. Keen's "best educated guess" about the
meaning of this art is that man may have identified his manhood through
his relationship with an animal, a totem. That special species would have
supplied identity for the man, its characteristics helping the individual man
to know himself.

Keen includes free-form meditation on the power of the flung spear
during the hunt—and how this power must be translated into visions of
prehistoric sex:

> I picture our first hunter-artist flushed with success after the hunt. Re-
> turning proudly with his kill he must have felt the potency of his act in
> his loins. Perhaps like the Bushman, whose penis even when not
> aroused rests in an up rather than a down position, the hunter felt the an-
> imal power as inseparable from his own masculinity. And perhaps he
> felt the same logic and the same mystery within the intimate act of inter-
> course. He must have thought something like this: As the spear wounds

and kills the animal that sustains life, so the penis wounds the woman who creates life.[4]

Sex in this view is the wounding of the female, a climax of the sexual hunt. That Sam Keen offers this supposition about the origins of sex, in the 1990s, even though he does not endorse them explicitly, demonstrates how deeply ingrained the predatory notions of sex are in modern men's minds.

I remember standing before the image of the monkey-faced bull in the cave of La Pasiega. Here was evidence that men hunted, and they pondered the meaning of hunting for who they were and the passions animals elicited in them. A modern man is so conditioned by all the mythology surrounding Paleolithic art, he can't look at an image like this wounded, aroused man-bull and imagine these men doing anything other than hunting. Our imaginations are dominated by the pictures they left of the animals of the hunt, and of themselves as hunters.

But why? Are those the only kinds of paintings they left?

In this same passageway I have seen many other images, painted by these same men, that nowhere figure in our thinking of who they were or how they imagined themselves. They seem to have nothing to do with hunting, at least as far as we can see. There's this mysterious and engaging little creature, a mannish figure called an "anthropomorph" tucked in one of the side pockets of La Pasiega. He looks for all the world like a Paleolithic Grover from "Sesame Street." He is engraved in the walls of many caves. One in La Pasiega was tucked behind a little side passage.

Most strange is the apparent calligraphy high on a wall deep in the cave, with symbols that look like they might have been left by extraterrestrials: upper-case *E*s and two bear paws. Did this have anything to do with hunting?

The great art that spans the twenty-five thousand years of the Paleolithic seems intensely immediate to us, but it remains a mystery, separated by a chasm in consciousness between us and them. But we attach ourselves to images that seem to make sense to us, and seize upon the meanings we want to attach, at the same time smothering the mystery that is what speaks so powerfully to us at a visceral, if not intellectual, level.

We are quick to jump to the conclusion that these prehistoric men were first and foremost hunters. The impulse to seize upon the hunter in all of this art says more about us than it says about the prehistoric artist. There are too many other images in the caves that suggest that hunting was not the universal truth about the lives of these people. They knew animals well, lived near them, learned from them. But hunting did not dominate their imaginations, in all likelihood, the way it has dominated our imagination of them. It is not likely that the hunting imagery can be used to justify a view of masculinity in which pleasure is linked to predation, and violence is eroticized. At least, this cannot be made into a universal truth.

Ironically, the interpretations of prehistoric art and the anthropology of early man offer one of the best ways to understand the modern meaning of the hunt.

Why has one image of men in prehistory come to dominate our views of their lives? And our views of evolution itself? To answer that, we turn not to prehistory, but to our own history. In this century, the obsession with hunting is a reflection of our own anxieties about the predatory nature of men. For men like Keen, the Paleolithic hunter-artist was a romanticized figure, even noble. But in the middle of our own century, an even more pathological hunter took our imaginations hostage—the "killer ape."

3

In May 1924, an anatomist named Raymond Dart was working in the School of Medicine at the University of Witwatersrand in the arid Transvaal of South Africa. Mining was king in the Transvaal, and in one of the limestone quarries in a place called Taungs, south of Johannesburg, a company director nipped a nice "monkey" skull as a kind of curiosity, and thought to use it as a souvenir paperweight. By an unlikely chain of accidents, the skull wound up in the hands of a student, Miss Josephine Salmons, and she took it to her anatomy professor to identify.

Raymond Dart knew it was no "fossilised monkey." It was the fossilized skull of a baboon with a hole in it. Since it was the first fossilized primate to be found in Africa south of Egypt, Dart sent to the mines to find more fossils.

A week later, Dart had obtained a number of fossil-full rocks from the same mines. He chipped them apart, and soon he held in his hands the makings of a scientific revolution—what has been called "the most important palaeo-anthropological discovery of the century."[5]

Dart had uncovered a spectacular find: the oldest protohuman yet unearthed. Remembering that moment decades later, when he held in his hand the face of "an infant only about 5 or 6 years old, which looked amazingly human," he wrote with a strangely cold and bloodless enthusiasm: "It was the first time that anyone had been privileged to see the complete face and to reconstruct accurately the entire head of one of man's extinct ape-like relatives. The brain was so large and the face was so human that I was confident that here indeed was one of our early progenitors that had lived on the African continent; and as it had chosen the southern part of Africa for its homeland I called it *Australopithecus africanus*, i.e., the South African ape."[6] This australopithecine "infant man-ape" became known, in the worldwide controversy that it engendered, as the Taungs skull. The grandiose and egotistical Dart, with an eye to scientific glory, called it "the missing link."

Dart's young hominid appeared to have lived in the early part of the Pleistocene, about a million years ago. From dental analyses of this single skull, Dart guessed the creature's age at about five or six. It must have walked erect, holding its head upright in the human fashion. He projected the adult to have been about four feet tall, weighing perhaps seventy pounds, and living in caves on the cliffsides of the Kalahari, looking out upon the frightening reaches of the open plain, which was populated with the most dangerous beasts to be found anywhere in the world.

As he pondered the skull of the baby, he thought of the hole in the top of the baboon's skull which Josephine Salmons had brought him earlier, the baboon skull that had led him to this protohuman. Was it possible, he wondered, that that animal had cracked the hole in the baboon's skull to extract the brain for food? Did the relatives of this baby man-ape, *Australopithecus africanus*, catch and eat baboons?

Dart declared with the certainty of an established fact that his "missing link" showed that we became humans when we left the bushes behind and began chasing animals. These apes were flesh-eating, bone-breaking predators. Meat, he declared triumphantly, made us men: "Wherever found, all prehistoric and most primitive living human types are hunters, i.e., flesh-eaters."[7]

As more fossils fell from the mines and hills of the Transvaal, particularly from the limeworks in the Makapansgat Valley in 1947, Dart's ideas about the earliest humans became increasingly horrific. He calls the australopithecine, famously, "the killer ape": "The predaceous habit is therefore 'living by preying,' i.e., hunting down and killing animals for food. On this thesis man's predecessors differed from living apes in being confirmed killers: carnivorous creatures, that seized living quarries by violence, battered them to death, tore apart their broken bodies, dismembered them limb from limb, slaking their ravenous thirst with the hot blood of victims and greedily devouring livid writhing flesh."[8]

Dart relishes the lurid images of violence, and he writes with an almost gleeful perversity of "ravenous thirst" and "writhing flesh." His rhetoric disturbs the easy liberal complacency of a fine and perfectible human image, the Enlightenment man of Diderot or the noble savage of the Romantic Rousseau. Dart isn't writing about bones here, but about human nature.

The moment and method of our emergence branded us. We were born in blood, and begotten by brooding, violent heroes. It's our birthmark. In Dart's own words this murderous impulse brands us as "Cain's children."

Our natural instinct is to kill with a weapon. Men are "confirmed killers," Dart claimed.

This is a kind of scientific Calvinism—we are sinners in the hands of an angry evolution. We're not the descendants of gentle chimps in the forests of central Africa. We were born in the hardships of the southern desert, tested in combat with fierce predators, proven in the moment of the kill:

> The australopithecine deposits of Taungs, Sterkfontein and Makapansgat tell us in this way a consistent, coherent story not of fruit-eating, forest-loving apes, but of the sanguinary pursuits and carnivorous habits of proto-men. They were human not merely in having the facial form and dental apparatus of humanity; they were also human in their cave life, in their love of flesh, in hunting wild game to secure meat and in employing implements, whether wielded and propelled to kill during hunting or systematically applied to the cracking of bones and the scraping of meat from them for food. Either these Procrustean proto-human folk tore the battered bodies of their quarries limb from limb and slaked their thirst with blood, consuming the flesh raw like every other carnivorous beast; or, like early man, some of them understood the advantages of fire as well as the use of missiles and clubs.[9]

Dart shoves a new hero onto the stage of human prehistory, and he bears a strange resemblance to our darkest selves. He's even a cannibal, this skulking forebear, and he competes directly with the romantic view of our spiritual birth as cave-dwelling artists, as hunters connected spiritually to the game.

Dart's view of the australopithecines as murderous hunters was accepted, not because he adduced evidence, but because it must have explained something to us about ourselves. We seemed to believe it instinctively, perhaps out of the horrors inspired by the unprecedented bloodshed of World War I. There were the skulls, but there was virtually no evidence upon which to base Dart's wild speculations about the australopithecines' lives. Dart had jumped instantly from bones to blood. Dart believed without reservation that all of the skulls he subsequently found lay amid the remains of their hunting meals, in a kind of kitchen midden. He was convinced that these man-apes must have killed all the other creatures they were found among. The species must have abandoned fruits and nuts in the forests farther north to be living in the arid regions of the Kalahari. Besides being found amid these baboon bones, the only real evidence for Dart's imaginative leap to carnivory was their teeth: like ours, they weren't made for grinding vegetables.

If Dart's speculations are an indulgence of a rhetoric of violence, why were they so compelling? Because he offered an origin myth to a desperate, scientific age. Dart's Procrustean man glides naturally through the ravaged landscape of the modern imagination. Reveling in death, Dart's protoman "explained" the slaughters of two world wars in the rubble of South Africa:

> The loathsome cruelty of mankind to man forms one of his inescapable, characteristic and differentiative features; and it is explicable only in terms of his carnivorous, and cannibalistic origin. . . . The blood-bespattered, slaughter-gutted archives of human history from the earliest Egyptian and Sumerian records to the most recent atrocities of the Second World War accord with early universal cannibalism, with animal and human sacrificial practices or their substitutes in formalized religions and with the worldwide scalping, headhunting, body-mutilating and necrophiliac practices of mankind in proclaiming this common bloodlust differentiator, this predaceous habit, this mark of Cain that separates man dietetically from his anthropoidal relatives and allies him rather with the deadliest Carnivora.[10]

A bloodthirsty australopithecine found his natural habitat and a new ecological niche in a similarly savage twentieth century.

But what begins as an explanation of human nature, by an unconscious elision, becomes very easily the justification and glorification of aggression. Dart's strangely unscientific and gory prose suggests he himself revels in his descriptions of these cannibals of the great dramatic scene of human origins. This isn't a scientist's clinical evaluation of data. Dart is a wild man, gleefully enthusiastic about his "killer ape"—whom he thinks of as an armed murderer.

Testosterone was the juice of our biological triumph. Aggression was the dirty secret of our survival. There must have been bleak comfort in Dart's sneering pessimism. Dart's guilty australopithecine hunter played to a huge audience in this century. The onetime playwright Robert Ardrey scripted an international best-seller out of the South African anatomist's four-foot-tall wild man. In 1961, *African Genesis* propelled Ardrey into fame as he pushed an "unsentimental" view of our animal origins. He portrayed us, à la Dart, as killers out of biological necessity. We are the guilty glory of creation, kings who assert our sovereignty over the world through our animal compulsions and our predatory instincts. We rose from the dust of the Lower Pleistocene into our present undisputed triumph by mastering the arts of murder.

Robert Ardrey also locates Dart's disturbing theories in the middle of the twentieth century: "in such desperate hours as those we now live in." He recounts asking Dart how he felt about advancing a theory of men as killers:

> I said that I understood his conviction that the predatory transition and the weapons fixation explained man's bloody history, his eternal aggression, his irrational, self-destroying inexorable pursuit of death for death's sake. But I asked, would it be wise for us to listen when man at last possessed weapons capable of sterilizing the earth.
>
> Dart turned from his window and sat down at his desk; and somewhere a tunnel collapsed, a mile down, and skulls jiggled. And he said that since we had tried everything else, we might in last resort try the truth.[11]

Australopithecus invented, not a tool, but technology, not a spear chucker but a nuclear bomb. Male destiny is adumbrated in its hunting origins, which Ardrey later called "the hunting hypothesis."

The same dark prehistoric savanna of Dart's australopithecine is the landscape of Stanley Kubrick's 1968 film, *2001: A Space Odyssey*. I remember seeing this film as a young undergraduate, when it first appeared, and even more than the scenes of the computer in space, I was haunted by the powerful image of a nightfall over the huge and predatory African plains. Kubrick portrays Dart's frightened australopithecines huddled together on the cliffs above the savanna, listening as menacing howls rise up to them in their cave on a cliff. And then these hairy humans fight each other, and a jawbone is flung as weapon, flying into the sky and transforming magically into an orbiting space station. Apes became men in that first weapon. Here is the predatory transition into manhood. The past that we fight over is our future.

Dart gave us our predatory origins, and draped his theory in the cloak of science. With Dart, the archaeology of our origins fixed in the modern imagination the notion that men by their very natures are hunters, and that hunting means violence, aggression, and a sadistic pleasure in killing. It upholds a particularly bleak view of human nature and male instinct. And at this distance, half a century later, it walks on political legs that look very wobbly now. But before reviewing how this archaeology has come to be displaced by another theory of human origins, one with little to do with hunting, we need to see how a whole cadre of American academics rationalized the hunting myth, tempering its emphasis on male aggression into terms suitable for middle-class respectability. These academics moved Dart's fur-clad and canine-toothed barbarian out of the caves and into a worsted business suit.

By the 1960s, the predatory prowler of prehistory had descended to a domesticated paterfamilias.

4

Scarcely a decade after Dart's essay on the predatory transition from ape to man, hunting had come to be viewed as the "master" behavior of human evolution. With its move into academic respectability, prehistoric hunting became less an origin myth of irrational brutality than a carefully plotted morality play. Not simply the activity of men, hunting became the key to unlock the mysteries of masculinity. It became at once the activity of masters and the mask of masculinity. According to the new theory, the male who wore this mask inherited the world because he had mastered the art of rational violence.

At a 1965 international conference entitled "Man the Hunter," hunting was described as not merely a way to get food, a means to meat. Hunting was described as a way of life—the most successful adaptation, the conferees argued, that man has ever achieved. Hunting was the invisible hand of evolution. It had created everything that we think of as distinctively human. For over 2 million years, men have been on the Earth. For over 99 percent of this time, they argued, men have lived as hunter-gatherers. And 90 percent of all the humans who have ever lived were hunter-gatherers.

If Dart had claimed that humans emerged as hunters, at this conference hunting became the single most powerful force in human evolution—the all-inclusive explanation for who we are as humans. Hunting not only was a universal behavior of all humans, the participants claimed, but we carried the results of our hunting past in our genes and genius. William S. Laughlin, for example, claimed it is nothing less than the "master integrating pattern of our species," which climaxed in the "relative rapidity by which he [man] developed civilizations. . . ."[12]

Here's how Sherwood L. Washburn and C. S. Lancaster viewed the global importance of hunting in evolution:

> Human hunting is made possible by tools, but it is far more than a technique or even a variety of techniques. It is a way of life, and the success

of this adaptation (in its total social, technical, and psychological dimensions) has dominated the course of human evolution for hundreds of thousands of years. In a very real sense our intellect, interests, emotions, and basic social life—all are evolutionary products of the success of the hunting adaptation. When anthropologists speak of the unity of mankind, they are stating that the selection pressures of the hunting and gathering way of life were so similar and the result so successful that populations of *Homo sapiens* are still fundamentally the same everywhere.

Washburn and Lancaster conclude that "the biology of our species was created in that long hunting and gathering period."[13]

Hunting as an idea organized human evolution into a single grand epic narrative, with the male emerging as hero. The epic hunting narrative of our evolution weaves tool use and the pursuit of game into a story of the emergence of full humanity.

Australopithecus is now thought to have emerged about 4 million years ago, in the Late Pliocene. Paleolithic culture emerged with pebble tools about 3 million years ago, still in the Pliocene epoch, and by 1.5 million years ago, *Australopithecus africanus* had developed. The first true man, *Homo habilis*, had appeared by 1 million years ago, using biface tools, living in caves, and hunting moderate-sized animals. *Homo erectus* (Java Man, Peking Man, and Heidelberg Man: seven hundred thousand years ago) continued the development by using numerous tools and specializing in large game. *Homo sapiens* took over about two hundred thousand years ago. *Homo sapiens* diverged into Neanderthals and Cro-Magnons. Neanderthals, *Homo sapiens neanderthalensis*, are a controversial species since experts still wrangle about whether these beetle-browed relatives, and powerful hunters of huge mastodons, were our poor distant cousins who exhausted their robustness in a kind of evolutionary implosion, or whether they were more directly our ancestors. But *Homo sapiens sapiens,* or Cro-Magnons, displaced them on their hunting grounds, with their superior brains and technology, using 240 kinds of tools, and they flourished from the Aurignacian period (forty thousand years ago) through the Solutrean (twenty thousand years ago), until the Magdalenian (ten thousand years ago). Their tools are exquisite—thin and narrow blades of flint, spear points flaked into shapes like laurel leaves, culminating in the exquisite and delicate "willow leaf" shape that defines the Magdalenian or latest stage of their material culture.[14]

How did hunting shape humans and give males possession of the world? We became not so much predators as hunters, growing smarter because we needed to track and trick big animals. So the brain ballooned to over four times its earlier size during the Pliocene. In addition, our memory gained retentive capacity because we had to remember where animals had been yesterday and last year. Our bodies also bear the stamp of the pressures of the hunt. We stand upright to be better killers. And our hands are the corporal signs of our intelligence—beautiful and delicate, our fingers let us grip the tools (weapons) with which we conquer the world. Intelligence and bipedalism and a hairy-chested strength—in capturing an animal, hunting is the origin and paradigm of the male's superiority physically and intellectually to the animals. It is an earnest of man's ultimate conquering of the world itself through strength and intelligence.

Inventing and using weapons stimulated the brain to grow more, gaining in power. We were locked in a prehistoric cybernetics, systems feeding upon each other, flinging us into our futures.

Even eyes, the organs of sense most intimately connected with reason and science, with being clear and enlightened, developed their power in the panoramic sweep of our gaze, through which we possessed the yellow savanna and the animals it hid. Scanning the field for animals is the origin of man's impulse to collect information.

Such is the theory. As Washburn and Lancaster write, "The extent to which the biological bases for killing have been incorporated into human psychology may be measured by the ease with which boys can be interested in hunting, fishing, fighting, and games of war."[15]

Hunting not only established the basic relations between men and animals, nature and culture, but it shaped culture itself, and the psychology of social relations. We expect to see animals flee from us—hunting shaped our relations with nature, wrote Lancaster and Washburn. Men learned male bonding around the fire at the hunting camp, telling stories, and on the quest. The tribal band of brothers is forged in the trials of the chase and cemented in the emotional release at the moment of the kill. This explains that strange combination of emotion and distance that is so characteristic of modern male relationships.

Women stayed at the base camp, in this mythic original tribe, and tended the kids. As Washburn and Lancaster wrote, culture became based on "an intensification of the division of labor."

> By hunting, men and women could specialize in their labors, with males chasing animals and females gathering or managing children by a home camp. Men brought the meat back to share with the women and children. The females and young became dependent on the hunting males, and the male took on the economic responsibility—fulfilling "the role of a socially responsible provider." These speculations constitute an an-

thropology of gender, and locate the birth of the human family in the
impulse to kill for woman and child: When males hunt and females
gather, the results are shared and given to the young, and the habitual
sharing between a male, a female, and their offspring becomes the basis
for the human family. According to this view, the human family is the
result of the reciprocity of hunting, the addition of a male to the mother-
plus-social group of the monkeys and apes.[16]

Males hunt. Females gather. And the sharing among them, and with their
children, is the basis for the human family. Men chase warthogs and
mastodons under the wide African sky. Women chase children near the
home fire.

And according to Washburn and Lancaster, hunting in prehistory created the pattern for economics as well: "The whole human pattern of gathering and hunting to share—indeed the whole complex of economic
reciprocity that dominates so much of human life—is unique to man. . . .
We believe that hunting large animals may demand all these aspects of human behavior which separate man so sharply from the other primates. If
this is so, then the human way appears to be as old as *Homo erectus.*"[17]
That is to say, between 1.5 million and seven hundred thousand years ago,
Homo erectus was already acting like a nineteenth-century capitalist.

Hunting created the biology of sex as well.

In this view, sex itself amounts to a female trick, women's bodies operating as a kind of lure or trap—note the hunting language—to capture men,
who would much rather be wandering the countryside together. In exchange
for spending more time at "home," helping with the kids, men are given the
chance to have sex with women at any time. The "continuous receptivity" of
the female, or the monthly menstrual cycle and the loss of estrus (when female primates' genitalia bulge and they are available for sex), meant men
could have sex without women conceiving. Sex became more complexly
linked with desire, and less with procreation. Hunting was located biologically in the structure of desire, the strategic ways in which males and females sought to satisfy emotional needs through sexual wiles. A liberal
feminist revisioning of the male as hunter in anthropology uses the same
paradigm but discovers power in the female role and female sexuality:

> Two linked developments occurred, however, which had considerable
> repercussions: continuous female sexual receptivity and elimination of
> morphological signals of ovulation. Chimpanzee males can ignore fe-
> males except at the stage of maximal perineal tumescence and recep-
> tiveness which predictably accompanies ovulation. Hominid females

evolutionarily divested themselves of cyclical estrus and perineal swelling and color change, and thus coerced constant attention from their mates. (The sole remaining dependable signal of reproductive cyclicity, menstrual bleeding, assumed disproportionate significance to both sexes.) The evolutionary origins of the feminine mystique lie in the burden of uncertainty (i.e., potential cuckoldry) foisted onto hominid males by the females.[18]

It's easy to watch the way in which, through hunting, we come to understand the battle of the sexes as a primal drama, a dispute of power through sexuality itself, inserted in our genes. Hunting supplies the terms by which power between the sexes is contested in prehistory. Men gained pleasure; women gained help in child rearing. But men distrusted women, and from the male point of view, they lost control over themselves. In this view, perfume and lingerie, for example, are the armaments of female hunting, but the fair game they pursue is a mate. They are also the products of hunting, as it were, created by the social geography of male hunting.

And so from the male perspective, sex became the woman's trap in a new kind of hunt. It took something as powerful as sex to get men to leave their hunting friends and come home to the female. In this view, hunting did not so much create the sex act itself, as sexual dynamics. It created the domestic arrangements for monogamous sex, and the basis for betrayal and infidelity.

"Man the hunter" seemed to explain men's identities, their relations with women, and their place in society. What the men writing about the hunt, theorizing the hunt and its significance in human evolution, have done is describe the meaning of the hunt for modern men. *This* hunt is then projected backward in time, in a magical circularity, to describe the original hunt. In this way, as the anthropologist Claude Lévi-Strauss wrote, our own values are "discovered" by science, and a culture naturalizes itself falsely.

If hunting had little evidence to support the hypotheses it generated, it had broad explanatory power. There was nothing hunting couldn't explain. Perhaps its greatest value was in explaining the pleasure men take in violence, that most troubling feature of the male. "Men enjoy hunting and killing," write Washburn and Lancaster,

> and these activities are continued as sports even when they are no longer economically necessary. . . . Part of the motivation for hunting is the immediate pleasure it gives the hunter, and the human killer can no more afford to be sorry for the game than a cat can for its intended victim. Evolution builds relations between biology, psychology, and behavior,

and, therefore, the evolutionary success of hunting exerted a profound effect on human psychology. Perhaps, this is most easily shown by the extent of the efforts devoted to maintain killing as a sport. . . . And until recently war was viewed in much the same way as hunting. Other human beings were simply the most dangerous game. War has been far too important in human history for it to be other than pleasurable for the males involved.[19]

The association with war and hunting occurs, as we'll see, throughout Western history, and yet the association is not universal. Eskimo hunters, for example, are not warlike, though they are hunters. These theorists simply assume that hunting means violence, uncritically. You may kill a quail because you're hungry. It does not follow that killing is informed with aggression and violence—those are emotions that Western men have felt particularly in need of locating within hunting. Hunting became both a vehicle and an excuse for violence in men.

Strip the theory of its anthropological apparatus and you have the modern male, naked and exposed. The original human hunter—he was a shorter, rougher, coarser, and unnuanced image of modern man. Prehistory gave us a series of "just-so stories" for the triumph of the modern male. The only thing that *Homo erectus* hadn't invented was the stock market.

There's a hopeless conflation of the prehistoric and the modern man.

No one makes the translation of the prehistoric hunter into the modern male more explicitly and succinctly than Desmond Morris. The hypothesis that man evolved as a hunter rationalizes modern life, as he shows in *The Naked Ape*. Like Robert Ardrey's books, Desmond Morris's work was immensely popular packaging of the anthropological and biological view of a violent, territorial, and predatory early man: "Behind the facade of modern city life there is the same old naked ape. Only the names have changed: for hunting read working, for hunting ground read place of business, for home base read house, for pair bond read marriage, for mate read wife, and so on."[20]

Perhaps the real reason hunting became so powerful in the theory of human origins is that it seemed to us, and still does, so self-evident. It is a mask in which we recognize ourselves. It compels us with its simplicity, its comprehensive range of explanation, and its clear narrative framework. The myth of the prehistoric hunter entered the popular mind with the force of a scientific fact, and created the scientific foundations for our current view of the male as a family man, in love with technology, the meatwinner, aggressive in hunting animals and competitors, protective of passive women and children. The male is, uniformly, conceived as dominant—over animals and women.

The idea of the hunter looked like a window onto the past. But shift your view just a little. Suddenly you will be startled to see your own image looking back at you in the glass. What we couldn't see in the prehistoric hunter, as we looked through the glass of paleoanthropology, was an image startlingly like our own, grinning back at us.

5

I am perched above a pile of Paleolithic bones fifteen feet thick, and I am wondering if men did in fact evolve through predation. Was my Pleistocene great-uncle an indomitable mammoth killer? Or is "man the hunter" a modern myth, suffused with the nostalgia of stifled men who have put on suits and need to believe in a utopian time when they felt freer, wilder, inhabiting a dangerous world, and somehow losing themselves even as they learned to conquer the world? For in the American myth of prehistory, hunting led to civilization, and remains our link to the deep and violent truth of our past. The moment of transition remains the crux of intense fascination, when the killer ape became the family provider. Perhaps this is the source of our fascination with a primate like King Kong, the lost ape inside, the ape in modern society, the roaring ape on a huge phallic tower, harried and harassed and done to death. He seizes the woman, while we gaze on from street level at some lost and towering version of ourselves, horrified and entranced and melancholy.

The weight of archaeological authority made it almost impossible, for much of our century, to imagine ourselves as anything other than hunters at our roots. And as I sit on a plank above my small square, excavating a living site of Paleolithic people from about fourteen thousand years ago, the evidence of human hunting is overwhelming. The family groups that lived in this small but spacious cave—and in the millenium of its occupation probably only a single family group at a time lived here—hunted a lot. This was a big pile of bones I was sitting above. One of the graduate students with a deadpan sense of humor says to me it is like "excavating a garbage dump. This cave must have been the New Jersey of the Upper Paleolithic."

This was a huge dump site from innumerable dinners.

The question is not, Did men hunt? The question is, What role did hunting play in their lives? And another question: What purposes did making hunting the single determiner, the only casual explanation, of human evolution serve for the people who once proposed it?

I knelt upon a plank above my little square of dirt, and I spent my day brushing loose the bones of countless numbers of dead animals. Dr. Leslie

Freeman, a professor of anthropology at the University of Chicago, was in charge of this dig, and was one of the foremost experts on Upper Paleolithic culture in Spain. He has been digging in this small cave, called El Juyo, for about a decade.

El Juyo had been inhabited in the Upper Paleolithic for only a thousand years, between fifteen thousand and fourteen thousand years ago, in the Magdalenian period. The bands that lived here tossed their remains all over the red-dirt floor of the cave, which is scarcely bigger than a large living room. We are digging through greasy dirt of decomposed animals and jumbled animal bones. Mostly we extract their favorite prey, red deer (which in America is an elk). But occasionally we lift the bones of horses and bison and even the long thin bones of birds. Perhaps they were herons from marshy estuaries, because in Paleolithic Iberia the sea coast was much closer to El Juyo than its current ten miles or so.

Freeman tells me that these people were exploring the area in "a thoroughly modern way by fourteen thousand years ago. Red deer especially were harvested as if they were a crop."

The strategy seemed to be to hunt until they'd depleted the region, then move on. When the game rebounded, a group of people would move back in, only to exploit the red deer until they'd vanished again. In the cave, they must have just tossed the bones from their meals in the darkness beyond the fire's circle of light. They literally lived on top of their own trash.

So these people were hunters. But despite the amount of hunting they must have done, the evidence that hunting was a universal, an inclusive, "integrating" behavior for early humans is not there.

The men who compiled the volume *Man the Hunter* were themselves aware that they had made hunting carry a weight of meaning it couldn't support. It creaked and groaned and nearly toppled the minute the theory went up. In one of the main papers of the volume, conference organizer R. B. Lee reported on his work with the modern !Kung Bushmen of the Kalahari Desert of South Africa. These men do not spend much time hunting, even though they are subsistence hunters in an apparently harsh environment. Lee estimated that the Bushmen devote only "twelve to nineteen hours a week to getting food." Frequently, the men hunt avidly for one week, and spend three weeks at home. What are they doing? They spend their time "visiting, entertaining, and especially dancing. . . ."[21]

Dancing! That has been a harder activity for academic men to theorize.

Yet hunting has not been so difficult for academic men to theorize, and the common wisdom held that this activity, hunting, was the dominant force in shaping maleness—though men spend scarcely more than a fourth of their time hunting.

What's more, Lee showed that meat provided only about 20 to 33 percent of the caloric intake for the !Kung Bushmen. Mongongo nuts were a larger part of their caloric lives than meat. Only in the Arctic is hunting the primary way of life. Hunting is dramatic, and it is easy for the imagination to fix on the drama of hunting. That makes it easy to focus on hunting, to "overdetermine" or "privilege" hunting as an explanatory activity and metaphor. Then the circle feeds upon itself: hunting becomes important in how men see themselves, and they see hunting as increasingly important as an activity in shaping them.

Still, to make hunting the primary force in men's lives, or even the primary metaphor, is at best misleading. As Lee wrote, even as others were making hunting the secret of manhood, "This emphasis on the dramatic may have been pedagogically useful, but unfortunately it has led to the assumption that a precarious hunting subsistence base was characteristic of all cultures of the Pleistocene. This view of both modern and ancient hunters ought to be reconsidered."[22]

I find the dig in El Juyo interesting because one of Freeman's goals is to study more precisely what other ways these late Paleolithic people got their food, especially in terms of gathering things like shellfish from the nearby sea and berries. In our dig, we frequently come across huge piles of seashells—limpets and periwinkles—shaped like sun caps. Freeman estimated that over 2 million shells had been removed from the cave so far—shellfish was a large portion of these hunters' diets. It's more shells than have been excavated from any other Paleolithic site.

Plus, one of the graduate students is evaluating the seeds we find in the layers of prehistoric dirt. Every bucket of dirt we dig from the floor of the cave, we sift through strainers and wash in buckets of water. Then with small cheesecloth nets, we scoop the timeless floating seeds from the water. When dried, they're studied and categorized to piece together how much of a component in their diet gathering might have been.

But these studies are a sort of liberal reconstruction of the ancient past. A more radical and revolutionary view of hunting has emerged in the last two decades that dismantles and refutes the old myth of hunting in human evolution. It also offers us a much less noble, or less savage, view of prehistoric men. Neither killer ape nor family hunter, the current theory makes early man look like a Pliocene corner hustler, a prehistoric Fagin with an eye always to the main chance. We didn't so much stride onto the stage of history erect and powerful. More likely, we snuck into the scene from the margins of the main drama, darting unflatteringly into view as scavengers.

Dart thought the early hominids had knocked the holes in baboon skulls, for example, to suck out their brains. But it doesn't hold up to scrutiny. During the 1960s and 1970s, C. K. Brain conducted tedious, painstaking analyses of the remains of thousands of animals in the caves of South Africa. According to Brain, the round holes in the baboon skulls, it turned out, are an exact fit for leopard fangs—not humanlike daggers.[23]

She comes to the exact opposite conclusion from Dart. We aren't the great murderous powerful hunters. We were the cowering prey. From the kinds of bones in the caves, and from the marks on those bones, Brain concluded early human bones were found in these caves in such large numbers because they, like baboons, were not hunters. Early leopards and prehistoric cats came to these caves, where they found sleeping primates, and hunted them. The predator, it turns out, was in fact the prey. They were the hunted.

She refuted Dart's "predatory transition."

Instead, Brain's research corroborated the work of Elisabeth Vrba, who found that the bone parts discarded in the caves were highly selective, suggesting that the men in Sterkfontein (one of Dart's caves) were not killing large animals and bringing them home, but bringing home parts of animals that had already been killed by other animals. Early men were not the heroes of a great dramatic moment of emergence, flinging a weapon and leaping into their future. They were more likely the furtive creatures on the plains, scavengers of other creatures' kills. Here's Brain's conclusion from her book-length study, *The Hunters or the Hunted?*, concerning the bones in the South African caves: "Yet the evidence, which flowed from the first researches of Elisabeth Vrba, does not suggest that the first men to live at Sterkfontein were more than amateurs at hunting. The nature of their antelope food remains, preserved in the upper levels of the cave, suggests that they depended heavily on the kills of professional carnivores *before* they progressively developed their own prowess as hunters. This interesting and significant conclusion is corroborated by the taphonomic studies described in this book."[24] Men were the hunted, with the same predators they stole from sometimes coming into their caves at night to feed on them. For a lion, an australopithecine was not much different from a baboon!

The question is not how hunting shaped humans. The question is, when did men make the transition from being the hunted to being the hunter?

With these and other studies, hunting was no longer a "scientific fact" of our evolutionary past. It became a model to be challenged, verified, or rejected. And as the challenges came, it kept losing ground. Slowly, hunting has been thrown over as a model of human evolution, or at least as the single inclusive explanatory idea of human evolution. Certainly, the "hunting habit," as some called it, is no longer used as the single analytical category for explaining the origin of human behavior. It's been knocked from its privileged seat.

During the 1980s a new consensus emerged, that early man was a scavenger. Studying the "cut marks" on fossil bones, Lewis Binford argued in 1981, for example, that the faunal remains in Olduvai Gorge had died of natural causes. The humans associated with these animals probably hadn't killed them. The high frequencies of bones that yield little meat, he said, as well as the patterns of bone damage and breakage, reflect hominid scavenging. Not hunting.

This view of our ancestors—the scroungers, not musclemen—has yet to penetrate the public imagination. Perhaps it never will, since it offers no mythology quite as conformable to our modern views of ourselves. But it is supported by four lines of evidence: placement of cut marks on nonmeat bones; cut marks that show that dead beasts were not butchered; microwear studies that show tools were used to process plant foods; and microwear studies on early hominid teeth, showing they ate fruits and vegetables. A leading developer of the view that men were "scavengers rather than accomplished hunters," Pat Shipman wrote in 1984 that men must only have learned to hunt between 1.5 million and seven hundred thousand years ago, "when we do see a shift to omnivory, with a greater proportion of meat in the diet. This more heroic ancestor may have been *Homo erectus*, equipped with Acheulean-style stone tools and, increasingly, fire. If we wish to look further back, we may have to become accustomed to a less flattering image of our heritage."[25]

The implications of the "scavenging hypothesis" stands the hunting myth on its head. After some anthropological bickering with Shipman about who really came up with the scavenging idea, Lewis Binford summarized its significance in 1985: "You can't be your own grandpa. Systematic hunting of moderate to large animals appears to be part of our modern condition, not its cause."[26]

In other words, hunting did not shape us. We shaped hunting. That means we are not the captives of our own theory any longer. We can begin to rethink what hunting means to us. We've cleared a space for us to begin to rethink what we are.

Perhaps we were opportunistic, agile scavengers at the start. Clearly men learned also to hunt at some stage, which archaeologists are now inclined to place with *Homo erectus*, about 1.5 million years ago. Yet even if men were hunters, it is hardly likely that that was the all-determining factor in their lives. Hunting was not a universal, and we do not live with its determinism. It is not necessarily written into our DNA. It was created then, as it is created now, and the view of the prehistoric hunt served a certain ideology of the modern male. Liberal men still use prehistoric hunting as a new sort of description and justification for a certain masculinity, more sensitive, more connected, more articulate in its sense of relationship to animals, but grounded in meat and killing. Ted Kerasote constructs a tale of respect out of the hunter's killing of the animal that is rooted in a biological and prehistoric compulsion:

> On my fingers I can smell elk breakfast sausage, and I imagine some part of his digested flesh charging my synapses when my hands start to move over the keyboard. I even wonder if he-in-me might be measured. After all, testing for toxic substances has grown sophisticated enough so that the E.P.A. can detect one part in a quintillion—less than a tablespoon of a compound dropped into the Great Lakes. Could we devise a test that would detect the venison my great-grandfather ate resident in my bones? Or one that might locate the ancient compulsion to hunt what the land grows hiding in the spirals of my DNA?[27]

Note the intertwining in this paragraph of scientism, biology, technology, and male genealogy around the subtleties of hunting carried in molecules in the bones. Later, he calls hunting "our first accord with animals," echoing Joseph Campbell's almost mystical view of prehistoric hunting.

The science is, though, a mask. And the meanings of masculinity that have disguised themselves under the scientific language of the prehistoric hunt are not factually grounded. This is male fantasy.

Remove the scientific foundation, and hunting can be considered as a cultural phenomenon, and so too can the meanings of masculinity that parade in the guise of the hunter. The hunt has justified a male image biologically rooted in aggression and violence, power and sex. And as cultural phenomena, the male agendas under the guise of hunting can be revealed—the mask separated from the face.

And more important, we can begin the process of rethinking what new shapes the masculine might assume. It need not conform to a single image, a single metaphor.

The effort to rethink our origins is in part an effort to reimagine ourselves. It is an attempt to construct new notions of what might have been at work in the complex worlds of human evolution, in the emotional and intellectual realities of men, in the worlds of desire and decision, that lie beyond the bones and stones that are the precious and minimal traces of the lives that these people once led. Feminist prehistorians have been particularly active in trying to reimagine life in the past. As Francis Dahlberg concluded in *Woman the Gatherer*, the hunting hypothesis is too constricting in its view of prehistoric life: "An accurate reconstruction of early hominid life is still being fashioned, minus the high drama of man the hunter. Heroic qualities seldom come into play in securing protein from catfish, termites, snails, gerbils, and baby baboons. But what is lost in drama is gained in diversity and complexity."[28] We are invited to reimagine the lives of prehistoric men, and particularly their lives when not hunting but spending that large portion of their time around the fire in their caves.

While I was excavating in El Juyo, I had an experience that set me to thinking about what men did at home, in the cave. I had been scratching in the dirt, poking after fragments from the lives of our ancestors. The project director, Les Freeman, sat next to me, excavating in what was thought to have been a part of the sanctuary. I had removed a huge pile of seashells, one by one.

These people gathered as well as hunted, and according to Les Freeman, in every society that gathers shells, it is the women who do the gathering. But feminists dispute that, citing tribes where women hunt and men gather.

I worked with brush and knife, delicately sweeping away the greasy dirt, rich from aeons of decomposing elk. I found myself working around a long, narrow bone. It was vertical in the dirt, in the rubble of big deer thigh bones and joints. This was exquisitely delicate and thin, and I thought perhaps it was a bird bone, something like a heron's leg.

I lifted it straight upward, and the bone slipped from the earth, like a jewel from its case.

It wasn't a weapon.

I didn't know what it was. I held it up in my fingers toward Les. The bone curved in a shallow, graceful bend.

Les's hoot almost filled the cave. "You've just found a perfectly preserved sewing needle."

I was staggered. Sure enough, it tapered to a point, and had a small eye, filled with red dirt. The needle was four inches long, and probably hadn't been touched since the person who once used it to sew animal hides dropped it in the pile of shells and bones fourteen thousand years ago.

A sewing needle is very fragile, and it is rare to recover one intact. Seventy had been found in El Juyo, but not many that were a full four inches long and completely whole.

Had this needle only been used by women? Might a man have used it? Might a man have used this to sew his leathery shoes, or his fur shirt?

Looking at the needle, I realized that all our modern social politics coalesced in its graceful bend. The old hunting grounds of prehistory have become, I thought, the battlegrounds of modern sexual politics. The value of returning to origins, I thought, is not really to get back to the primal truth. It's to get back to a place where we can start all over again.

A sewing needle is a powerful and intimate tool, with its soft curve and smooth bone and its open eye. It's a trace of the domestic life of these people, a domestic and emotional life that is scarcely suggested in any of the theories of man as a hunter. It invited me to imagine the ancient male sitting in this same cave, eating and sewing, chatting and laughing.

What would a hunter do at home? How would he measure his life and his manhood? In the high drama of the hunt? Or perhaps in some idiom other than the grand achievement, the beast defeated or woman subdued to his needs. Perhaps his life took meaning for him in some image other than the trajectory of the flying spear, the crashing club. It is almost certain that it must have. Would his métier be known only in the large gesture by which the spear is flung? For even now, when men still define themselves in terms of great achievements and crushing disappointments, our lives are also measured in smaller, more intimate rhythms, the almost invisible gestures of care and love that are never made heroic, but without which life would lose all meaning. Our lives are traced in the motions of the thread and needle.

Certainly there is little of this imagery, of seashells and berry seeds, of sewing needles and gentle words, in the image of the man as hunter. But picture the hunter at home near the fire. Perhaps his life was measured most truly by the stitches that held him together, body and soul, heart and mind.

6

I'm standing in the womblike cave of Altamira, looking at one of the only two known images of copulation in the entire corpus of known prehistoric art. The other image looks like this one, and is also in Altamira. It's in a tiny tunnel in the back of the cave, hard to get to visit, full of even more surprising images. And I've just been given permission to visit that tunnel, Cola del Caballo or "tail of the horse," after I leave this stunning central salon.

One of the most miraculous sites of human imagery in the world, Altamira—the "high look" or "spectacular scene"—is most famous for the sculpted and painted bison adorning the ceiling of its central salon. But all the animal imagery in the art, along with several provocative sets of symbols that seem phallic or vulval, stir powerful sexual feelings in modern viewers and commentators on the art. Still, there are only two known images of actual sexual relations, and those disputed; but we persist in locating our conflation of hunting and sexuality in the evocative darkness of these prehistoric caves.

I am here, on this visit, because I want to study the images of copulation closely. They give a clue to the link between predation and male desire, hunting and sex, that has vexed us for centuries. Altamira gives us a glimpse of the prehistoric face of desire in nature.

In his exuberance of national pride, my voluble Spanish guide is calling the ceiling of the small grotto the "Sistine Chapel" of Paleolithic art, and for good reason. In the low, cramped space of this intimate chamber, the painted ceiling dances with a joy of animals.

The ceiling is crammed with the images of over twenty animals, polychrome creatures that lounge and romp, walk and leap across the reddish rock. The main group of animals looks like a herd of bison gathered in a meadow in the rocky foothills outside the cave.

The animals are staggering to behold, and with your head turned awkwardly upward, the effect of the leaping and resting animals is dizzyingly wonderful. What is probably a boar leaps through a corner of the ceiling near the entrance. On the far side, a large-rumped deer seems to be walking out of the meadow, away from all the other gathered creatures. High on the left, a small pony stands with placid dignity, full of sweetly affectionate peace. But the whole menagerie is dominated by about sixteen bison, males and females, huge polychrome figures done with powerful energy and inspiration. Most of the males are standing amid what appears to be a herd of recumbent females. Several large bosses of rock depend from the ceiling, and the female bison are curled around these hanging chunks of stone, nose to hind feet, as if curled in a field, resting. One bison lifts her hind legs to reveal a full udder. The effect is so strikingly lifelike, they appear to have been sculpted.

These animals were painted by people who knew animals well, who loved animals, who came to understand themselves and their own lives in terms of the animals. Animals seem clearly to have been part of our first visual vocabulary, the imagery that shaped human psychology. We think and feel through animals. In the upper part of the herd of bison, a cow stands on all four legs. She is mooing. Vigorously painted, her tail is lifted, her back is arched, her brown body is taut with excitement. She seems to be standing on the tips of her superb black hooves. Her chin is uplifted and her puckered mouth is raised as you almost hear her moo. Immediately below this energetic cow is a male. The head and horns of the bull are powerfully outlined in black. Its lower body is fused with the rear end of the mooing female.

Leslie Freeman believes that the picture is a representation of the female mounting the male. It is he who reinterpreted this image, which has never before been understood. The engraving in the Cola del Caballo appears to be of the same behavior. This is a sexual posture, according to Freeman, typical of bovine behavior. During rutting season, females grow so excited they frequently mount males. It's a precopulatory act, so common that it was observed by Aristotle in cows.

Leslie Freeman believes that there is powerful symbolism in Paleolithic art, but as in the case of these two copulating, or precopulatory, bison, the symbolism is not clear to us. For Freeman, the image is an example of Paleolithic naturalism—the art of a people who observed animals carefully and painted what they saw. But for most interpreters of Paleolithic cave art, animals are the symbols through which hunting and sex are linked in the human psyche. We internalized them through this art, not simply as hunters, and we learned to think ourselves, we established our human identity, by learning to make images of them as "others."

The best known, and largely abandoned, theory links hunting and the sex act through primitive magic. Herbert Read was an art historian who provided a valuable summary of the ways in which hunting and sexuality were thought to be magically linked for the primitive people who made these paintings. The focus on animals in the art, he maintained, was the result of these men's preoccupation with securing meat. Over the millennia, that preoccupation was drilled into the male imagination as a central archetype, an image with a powerful and universal meaning for humanity. The imagery of the caves is full of a "psychic energy," he claims, that moves immediately to speculation on what "was going on in the mind of prehistoric man? What were his conscious thought processes, what were his *unconscious* dream processes?"[29]

According to Read, the primitive mind operated through a magical identification between an image and reality. At the primitive stage in our evolution represented by the cave art, image and reality were not in fact clearly differentiated in our minds. As a result, he claimed, the painted image could help beget reality. A wounded bison in the cave could lead to a wounded bison in the hunt. Sexual images, likewise, could help ensure the reproductive success of the animals, and abundant numbers of deer and bison would mean the survival of the tribe or family which hunted them.

In this magical landscape, hunting and sexuality defined our central preoccupations in art. They were linked at the primal core of our imaginations, when we were poised on the dark edge of history. They are archetypes in our consciousness, a part of our imaginative legacy, not merely on walls, but actually carried in our psyches:

And no doubt certain images had a priority in this development [of specifically human intelligence]—images connected with the primary instincts of food-getting and sex . . . and if we may assume that man inherits a physical predisposition towards images that conform to these patterns, then we arrive at [Carl] Jung's conception of the *archetype*, a term in his psychology which indicated an inherited structure of the brain predisposing the human race, at certain epochs, to the invention of particular kinds of symbol, or to the creation of particular mythical figures. These structural features of the psyche can only have been evolved by collective experiences of long duration, and of great intensity and unity. The life-or-death struggle with the animal, at a certain geological epoch when the human race depended for its survival on the killing of such animals, was precisely one of those profound social experiences which, in Jung's hypothesis, are creative of an archetype.[30]

Sex and hunting were in this view the central preoccupation of our imaginations from the earliest times.

The argument has a powerful appeal to men. It survives even in the men's movement, which is largely based on Jungian ideas. And it often evokes cave painting to ground its ideas of maleness, imagining initiation rites and magical ceremonies deep in the recesses of these caves. These magic rituals not only focused on the hunt; they would transmit the mysteries of manhood to young boys. Yet there is not one piece of evidence that ceremonies were performed in these caves—not one that anthropologists accept uncontested.[31]

And the use of the art for hunting magic? Certainly it was sometimes used. I've seen one image in a cave—La Pasiega, in fact—that is certainly a bull trapped within a cage. But this is the only image in European cave art that is certainly of a captured animal. It is significant for its rarity. The art was used for much more than rituals of hunting and sex. We know, for example, from bone remains that reindeer was the staple food for hunters during the period of the great cave painting, the Magdalenian period of the Upper Paleolithic, from seventeen thousand to ten thousand years ago. Yet reindeer are extremely rare in Paleolithic art. And less than 10 percent of all animals in this parietal art are wounded in any way.[32]

Another theory provides an example of the way this art of hunters is used to posit the origins of the psychology of sex. In *The Tender Carnivore and the Sacred Game*, Paul Shepard idealizes the association between sex and hunting. It's a primal reality, he claims, in shaping men's emotional lives:

> The symbiotic interplay of the hunt and love, of predation and copula-
> tion, is a primal motif, surely preliterate, and older than the agricultural
> theme of the cycle of birth and death, regeneration for the decay of life,
> and the dead as a source of the living. The spear's interpenetration of the
> body and the flesh as the source of all new life are the iconography of
> venery—at once the pursuit of love and game. . . . Both have to do with
> the most profound of life's passions, the demonic moment of the kill
> and of orgasm. These two powerful expressions are related. Both lead to
> life and death, which, like maleness and femaleness, represent a funda-
> mental polarity.[33]

It is a remarkable passage, as is the entire section in which it is embedded.
His is a liberal rereading of prehistoric hunting and its link to sexuality, a
palliated version of male domination.

He links menstrual blood with the idea of a bleeding wound—it is an
"inescapable" idea in the male imagination, he asserts. "Genital anatomy,"
he maintains, also upholds the symbolism of sex and hunting, love and
death, killing and orgasms. The female's job in sex is to act as "sexual prey
of the wild huntsman." The woman magically, artfully, deflects his violence and entertains it. Shepard claims the link between sex and hunting is
not symbolic. The sex act is "the demonic moment" in which a man kills
the female in love, the moment "of the kill and of the orgasm."[34]

Her submission, though, creates something new in the male: "new sensitivity." The women, in this model, are to blame if men are violent to
them, since they haven't sufficiently "appeased" the male: "In courtship,"
writes Shepard, "the appeaser is not a true prey but the human female." He
crowns his native aggression with a surprising new tenderness. This softer
feeling, this love, in turn becomes part of his hunting, part of his act of
killing the beast: "The human hunter in the field is not merely a predator,
because of hundreds of centuries of experience in treating the woman-prey
with love, which he turns back into the hunt proper."[35] This is how the
hunter can love the thing he kills.

We see the familiar attempt to universalize a particular view of masculinity in hunting, carefully defined and maintained gender roles, and
most startling, a definition of "normal" sex as "face-to-face copulation."
Shepard says this new sexual position, common only to primates, also defines a new psychology of relationship. "Sexual intercourse," Shepard
concludes, "has become the most powerful imaginable experience of re-
latedness." The art of the caves reenacts the sexual act: "Supine in the act
she may be, but the woman is more a partner and less an object. The male
does not simply penetrate; he is engulfed. He is also engulfed in the sacred

cave, in the ceremonial confrontation of the symbolic gender of animal art."[36] Shepard's theory of the sex act is pure fantasy, a sanctimonious romanticizing of male domination. He offers no evidence because there is none to adduce. But he tells us how deeply ingrained the associations of women and prey, desire and predation are in the modern male psyche.

He makes the Judeo-Christian position a metaphor of all human sex. It's easy to dismiss because, like the theory of hunting which it parallels, it leaves so much out. And what the man-on-top position leaves out are all the parts of sex that make it interesting. Shepard's is not only a male-superior theory, but it isn't even a fun version of sex. Of course sex is a corporeal representation of the desire we feel, giving it a body and a name: what turns you on is a description of how you relate.

Such an image of the sex act is not true now. And it wasn't true for prehistoric people either. At least, they had enough imagination to realize that a cow can mount a bull, in Altamira, in the only explicit image of the sex act they painted.

For Shepard, the woman is interchangeable with the animal—relationship between the two is merged in the mind of the male as hunter. Sex and death, power and love, killing and orgasms—hunting is a figure of erotic domination. Through hunting, more than any other metaphor for the sex act and the psychology of sex, this confusion has been developed and perpetuated.

The most important attempt to link hunting and sex, the one which achieved the credibility of evidence, came in the 1960s and 1970s, not through theories of magic, but through a careful scrutiny of all the cave imagery by the famous French scientist Andre Leroi-Gourhan.[37] The meaning of this art, he claimed, does not reside in specific images. Rather, it is part of the implicit structure of the artistic compositions of the caves. Images of male and female, phallus and vulva, spear and wound—these are the organizing structures of meaning in the human mind.

Leroi-Gourhan inventoried every image in over sixty-six caves in France and Spain, carefully mapping their locations, statistically analyzing placement and associations. He was interested in discovering something deeper than the meanings of a particular image, or of a particular panel. He used Paleolithic art to try to decipher the fundamental structure of the human mind itself. This made him a "structuralist." As Terence Hawkes describes it, the "ultimate quarry of structuralist thinking may be the permanent structures into which human acts and perceptions fit. . . ."[38] It is the pursuit of the universal structures in the human mind within which acts and images, thoughts and deeds, find their meaning.

Leroi-Gourhan swept away the focus on magic, and replaced it with the idea that in the art of the Paleolithic peoples taken as a whole we could

read a universal "mythogram" of our own thinking. His work was powerful, revolutionary, stimulating. His mapping of the imagery in the caves led
him to treat the cave as a "mythological vessel," a text through which we
could access the traces of our deepest metaphysical thought. What he found
was a kind of "syntax" in the imagery, a set of relationships between symbols and animals that bears meaning. The caves were not about magic.
They were about the human mind.

What did they reveal? "Whether the figures correspond to magical or
any other sort of religious intention," he wrote, "the order and frequency of
these figures were bound . . . to express the image—even if unconsciously
or incompletely formulated—which their maker had of the world upon
which those practices were exercised."[39]

In the Paleolithic bestiary, the meaning of the animals in the ideology
or metaphysic of its makers is sexual. Leroi-Gourhan found that the group-
ings fell into two classes—animals and signs or symbols. Of the animals,
over 60 percent of the representations were of horses and bison/aurochs.
When found in association with the symbols, the horse was associated with
images that we view as phallic and male. The bison/auroch images are associated with images we typically view as vulval or female. The animals,
then, came to define two classes, into which Leroi-Gourhan believed he
could dispose all Paleolithic (and human) meaning. The paintings were
about sexual "couplings," even though copulation itself is so very rare. The
caves are about "sexual polarization."

The classic structural meaning of the art, according to Leroi-Gourhan,
is that the caves contain statements about the dependence of life and death
upon each other. Males, horses, weapons, and death-dealing animals are
opposed to females, animals traditionally hunted by Paleolithic peoples,
and wounded and dying animals.

As Leroi-Gourhan writes in his classic and comprehensive study, *Treasures of Prehistoric Art:*

> Without overly forcing the evidence, we can view the whole of Paleo-
> lithic figurative art as the expression of ideas concerning the natural
> and supernatural organization of the living world (the two might have
> been one in Paleolithic thought). Can we go further? It is possible that
> the truth corresponds to this frame of reference, which is still too
> broad. To gain a dynamic understanding of cave representations, one
> would still have to integrate into this framework the symbolism of the
> spear and the wound. Taken as symbols of sexual union and death,
> the spear and the wound would then be integrated into a cycle of

life's renewal, the actors in which would form two parallel and complementary series: man/horse/spear, and woman/bison/wound.

In the last analysis (which is still provisional) we may conclude that
Palaeolithic [*sic*] people represented in the caves the two great categories of living beings, their corresponding male and female symbols,
and the symbols of death which feeds the hunter. In the central zones [of
the panels of images] the system was expressed by the aggregate of
male symbols around the female principal figures, while in other parts
of the sanctuary the male representations were exclusive, apparently
complementary to the cavern itself.[40]

Once again, cave art links sex and death, hunting and love, the spear and
the wound. And these are posited as fundamental to the male psyche—the
universal structure of our mental lives.

The structuralist enterprise of Leroi-Gourhan has been influential in re-
focusing archaeology on theory, and on treating the art as a kind of "language." But it is no longer in favor because of its quest for universals. As
Terence Eagleton writes, it is "hair-raisingly unhistorical." It's also illogical: for Leroi-Gourhan, a horse is a male image, whether the particular image is itself male or female. And a bison is a female image, even if it's a
bull. It's hard to imagine the artist's thinking this way, even unconsciously.

Margaret Conkey, an anthropologist from the University of California
at Berkeley, puts the objections to all these theories about cave art most
powerfully and succinctly. By trying to explain these cave paintings in
terms of hunting, she claims we have tried to find a single explanation for
all the many styles of art that spanned at least twenty-five thousand years of
prehistory. No single theory, and no single theme, is likely to account for
the incredible variety of styles and themes this art portrays. There are, for
example, at least twenty-two easily recognizable styles of horses in Paleolithic art.[41]

The female as prey, intercourse as a wounding, orgasm as a death—
love as a kind of hunt postulates a psychology of relationship in the male
mind that needs to be carefully examined, carefully deconstructed. It is a
model of erotic domination, of sex and violence posited as an inescapable
unity in the cortex of the male. How did it get so ingrained in us that we
have been willing to make it the single interpretive theory for the nature of
desire in prehistory?

The emphasis now in the study of cave art is no longer on finding a
single narrative to account for all the art, but on the diversity of styles
and meanings that are likely to inform, not only the art itself, but even a
single cave.

Leslie Freeman believes, for example, that each cave must be studied individually, and the images understood in the context of the particular cave and the concerns of the particular people. This he thinks was one of the great contributions made by Leroi-Gourhan: he studied each cave painstakingly, for its precise and unique distribution of images. Altamira, for example, contains mostly images of bison, which seems to reflect a peaceful tribe or period. There is little fierceness in any of the cave's imagery. But the Cola del Caballo contains stunning images that show these hunters learning to imagine themselves through animals that don't have anything to do with killing them.

7

Well beyond the chamber with the Great Ceiling, a small passageway leads into a rock wall off the top of an inconspicuous high ledge. Tourists never visit this part of the cave, and Les Freeman in a recent study discovered several new magnificent images here. It's a tiny, cramped, dead-end corridor, a small fissure in the rock.

In this narrow crack in the rock, the Cro-Magnons sculpted a series of images that showed them using animals to try to imagine themselves as human. They imagined desire not in terms of a wounding, but in terms of a transformation.

You have to scoot and scuttle in this passageway, almost crawl in places. It's long, but only two meters wide and only waist-high in some spots. Large, sharp rocks jut from the walls, and rubble on the floor makes it easy to trip.

The entrance to the Cola is marked with primitive forms, vaguely like finger-paint squiggles—indecipherable lines that researchers call "macaroni." Goats and deer are incised on the rock walls at various points, as are strange black marks, lines really, whose meanings have been fiercely but inconclusively debated. Whatever this place was to its decorators, it's a darkness filled with meaning.

The defining images of the corridor of the Cola are the bison. Their faces are carved on large stones that poke out from the wall and ceiling. As so often and so beautifully in prehistoric art, the shapes of the rocks and cave have themselves been exploited, made part of the art. The artists took a long crack on a projecting rock, etched it out longer, and made a nose out of it. Or black paint, added to a hole on the rock, emphasizes an eye.

These faces occur at dramatic points along the cramped passageway.

They are immensely haunting, both because they are simply faces, or "masks," and because they loom out at me, in the jut of the rock, barely discernible at first, but unmistakable and unforgettable once I've seen them. They seem to come at me out of the dark cave itself, like optical illusions. I stare at them each, concentrating until I see the face take shape in the natural contours of the rock, augmented by incisions, gouges, streaks of black paint.

The first bison image is barely ten meters from the entry, chunked out of a squarish block of stone, enigmatic eyes gouged roughly and painted black, a long vertical fissure in the rock forming the nose. At the bottom of the stone, the fissure bends from my right to left, and has been scraped by some tool, and a line for a mouth was formed. It is the image of a beast, but the face is also eerily human. It's half-beast, half-human—a human-animal double.

There are nine masks altogether in the Cola. Just before the end, the narrowness widens perceptibly into what Les Freeman calls the "Chamber of the Masks." In this space, the prehistoric sculptors carved five faces. Two are clearly animal faces, both bison, easily identifiable because they're in profile, with long snouts. Two other bison, however, merge the bestial with the human. One of these is carved out of a long vertical rock hanging from the ceiling, an almost threatening projection. On either side of a sharp vertical ridge in the rock, which serves as a nasal shape, two dark circles have been painted in, black and ghostly eyes, like those on the white sheets of Halloween ghosts.

At the bottom, a curving gouge serves as a heavy, slightly gaping but silent mouth. The human-animal double is powerful for its crudeness, so at odds with the technical sophistication of the bison in the large main chamber of the cave. There is a kind of tentativeness in the image, a wavering in the dark borders between human and animal. It's in this darkness that the subjectivity of humans seems to take shape, worked out of the image of the animal, teased from it.

Just beyond this human-animal double is the startling culmination of the masks. I have to look hard to see it, turning around in the tunnel. My guide lights the stone from below with a flashlight while I squeeze up against the far wall, a few feet away, for the needed perspective. In the strange light, emerging from the play of shadow and rock and light, the image begins to appear.

It is utterly recognizable, even in the unsteady beam of a weak flashlight—an engraved human face. Heavy, pondering brows hang above deeply recessed, darkly peering eyes. One of the eyes is huge, punched into the stone. The other is tight and small, as if squinting, even winking at you. The nose is more subtle than on the other masks, and the mouth has small human lips, vaguely like the rosebud mouths of Gothic paintings, tight-lipped and pursy, almost scowling. It is a lonely, tense, brooding face.

Freeman believes that these masks demonstrate that, for these early *Homo sapiens*, the symbolic capacity was already fully developed, and played as prominent a role in evolution as did material culture. These people were making a metaphoric connection between themselves and bison, human and animal. No doubt this derived from the close relationship they had as hunters with their prey. And as you enter and leave the Cola, Freeman argues, you enact a process of transformation, from animal to human and back again.

I'm struck by how these people, the Cro-Magnons, seemed to be groping, through some dark desire, to know their own image. This may be the ultimate human desire—to make meaning itself out of our lives. And if desire emerges in relationship to what is not, one form it can take is in the connection that gives shape to a sense of self.

As I squat against the wall, I am startled by the sudden recognition of a human image out of the animal "mask." The two images seem to waver in and out of each other, unstable. They interpenetrate. The consciousness of being human emerges out of the consciousness of the animal. And sinks back into it in the dark. I have been startled by images in prehistoric caves before. I have been moved by encounters with animals that changed the way I see things, even see myself. And I find myself thinking of the Green Man carved on the capitals of the Chapter House in Southwell Cathedral in England, that dynamic and unstable sense of self, the human allied to the natural. But I've never before had such a powerful feeling, such a breathtaking moment of recognition in a piece of art that is also in nature, as I have this very minute.

But this is different. Not just because I'm deep in a cave. And not just because these images are at least fifteen thousand years older than a medieval cathedral.

These creatures may have been painted *by* hunters, but they are certainly not *about* hunting. We don't actually know if hunters painted them, or if they were painted by men (or women) who might have lived with hunters and were not themselves hunters. But the concern is about knowing themselves through animals. We see ourselves through the animal. We cannot, it seems, imagine ourselves without them.

Animals are the language of these earliest of human images. Animals are an original vocabulary for men to use for self-exploration and self-discovery.

The crudeness of the image is part of its power, rough lines and scratches. Little chips of rock, a smudge of black paint, a ghostly circle of eyes. This moment of emergence, this process of transformation, this connection between beast and human—on the rock, in the cave, in conception: all our urge for a stable identity, a powerful and fixed sense of self, belies the dynamic of a self struggling to make an image of itself out of the creatures it identifies with. These animals are scratched in our brains, as surely as the human image is scratched onto the rocks. It is part of our psychology that we imagine ourselves out of our relationship with animals, with the other that compels us.

We are rough hewn in the images of the creatures we adore. The self is not an entity but a complex and unstable set of relationships. We see and suffer ourselves in the eyes of others. Like the artist or artists who carved and painted these "masks," we are always moving in and out of ourselves, sliding back and forth, glimpsing ourselves for a moment, slipping back into the darkness. Our emergence into consciousness comes not simply with domination, but with identification. Even more, it comes with this struggle to spot ourselves in the image of the other. The creature is deeply implanted in us, and our vision of ourselves is carved and hacked and teased out of it, in scratches and paint.

We are forever becoming ourselves. We want things to be certain, solid, determinant. We want control of our sense of ourselves. We want to believe in a stable and substantial self. We want to believe in hunting because it gives us the image of our selves in control of animals, in control of the world, in control of ourselves. These are images of transformation and change. Under our images of control is this more delicate and vulnerable image of the human face always taking shape to itself. Always coming as a surprise to itself when you actually see it.

Is the vision of the emergence of the human image in the Cola based on a hunting motif? What seems important is not that these bison were hunted, not even that they were eaten. It is that they were food for thought. These bison are vehicles for thought, original metaphors of that deep desire to picture the human face—to face ourselves at last.

And only for brief moments. Then to return to our quotidian lives, but with that heightened sense of awareness that knows there are animals inside us, in the depths, like the faces carved in the guts of these caves.

I myself come out of the cave of Altamira seething inside, changed. I step out of the dark cave into the bright Spanish sun. A thin mist gleams over the fields. The images of those animals and humans are inside me. They remind me that we exist, we invent ourselves, somewhere between memory and desire. We slip along the inner boundary between the beast and the human. In this inner space, our mental evolution takes place. The boundaries for a moment become less clear, between past and future, animal and human. Identity is less a matter of my isolated self, and more a matter of relationship.

The sun is bright and heavy with mist when I emerge and am filled with the beautiful, brooding darkness of faces.

3

THE HUNTER IN MIND

Canst thou bind the sweet influences of the Pleiades, or loose the bands
of Orion?

—Job 38.31[1]

Orion went away to Crete and spent his time hunting in company with
Artemis and Leto. It seems that he threatened to kill every beast there
was on earth; whereupon, in her anger, Earth sent up against him a scorpion of very great size by which he was stung and so perished. After this
Zeus, at the prayer of Artemis and Leto, put him among the stars, because of his manliness, and the scorpion also as a memorial of him and
of what had occurred.

—Hesiod, "Astronomy"[2]

In 395 B.C., the celebrated general Xenophon returned to Athens to find a
city he no longer recognized. With his mercenary force of ten thousand
Greeks, he had fought with Cyrus the Younger, the pretender to the
throne in Persia. Xenophon's campaign was more notable for its famous
and spectacular retreat than any great victories, and when he returned to
Athens, he discovered that his adored friend Socrates had been put to
death in 399 B.C. A new decadent kind of men had taken over the city. In
Xenophon's eyes, these sophists and rhetoricians were corrupters of
young Athenian boys, destroyers of the state.

He left Athens with his friend Agesilaus, the king of Sparta, and was
formally exiled from the city in 394 B.C. Retiring to his country farm at
Scillus, on the sunny Peloponnisos near Olympia, he passed his time in
hunting and writing.

In his leisure at Scillus, Xenophon probably wrote the first known tract
on hunting. His treatise is called *On Hunting*, sometimes called *Cynegeti-
cus*, and in Greek means literally "leading out the dogs."[3] It's a training
manual, really, for privileged young sons of Athens who would become the
ruling class of adult men. It's a practical document, and interesting reading,

betraying Xenophon's particular love for his favorite sport of hare hunting in the countryside just outside the city. It lays out all the necessities for clothing and equipment and technique. But the treatise is much more than a checklist of outfits and skills. It also describes the hunter himself. It fact, it prescribes what the hunter should be.

For Xenophon and other prominent Greek thinkers, hunting was an educational program, not in letters, but in masculine mores. For Xenophon, hunting taught young men how to be virtuous, by which he meant a certain ethics of virility.

Xenophon described hunting as a sort of technique for boys through which they could be shaped into men. It was one central strategy in a broader, conservative social agenda whose goal was producing socially responsible citizens. Hunting was a sort of practice, a physical regimen. But more, it was a social institution and a social practice, a social technology even, by which Greek ruling-class men could reproduce the kind of men they wanted.

Under this scheme, hunting was not particularly important in producing rabbits for domestic meals. Nor was it really important to protect rural areas from marauding predators. Xenophon's love of hare hunting can hardly be required for defending the city. Both acquiring food and protecting agricultural fields were important reasons for hunting for still-emerging civilizations. But as it was taken over by philosophers and social thinkers in ancient Greece, hunting's value lay in recreation and, even more, in politics and ethics. The hunter in mind had social meaning, and was a social creature.

Hunting had a long pedigree already, before Xenophon, as the proper calling of heroes. It could then easily be marshaled as the image of manhood. As J. K. Anderson puts it, hunting in archaic and classical Greece was "a masculine, and in a sense, a manly activity."[4]

On Crete, the ancient geographer Strabo describes how the fourth century BC men of the assembly formed "Troops" of boys, with each leader an older man. These "Troops" were taken out to hunt and run races and learn how to form ranks for battle. If disobedient, they were beaten. Their "particular custom" in hunting had to do with "love affairs." Noble young boys were pursued and then "ritually abducted" by the older men of the island. The abductor gave the boy presents, took him to the country, and entertained him with feasting and hunting. The adult was called the *erastes*, or lover, and the boy was called *eromenos*, or beloved. After two months, they returned to the city, where the boy was released and lavished with presents: an ox for sacrifice to Zeus, a cup, and military equipment are the presents required by law, but the gifts exceeded these, too. Ritual and erotic hunting retreats served as the initiation into the world of warrior men for the boys of Crete.

In Macedonia, boar-hunting provided the test of manhood. Only those nobles who had killed a boar without the use of a net—that is, only through the more heroic means of a spear in direct confrontation with a boar—were allowed to recline at banquets. One king's son had to sit in a chair, like an adolescent, until the ignominious age of thirty-five.[5]

As social ritual, as educational program, and as literary motif, hunting moved the true natural habitat of hunting from the countryside to the city. The hunter may actually hunt in the fields beyond the city walls. But the true locus of the hunt, its meaning and purpose, was shaped inside the city. And even as hunting assumed its symbolic range in the marking out of territory for full manhood in the ancient world, it assumed its dark and subversive side. It became the image at once of social responsibility and social disruption, of rational political order and a dangerous wildness.

But this hunter was known not only by the beasts he opposed, but also by the kinds of men he opposed. He was a political image—*for* one kind of manhood and *against* another. Hunting promoted a specific image of manliness. In Xenophon's "On Hunting" as well as in all instances when hunting bears a social burden of training men into a specific image of masculinity, hunting is about social power. As hunting is socially deployed in debates about masculinity, is made part of a social agenda, it inevitably expresses a politics of identity and a politics of social dominance. It politicizes the options available to a boy. For Xenophon, for example, the virtuous hunter chasing beasts and fighting as a hoplite in the Greek army was contrasted with the despised male, who was variously described as a "sophist" or a "politician." The hunter by contrast was a lover of toil and virtue. He was a philosopher or a general: men of truth and action. The sophist taught language and political speeches. He loved pleasure and idleness. As Xenophon said, sophists and politicians strove "for victory over their friends," and they "hunt the rich and the young." But the true "huntsmen offer their lives and their property in sound condition for the service of the citizens. These attack wild beasts, those other [sophists and politicians attack] their friends." The hunter was the image of the virtuous soldier defending the entire city.[6]

Specifically, Xenophon justified hunting because he felt it produced an ideal citizen out of a young boy. After introducing hunting by giving its pedigree among the gods, Xenophon moved to a succinct justification for using hunting in the education of boys:

> Therefore I charge the young not to despise hunting or any other school-
> ing. For these are the means by which men become good in war and in

all things out of which must come excellence.... The first pursuit, therefore, that a young man just out of his boyhood should take up is hunting, and afterwards he should go on to other branches of education, provided he has the means.[7]

Hunting was the foundation of knowledge and ethical action, and was reserved for those of means. The young hunter learned the duties and disciplines required by his rank.

The young Greek hunter praised by Xenophon also learned the powers and prerogatives of his social station. And, he learned his duties and discipline. He will be a soldier and a voting citizen. Virtuous hunting involved not only a social politics in a contest with sophists over the boys of Athens—whose educational systems would prevail?—but is was also cut with class concerns. As the symbolic content of hunting took on an ideological cast, its value as a subsistence activity not only atrophied, but in fact was suppressed. It's a common theme in the history of hunting that the elite hunters, for whom hunting trains men in a certain ethical behavior, condescend to and perhaps even despise the practical hunting of lower classes. In a long passage at the end of his treatise, Xenophon explains how the ideal male would be elevated by his sport, how he would serve the state, and how this justified privileging these city hunters over farmers and the nocturnal hunters around the city who would usurp the game:

But the advantages that those who have been attracted to this pursuit [hunting] will gain are many. For it makes the body healthy, improves the sight and hearing, and keeps men from growing old; and it affords the best training for war. . . . For men who are sound in body and mind may always stand on the threshold of success. It was because they knew that they owed their successes against the enemy to such qualities that our ancestors looked after the young men. For in spite of the scarcity of corn it was their custom from the earliest times not to prevent hunters from hunting over any growing crops; and, in addition, not to permit hunting at night within a radius of many furlongs from the city, so that the masters of that art might not rob the young men of their game. . . . For it makes sober and upright men of them, because they are trained in the school of truth (and they perceived that to these men they owed their success in war, as in other matters); and it does not keep them from any other honourable occupation they wish to follow, like other and evil pleasures that they ought not to learn. Of such men, therefore, are good soldiers and good generals made. For they whose toils root out whatever is base and froward from mind and body make desire for virtue to flour-

ish in their place—they are the best, since they will not brook injustice
to their city nor injury to its soil.[8]

Hunting was already a heroic story that linked self-education with the
preservation of the nation. These values coalesced in the image of the active young boy running through the fields. Hunting was the activity that
made possible the founding and the preservation of the city. As such, it was
the privileged activity of a privileged class.

In many instances, hunting for utilitarian purposes came to be despised
as a sign of inferior status. Its very uselessness—men explicitly did not
hunt for food—became a mark of social superiority. It was pursued as a
symbol of superiority and as a means to build character. The association of
hunting with an elite class, and its use in educating the young in the standards of that class, is found also in Persian and Mogul traditions, as well as
in the aristocratic hunting of the Renaissance and in nineteenth-century
big-game hunters.[9]

Plato took Xenophon's side in the promotion of hunting as an educational program and social institution. In the Laws, Plato spurned any kind
of hunting that is "too illiberal," not gentlemanly enough. His goal, both in
the laws used to regulate hunting and in the morality that hunting should
inculcate, was to create the "perfect citizen." Plato recognized hunting as a
social metaphor and form of social policy, tantamount to a sociological theory. "Hunting is a large and complex matter," Plato wrote, and provided a
whole series of distinctions in hunting, dissecting society as essentially
constructed out of these many types of social hunting (for friends, wealth,
fame, and so on).

Most important, though, was the education of youth through good
forms of hunting. Good hunting was determined by its ability to "render the
souls of the young better." Fishing, bird snaring, hunting by night—these
among others Plato dismissed as base, all smacking somehow of laziness
and practicalities. He disdained the cunning that was implied by using
nets—"no gentlemanly pursuit"—and the deceit implied by hunting in the
dark. Only the stalking and capture of land animals, in his view, were frank
and courageous enough to use in teaching virtue to boys. He was thinking
primarily of athletics, and the ways in which the physical contest could
teach courage.

Men are known by their hunting methods, Plato asserted, which reveal
a man's soul. Only mastering beasts through "the victorious might of the
toil-loving soul," he wrote, is the best hunting. Plato urged only the hunting
"of quadrupeds with horses and dogs and the hunter's own limbs." Such
hunting lifts men in a "godlike manliness."[10]

As a social idea, hunting was being transformed. It is not linked to a notion of selfhood as a discovery of identity in nature, despite its ethic of confrontation with beasts in the field. Hunting represents the conscious and careful fashioning of boys into model citizens. It served cultural ends, and reflects conscious political and social interests. It supported a specific code of ethics for governing males—an ethic made by men for men.

Hunting was thought of as both maker and marker of social power.

More fundamental, hunting had been converted from a natural to a symbolic activity. It now existed inside the imaginations of men. And if it had ever been possible before, it certainly will not be possible in the future, at least in the West, to separate the symbolic from the practical functions of hunting—however they may change in various cultural and historical circumstances. Or rather, the Western hunter will always enter a hunting terrain that is marked by symbolic demarcations. The hunter took up residence in the male's head.

Still, this philosophical hunting, this idea of the good citizen-hunter of Plato and Xenophon, was a sort of grid imposed upon an inherited mythology of the hunter. Developed in early Greek culture, myths dating from before Homer gave an early genealogy to both hunter and male. The genealogy of the hunter is the genealogy of the male by the time Plato and Xenophon rationalize the mythic inheritance. Xenophon and Plato's notions of the philosophical and military values of the hunter, of the good citizen-hunter, were a grid imposed upon these more crepuscular hunter-heroes inhabiting the borderlands between nature and culture. If the philosophers had the imprimatur of the gods and heroes whom Xenophon said invented the sport, so much the better. But the myths did not describe so much the training of a good citizen. They described the emergence and career of the great hero, and there's something much more unruly about them, something much more dangerous and primitive in the impulses that hunting described in the male psyche. The philosophers tamed the image, grooming the hunter to leave the wilds and take his place in the town assembly.

In the great myths, all the heroes are hunters, and all the great hunters were heroes.[11]

What was fundamental to the notions of the male as hunter in the philosophers and the myths, is that he was created by adversity. The male was somehow created, he somehow realized his identity, in the battle with an adversary. Manly identity required opposition, and the battle is actually generative, as we'll see in reviewing some of the most important myths of the hunter as hero.

Identity in this hunterly model is defined not only by what it *is*, but simultaneously by what it is *not*.

If generals and philosophers, heroes and gods, both approve this noble image of the hunter as a model of masculinity, can we be surprised at its tenacity? After all, we have it from Zeus and Xenophon, Apollo and Plato.

2

Shining, heroic, belted with bright stars, Orion circles our heads every fall and winter. For many, Orion is the most easily recognizable constellation in the heavens, one of the best-known star groups. It's a star group many use to orient themselves in the night. Orion is the great hero of the early Greeks, a hunter and a night stalker. Orion is the image of the great hunter still. He still stalks the night sky, close behind Taurus the bull, carrying his club in one hand, holding a skin in the other. He sends us messages down from the sky, old messages from ancient mythology about the greatest of the early Greek heroes. Stories of the way manhood was first defined by hunting for the Greeks. He remains a presence for us, circling our heads at night, familiar but somehow distant and strange. Few still know his stories, few still realize how manhood was shaped by this gigantic, terrifying hunter in the heavens.

No image better defines how the hunter planted certain notions of violence and rapacity into the deep structure of the male psyche.

I love finding Orion in the winter sky. Late in the fall, when men in their blaze-orange hunting hats and vests stalked the midwestern hardwood forests, looking for white-tailed deer and black bear, I often used to retreat to a one-room log cabin by a secluded lake in the Minnesota hardwoods. It was the only cabin on the shallow lake, and I had perfect privacy. During the day, I would write and watch the buffleheads flocking for the migration. At night, the air got so cold and clear that stars would flare in the sky.

After dark, I often paddled the Grumman canoe out onto the dark lake. I would lie backward on the bottom of the canoe and drift under the white sweep of the Milky Way, studying the constellations with a flashlight and an astronomy book. As I learned my way around the sky, I felt more and more at home on that lake. It was somehow comforting to me to know that the constellations I was getting to know were the same ones that had been seen—and named—by the ancients.

Orion the hunter announces the fall, heralds the winter. I loved to watch him rise low over the marshy end of the lake, down where the loons often nested. His slanted belt, his dangling sword, his club raised over his head, about to whack Taurus the bull—he is a star group of cold white brilliance, one of the most dependable ways to orient myself through the sky. I always began with Orion.

Orion is perhaps the most ancient of the Greek heroes. His stories were not written down, and he was later eclipsed by other heroes—Hercules, Theseus, Perseus, and others. He comes down to us in fragments, snippets of stories with many variants and contradictions. He was the hero of a rough and unvarnished age, and he is so old that he comes down to us only in fragments and allusions. Homer refers to him in the *Odyssey*, beautifully describing how he was abducted by the goddess of the dawn, who took him to her lovely bed.

Orion's fame rested, first, on his prowess as a hunter. Even in the heavens, he continues to hunt the bull that is frozen tantalizingly just in front of him. In his left hand, Orion holds the skin of some prey, perhaps a lion. As the prototypical hero of classical mythology, Orion's exploits as a hunter achieved for him his greatness and fame, and he was lifted into the skies in the apotheosis of the hunter. As with Hercules, the Greek hunter not only moved between nature and culture, but his true margin was between manhood and godhead.

He's an idealized figure, his image outlined by gorgeous stars that burn white and blue in the winter sky. His familiarity in the skies suggests the power he has exerted in shaping men's consciousness of themselves. Yet Orion's stories don't suggest an ideal hero. There is some suggestion that he was a culture hero, helping to protect kings from wild beasts. He was also loved by goddesses, a man of charisma and power. But he comes to life most vividly as a man of dark and aggressive desires. The spirit of Orion the hunter emerges in the violent passions that impel him to cross boundaries, to break rules, to transgress proprieties. He was connected with all those forms of hunting, for example, that Plato labels as unacceptable in his educational scheme for Athenian boys. Orion is a nocturnal hunter, and he loves to hunt by craftiness, especially with snares. And he's a giant, as well. He is able to stride across the earth, and even across the sea. As he walks, he casts a terrifying shadow, and there's some mention of earthquakes. His constellation is beautiful, and goddesses fell in love with him. He must have been a powerful figure. But it's hard to see, in the fragments we have of his stories, other than a kind of outlaw's charisma, just what the source of his attractiveness was, for his stories all stress a kind of destructive darkness, a rapacious appetite that terrifies kings, women, and the goddesses who love him.[12]

A force of nature, even a threat to the stability of social relations, Orion the hunter moves back and forth across the threshold of civilization. He becomes more bestial than human, chthonic and even demonic—a nocturnal hunter who strides like a giant across earth and sea. Strangely, the depredations of Orion are largely social in nature, and his violence is a kind of social subversion. Orion's stories, for example, are less about hunting than about sexual violence, and the passions that animate him as hunter and hero—his transgressions are really not a kind of fighting but a kind of rape. Hunting suggests this rapacity in several guises, and although I discussed Orion in the first chapter, it's worth examining his stories in more detail, since they reveal the way the hunter as a hero myth moves across contradictions and paradoxes in defining the heroic male within us.

While the stories vary as to his parents—all agree on Poseidon as father, and only a few important sources call his mother Gaea, or Earth—it's clear Orion is linked to the elemental forces of the land and water and body. One tradition has it that he was conceived when Poseidon, Zeus, and Hermes urinated on the hide of an ox, which was buried in the ground. After the proper time, Orion was born from the buried hide—that is, from the earth and "water," Gaea and Poseidon. He was named Urion, after *ouron*, to urinate, which later became Orion.

He may have married a woman named Side, so beautiful she rivaled Hera and was exiled to the underworld. After she vanished, Orion traveled to the island of Chios, where he hoped to wed the princess Merope. He asked her father, Oinopion, for her hand, and he set the hunter the task of clearing the island of its infestation of wild beasts. Orion proved his prowess by his hunting success. Hunting gave him his credentials as a hero or great man.

Oinopion seems to have backed out of his promise, however, postponing the wedding date that was to be the hero's reward. Orion grew impatient. One night, in a fit of drunken lust, he broke into Merope's chamber as she slept and raped her.

Oinopion was enraged. As the stupefied Orion slept off his wine, the king burned out his eyes and threw him from the castle. The blinded Orion wandered through the forests and along the seashore, sightless like another ancient hunter, Samson in the Old Testament. Somehow, Orion found a boy named Kedalion, whom he lifted onto his shoulders. The boy guided the blind hunter to the east, where the rays of Helios the sun god healed Orion's eyes.

From conception to rape, this story is a stunning fantasy of potency—beginning with men conceiving without women, peeing on an ox hide, progressing through the grandiosity of eliminating all animals from an island, and leading to the rape of the King's daughter. This intersection of the hunter and the rapist, of hunting heroics and sexual appetite, is disturbing. The killing of animals, the seizing of women—by an unstated but unmistakable elision, the two slide into each other in the story. Both seem to express an overweening libidinous impulse—killing is eroticized, sexuality is brutalized. The elision can take place in the psyche of the great hunter because identity means all others must be reduced to serving his appetite—both hunting and sexuality coincide in narratives of erotic domination.

Hunting and sex, desire and death, are linked in this early myth. Orion defines the darker terrain in the male psyche, the underside of the myth of potency. Many men, I suspect, if they were honest, might admit that they fear a figure like Orion lurking in the nether regions of the soul—unbridled, drunken, violent. The stories of William Golding suggest that this nightmarish descent into primitive violence is a modern obsession as well, that under the thin veneer of civilization is a violence and rapacity embodied in this primitive hunter.

Another feature of the Orion story is more touching. Orion is also a blind man.

He wanders blindly across the island, carrying a young boy on his shoulders, looking for the healing rays of the sun at dawn.

Orion's blindness is an eloquent image of men's confusion right now. For an image of manhood built upon motifs of power, his blindness is an image of both punishment and emasculation. It suggests, I think, the ways in which men feel indicted and under attack, perhaps even guilty in some deep part of themselves—that perhaps male sexuality and desire are deeply flawed in their aggressiveness. And yet, also, feeling some sense of being less than men, some sense of having lost some power. Of being blind and impotent and wandering.

The hero usually likes to think of himself not as a learner, but as a knower. Yet we might now be at a stage where we are groping in a kind of blindness for new sight.

Then the scene shifts, from the island of Chios to the island of Delos, where a second set of stories takes place. They repeat the themes of the first—hunting and sexual desire, venatic and sexual violence. In these stories, though, male domination is met with female resistance. On Delos, the goddess Artemis wins her revenge. When Orion regains his sight, he is snatched away by the goddess of the dawn, Eos, who has fallen in love with him. "Radiant Dawn," writes Homer in the *Odyssey*, "took to bed Orion."

In Homer, Orion is slain by Artemis for his presumption to sleep with a goddess. The other gods are jealous of his affair with the goddess, and Artemis hunts Orion down on their behalf, "in Delos with her arrows."[13]

Despite his lovely affair with Eos, Orion's violence seems by most accounts to be incorrigible. On Delos, he turns hunter/rapist again.

Despite the many variations of the story, the hunter and huntress are used to explore the complex relations between male and female. The best-known version makes Orion and Artemis hunting companions, a discreet way of suggesting they are lovers, or would-be lovers. Orion tries to woo the goddess, and she will only hunt with him if she favors him. Artemis is the sister of Apollo and the goddess of both chastity and the hunt— Xenophon says they two together invented hunting and taught it to Chiron the centaur, who taught mortals.[14] Though Artemis is devoted to chastity— preferring the company of her nymphs (who are sworn to chastity) and of animals to that of men—the goddess of the golden belt and the silver bow falls in love with the greatest hunter among mortals.

Together, Orion and Artemis chase wild animals, racing across the island with lop-eared hounds that are fierce enough to capture lions. His passion gets the better of him, and he seizes the beautiful goddess by her tunic, a sleeveless gown that reaches to her knees. He tries to rape her.

The armed goddess fights back. According to Apollodorus, she escapes his grasp and, aiming her bow, shoots him with an arrow.

He dies, and she immediately regrets his death, at least in one version. She prays to Zeus, her father, to save the dead hunter and hero. He grants her wish, and places him in the night heavens.

In Hesiod and Ovid, there is no attempted rape. Instead, Orion boasts that he is the greatest of hunters—apparently like an adolescent trying to make an impression on his girlfriend. He says he will kill every wild beast on Earth. He may even feel contempt for Artemis, belittling her and boasting that he is a better hunter than she. Earth herself, the goddess Gaea, is offended by Orion's contempt for animals and the goddess, and sends a scorpion after him. Its deadly sting is the Earth's revenge for boasting he'd kill off all the animals on Earth.

Whatever the details of the story, and even when Ovid tries to palliate Orion's guilt by making him defend one of Artemis's hunting companions, the hunter is a figure of prowess and plunder. His appetite is for both—or either—animals or females. Hunting is portrayed as a contest for the hero, and the contest can easily be with either nature or goddesses who represent the earth and the female simultaneously. Gaea and Artemis fulfill the same function in the story.

According to yet another version of the myth, Artemis doesn't intend to kill Orion. She loves him and plans to marry him—the two hunters share one bed. But she is tricked by her twin brother, Apollo, who is also a hunter. He is jealous of her affection for Orion. When he spots Orion one day swimming far out to sea, a mere speck, he tells his sister—cunning god that he is—that he doubts she could hit the distant black spot. Artemis shoots her bow, wins the challenge, and kills Orion. In addition to suggesting a mutually erotic attraction between antagonists, this story helps to rehabilitate an otherwise intractable Orion.

So Orion is a great hunter, he makes the gods jealous of his liaisons with goddesses, he clears islands of wildlife, he boasts of his great hunting abilities, he tries to rape women and goddesses, he offends the Earth, and he is killed either by Artemis's arrows, or by Skorpio, acting for Artemis and the Earth.

Then, in the heavens, he remains the hunter. A different, later story supplements his apotheosis. While on earth, Orion falls in love with the daughters of Pleione—these are the Pleiades. They arouse his lust, and flee from him. The hunter gives chase. In his pity for the girls, Zeus makes the Pleiades into stars, fixed ever just ahead of Orion in the skies.

They are visible in the shoulder of Taurus, a faint and beautiful cluster of stars. Orion still chases them perpetually through the heavens, forever in pursuit, cold and brilliant. It's an image of a desire that is at once insatiable, rapacious, and built upon its own impossibility.

Apart from being a hunter largely of women, what's compelling about these stories of the original hunter is that Orion defines himself, achieves his identity and apotheosis as hunter, by an ethic of opposition and conflict. Psychologically speaking, he defines a crucial and fundamental pattern for male self-identity: he knows who he is, he comes into existence as hero and male, through opposition to an Other. Desire itself is grounded in this opposition, which pursues not relationship, but its own appetite. Identity is in some sense opposed to relationship in this model, a model not simply of ethics and behavior, but of consciousness. The relations he establishes with others, with "objects" in his world, are really subsumed by the more important business in the hero of identity formation. The male creates himself by defeating "the other."

If women define themselves "relationally," men define themselves through individual identity in this model or myth—an individual identity that coalesces through opposition to humans or animals that, in the process, get defined as alien and inferior. In other words, this sense of self is most energetically alive and intensely realized when it has an enemy to conquer. And the enemy can vary—beast, barbarian, female, slave.[15]

Orion's legacy to us combines these themes of identity and desire and power—he at once chases the bull Taurus and the Pleiades sisters through the heavens. And he's pursued by Skorpio. I imagine Orion longing for the prey—bull and sisters—always just out of his reach. Club raised, he's condemned to his own eternal hunt, to an endless repetition of his own lust, to the coldness of his own winter and nocturnal desires. He wears his bright sword at his side, with his belt slanted across his hips. The stars Betelgeuse and Rigel, two of the brightest winter stars, shine from his body. And he's accompanied, even in the sky, by the Dog Star, Sirius.

Orion is one of our first heroes, and his drama continues to circle our heads every year, a silent message to us inscribed in the night sky. Locked in his own perpetual chase, Orion might be regarded as the victim of his own venatic longing. Until we become more aware of the stories that define masculinity, and until we construct new narratives for masculine identity, men are likely to be trapped in cycles of blind repetition like Orion.

3

Though Artemis was a female goddess and huntress, women probably didn't hunt a great deal in the ancient world. The Roman poet Ovid, writing under Augustus, imagines the beautiful maiden Hero writing a letter to her lover, Leander. Ovid includes her letter in the *Heroides*, a book of love letters by legendary, mostly mythical lovers. They are mostly laments, and mostly from women to their absent men. Hero writes longingly to Leander, and she's full of the passion of youthful romance. But she has a complaint, as well, wishing she had available to her the same distractions he has during their lengthy separations. He gets to ride horses and hunt, she says, fish, and catch birds with snares. But she, a woman, is "denied these things." What is left for her, in his absence? "There is nothing left to do but love," she sighs.[16]

Men hunted, and women loved, supposedly.

Hunting helped men to mark out a uniquely male, uniquely private masculine arena, from which women were largely excluded. Its function was not merely to exclude women from male activities, though it did that. It's that, conceptually, hunting marked out the social terrain, the social roles. Men didn't find their identities through love, primarily. They used the hunt as a way of finding and affirming identity. This is marked as a male terrain, a male activity. Men used it to create, first, a space in which they might escape from women, but second and more important, a space outside of the domestic and even the civil, home and city, where they might test their mettle, challenge themselves, prove their identities.

The hunt controlled the way people *thought* about gender and identity, as much as it defined behaviors for the sexes.

It's not that women weren't portrayed as hunters. Dido of Carthage sallied out to hunt with Aeneas, and Phaedra was devoted to the hunt. Plus, myths related to Artemis show numerous goddesses and nymphs hunting. But they were exceptional women, probably. As J. K. Anderson writes in his book-length study of hunting among the ancients, hunting in classical and archaic Greece was a "masculine, and in a sense, a manly activity."[17]

Even in Sparta, that most vigorous and rigorous of Greek states, he could find no evidence of women actually hunting—it was part of how men were trained for the discipline of war. Artemis was mythical: "If the nymphs, the daughters of Zeus who gladdened the heart of Artemis on the hunt on the long ridges of Taygetus, had not flesh and blood counterparts in Sparta, there is little use in seeking huntresses in those city-states whose educations encouraged a less strenuous way of life."[18] The social value of hunting lay in training a class of boys in the responsibilities expected of them as men. The metaphorical value of hunting lay in giving men a way of conceiving of themselves as heroes. The ethic of the hero was, in essence, the path to a coherent identity.

Hunting was not usually, however, the way men might become heroes. Orion might in some measure prove himself a hero to the culture by his ability to hunt—to kill all the animals on Earth. More typically, though, hunting doesn't provide the classical hero with his greatest exploits. Rather, it is through hunting that the hero announces his imminent great-ness. In hunting, he serves notice of his maturing prowess. In its purest forms, the prowess of the classical hunter is unremittingly physical. But the ethic of the hero in hunting is more than the accomplishment of a great feat or deed. Most important in the ethic of the hunter as hero, the hunter gains his identity through conflict and conquest. Male identity is established in opposition to something else. Animals are symbols, really, of "the Other" against which the hero learns to create a self. Without an Other, he doesn't know how to exist. Hunting works in this psychodynamic of identity be-cause it can place the man in opposition to animals. Or, more precisely, the ethic of the classical hero exploits the sense of opposition to animals that hunting comes to mean in the West.

This creation of identity is a dynamic in the psyche of the hunter, not a static fact of the hunter. The identity is created in the act of defeating ani-mals or others. Because it's a dynamic process, it must be continually re-enacted, so that the hunter-hero can sustain a sense of self. As a hunter, the male must keep hunting to keep re-creating himself.

No story better illustrates the power of hunting in the identity of the hero than that of Odysseus, an archetypal Greek hero. Homer tells the story of Odysseus's hunting expedition to Mount Parnassus in the famous recognition scene between the old hero, twenty years gone from home, and his childhood nurse, Eurykleia, in the *Odyssey*.[19]

Odysseus is the clever Greek hero, the man of ruses and trickery. Yet his identity as a hero is carried, or revealed, not in his brainpower, but in his body. We know him as a hero because he has a scar on his thigh. Through this scar, Odysseus is recognized by his old nurse when he returns to his home after his long absence in the Trojan War. He received the scar on his thigh when he was a boy—"An old wound, a boar's white tusk inflicted."

As an adult, the hunting scar marks Odysseus's body and is how he is known as the returning hero.

Odysseus returns home after ten years of war in Troy and another ten years of wandering adventures. He finds his wife beset by suitors, who lounge in his castle and eat his food. To avoid detection, he dons the disguise of an old beggar. In a very poignant moment, he is inside the castle, and an old woman, his boyhood nurse, offers to bathe him. She does not realize this old beggar, to whom she offers a kindness, is her master. Odysseus also forgets himself. He agrees to let her bathe him. They are in a room warmed by a fire, and she lifts his leg above a bronze basin, gleaming in the firelight. Her fingers rub up against an old wound. An old hunting scar.

She bares her lord's leg, bends near, and knows the wound at once. Odysseus's identity, the whole story of the wound, comes rushing into her mind.

Eurykleia remembers Odysseus hunting at his grandparents' castle on Mount Parnassus. He went out with his uncles early one morning, hunting boar, the fiercest of prey, climbing through the green forests of the lower reaches of the mountain. The boar hid from them, hiding in the dense underbrush, sleeping, protected from the heat of the sun by thickets.

Odysseus leads the men. He charges ahead. Out in front with the barking dogs, he carries his "long-shadowing spear," emblematic of his youthful manliness. Already the boy casts a long shadow.

At noon Odysseus and his men enter a cool, dense glen. They can see the Mediterranean Sea glittering in the dreamy distance. They startle a great boar, couched in the shadows. It rises to meet them:

> Patter of hounds' feet, men's feet, woke the boar
> as they came up—and from his woody ambush
> with razor back bristling and raging eyes
> he trotted and stood at bay. Odysseus,
> being on top of him, had the first shot,

> lunging to stick him; but the boar
> had already charged under the long spear.
> He hooked aslant with one white tusk and ripped out
> flesh above the knee, but missed the bone.
> Odysseus' second thrust went home by luck,
> his bright spear passing through the shoulder joint;
> and the beast fell, moaning as life pulsed away.

The moment shifts quickly back to the nurse, washing Odysseus's leg. She traces the scar under her hand, knowing it by the touch, then lets go of his leg. It crashes into the basin. She is overcome with emotion, and whispers to him: "You are Odysseus!

"I could not see you till now," she says, "not till I knew my master's very body with my own hands."

His identity is revealed through his hunting, as young man among his uncles, and as old man returning as hero. The way heroic identity breaks through to reverberate in a supremely domestic moment, is conveyed in the simple image of Odysseus's leg falling into the bronze basin. The bronze clanged, sloshing the water out.

As an adult, Odysseus's identity is quite literally written on his flesh. He's marked by the old hunting scar, and it betrays his identity to the nurse. Much of the appeal of hunting, as a marker of identity, lies in the confrontation of two bodies, man and beast, and the very material nature of the struggle. As bodies in conflict, hunting seems more than dramatic and epic—it seems somehow incontrovertibly real. There is something reassuring in the wound that carries such a complete story, woven into the very tissue of the man himself. The story seems part of his flesh.

Hunting is a discourse of male bodies, wounded and scarred, and the male identity is given the apparent and inescapable solidity of the flesh. It is the power of hunting, as we've seen in scientific discourses of archaeology, to use a language that makes it seem palpably real within the values of the culture deploying hunting as a masculine ethic. The twentieth century gave the hunt a scientific sanction—that is the language that gave hunting a certain kind of reality for us. The Greeks gave the hunt the sanction of the body. The touch and gleam of the flesh, the contest of two bodies, the self embedded in the wounded flesh—these have the weight and heft of something real.

This same ethic is carried out in the climax of the epic, when in a flurry of hunting metaphors, Odysseus destroys the suitors who have tried to steal his wife. Most touching of all in the story, Odysseus is first recognized when he returns to Ithaca, not by any person, but by his old, beloved hunting dog.

In a fundamental way, at once literal and metaphorical, these ancient hunters were created in the act of killing the beast. The hero required the beast to kill.

The preferred prey of heroes were boars or lions—the lions carved on the gates of the heroic Greek fortresses testify to the ferocity of the heroes, so closely were identity and prey linked. Hercules was the greatest of Greek heroes, and a hunter bar none. Chaucer, for example, considered him the model of the ascendant hunter. He was the perfect image of the strong man as hunter. Chaucer summarized the great Hercules's twelve labors as forms of hunting—the boar Erymanthus that got "scum" all over him, the monster Cacus, the Nemean lion (whose skin Hercules wore on his back), the bull he captured on Crete, the Lernean hydra whose heads kept multiplying, the Ceryneian stag with the golden horns, sacred to Artemis. He finally was made a god. "Ye strong men," writes Chaucer, Hercules is "the heye wey of the grete ensaumple" (the high way of the great example), showing how heaven may be won by great exploits.

Meleager was another hero, famed for killing the Calydonian boar when all other heroes had failed. Achilles, too, was a hunter. Xenophon said he learned hunting from Chiron, the centaur. On his divinely made shield, in Book Eighteen of the *Iliad*, the great hero Achilles has only one hero pictured, Orion, and a scene of hunters and dogs attacking a pair of monstrous lions and a bull. Hunters also had to defeat strange and mythical beasts—chimerical creatures. Bellerophon, for instance, killed the fire-breathing Chimera—composite she-monster, part serpent, part lion, part goat. Perseus killed the Gorgon, the snake-haired Medusa.[20]

One could go on at length about these stories—there are so many of them, and they're all immensely fascinating, both as stories and as psychology. It's an odd pedigree, but the route for men to the heroes' pantheon was through hunting. This particular version of hunting, this story of facing the beast in hand-to-hand combat, isn't today as commanding in men's imagination, since men are so used to hunting at long distances with high-powered rifles. Technology is a more commanding dimension of the modern meaning of the hunt—men's ability to use weapons and other ways of manipulating nature and animals. But even with rifles, we're still likely to find the story of the hunt most compelling that pits the individual man against a strong and fierce animal. Predators make the most masculine of prey. We rarely hunt like the old heroes, but men still squeeze their different stories in their imaginations into a mold that looks something like the hero. The story gives the imaginative and the emotional meaning of the hunt for men. The story tells how they take the hunt inside.

Heroic confrontation remains at the heart of modern notions of masculinity. Men still tend to feel most like they are men when they face something head-on, take on their problems, wrestle with the enemy. We like to confront the beast in its den. These metaphors have the distant odor and faint scent of the hunt.

4

Once, I decided to join men in the mountains of Spain on a wild boar hunt, to compare the literature with the experience of the boar hunt. It is an exquisitely beautiful Sunday in the mountains, and over the course of the day I discover just how alive this particular story of the hunt—the hero confronting the beast—still is. We are hunting in the rugged mountains of Cantabria, with the austere magnificence of the snow-covered Picos de Europa right behind us. The day is warm, the air heavy, and as the afternoon heads into the coolness of a mountain evening, a heavy mist gathers in the air, golden and glowing with the slanting sunlight. The boar hunt, or *caza de jabalí*, is the classic machismo hunt in Spain.

The modern boar hunt in most of Europe is a quasi-military operation. The men wear hunter green sweaters and pants, as though they were in military uniforms, and are organized in teams, *equipos*, deploying themselves through the hills in strategic locations. They use radios to talk back and forth about the progress of the hunt. I accompany José Luis Gonzalez, a thin man with a mustache and sharp, moving eyes. He is the *guarda* of the Reserva de Saja, the man from the government who is essentially like an American park ranger on the wildlife reserve. But José does not so much regulate the hunt as lead it. He and I move in my tiny orange Renault Cinco among the hunters, who are stationed through the ridges, where they wait. We wait with them, and José Luis keeps track of the movement of the boar with the radio.

Below us, we can hear the dogs yelping. Certain designated men take their dogs and work the *pinares*, or pine stands, at the bases of ridges, where boars secrete themselves during the day to hide and sleep. The idea is that the dogs will flush the boars, and send them running up the hills, where they will pass the positions of the hunters. If you are one of the lucky hunters, the boar might pass you and you will be the one to shoot it.

I have already been told many times by friends that sharp-tusked boars are dangerous, and I should be ready to climb a tree if we see a boar. An aura of heroics surrounds the tradition of the boar hunt. By lunchtime, José Luis and I have driven to the top of a high peak just below the range of mountains, looking down on a stand of pines. We share sandwiches, and José Luis learns over the radio that one boar, early in the morning, has attacked the dogs which roused it. It gored one of the dogs and got away.

By late afternoon, it seems we aren't going to get a boar. José Luis is digusted. We move to a lovely spot, high above a small village named Carmona, with red-tiled houses where people still live on the second floor, and the animals live in the barn on the first floor. We are at the top of a draw, and hunters are stationed below us.

Suddenly, the dogs on the far side are chasing the boar through the brown ferns up the ravine, toward us. The dogs come rushing through the green thickets at the base of the draw, howling excitedly. José Luis gets excited as well, and barks into his radio. "*¡Atención! ¡Atención! ¡Jabalí!*" A boar has been flushed, and we are in the perfect place to see the hunt unfold.

We are actually command central, and José Luis directs the hunters over the radio.

I don't see the animal at first. José Luis warns the men directly below us to be prepared to shoot.

The boar races up the draw, though I still don't see it, then through the thickets, and begins to head along the base of the steep hill directly below us. By this time, the dogs are insane with the chase, their barks a frenzy. They've left their struggling owners far behind, scrambling through the brush, still on the far side of the draw.

José Luis barks once more into the radio, warning the men below us once more that the boar is coming. He gives its precise location, coming our way. I spot it just as it passes the hunters.

I hear a rifle shot. The boar squeals just like a pig.

The boar looks like a pig, too. It isn't a big animal, but is the size, say, of a spaniel. It is young. It hardly looks like the opponent in a heroic contest.

By now it's running away from us, down the draw. With the next shot, its back legs collapse. It falls in the dirt of an open patch on the hill. But it jumps back up and tries to climb upward and away from us, running through some dead ferns. More shots. More sharp pig squeals.

Then it goes down for good.

In its military formality and its cold efficiency, there is something profoundly male about this hunt. I also know that I am very excited at seeing the boar and watching the hunt. After the boar drops, I run down the hill to see it up close. Several dogs attack it, and three hunters arrive to exult over it.

But the little boar somehow embarrasses us a bit, too. It's very young. It has no tusks. It is a dark brown, with a small snout and bristly fur. But nothing about it that would be likely to send a hero to the hospital. No danger. The moment of greatest physical confrontation comes when the hunters let the dogs snap and tear at the dead *jabalí*, jerking it around the ground as if they were wreaking some postmortem vengeance on its corpse.

Still, the machismo and quasi-heroic feel of the boar hunt—the way masculinity turns into a physical statement—seems to pervade the "feel" of the hunt. It can be glimpsed in a final exchange I had with José Luis. Physical prowess remains part of the validation of the hunt, even when the narrative can only very tenuously sustain such a message. After the boar has come up, and we are gathered around it, I tell José Luis how impressed I am that he saw the boar so well. You have, I tell him, *ojos fuertes*. He laughs uproariously, repeating to all his friends, with a sly mischief in his eyes. Then I realize what I'd implied: strong eyes, strong balls.

He winks at me. Returning the compliment, José Luis tells me that I have good Spanish, too. He laughs again. Some bond has formed in this instant that only indirectly had to do with the boar, but has everything to do with having hunted together. And my good Spanish, José Luis says to me, shows I had *cojones fuertes*.

5

Apollo was born on the island of Delos, a premature baby. He was delivered after seven months. His mother was Leto, his father Zeus. Fed on nectar and ambrosia, the child-god grew quickly. On the dawn of the fourth day, the baby Apollo called for a bow and arrow. He is sometimes pictured on pottery hunting with his weapons, still a young boy, from his mother's arms.

Hunting may have been the sport of men, but it was the invention of the gods. The Greeks gave hunting a divine sanction, more than was ever really established for the hunt in the Christian tradition.[21] In *On Hunting*, Xenophon says that Apollo and Artemis invented hunting. As the archer who shoots from afar, as the god of brightness and glory, Apollo himself gave to hunting the imprimatur of manly luminosity. He stamped hunting with a god's blessing. Orion as demonic, Odysseus as heroic, and Apollo as divine—taken together, they give three separate routes to the heroizing of the hunter. Apollo's exploits as a type of hunter identify the act of overcoming the beast as a specifically male activity, one in which the opponent, as Joseph Fontenrose puts it in his study of the Greek myths of combat, *Python: A Study of Delphic Myth and Its Origins*, could vary without regard to sex or species.[22] In the story of Apollo and the Python, the main part of the story suggests that the male god came as hunter to overcome the beast and establish his own shrine.

Apollo's connection with hunting has faded in our minds, as he has become increasingly associated with the arts and rationality, the flute and the sun. He was called Phoebus, the shining god, but he never lost his bow and quiver. His epithet remained the one "who shoots from afar," and he made the other gods tremble. In one of his early epithets, he is called Lykeios, which is uncertain in origin and meaning, but it suggests *lykos*, the word for wolf, connecting Apollo with shepherds and predatory animals.

According to the Homeric Hymn, "To Pythian Apollo," the god left Delos to find a suitable place for a shrine to himself, and went immediately to Mount Parnassus, the same mountain where Odysseus was said to have shown his youthful valor as a boar hunter. On the craggy side of the mountain, he came upon Delphi, the site of the ancient sanctuary in Greece. The Mother Earth, Gaea, had made the site sacred, and in the cavern she heard the rumblings of the Earth and made her prophecies. A large stone, the omphalos, marked the navel or center of the world. And with Gaea, Mother Earth, was a great she-dragon, which protected and guarded her. The shining Apollo killed the she-dragon to protect men.

> But near by was a sweet flowing spring, and there with his strong bow the lord, son of Zeus, killed the bloated, great she-dragon, a fierce monster wont to do great mischief to men upon earth, to men themselves and their thin-shanked sheep; for she was a bloody plague. . . . Whosoever met the dragoness, the day of doom would sweep him away, until the lord Apollo, who deals death from afar, shot a strong arrow at her. Then she, rent with bitter pangs, lay drawing great gasps for breath and rolling about that place. An awful noise swelled up unspeakable as she writhed continually this way and that amid the wood: and so she left her life, breathing it forth in blood.[23]

Confirmed as a hero, Apollo boasted over the dead body of the she-dragon: " 'Now rot here upon the soil that feeds man. You at least shall live no more to be a fell bane to men who eat the fruit of all-nourishing earth, and who will bring hither perfect hecatombs. . . .' Thus said Phoebus, exulting over her: and darkness covered her eyes. And the holy strength of Helios made her rot away there; wherefore the place is now called Pytho [to rot], and men call the lord Apollo by another name, Pythian; because on that

spot the power of piercing Helios made the monster rot away."[24] The lord
of light and reason, the god of sun and the young divine hunter—Apollo
slays the female dragon, and takes over the shrine of Gaea, Mother Earth.
He brings clarity and reason, Helios and weapons, to cleanse the Earth of
dangerous animals. Like Orion's, Apollo's story suggests the hunter brings
male culture, male order, into the world. The hymn stresses the virtue of a
god protecting an agriculture society. But more than that, Apollo is a virile
god, establishing his shrine on Delphi out of his vigor and violence.

Unlike the myth of Orion, which stresses the darkness of the hunter's
passions, the myth of Apollo at Delphi shows the hunter's violence rationalized. He brings culture, or at least defends culture. Perhaps the most important point, the most fundamental point, to notice about all these stories
of the hunter as hero is that the male identity is defined in opposition to
something. It is defined at least as much by what it is *not* as by what it *is*.
The other can be animal or female, nature or emotions, but the hero must
have an enemy. At an early stage of men's psychological history, they
learned not simply that they had to be heroes to be men. Even more insidious, they learned that the hero wrests his identity from the subjugation of
another creature.

The story of Apollo hints at the early displacing of the worship at Delphi
of an Earth goddess called Gaea, who was associated with another female
deity, Themis. As H. W. Parke says in his history of the Delphic Oracle,

> So Delphi was originally devoted to the worship of the Earth goddess
> whom the Greeks called Ge. Themis, who was associated with her . . . is
> really another manifestation of the same deity. . . . The worship of these
> two, as one or distinguished, was displaced by the introduction of
> Apollo. His origin has been the subject of much learned controversy: it
> is sufficient for our purpose to take him as the Homeric Hymn repre-
> sents him—a northern intruder. . . . His conflict with Ge for the posses-
> sion of the cult-site was represented under the legend of his slaying of
> the serpent [or she-dragon]. The motive of the young god who slays a
> dragon may be more primitive than its immediate association with Del-
> phi. There, however, it would take on special meaning. Snakes were
> regularly supposed to be born from the ground, and this female serpent
> evidently was originally the visible manifestation of Ge herself, a belief
> which can be traced in Minoan religion.[25]

These stories of great classical hunters, like Orion and Apollo, suggest
that both in an individual and in a cultural sense the male learned to become himself in the subjugation of something outside himself. It's easy to

see how feminists might find these myths objectionable. Hunting describes, not simply a masculine social space, where men can be on their own, apart if they like from women. As a myth and a metaphor, it goes much deeper, to describe a psychological dynamic in the formation of identity in which the coherent self realizes its existence by defeating some other—it can be beast or female. The she-dragon guarding the oracle at Delphi, the stand-in for the Earth goddess Gaea, summarizes this. The hunter serves as a primal hero because he defeats a feminized earth.

Sherry B. Ortner is one feminist who, in a very important essay called "Is Man to Culture as Woman Is to Nature?" examines the ways in which nature, beasts, and females have been aligned in our psyches. She claims hunting, like warfare, is a way men have preferred culture to nature, mind to body, control to involvement in nature. Hunting functions in the male psyche not simply to distinguish men from women, male from female, but to invent the male in the transcendence of the female:

> In other words, woman's body seems to doom her to mere reproduction of life; the male, in contrast, lacking natural creative functions, must (or has the opportunity to) assert his creativity externally, "artificially," through the medium of technology and symbols. In so doing, he creates relatively lasting, eternal, and transcendent objects, while the woman creates only perishables—human beings. [This] speaks, for example, to the great puzzle of why male activities involving the destruction of life (hunting and warfare) are often given more prestige than the female's ability to give birth. . . . [W]e realize it is not the killing that is the relevant and valued aspect of hunting and warfare; rather, it is the transcendental (social and cultural) nature of these activities, as opposed to the naturalness of the process of birth. . . .[26]

In risking their lives hunting, she argues, men actually in a sense confront death and lift themselves above nature and its cycles of life and death. They inflict death, but the real accomplishment is a kind of transcendence. Men do not kill animals for sport or for the sake of killing, she argues. Rather, they do it to assert their superiority over nature. This view makes hunting a profoundly cultural act, not "natural" at all. It becomes a reaffirmation of culture and patriarchy over nature and the feminine—achieved through reason and violence.

This kind of examination of the deeper psychological significance of hunting might upset many hunters. It is not how hunters or heroes usually choose to imagine themselves. Every man understands the way the hunting story structures the male imagination—we quest, we encounter, we triumph over an enemy. And we achieve some greatness. We become heroes. Certainly, *I* have had many fantasies of being heroic in this old-fashioned, triumphant way.

But this deeper structure of the hunt includes an insidious dimension lacking in other competitive male games, like warfare or, say, wrestling. In war and sport, the opponent is usually another man. The world is male, but so too is the victim. Hunting, though, seems more primal in its encounters. That is its attraction in the mythical story—heroes move in close connection with human roots, with land, with animals. But hunting risks demonizing animals. What starts as a dragon in the imagination is also the hare running through a farmer's fields. And more insidious is the way the hunting myth has structured our psyches, so that we find demons in the other sex as well as in other species. At the root of our notions of greatness, planted in our psyches from these profound stories of the heroizing of the male, these stories of the early hunters suggest just how powerful a story can be in influencing how we imagine ourselves.

And how important it is to choose our stories carefully.

6

The great French anthropologist, Claude Lévi-Strauss, marks the triumph of Apollo as a decisive moment in our history. Apollo is in many ways the rational god, and his "overthrow" of earlier gods, to use Lévi-Strauss's word, allowed the emergence of scientific thinking, beginning with the invention of philosophy and the establishment of rational thought. The idea that reason is a kind of hunter, and its movements in the mind is a kind of stalking and chase, is as ancient as formal philosophy itself. The famous Thomas Henry Huxley quoted David Hume as writing, "There cannot be two passions more nearly resembling each other than hunting and philosophy." Our notions of pursuit of truth and knowledge are intimately connected with concepts of hunting. The word "investigate," for example, comes from the Latin word *vestigium*, meaning a footprint, a track, or a trace. Apollo-the-hunter lives inside our concepts of reason.[27]

For the Greeks, the philosopher-hunter is a standard figure. Plato uses the word *thereutes* for the philosopher, from the word *thera* for wild animal. The "hunter" is one of Plato's favorite images for the philosopher. A philosopher is one who tracks down wild or elusive knowledge. In the *Euthydemus*, Plato writes that the most important part of thinking is the chase and the capture, as it is in hunting, not the practical use of the booty afterward.[28]

In the *Republic*, Plato uses the image of both the chase and the drive in a hunt to describe the philosophical method of reasoning through a dialogue. If philosophers are to define the elusive concept of justice, Socrates says, they must be like hunters:

"Now then, Glaucon, is the time for us like huntsmen to surround the covert and keep close watch that justice may not slip through and get away from us and vanish from our sight. It plainly must be somewhere hereabouts. Keep your eyes open then and do your best to descry it. You may see it before I do and point it out to me." "Would that I could," he [Glaucon] said; "but I think rather that if you find in me one who can follow you and discern what you point out to him you will be making a very fair use of me." "Pray for success then," said I [Socrates], "and follow along with me." "That I will do, only lead on," he said. "And truly," said I, "it appears to be an inaccessible place, lying in deep shadows." "It certainly is a dark covert, not easy to beat up." "But all the same on we must go." "Yes, on." And I caught view and gave a hulloa and said, "Glaucon, I think we have found its trail and I don't believe it will get away from us."[29]

The Socratic dialogue itself enacts a venatic model, the enlightened philosopher acting as hunting guide for the foils who follow his intellectual lead. Glaucon is the philosopher-hunter's "squire," if you will.

Plato links hunting, in fact, to a whole class of social activities, all defined by their emphasis on "coercion" and "acquisition" in the *Sophist*. After discussing creative arts, he says, "And after this comes the whole class of learning and that of acquiring knowledge, and money making, and fighting, and hunting. None of these is creative, but they are all engaged in coercing, by deeds or words, things which already exist and have been produced, or in preventing others from coercing them; therefore all these divisions together might very properly be called acquisitive art. Plato follows this with a long disquisition on the pervasive nature of the hunting metaphor in society, structuring virtually all human relationships from war to love. This is what he calls "a hunting of man."[30]

The philosopher-hunter is also a prominent Greek dramatic character. Oedipus is not literally a philosopher, but Sophocles is a profoundly philosophical playwright. In *Oedipus the King*, Oedipus is frequently described as a hunter, or his quest is framed in the language of the hunt. He is a hunter of truth. He thinks he seeks the killer of the former king of Thebes. Without knowing it, the truth he seeks is the knowledge of his own identity—it's a hunt for self-knowledge, and if it turns out that in this quasi-

murder mystery, he is literally tracking down himself, that intensifies the
ironies. The hunt for self-knowledge frequently takes one on an excursion
into the menacing reaches of the self. Following the tracks of his own guilt,
Oedipus is both hunter and prey, philosopher-hunter and hunted beast, king
and fugitive criminal. "A man who hunts with care," writes Sophocles
early in the play, "may often find what other men will miss."[31]

In Aristophanes, the philosopher-hunter has become so familiar he is
put on public display as a joke. In the *Clouds*, Strepsiades is a fool, the man
with his head in the clouds, lost in arcane and airy ideas. "We greet you,"
says the chorus, "hunter of the Muses' lore!"[32]

The metaphor of the hunt for knowledge continued among the Romans
as a commonplace. Cicero speaks of the *speculatorem venatoremque naturae*, the inquirer and hunter after nature, in which the hunt is an explicit
metaphor of the attempt to know and possess nature, which is always the
end of hunting. In the Middle Ages, Saint Thomas Aquinas uses the Latin
word *venator* (hunter) for the philosopher.[33]

Ortega y Gasset brings the idea into our own century. The philosopher of
hunting uses hunting as a way of describing how the thinker actually takes
possession of ideas, of nature, of knowledge—his excursions into the fearful
jungle of ideas and ignorance, hoping to return with the captured game:
"Like the hunter in the absolute outside of the countryside, the philosopher is
the alert man in the absolute inside of ideas, which are also an unconquerable
and dangerous jungle. As problematic a task as hunting, meditation always
runs the risk of returning empty-handed."[34] The metaphor of hunting builds
into this notion of thinking, of rationality, a structure of contest and conquest.

One implication of the metaphor of hunting in the use of reason is that,
as Plato suggested, our relations even to the objects of thought are structured as an opposition. Thinking becomes in some sense the process of taking over an idea, acquiring it. The reason of Apollo and the philosophers
has given us possession of the world, but the hunting metaphor plants violence in the heart of reason.

7

Two parables. One by a modern man. One by a modern woman. They mark
the reach of the classical hero, at this far remove, and show how the images
of the hunter as wild man, conqueror, and philosopher continue to live
within our minds and culture. And they mark, as well, the way the hunter
continues to be used, not simply to mark out different gender roles, but different psychologies.

Robert Bly's *Iron John* might be called the central document of the contemporary "men's movement," the attempt by men to begin to find for themselves some way into new images of masculinity. Bly writes to help men recapture some lost sense of themselves. He wants men to get back in touch with a long-vanished sense of their primitive, wild selves. In *Iron John*, the hunter is the figure who discovers this lost masculinity—exploiting still the old notion of the hunter who carries us to the margins, who helps us discover ourselves, who brings us to our more heroic destinies. In the parable, it happens that all the hunters going into the woods disappear and never return. One day, an "unknown hunter" shows up at the castle, offers to help the king solve this mystery, and goes into the woods with his dog. There the hunter discovers a pond, in which resides the primitive wild man, Iron John—hairy, tough, symbol of men's lost masculine energies lying at the other side of the "feminine" pool. Bly once called this the "deep male," not so much exemplified by the hunter, but discovered by the hunter in his sojourns in female nature. Iron John is the wild man.

This iron man Bly also associates with Odysseus. He introduces his story of Iron John with the story of Odysseus and Circe. The winged god Hermes, Bly writes, tells Odysseus how to deal with Circe, who is the enchantress who can change men into beasts: "In the *Odyssey*, Hermes instructs Odysseus that when he approaches Circe, who stands for a certain kind of matriarchal energy, he is to lift or show his sword. In these early sessions [he's discussing early workshops with men on masculinity] it was difficult for many of the younger men to distinguish between showing the sword and hurting someone. One man . . . found himself unable to extend his arm when it held a sword. He had learned so well not to hurt anyone that he couldn't lift the steel, even to catch the light of the sun on it."[35] Circe is the female who turns men into beasts. And with the use of his phallic weapon, Odysseus is able to defeat Circe, to conquer her and subdue her to his terms, and at the same time avoid being turned into a beast. It contains all the elements of the hunt, without actually stalking an animal.

What's problematic in Bly's parable, in his representation of male power, is that it depends precisely on this oppositional structure built into the hunter myth. We get power through weapons. Men are defined here still by what they can defeat. Through "showing the sword." Bly's search for a deeper experience of masculinity, for the inner substance in the lives of modern men, speaks powerfully to men who feel lost, out of touch with themselves. Male identity is now up for grabs, a contentious issue. It's hard not to sympathize with his claim that the old images of manhood are worn out. But Bly turns to the founding myths of our culture, like the myth of the hunter as hero, as offering some answers. These are the same images, and the same patterns, that lead us to the current impasse. They enforce myths of privilege and prerogative, power and prestige, all over again. And they reinforce cycles of battle and wounds, violence and loss—the very patterns many men would like to get beyond.

Margaret Atwood tells a different story about men as hunters, relating not to the wild man and conqueror, but to the philosopher. After discussing the female brain, she says that men's brains are themselves like weapons.

> The male brain, now, that's a different matter. Only a thin connection [between the two halves]. Space over here, time over there, music and arithmetic in their own sealed compartments. The right brain doesn't know what the left brain is doing. Good for aiming, though, for hitting the target when you pull the trigger. What's the target? Who's the target? Who cares? What matters is hitting it. That's the male brain for you. Objective.
>
> This is why men are so sad, why they feel so cut off, why they think of themselves as orphans cast adrift, footloose and stringless in the deep void. What void? she asks. What are you talking about? The void of the universe, he says, and she says, Oh and looks out the window and tries to get a handle on it, but it's no use, there's too much going on, too many rustlings in the leaves, too many voices, so she says, Would you like a cheese sandwich, a piece of cake, a cup of tea? And he grinds his teeth because she doesn't understand, and wanders off, not just alone but Alone, lost in the dark, lost in the skull, searching for the other half, the twin that could complete him.[36]

Both Bly and Atwood see the modern male as alone and alienated from himself, wandering, searching, still hunting. Bly imagines men able to find some wild power through the searching of the hunter and his weapons, some ferocity. He treats myths as though they're unchangeable, and our problem is that we've gotten away from these parts of our deep unconscious lives. Atwood imagines men lost because they have been hunters. The hunt was invented in mythology as a way of marking out a powerful and clear male identity.

They both turn to the classical images of hunter—Orion types with wild hair, and Apollo types, coolly rational, minds like steel traps.

We need not simply reassert some ancient sense of heroism, in which men are defined by what they can defeat. Myths are not simply archetypes, images that live in some special and universal part of the brain. Myths are not, that is, simply inherited. They are also made, a culture's response to its own struggles with issues like sex and identity. We need to be rewriting some of our myths of masculinity, finding new models.

8

One way to begin to develop new images of the male is to find old images that define new possibilities: images of men as powerful and emotional without being destructive. The cool, objective male who lives within his controlled mind is an easy target, but the grasp of this figure on the imaginations of men is strong. That must be for several reasons, not the least of which is that many, if not most, men can't see past it. His very rationality makes him unable to experience the limits of his own vision. But another reason men hold themselves together with reason, bind themselves like Odysseus to the mast, is that the song of the world seems so dangerous to them. They can barely see that its dangers are largely of their own creating, a projection largely of their own values onto the face of nature. The predator sees predators in nature.

But another reason is that the alternative for a rationalist looks frightening. Underneath the serene calm of Apollo, who shoots from afar, is the turbulence and destructiveness of Orion. But before the great hunter defined masculinity, another image of the male relationship with nature suggests what might be possible for us in our relationship with nature.

The Epic of Gilgamesh, written about 2000 B.C., is the great poem of the oral tradition of the Babylonian Semites in Mesopotamia. Named for its central hero, Gilgamesh, the poem celebrates his great triumphs as a hunter. Gilgamesh proves his manliness and his puissance through hunting, and magnificent hunting rituals were common among rulers in the ancient world. Nimrod, the "mighty hunter" in the Old Testament; Ashurbanipal in Assyria, who fancied himself the ruler of the universe; the Persian satraps extolled by Xenophon; the Roman rulers like Caesar who mounted huge *venationes* or hunting entertainments in the Coliseum; extravagant hunting of gazelles by princes in ancient India—these all testify to the value of hunting in supporting the regimes of rulers.[37] *The Epic of Gilgamesh* is usually read as a tribute to the great hero of the first Uruk dynasty. "I have killed the bear," he boasts, "and the hyena, the lion and the panther, the stag, the ibex, all sorts of wild game and small creatures." His great exploit is in defeating the mythical creature Humbaba, a monster with "seven-fold terrors." Humbaba guards the cedars. He is "the watchman of the forest."

Gilgamesh's relationship with his wonderful friend and hunting companion, Enkidu, almost steals the focus of the epic. Their friendship begins as a contest, as is often the case with giant figures. When Gilgamesh first comes to Uruk, he resembles Orion. He has a voracious appetite. His "lust leaves no virgin to her lover." The man who rises up to resist Gilgamesh is Enkidu, and though he is defeated, we glimpse in him perhaps something of an older order of masculinity.[38]

Enkidu was created out of water and clay. His body was rough and covered with hair, symbol of wildness and potency. It was matted like Samauquan's, the god of cattle. Enkidu has a close relationship with animals. He knows nothing of agriculture and cultivation of fields. He is a man, but he is uncultivated.

Instead, Enkidu eats grass in the hills with the gazelle, and lurks with the wild beasts at the water holes. He "has a joy of the water with the herds of wild game." Enkidu protects these animals from hunters and trappers. When a trapper comes to capture the gazelles, he sees Enkidu and is frozen with fear, "benumbed with terror." Enkidu fills in the traps laid for the animals he loves, and scares the hunters away.

One trapper sees Enkidu and returns from his hunt altered, like "one who has made a long journey." In awe, the trapper tells his father of Enkidu, who comes "down from the hills. He is the strongest [man] in the world he is like an immortal from heaven. He ranges over the hills with the wild beasts and eats grass; he ranges through your land and comes down to the wells. I am afraid to go near him. He fills in the pits which I dig and tears up my traps set for the game; he helps the beasts to escape and now they slip through my fingers." Enkidu is defeated by Gilgamesh, who seduces him with the image of a "harlot, a child of pleasure." Enkidu is never the same. After sex, he forgets the animals, and they flee from him. Then he learns to guard the flocks of shepherds at night, protecting them from lions and wolves, until he goes with Gilgamesh as his hunting companion for Humbaba, and is finally killed in a battle with a bull.

Before he becomes civilized and learns to hunt, Enkidu lives a peaceful life in the fields with the animals, protecting them from trappers. Hunters like Xenophon and philosophers like Plato have largely been in control of how virtuous—that is, "manly"—men have been represented. Enkidu is freeing, in a sense, because he gives a different representation, a man opposed to the dominant image of men as killers, a man of peace. Yet he is strong. He's an oxymoron for us: a strong man who is a vegetarian.

But Enkidu, who "ate grass in the hills with the gazelle," perhaps suggests there is a different model of strength and power for men, without proving you can dominate. Perhaps Enkidu was an earlier image of man, the image of man that the hunter defeated. This is Enkidu's legacy—that we could again begin to think, for example, that the strongest man in the world ate grass and defended animals.

9

I visited Delphi once, on Mount Parnassus, with a good friend of mine, a philosopher. Educated at Cambridge University in England, he's a confirmed rationalist. As we walked through the toppled columns and crumbled temples, we talked about the legacy of Apollo and classical Greek civilization. He saw Apollo and the rationalism of Greek philosophy as an unequivocal boon for civilization, which it is our job as educators to preserve and defend and pass along to the next generation. His view of Apollo was entirely honorific.

He loved Odysseus, for example, because he was a figure of restraint and reason—tying himself to the mast so that he would not respond to the music of the sirens was, for my philosopher friend, an image of the value of reason. It binds us.

My view was more complicated, more troubled. As we ambled on the uphill path through the ancient shrine, we reached a spot where we could look down to the location where Gaea, the Earth Mother, had had the original shrine. It was the site where Apollo was supposed to have defeated her and her dragon. I told my rationalist philosopher friend the story of Apollo's usurpation of the shrine at Delphi, and that I didn't like his repressiveness and his violence. My friend was unimpressed, remaining utterly at peace with his own sense of the right of reason to rule our lives.

He and I parted company for a while as we hiked up the craggy mountainside. I climbed above the shrine, rising through the sparse trees with their olive-colored leaves, until I came to a sheer cliff. It seemed to me, despite my friend's impassioned defense of rationality, that something has been lost for men, and that many men, the men I most respect, sense that something powerful has been lost in our lives. When I got to the cliff, I rested my back against it. The black rock was warm. I could hear a bird calling from the top of the cliff, its liquid song drifting down to me. I looked out at the Mediterranean, so dreamy in the distance. I looked down at the lovely temples of the shrine.

And I thought about the shrine as a site of pilgrimages for the ancient Greeks, where they came to hear the riddles of the priestess of Pythian Apollo, putting themselves in strange trances and returning to offer riddles and conundrums—teasing prophetic wisdom. Sometimes, the priestesses were lowered into a chasm, reminiscent of the older worship of Gaea, or the earth, from which they'd return with their riddling solutions to the problems posed by pilgrims.[39]

I know men are longing for some new wisdom, some new power. I have been a member of an all men's group for some time, and I admire how these men are working together to find a new way for themselves into their lives, out of their heads, into their hearts and souls. And I have loved to learn that I can learn from them. Leaning against the cliff face above Delphi, I thought about the blinded Orion. And I thought about the wound of Odysseus, gored on his thigh by a charging boar. And I thought about Apollo's triumph over the Python, the she-dragon rotting away in the sun.

Men triumphed, over the "other" outside and inside themselves. They created the image of themselves as powerful hunters. But they have carried with them some wound, a cultural wound, that we're trying now to heal. It's a wound in our own psyches. As I looked down on the shrine, I realized that we can't kill the beast without also killing something inside ourselves.

The price was some animal vitality, which connects us to life. Apollo killed some of his own feelings when he killed the Python. Like Apollo, we've always turned to women, if you will, to teach us about these feelings, to guide us through the emotional world we separated ourselves from. We have sought that part of ourselves we lost in women.

Suddenly, I felt like a pilgrim myself, coming to the shrine with my own problems and questions.

The bird kept singing above me on the cliff. I decided to try to identify what species it was. Its fluted song wavered and floated down along the cliff face, like a thrush. High along the top, a gray-bodied bird leaped from a rock, its black wings fanned to ride the hot afternoon air. It was a blue rock thrush. I sat back down, satisfied.

How will men find new images for what to be? I thought of the oracle below me. Listening to animals, I realized, is one way. Listening. And I looked down, where my philosopher friend was waiting for me, amid the shrines. For a happy moment, I had the vivid image of Apollo the hunter with his ear to the Pythian ground, straining for new answers, listening to the voices of the creatures he had once struggled to conquer.

In the harsh sun of a Greek afternoon, the blue rock thrush kept singing on the face of the cliff above Apollo's shrine. Be here, be present, right now, it seemed to sing. You are not alone.

4

THE METAPHORS OF MALE DESIRE

O Cupid . . . The hunter pursues the fugitive quarry. What he captures, he always abandons, and goes after the next prey he can find; and those of us who have surrendered to you, Cupid, feel the sting of your weapons.

—Ovid, *Amores*, 2.9.9–11[1]

Sulpicia at home to her lover Cerinthus, who is hunting: Still, I would wander with you, Cerinthus, and I myself would even carry your hunting nets for you through the wild mountains. I'd even pursue the tracks of the running stags, and I'd even loose the iron chains from your fast dogs. If I were with you, the wild forests would delight me, my light, and I'd be happily discovered lying beside you, entangled in love, just in front of those very hunting nets. Then the wild boar, if he comes to the nets, will run away unhurt, and he won't, I promise, interrupt the joys we'll share in love's desire. Let me be your only Venus. . . .

—Tibullus, 4.3.11–19[2]

Sandie polished her gun, tender and ominous at the same time. The affection she bestowed upon the weapon seemed dangerous and misplaced.

She stood on a stage in an A-line skirt and loose blouse, straight out of Nordstrom. She had pulled her curly hair back into an ebullient ponytail. This was a performance, and Sandie had captured an instantly recognizable persona—a modern woman in the workplace. She was dressed in the guise of a bank teller, innocuous and cute. If she'd had a car, it would have been a Honda Prelude. This cuteness, associated with one type of the American female, is calculated to be unthreatening, even diffident. The affection Sandie was devoting to a gun would normally be given to, say, a baby or a pet dog.

But Sandie stood on stage and coddled her gun.

A well-known performance artist in Seattle, Sandie was on stage in a piece about a mild-mannered bank employee talking about sexual harassment. The performance seemed harmless enough at first. There was no gun. Sandie had simply stood talking, acting shy. But then, dramatically, she reached in her purse and pulled out the gun. The audience gasped.

Sandie's eyes took on a daggerlike edge, fierce and narrow. The character on stage was going through a transformation. Her voice grew taunting. She'd had enough. She was sick of the harassment. She talked of a recent rape in north Seattle. She was ready to fight back. She'd use the gun, why not?

Because, she said, glaring at the audience, "Women are prey."

I know Sandie personally. She hates violence, yet she owns more than one gun. She's a crack shot, a markswoman who's proud of her skill. Like other women I've known, she asked me once if I wanted to go to the shooting range with her. And she's fascinated by sexual violence. She maintained a friendship, or at least an acquaintance, with a man on death row in Washington, Charles Campbell. She visited him in the penitentiary, and they talked on the phone. She introduced me to him. He's since been executed for the rape and murder of two women. She's angry and fascinated at once.

Women as prey—it's only one of the ways in which hunting language and hunting concepts are implicated in our notions of desire. Cleaning her gun so affectionately on stage, Sandie also seems almost toxic with female anger and female rage. But how central and pervasive to male notions of desire are hunting metaphors like "women as prey"? Are they adventitious, or are they central to our notions of desire, and particularly male desire? I'd like to look at how men have defined their own sense of desire and sexuality. I think they're central, and I'd like to examine how they have shaped male fantasies of their own sexuality, and as a result defined men's relations to the self as well as to women.

To do that, we need look at the sources of our associations between sexuality and hunting.

The language of predation is common enough nowadays, and has in fact been common enough in most Western literature. Many early poets exploited the possibilities in hunting as a way of defining their desires, and they did it with pride, even boasting that they were hunters. The hunt offered a great vehicle for expressing longing and desire. Now, though, the perspective on male sexuality is changing, and the venatic language of the hunt is more embarrassing, at least, and horrifying at worst. The hunt has entered our public discourse on male desire in scandalous ways. O.J. Simpson stood trial, and whether or not he killed his ex-wife, he certainly beat and stalked her. And she feared he would kill her. Robert Packwood has been expelled from the Senate for sexual harassment, and even the President, Bill Clinton, has had to defend himself against charges of adultery and harassment. These examples suggest how straight, heterosexual masculine sexuality is on trial, and certainly under scrutiny in ways that have many men feeling defensive.

But when as many as 40 percent of all women may be the victims of an attempted rape at some point in their lives, it seems that the issue goes to deep cultural notions of desire.

A whole vocabulary, as ancient and as powerful as our most cherished Western myths, supports a construction of desire as a hunt, largely by men for women. Certainly women can be erotic hunters, but it is not the primary way the metaphor or trope works. Tibullus in the quotation introducing this chapter has the female, Sulpicia, plead with her lover Cerinthus to leave the hunt and come home. She only wants to join him, she says with a wit that is sophisticated and urbane, if she can lie with him in his nets. When the metaphor does make women hunters, the reversal of roles gives the narrative additional force and menace and even terror. If hunting metaphors are not the most common figurative language we have for the hunt, I'd be surprised. They structure entire myths, and frame many of the most compelling and definitive stories in which the West gave a voice and a meaning to desire, including the great shaping stories of the ancient world, from Bacchus to Ovid's many myths, to Virgil's epic of Aeneas and Dido.

Most of us experience desire as a powerful and uniquely personal feeling, one that seems to define us as individuals and derive directly from the deepest self, from our cells and our blood and our heart. Yet fantasies can be cultural as well as personal. Desire is generated and structured by cultural images. Those images are more than metaphor, more than merely language. They define the way we feel, the way we think. We can look to the images and stories we use to understand ourselves. It's the task of great poets to teach us how we feel—or more precisely, to give us the language that helps us interpret our feelings. So pervasive is the language of the chase in our understanding of desire, so thoroughly integrated into our primary myths of longing, that they are more than language. They are figures of feeling. They are tropes of thought.

We experience ourselves through the lens of our language.

If we live in a culture of desire, it's largely a narcissistic desire now. One of our greatest emblems of desire, Narcissus, was himself a hunter, lured by an echo to the bewitching sight of his own reflection. Our own chase now is to follow our own words to an image of ourselves.

The epic hunt is about identity—heroic identity. It imagines the hero—

Odysseus or Hercules or Orion—largely independent and alone, an agent of will and appetite, conquering enemies and women. It imagines that the hero lives apart from relationship, somehow, not recognizing that this notion of identity itself creates a version of relationship based on opposition.

The erotic hunt is about desire. It seems to be largely about relationship. But in its early incarnations, the erotic hunt was imagined to have relatively little to do with identity. Desire was about a power and a hunger. It was about the ways in which we've learned to imagine sexuality in terms of dominion and desire, pursuit and power, contest and conquest. It was viewed, at least initially it seems, as having little to do with identity. It was an external force, a power from the gods which was irresistible, and it was concerned with winning and losing in love. It was about battle and winning, chasing or being chased. But desire in the old stories seems always somehow generic and apart from the hero, and his concern is always with being the hunter, not the hunted. The force of desire did not come from inside the hero, though it could knock him to his knees and even ruin a hero. But its very threat suggested that the power of desire might also be closely linked to identity. That's why, when Narcissus realized that his desire had taken him back to the image of himself, he drowns. With that image of drowning in self, the ancients were on the verge of recognizing our more modern notion of the relation between identity and desire.

In addition to offering a narrative structure for desire, a narrative of searching and longing for the elusive creature, the hunt also poses one of the central questions through which power is negotiated and structured in a relationship: Who chases whom?

2

As much as anyone, the Roman poet Ovid taught the world how to love. It's a large claim, supported at least by convention and tradition if not by fact. It certainly does not mean that people before Ovid didn't love, or that all people after him only loved as he prescribed. But by his own claim, by the immense influence his poetry exerted on subsequent poets of love, and by general critical assent, Ovid gave us the concrete images that largely summarized for two millenia the main postures and attitudes of erotic feeling—the parameters of our experience of desire.

Ovid was born in 43 B.C. and wrote at the height of the brilliant Augustan Age in Rome. He was sophisticated, urbane, and brilliantly ironic. In his playful wit, Ovid described himself as the only man in Rome worthy to teach other men how to love. He styled himself, in fact, "*praeceptor amoris*," the teacher of love, and even "*magister amoris maximus*," the greatest teacher of love. In some sense, he may have been more right in his self-assessment than he knew: he was Shakespeare's favorite poet of desire, and the *Times* of London repeats the conventional wisdom about Ovid when it claimed in an article on this poet that he "influenced the content of European literature probably more than any other of the ancients."[3]

This poet loves the myriad situations of love and the strange labyrinth of desire, and because of his expertise he took it upon himself to put his erotic wisdom into a clever handbook for would-be Roman lovers. The *Ars Amatoria—The Art of Love*—is a poem in three books, derived he asserts from long experience, and amounts to a kind of hunting manual for the youth of Rome.[4] It's a mock-didactic guidebook promising the reader a complete education in love as it was understood then—and it gets down to very concrete specifics. It tells young men what streets to cruise to find the most beautiful women, how to deliver good pick-up lines, what to do with bothersome husbands, how to dress and perfume yourself, and when to make your best moves. It also gives advice on how to get out of an affair that's run its course. It's a practical, tongue-in-cheek little book, and it does for erotic hunting what Xenophon's "On Hunting" did for the wealthy young citizen-hunters of Athens. For Ovid, hunting is a metaphor of manly desire; for Xenophon, hunting is a metaphor of manly virtue.

The hunting metaphor dominates Ovid's notion of desire in this book. He links hunting, sports, and the military in a single word which he applies to the female object of desire: she is "*praeda*," which means either spoil or prey. The Latin word embeds the prey in a larger set of hunting metaphors that encompasses all types of sexual desire; *praeda* as prey are the victims of the predator, or "*praedator*," which in Latin, as in English, means a hunter.

Women as prey are one facet of a much larger set of metaphors that structure desire in the male psyche. Ovid in *Ars Amatoria* advises that two sorts of skills are involved in the erotic hunt. First the young Roman males must know how to do their stalking, where to prosecute their chase. Second, they must know how to capture their women. Men should set their traps, he advises in Book 1, where they have the best chance to bag their limits:

> While you're free, and can go everywhere with a free rein, choose who you'll tell, "You alone please me." She isn't going to drop in your lap, floating out of thin air. You've got to go seek the girl who will be most pleasing to your eye. The hunter knows the haunts of deer very well,

knows where to spread his nets. The hunter knows which valleys are the favorite of the boar with the gnashing teeth. Bird hunters know well the bushes of their favorite birds. And the fisherman with his dangling hook knows exactly where to find the big schools of fish. You also, who seek the object for a long love, first have to learn the places the girls hang out. (1.41–50)

The best place for this love hunt in ancient Rome, according to Ovid, was in the round theaters, which is where he guides his young students of the game.

Once you've found a woman that strikes your fancy, Ovid says, you've got to know how to capture her. Ovid's expert at that too. When Ovid captures a girl, he's ecstatic at the thought: "Shout Paeans, scream hooray. Yell it over and over. The prey I chased has run into my snares" (2.1–2). This opening to Book 2 announces the theme of the second stage of the chase: how the love hunter should capture the object of his desire.

The best way is with nets, it seems. At least, that's his favorite metaphor of the capture in this witty pamphlet. Ovid sticks to metaphors of the net, shying away from the more grotesque possibilities of the capture, notably rape. The full territory that the metaphor of hunting outlines—the desire mapped out by the metaphor of the hunt—is explored in more detail in a number of other myths and stories from the ancients.

All women are spoils, says Ovid. Even the most chaste want to get caught, or at least can be caught. They may gather together in big bands, at notable places, apart from men. They may seem, like the chaste goddess Diana, to shun the company of men and prefer chastity. But these are rather "perfect spots for hunting" (1.258). These are spots to spread your nets. The grove of Diana just outside of Rome, by the lake of Nemi, was a favorite resort of ancient lovers. The important thing for men to remember at this crucial stage of the hunt, according to Ovid, is that all women want to get caught: "First, have faith in your mind that the entirety of women can be caught; you can catch them easily, all you have to do is set your snares. Birds will go silent in spring, or grasshoppers in summer, or Maenalus's dog will be pursued by the hare, before a woman who has been well tempted will resist her young lover" (1.269–73). The chase and capture are conceits for seduction. Nets are the preferred images because they work so well as a metaphor for strategy and ruse. The nets might be words, wine, or lovers' gifts, often themselves hunted animals like hares or, famously, Catullus's girlfriend's envied little sparrow.

The point to note in Ovid's view of women is not only that men are justified in coercing them—an idea that seems to have culminated in our times in the insistence that men learn that when women say no, they may actually mean yes. More than that, it is the way the hunting metaphor has been used as the point of reference, the ground which naturalizes this notion of desire. An unwilling woman, says Ovid, would be a reversal of nature, a freak of nature. The metaphor of hunting gives the authority in this passage to a predatory notion of desire. It casts women's reluctance and men's aggressiveness in matters of desire as "natural." This way of deploying the metaphor of the hunt, to give a natural cast to notions of both virtue and desire, is one of its most insistent functions through history.

In *Ars Amatoria*, we have the lucky opportunity of seeing men actually being instructed in predatory notions of desire. There are two things I'd like to point out here. First, the idea that women are prey has an ancient and honorific lineage. Desire as predatory is not viewed as an aberration, but as absolutely central to the concept of desire. The erotic hunt defines desire, and for the most part defines for men what *amor*, which means desire more than it means our notion of romantic love, could be. Ovid's metaphor is part of a textbook for seduction, and it is a structuring idea for relations in love and desire. Men are usually the hunters (though in Book 3 Ovid gives advice to women), and women are the *fugaces*—the fleeing prey. Women are imagined as objects of desire, or sometimes as objects that might themselves desire.

Second, men must be taught this notion of desire. Currently, we give to desire a privileged place in our sense of self, viewing it as a primary experience, along with fear. It seems to come right from the body. It seems to be a force of nature. We call it an instinct. But Ovid is educating men in this notion of desire as a chase. Though the hunting language pretends this eroticism has a natural setting and origin, it is really a thoroughly urbane and citified notion. The hunt, ironically, gives desire a cultural locus and framework. What must be taught so systematically, even in desire, cannot truly be said to come naturally. Desire may be instinctual, but how we express that desire has been taught and learned.

The hunt is one of the favored tropes for sexual desire for us, and we inherited it from ancient sources like Ovid. With all his worldly charm and disarming candor, Ovid lends to the connection between sexual desire and the chase a powerful authority. *Amor* is desire, and someone like Isidore of Seville argued in the Middle Ages that the word itself comes from *hamus*—Latin for fishhook, and related to a similar word in Sanskrit.[5]

The erotic hunt is a topos, a locus of feeling in language. As a narrative structure, hunting gives a sense of the erratic nature of Eros, its restlessness and wandering. It is a sort of journey into the wilderness, the perfect vehicle for a story, culminating in a climax or confrontation. The hunter belies a deep psychological impetus and impulse. The erotic hunter taught men that desire comes before love, that desire is a game, that women are fair game, and that the goal of the game is to score as often as possible.

It remained for other stories, many of them also told by Ovid, to enter into the deeper psychological dimensions of the erotic hunt. Many of the best myths from the classics define love as an erotic hunt. From my reading, the most important representations of love in the ancient myths are really in fact stories of erotic desire, not love as we think of it now. Or, they are conflations of Eros and love. This legacy of desire as a hunt still very much exists. Certainly, romantic love has not displaced these notions of Eros, just as a woman like Sandie might stand on stage and say, angrily, "Women are prey." Love as we think of it, as a romantic ideal and the foundation of a lasting relationship, is hard to find in ancient literature. But our notions of love still bear the stamp of these ancient notions of predatory desire, and our emotional evolution is marked by these notions of desire. We continue to imagine love as emerging from desire, for example—desire is a crucial sign of love, the beginning of love.

Yet we still also see desire and love, established love, in conflict. Desire and love can easily be imagined as mutually exclusive. Romantic love may begin for us in desire, and it may culminate in marriage. But we don't usually think of marriage as the scene of great passion. Marriage among the classics is not based on romantic love, but it is inimical usually to desire, also. For example, Eros spurs the married but amorous Jove to his incorrigible career of flings, seductions, and rapes in the ancient myths. The great myths of the ancients gave us the erotic hunter, and taught us a schooling in desire, a desire we have not left behind. The challenge posed by this concept of desire defined by the hunter is nothing less than to begin to confront, and reimagine, what we understand as male sexuality.

3

The hunt worked two ways in the psychology of desire for men: it eroticized nature, and it naturalized an erotics of power. The imagery of hunting took on an erotic flavor, even when describing actual hunting stories, as in the case of Sulpicia writing to her hunting lover, Cerinthus, in the epigraph. The nets of the boar could be the location of lovemaking in the woods. Mythic hunters, on the other hand, move into the wilderness inside, the wilderness of passion. Men move through the landscape of the heart as

hunters, impelled by desire. The erotic hunt links a favored *
the narrative impulse, with the movement of desire.

The hunting narrative gave men a structure and a psychoiog,

I'd like to suggest that the erotic hunt corresponds to two defining ways
in which we've learned to experience desire. They both challenge the notion that desire is merely an instinct, or is so fully grounded in the body as
to be a biological imperative. The erotic chase and capture describe the
most powerful feature of Eros—we experience it as the pursuit of something we need. It is a lack, an absence, an emptiness we want filled.[6]
The chase and capture correspond perfectly to, follow almost inevitably
from, this notion of desire as lack. Experienced as not having something,
desire impels the hunter/lover to pursue the elusive creature. But what is
pursued is lost in the moment of capture. Like Ovid in the epigraph, the
lover/hunter learns he must always pursue the next thing. "The hunter pursues, and the quarry flees, and what he captures he always leaves behind, to
go after the next prey he sees."

The other type of desire is full of power, articulated brilliantly by the
myths of hunters as diverse as Jove who dominates and Dionysus who subverts. The erotic hunts define desire through narratives of repression and release. It can both enforce conventional powers—gods, state—or it can, most
interestingly, subvert them. Desire sets its sights on the forbidden object, the
illicit target. This is exactly the way Jove in the guise of the hunter loves to
pursue, in so many of his mythic stories, the chaste nymphs of Diana. The
French poststructuralist theorist Michel Foucault describes this type of desire throughout his work. The erotic hunter, patrolling the boundaries between culture and nature, works subversively to undermine the conventional
forms and ideals of sexuality—especially chastity and married sexuality.
This is desire imagined as a violation, as a struggle, and yet somehow productive of new forms and modes of insight. The image of the fight or even
the rape—violence itself—is the sign of both resistance and domination.[7]

To see the way hunting intersected with desire at these psychological
and political levels, Ovid is a good guide. The *Metamorphoses* is his superb retelling in poetry of nearly all the great myths of ancient Rome and
Greece. He finished this collection in A.D. 7, and its myths trace a landscape
of human longing more intricately than perhaps any other work. Ovid's
wooded landscapes are filled with hunters, and they are only incidentally
hunting for animals. The real game is sex. One story can stand as representative of the many myths that describe desire as a chase and a contest, as a
longing for what is missing and a power struggle. It's the story of Daphne
and Apollo.[8]

As Ovid tells the story, the god Apollo has just returned to Olympus, home of the gods, from his great triumph over the Python at Delphi. Before this victory, this "god of the glittering bow" had only used his arrows "in hunting does and fleeing goats." But now he's a hero and he feels exultant. When Apollo sees young Cupid struggling to string his bow, Apollo can't resist mocking him. "What have you got to do with powerful weapons, lascivious little boy," says Apollo. "These weapons are for my shoulders, who is strong enough to wound wild beasts mortally. I just now destroyed the swollen Python with arrows too numerous to count. The pestilent serpent was so large, her corpse sprawled across several acres" (456–60). As a hunter, Cupid is no match for the great Apollo. Or so the boasting god thinks.

Cupid has other notions. He's a malicious boy, and a flash of subversive desire bursts out. Cupid tells Apollo that he will get even for this insult. Apollo can hunt everything in the whole world with his arrows. But Cupid can shoot Apollo himself with his darts. Apollo can only take living creatures. Cupid can take even gods. By so much is Cupid's glory greater than Apollo's.

Cupid flies up to Mount Parnassus. He takes out two darts, one of gold and the other of lead. The sharp gold arrow instills desire. The dull leaden arrow makes one flee love. Cupid shoots Apollo with the golden point, piercing him to the marrow. He immediately burns with desire for Daphne, daughter of a river god named Peneus.

With the leaden tip, Cupid shoots Daphne, to make her hate Apollo.

This is the first great lesson of desire in Ovid: Eros is irresistible. The instant Apollo sees Daphne, he's ready to give chase. His passion is an appetite, a hunger like that of predators for their prey. He tries to convince her to love him, but she's uninterested. He begs her not to run, but she flees anyway.

> He wants to say more, but the timid nymph flees and he's stuck with unfinished words. Even as she runs, she seems more beautiful. The wind blew bare her body. Her gown blew lovely in the breezes. Her delicate hair streamed in the soft air. She was even more beautiful in flight. The young god abandoned words. Moved by Cupid himself, Apollo pursued her tracks. He was like a hound that spots a hare in an open plain, chasing his prey on foot. The hare wants safety. The hound catches at her with his muzzle, and thinks he almost has her. She's not sure if she's been caught, and only just snatches herself away from his biting mouth. Apollo and Daphne ran just like this hound and hare. He was fast, she was afraid. He had the advantage because he was carried on the wings

of Cupid himself. She could only flee, with her hair flying over her shoulders, exhausted by the terrible flight. . . . (525–44)

This is the locus classicus of love as a chase. The god of reason pursues a fleeing nymph as a "lamb flees a wolf, or a deer a lion" (505).

Daphne is herself a huntress. Even before she was shot by Cupid's leaden bolt, she was like Phoebe or Diana—the Roman names for Artemis: she wants no part of men. Ovid says that Daphne "flees the very name of love, and joys in the deep retreats of forests and in catching wild animals, just like the virgin goddess Diana. A single band held her lovely hair loosely. Many men sought her, but she scorned them all, roaming the deep woods without a thought for men, or Hymen, or Cupid" (474–80). She's a virgin huntress, but she cannot escape Apollo.

Just as he's about to seize her, breathing on her shoulders in the chase, she prays to her father Peneus. She begs him to save her from Apollo. "Destroy the beauty of my body," she pleads, "which gives too much delight." Even while she's praying, she begins to change. Her father saves her by turning her into a laurel tree: her skin becomes bark enclosing her beautiful breasts, her fingers change into twigs, her hair becomes leaves, her toes stretch into tendrils and roots.

Apollo places his hand on the bark of the tree, and he can feel her heart beating within.

He loves her still, even in her new form. Rather than lose her, he promises to wear her leaves in his hair. She will always be Apollo's tree, and victors in poetry and war will wear the laurel wreath as a sign of their success. He made her leaves to be perpetually green, just as he is perpetually young.

I remember seeing the sculpture of Daphne and Apollo by Bernini in the Villa Borghese in Rome. The god Apollo is just touching the young nymph at the climax of the story. The marble is carved into an exquisite delicateness. Daphne is just changing into a tree. Her fingers are sprouting leaves, the bark is climbing up her body. It is so beautiful, so idealized. I've always found this image haunting. And troubling, also, without always knowing why. Ovid lingers over the transformation of Daphne, also. He dotes on it. His charming poetry idealizes the story, casts a luminous glow over the loveliness of Daphne. Even as she flees, even as she resists, she is only more lovely. Daphne *fugax*, the fugitive.

The story illustrates the structure and the dynamics of one form of male desire. Many hunting stories are explicitly about male versus female roles. Atalanta, for example, was a huntress who wanted to hunt the Calydonian boar, and her gender was ambiguous—"She truly looked like a virginal boy, or a boyish virgin" (8.323). She violates gender roles in both hunting and love for Meleager, usurping the male roles.[9] The male is the hunter, the female the prey. The male desires, pursues, captures. The female flees. Desire is conceived as largely male, something the female avoids. She is at best prey, able to flee but not escape. Even in her transformation, she cannot escape the god Apollo. He may not be able to possess her in her female form, but he can take her over as his in her form as a laurel tree. She belongs to him, in life or death. Desire is about the acquisition of what was lacking. She is transformed into something else, something he can possess as well as pursue. She becomes his laurel wreath, the tree sacred to Apollo. The image is idealized in Ovid and in Bernini, but it is an image of appropriation and acquisition. The female is fully identified with nature—in various stories, she can be hare, lamb, deer, cow, or tree. In whatever guise, the erotic hunter asserts the prerogative of ownership.

Ovid's pathless woods are filled with hunters that bear various relations to Apollo and Daphne. The story of the hunter or huntress in love can assume myriad forms, and while in this story Daphne more or less succeeds in escaping, it's clear that Apollo is willing to assert what he views as his prerogative. He'll not only chase, but if he can, he'll seize her as well. Making Daphne's laurel into an emblem of Apollo symbolizes the way in which idealization covers a deeper darkness. This desire is given a divine sanction. Under the grace of Ovid's story, desire is predatory and rapacious. The hidden secret of the erotic chase is that Apollo is willing to take what is not given, and Daphne as a tree is a symbol of the way desire and dominion operate simultaneously in men's imaginations on both women and nature. This is the verge of Eros as rape.

In the ancient myths, desire is a chase, a longing for the thing that flees, a story of pursuer and pursued. Desire is born in that fugitive moment, when we realize something is missing, something just left, something flees our outstretched reach. And the thing we desire always somehow escapes us, changed in the very moment in which we succeed. In desire, by definition, we can never win the thing we lack.

It is not only that the female was transformed into an object, a tree, to escape Apollo's desire. When desire is a chase for the thing that flees, satisfaction is always just out of reach. Apollo loses the very thing he longs for. Loss and longing are the twin sides of the chase. Absence and lack are the stuff the erotic chase is made of. There is some sweet melancholy in the heart of desire. Beauty flees just before us, perpetually out of reach, at our fingertips, always fugitive. The best we can do, the male is taught, is to possess the female. She becomes a symbol of his power and his strength.

She becomes, like Daphne, a symbol of the hero's victory. He idealizes her, and her idealization is the transformation of the creature into the symbol, nature into art. Woman and nature—they are both his. Apollo is identified with art and culture. Apollo takes possession of the arrested female in nature. In succeeding, he loses the thing he loves.

4

In the *Metamorphoses*, Ovid tells about a hundred myths and legends. It depends on how you count, of course, because along the way, there is a seemingly infinite number of incidental stories. The tales go from the creation of the world and the golden age to the deification of Julius Caesar: a poetic history of the earth. Desire and lust are prominent themes, and are largely defined by hunting. In at least twenty of the stories, hunters are the image of the lover in the woods. This is far more common than any other image. In another group of about eight stories, hunting or predation is central as metaphor for the relations formed.

The following list illustrates the mythic exploitation of the hunt as a vehicle for exploring certain imaginative postures for men in desire. These gods and their stories are more or less familiar to us. The stories are given more or less in the order in which they are told in the *Metamorphoses*: Apollo and Daphne, Pan and Syrinx, Jove and Callisto (Jove disguises himself as Diana to seduce the huntress-nymph, and she ultimately becomes a bear, and Ursa Major in the sky); Actaeon and Diana; Echo and Narcissus (Narcissus is a hunter in pursuit of a woman who disappears into an empty sound); Pentheus and Bacchus (Bacchus or Dionysus is himself a hunting god); Venus and Mars; Salamacis (who is loved by a nymph and becomes male and female, Hermaphroditus); Arethusa, Cephalus, and Procris (Cephalus the hunter falls in love with the dawn or "Aurora," and his wife Procris, overhearing the hunter sigh for Aurora, kills him); Meleager and Atalanta (he kills the Calydonian boar and wins her love); Cyparissus (he loves a deer with golden horns, which he accidentally kills, becoming a cypress tree in his sorrow); Apollo and Hyacinth (Apollo accidentally kills the beautiful youth whom he loves); Venus and Adonis (both are hunters); Orpheus and the Maenads (wild hunting women kill Orpheus like hounds on prey); Galatea and Polyphemus; Circe and Picus (Picus the boar hunter becomes a cackling, insane woodpecker to flee Circe); Hippolytus (who refuses to love, in preference for the hunt); and Jove and Ganymede (Jove becomes a predatory eagle to snatch his beloved boy into the heavens).

In all cases, desire is understood largely in terms of desire and fear, longing and flight, lust and chastity. The hunting motif in Ovid is so pervasive, and so important, in defining desire because it condenses in a single image Ovid's view of life and time themselves: pursued, pursuing, forever fugitive, forever new. We are always changing, he writes in the *Metamorphoses*:

> Everything is in flux, and everything is born into a wandering life. Time itself flows like a river, and neither time nor the river can stop flowing: wave pushes wave, and each wave as it comes urges the one ahead, which itself is urging another, and fugitive time is always equally following, forever new. What was before, is left behind; what didn't exist, now is. Time and all things are forever being reborn. (15.178–84)

The hunt is an image for life itself, for life within the flux of time. Desire is at the heart of nature.

More important, though, desire becomes energized when it is connected with structures of power—largely with domination, and flight in Ovid. In Ovid, and in desire as we largely understand it, hunting is a central metaphor because it enables an exploration of the way power is deployed in sexuality. The chase largely implicates Eros with male dominion. But stories of domination—intrusion, penetration, voyeurism—can inevitably and suddenly lead to their reversal and inversion. The hunter can be the victim of his own sexual politics. He can suddenly be the prey.

No story is more famous or compelling in this regard than that of Actaeon and Diana.

Before telling this story from Ovid, I have to speak of Diana, the Roman name for the goddess Artemis. Diana is the goddess of the hunt, the virgin who typically prefers chastity, the company of her nymphs, and the pursuit of wild animals to men. We've already had occasion to discuss Diana in the stories of Orion, where she is the hunting goddess he hunts with, desires, and tries to rape. The story of Orion and Artemis is the prototype for many stories about hunters and huntresses, through which the complex erotic interactions of males and females were explored and defined in the classical world. Apollo and Daphne derive from this prototype. Daphne is the chaste nymph who hunts in the woods and flees men. The stories of Jove and Callisto, Cephalus and Procris, and Meleager and Atalanta also derive from this type. The most famous story of the hunter and the goddess, Actaeon and Diana, is from the same rough group of stories. The goddess Artemis or Diana is the virgin huntress, and her image focuses an intense vision of moral purity and chastity in the image of the hunt. It seems a sort of renunciation of sexuality in favor of ethical purity, of the sort Xenophon and Plato might endorse. There's a male version of this renunciation—the male who renounces women to hunt in the forests, like Melanion, a misogynist "Black Hunter" referred to by Aristophanes in *Lysistrata*.

Yet the ideal of Artemis or Diana makes her much adored, one of the loveliest conceptions in the Greek pantheon. She expresses a deep and beautiful spiritual vision. She was free and untamed, combining chastity and desire in one image of the female. She was everywhere in nature, and could appear as a bear or a doe. Callisto, her double and nymph, appeared as a bear, and circles in the sky to this day, the nymph who became Ursa Major, the constellation. Young Athenian girls danced as bears in honor of Artemis, and in initiation rituals became bears. She is surrounded by beautiful nymphs, accompanied by stags and other wild animals, and as huntress is mistress of game. In some of the finest conceptions of the goddess, Diana gives an image to pure spiritual longing that makes her at once a chaste female and the "Mistress of the Animals," the female who runs with wild creatures. She is the twin sister of Apollo, and her description by the poet Callimachus from the third century B.C. gives her in her idealized form.

As a three-year-old girl, she is already challenging her father and her brother. She reaches up to her father Jove's chin and asks for all the gifts he's already given her brother, plus the addition of one more, virginity: "Give me to keep my maidenhood, Father, forever," she implores,

> and give me to be of many names, that Phoebus [Apollo] may not vie with me. And give me arrows and a bow—stay, Father, I ask thee not for quiver or for mighty bow: for me the Cyclopes will straightway fashion arrows and fashion for me a well-bent bow. But give me to be the Bringer of Light and give me to gird me in a tunic with embroidered border reaching to the knee, that I may slay wild beasts. And give me sixty daughters of Oceanus for my choir, all nine years old, all maidens yet ungirdled; and give me for handmaidens twenty nymphs of Anmisus who shall tend well my buskins, and, when I shoot no more at lynx or stag, shall tend my swift hounds. And give to me all mountains; and for city, assign me any, even whatsoever thou wilt: for seldom is it that Artemis goes down to the town.

She is accompanied always by hounds and nymphs, and she has a special herd of deer, sacred to her, with horns of gold.[10]

Still, it would be a mistake to imagine a goddess like Diana or Artemis, in her guise as virgin and huntress, as a simple denial of desire as a crucial element in the male conception of hunting. On the contrary, she reveals the desire that is latent in chastity. As a goddess of hunting, Diana stresses two themes: chaste desire, and female power in response to male aggressions. Both are focused through the lens of hunting. Within Diana the contrasting principles of chastity and desire are fused. Orgiastic dances were held to glorify her in some locales, and fat men sometimes sought to invade these fertility dances. As protector of life, she was a sort of fertility goddess as well as chastity goddess, and phalli were offered to her in some rituals, as well as fruit and all species of animals. She is the divine feminine in nature, in its wildness and its strangeness, its innocence and its otherness. She gathers a power into the female image, and can strike animals and hunters dead in her anger.

And these female goddesses and nymphs operate within male landscapes, find their terrain crossed by male hunters, who threaten and compete and rape. Hercules for example may have violated Artemis's world when, in his third labor, he captured the Cernynian deer, sacred to her.

The chaste female offers an ideal for both men and women: for men, it offers a chastened and purified desire, for women a renunciation of male desire. And the huntress who fights back, as well as the huntress who renounces, places a certain self-determining power in the image of the female. And this female embodies, as well, a fantasy of male fear of women. Whatever agency these female hunters may achieve, they are still figures and objects for pursuing men, defining ways in which they experienced their desire as a problem to themselves and their quarry.

Diana's militant or venatic renunciation of sexual desire, displaced onto animals and hunting, is itself a sign of the way a contradiction confirms the importance of an issue. Her denial is at once a spiritual and emotional ideal, and her chastity is itself a spur to men's desire. Desire and denial are connected in Diana, just like the pursuer and pursued.

Just as Diana might love Orion in some stories, she is also his adversary in others. She can be both consort and enemy to male hunters.

One of her jobs is to set boundaries to hunters' desire. Diana was a golden ideal for a highly civilized culture—a powerful female image women might strive to emulate in her strength, an austere female image men might use to discipline their more unruly predatory instincts. It is a violation of her godhead to invade her sanctuary, as Agamemnon discovers. For killing one of the "dappled stags" in her sacred grove, and then vaunting of his hunting prowess, Agamemnon incurs the wrath of Artemis, and has to sacrifice his daughter Iphigenia at Aulis before receiving a favorable wind to sail to Troy. Actaeon makes an even more spectacular mistake, and it costs him dearly.

5

Of the many versions told of Actaeon and Diana, Ovid's story of the hunter who sees the goddess naked is the most famous. He tells it in Book 3 of the *Metamorphoses*.[11] A grandson of Cadmus, the city's founder, Actaeon loves to hunt with his companions on the mountain outside of Thebes, Ovid says. By noon one day, Actaeon and his men have killed many species of game. With their nets and spears dripping "with the blood of our successful hunting," Actaeon orders his men to rest for the day. "Tomorrow," he tells them, "we try again."

On his way down the mountain, he comes across a valley called Gargaphie, sacred to Diana. It's highly feminized in its description, a "secret grotto," dark and shaded. A slender archway in the rock leads to shining water, a crystal pool with grassy banks all around it. After pursuing animals, Actaeon has stumbled upon naked women in the woods. In this pool, he discovers Diana, bathing in her secret place after the hunt. He watches her undress—the lucky mortal spying on the nakedness of a goddess. She puts aside her arrows and quiver and spear. She takes off her robe and gives it to one of her nymphs. A nymph unbinds her sandals. Another, Crocale, ties the goddess's flowing hair up in a knot. The rest of the nymphs bring urns of water, which they pour over the goddess's lovely limbs.

Ovid makes Actaeon innocent, getting lost and inadvertently barging into this secret world of naked women. He is more erratic then erotic. Other versions tell of Actaeon hanging from a tree, watching—much more obviously the guilty spy upon women's secret and private moments. In either case, he's uninvited, bursting into the "cool and dripping grotto." He's intruded upon women's space, a voyeur on female secrets. Nature has been feminized, and the female naturalized. This is her natural habitat, the secret grotto of desire—goddess and nymphs in a woodland pool. He's a man in no man's land. This is very much about what is male and what is female. He barges through the woods, and the minute the nymphs see him, they begin to pound their naked breasts and scream. "They were naked, the nymphs, and seeing the man, they beat their breasts and filled the grove with their wailing and circled Diana to hide her body with theirs. But the goddess herself stood taller than them and rises above them up to her breasts" (3.178–82).

Unable to hide her sexual parts, Diana "blushed at being seen." She looks for her weapons, but she's placed them far away. So instead of arrows, she scoops a handful of water from the pond and flings it in the young, bewildered hunter's face. Female imagery, female weapons—water against his "virile visage." He may have meant no harm, but to Diana, this is "avenging water." She scorns him with prophetic anger: "Now you can tell anyone you want that you've seen me without my clothes, if you're able to talk" (3.192–93). He won't be able to speak. He'll never report what he has seen.

The water transforms him into a beast. Limb by terrifying limb, he turns into a stag. On his forehead, where the water has been splashed, he feels the horns begin to sprout. His nose stretches into a long snout, like a deer's. His neck extends. His ears grow long and pointed, his skin turns into dappled fur. He has become the beast he has always loved to hunt. And last of all, the goddess plants in the heart of the young hero the feelings of fear. Immediately he runs, more swiftly than he's ever run before.

Running up to a pool, he sees his features, the horns on his forehead. He tries to moan. Actaeon is mute. He can no longer speak, can no longer tell anyone who he is or what he's seen. His identity has dissolved in the water. He has lost body and word, dignity and language. The power of the hunter has been reduced to the impotence of the prey.

Language is power. Through language, a man controls the way he sees himself. Actaeon's loss of language is directly related to his loss of self. He's dissolved, in a way. As he wonders where to go, he sees his own hounds come baying over the hill, full of the lust for blood. When they see him, a stag now, he cannot tell them he is their master. He tries to tell them not to attack. He tries to tell them who he is. But he can't speak: "He longs to exclaim, 'I am Actaeon. Know your master!' But words desert his desire" (3.230–31). He can no longer name himself or command his dogs. Without words, he is impotent. Only words, the ability to name yourself as master, separate hunter from hunted: "Actaeon, so frequently the gladiator-like pursuer through these very places, himself is pursued by his own servants" (3.227–28). The dogs bring Actaeon to bay, biting and nipping and slashing. Actaeon fills the mountains with his moaning, uttering a groan neither human nor cervine—and drops to his knees like a man praying. He falls in mute supplication to his own dogs. He has no arms to plead with, but his eyes are full of mute appeal. The dogs dismember the body of their former master: "They circle him on every side, slash his body with their teeth, tear him to pieces, and mangle their master, whom they don't recognize under the false shape of the deer. Finally, when his many wounds had killed him, the anger of quiver-bearing Diana was sated" (3.249–52). It's hard to know which is the metaphor and which the meaning in this story—

male relationships with nature, or male relationships with women—so deeply entwined are the two in the male imagination. It's a contest between our engendered bodies as we have imagined them in nature. The female body: chaste, hidden and protected, exposed and violated. The male body: guilty, wandering and intrusive, attacked and broken.

This is the politics of desire. The myth of the hunter enables the exploration of various postures and poses in desire. Hunting is a language of sex. It is a knowledge of sex.

Hunting has created a certain knowledge of sex by naturalizing domination in desire.[12] Power is thoroughly articulated in the natural imagery of the women in grottos and men with hounds and weapons. This distributes the roles and the power—men are active, women are passive. Men intrusive, women retiring. In this story, the contest is over who is master and who, so to speak, is mistress. Who is the hunter, and who is the hunted. It is a contest between who dominates and who is dominated. What is interesting, though, is that it's also a fight over who gets to speak for himself or herself, who gets to describe who each is. It's a battle over bodies and identities, vision and voice. Diana does not want Actaeon being able to speak to others about what he's seen—her naked body. She alone controls that. And Actaeon can no longer announce who he is, who resides inside the body of the stag that is now him.

Hunting is a knowledge of power in desire. Here, it is about domination between bodies, carried out not with the weapons of the hunt, but with water and words. If hunting is for men about power, it is also about impotence, necessarily. In such an obsessive concern with power, hunting explores the limits of power, and contains in its myths the exploration of its own subversion. Actaeon violates boundaries, sees the naked body of the goddess, and is turned into a beast. His own body, source of his desire, is torn to pieces. He embodies the image of the greatest of hunters, but he is dismembered—torn limb from limb. He loses himself as hunter by becoming the hunted. The obsession with power and self-containment that is represented by the chaste hunter is almost literally asserted and deconstructed in this single myth.

Power is torn apart and redistributed, between the male master and the violated female quarry. Actaeon is the broken body of the male, unable any longer to articulate his own desire. He can no longer speak his name. Perhaps the way this story puts two ideals together—the great hunter and the chaste goddess—as a way of asserting the values of the hunt and also deconstructing it, like the body of Actaeon, accounts for its enduring popularity. It seems to reach some real deep anxieties that lie within the male as hunter.

Actaeon is a type for a number of other hunters who press past limits, whose hunting is a way of undermining the ethos and the erotics of the hunter. Dionysus is a hunter, and he subverts every principle of the heroic and virile hunter. In *The Bacchae*, by Euripedes, this god arrives from the east wearing a fawn skin and carrying a thyrsus—a phallic staff of fennel tipped with a pinecone. His favorite animal is the panther (which was slang in Greek for prostitute), who can lure prey right up to itself with its perfumed breath. Dionysus is "sweet upon the mountains. He drops to the earth from the running packs. He wears the holy fawn-skin. He hunts the wild goat and kills it. He delights in the raw flesh."[13]

This new god is a savage hunter of the passions. He violates gender roles, being described not as a hero but as an "effeminate stranger." He confers a mystical, mantic power on his followers, who are largely women. They pursue animals in the mountains with an orgiastic wildness, tearing them apart. These Maenads might be thought of as women of license, but that's an oversimplification. Their wildness expresses itself in a contradiction of the values of the Greek city, a subversion of the values of the chorus. They transgress the laws and follow a new god.

In the story of Dionysus, one member of Thebes won't worship him— Pentheus. Dionysus stalks the young man, a chaste prig, and gets him to stalk the Maenads in the hills, disguised. Pentheus becomes an Actaeon-like figure, watching the women in their hunting rites. When they see him, they tear the young Pentheus apart, mistaking him for a mountain lion. He is another dismembered hunting hero.

Both chastity and violent lust are tropes of the erotic hunt. Another standard theme of the erotic hunt is the contest between the hunter and huntress. The hunter who becomes the hunted expresses another. And so is the heroic hunter—sometimes virtuous, sometimes not—who is dismembered or destroyed by vengeful females. The heroic hunter, like Apollo or Pentheus, who is victimized by the erotic hunt is another standard motif. These tropes identify places in our psyches. They define important features in our psychic landscape.

Were I to guess, I'd say that now most men are likely to identify with Actaeon more than Orion. It's not that there aren't many men who overtly chase and womanize, but it is not fashionable and has grown more and more unacceptable. Male wildness, like Dionysus's, appears more problematic now with its savage violence, despite its wild sexual energy. Actaeon suggests how male desire seems tinged with a sense of guilt. Few men admit it publicly. But in an era when every woman sees herself as a goddess, as is the case now, men seem inarticulate and dumb. Men seem on the defensive. Men seem unable to say their own names very clearly.

Like Actaeon, they are likely to feel they've somehow been torn apart in revenge. Their own bodies have been mangled. And they are likely to feel mute in their ability to name their desire, to know for sure who they now are. Or, like Dionysus, perhaps they cling to some vague notion of wildness—its own illusion. Men are ready, I suspect, to relinquish the metaphor of the hunter that makes them the predator. But not the one that makes them feel at once hunter and hunted. They have become, in a real way, the victims of their own metaphors.

In the silence that now hangs around male desire, at least the silence of men, perhaps we see the conditions for developing a new language for desire. This muteness men feel is perhaps the beginning of a new way of thinking about sex, less trapped in its phallic metaphors of weapons and wounds, predation and penetration.

6

Hunting is the privileged, ethical activity of young men on their way to responsible, even heroic, identities—the language of Xenophon and Plato, the language of a boasting Apollo and a heroic Actaeon before he meets Diana. It is the language of chastity and grace—of Diana and all her virginal nymphs in the woods.

Hunting is also the language of Amazons who dress up like men and threaten great heroes like Hercules. Erotic hunting is also about gods like Jove and Dionysus, who dress up like women. It shows how men become great, like Apollo killing the Python. And how those same men are brought low: Hippolytus and Pentheus are chaste heroic hunters who succumb to Venus's hunting. Actaeon incurs Diana's revenge, and Apollo is shot by Cupid. All these heroic hunters become victims of the erotic hunt. The standard motif: the hunter is the hunted.

It is precisely because hunting circumscribes these paradoxical impulses in the human spirit—for lust and chastity, responsibility and freedom—that it is so powerful and enduring as a myth. If a myth is a collective social fantasy, the enduring myths are the ones that need to be continually retold and reconfigured. They need this because they deal with problems that seem apparently insoluble, and can be handled from contradictory perspectives. The persistence of these hunting myths is testimony as well to the enduring problems, the murky cruxes of psychology and ethics, that it tries to encapsulate in its imagery.

Cupid, or Eros, is himself a great hunter. The conception of Venus's son as hunter has an extensive history. The boy with the bow is easily associated with hunting. The Greek poet Bion makes the association between Eros and hunting in his poem about a bird catcher: "A bird-catcher yet a boy in a woody grove / Was hunting birds when he saw winged Eros / Perched on the young shoot of a box tree."[14] Tibullus and Propertius among the Romans repeat the trope of Cupid as young hunter. And in the Renaissance, many poets drew on the motif. Edmund Spenser pictures "lusty Love"—or Eros—as both an aggressive hunter "manfully" shooting "at his game" (26–27) and as a young bird "entangled in a fowling net." In tricking Beatrice to confess her love for Benedick, Shakespeare's character Hero says, "Some Cupid kills with arrows, some with traps."[15] But the philosophical roots of this idea can be found in Plato's *Symposium*, his dialogue on love. Our very idea of desire, of Eros, is grounded in hunting.

With his bow and arrows, Cupid himself is a hunter.

Socrates professes to have always been a lover, a charming notion. He relates the lessons he professes to have learned about love from an old woman named Diotima, a prophet. Diotima tells Socrates that we can understand love—she means Eros—by his parentage.

Eros was born, she says, of a mother named Penia, which means poverty, want, or lack. And Eros was born of a father named Poros—strategy or guile. Diotima explains:

> Now, as a son of Resource and Poverty, Love is in a peculiar case. First, he is ever poor, and far from tender or beautiful as most suppose him: rather is he hard and parched, shoeless and homeless; on the bare ground always he lies with no bedding, and takes his rest on doorsteps and waysides in the open air; true to his mother's nature, he ever dwells with want. But he takes after his father in scheming for all that is beautiful and good; for he is brave, impetuous and high-strung, a famous [or, terrible] hunter, always weaving some stratagem; . . . a master of jugglery, witchcraft, and artful speech.[16]

Eros or Cupid or *Amor* or Love, as he is variously called, is "the terrible hunter." His two major attributes, as posited by Socrates, are lack and strategy. These correspond roughly to the characteristics of desire in the erotic hunts of Apollo and Actaeon. Love is the perpetual chase for what is forever out of reach, receding, and missing—that Lacanian sense of desire as absence and need. Love is also the ubiquitous and calculating deployment of political intent—it is power in Foucault's sense.

In *The Sophist*, Plato writes at length about what he calls the "lover's method of hunting."[17] He means that lovers use tricks and traps to win what they want. Love is essentially, he says, an acquisitive art—a way of taking possession of someone as the beloved. Seduction is merely a way of setting a trap with words and gifts.

How are we to understand a psychology of desire that can be summarized so succinctly by the figure of the hunter? Are we to assume, because it is so pervasive and deeply rooted in our feelings, that the metaphor of the erotic hunter defines an objective truth about desire—it is by nature defined by lack and strategy, by chase and power? Or we might ask, How is it that a culture would come to view desire in terms of lack and strategy, chase and conflict, arrogance and agony?

If you take Socrates at his word, men desire because they feel something is missing, something is lacking. They turn to strategy and guile to recover what has been lost.

As a myth and metaphor, hunting is isomorphic with our basic division of experience into paradoxical categories. The hunter moves along the boundaries between culture and nature, mind and body. Hunter and hunted: they define the break between self and other. He articulates the dualism that defines Western consciousness. What is not self, what Apollo defeats, what the hunter chases is automatically defined as the other—the prey, the pursued, the thing that can be captured. Into that category of other can fall nature, animal, lesser humans, lovers, women. It is a capacious category, and marks the division in our minds between subject and object.

Hunting describes desire as we know it because it represents this basic philosophic dichotomy in our consciousness. Desire as a hunt is born in the gap we have created between self and other, subject and object. The pursuer is the subject that desires. The pursued is the object that is desired. The erotic hunter is at one moment the chaste Diana, at another the debauched Dionysus. The erotic hunter traverses and patrols the margins and boundaries we have ourselves created. He can either enforce those boundaries, or traverse them.

These categories—desiring subject and desired object—can be flipped on their heads, and suddenly the chaste/chased object exacts her revenge. The hunter becomes the hunted.

The hunter can transgress boundaries. He can become the victim of his own hunting impulse. What he cannot do is make the boundaries disappear. What he cannot do is step outside of the hunting mythos. He is trapped in a certain mental terrain. How could he step outside the terms of the hunt? That would be impossible for him—he would have to disappear himself.

Since both heroic and erotic hunters helped invent the myths we experience ourselves by, it would require him to see beyond himself. It would require him to see that these myths—these group fantasies—were projects of his own consciousness. He would have to be able to see beyond a world organized into categories of self and other, subject and object, desirer and desired, male and female, hunter and victim. How could the hunter help us see beyond himself? He couldn't, this mythic hunter, because he so thoroughly believes in the categories he's created.

Desire drives the erotic hunter back and forth across the frontiers of self and other, seeking contact with what was once lost. What is sought is contact with the expelled and defeated other. The hunter, always chasing, always abandoning what he has caught, is doomed perpetually to reenact the original drama that articulates how his separation of the self from the world was created. He must constantly chase back and forth between loss and strategy. This is Freud's concept of "the return of the repressed." In a forever-unfinished drama, the male hunter continues to seek the beast or woman or lover—the other—he separated himself from in the first place. Apollo defeats Python and Gaea, and then finds himself chasing a young nymph. It is Cupid's revenge—coming just after the original triumph.

This is how the hunt defines not only identity, but relationship with the other. The male as we understand him in our myths was born when he defeated woman and nature and beast. Reason triumphed over emotion. But he is doomed to desire what he lost, which continually returns to him, and he continually seeks it, experiences it, and subdues it. He is caught in a cycle of unfulfilled, or momentarily fulfilled, desire.

What we discover in these ancient myths, what we can glimpse as we train our vision just past the beautiful moral of the hero winning great victories, just past the image of the noble lover driven by irresistible passion, is not the truth of their representations of either the male or male desire. We discover what Foucault calls a "genealogy of values, morality, asceticism, and knowledge." What is revealed in the details are the "accidents that accompany every beginning." What he means is that it is not necessity we discover in the origins of the hunter. These myths don't speak to us in a prophetic voice, telling us of Truth—the male is predatory, desire is a "terrible hunter." What the myths expose in the structure they reveal, is the shadow of all that might have been. The defeated beast becomes the shadow, a part of the unconscious. The external drama is also an internal struggle. What we glimpse, like Apollo holding his laurel wreath, is the hint of what was lost. When we excavate the depths, when we enter the labyrinths of desire, we find both intention and the shadow of ourselves.

We get glimpses of our own unconscious in the form of nature, beast, and female. We find in the prey an image of our shadow selves. What we find, attending upon the ideals and atavisms of our origins, is "the face of the other."[18]

The origin myth is a chimera, a fictive and collective social dream: not a lie, but a fiction.

The power and persistence of the image of the hunter, both heroic and erotic, can be traced to this: At one and the same time, the categories of predator and prey, hunter and hunted, give men a place to put all sorts of problematic "others"—beasts, nature, women, lovers, slaves, competitors. Even more, it gives men a strategy for maintaining contact with the displaced others that they now lack but need. As a metaphor, hunting defines a psychology in which men are cut off from the other and connected to it by a certain venatic desire. The erotic hunter defines perfectly the ambivalence of men's desire—longing to be at once connected but separate, near but apart, passionate but controlled. The voyeuristic Actaeon watches the naked huntress Diana from the bushes. Apollo chases a hunting nymph, and makes a laurel trophy out of the beauty he can touch but cannot keep. And always there is the danger that the hunter's schemes will backfire. Always, there is the danger that the hero will be shot by desire. Cupid will wound Apollo. Actaeon will be the prey of his own dogs. Pentheus will be destroyed by his rabid Maenad mother.

As he moves along the margins, in the crepuscular light of a shadowy forest, the hunter is himself a moving target. He's hard to see clearly, hard to pin down. It's part of his strategy. In moving through the landscape of desire, he doesn't want himself to be seen. He wants to be the hunter—the one who sees and who names the prey.

7

As a graduate student, my favorite place to read Latin was the classics library in Folwell Hall at the University of Minnesota. I read Ovid in the spring, found the *Ars Amatoria* to be witty, funny, entertaining. Ovid's myths fascinated me. But I had yet to discover Ovid's real power. I was less interested in desire then. Much as I enjoyed desire, I did not want to know about it.

It was Virgil who gave me the posture toward desire that carried me into manhood. I read Virgil during the winter, trudging to the library in temperatures often reaching twenty degrees below zero. It was the *Aeneid* that I read, and I loved Virgil's stately, marmoreal Latin. More than that, he gave me something more. The stoic Virgil defined for me the purpose and direction in life.

I took Virgil's lessons to heart. I found Ovid entertaining at the time, but somehow strange. I suspect that most men might find Ovid's stories of a tumultuous world of sex and transformation both compelling and bizarre. Few will explore the inner world of desire, with its alluring sexuality and dangerous reversals, with the open-eyed delight of Ovid. This venatic inner terrain is too self-indulgent, too threatening. Most men are likely to follow the path of Aeneas, Virgil's great hero. Most men will have learned, I suspect, to handle desire the way Virgil has taught us. They will follow work over desire, duty over pleasure.

Virgil set the two hunts—the epic hunt and the erotic hunt—in a direct confrontation. What Ovid did with Apollo and Cupid, in a single myth, Virgil made the subject of the first half of the *Aeneid*, which he was still polishing when he died in 19 B.C. The poem became an instant classic, the allegory of the founding of a nation, the allegory of the virtues of a new, Roman hero. Aeneas links the quest for a personal destiny with the demands of empire.[19]

He is a heroic hunter who flirts with an erotic hunt.

A fugitive, Aeneas flees the burning city of Troy, one of the city's young heroes. It is an explicitly male quest he embarks upon. As he flees the burning city, he carries his father, Anchises, upon his back and holds his son Ascanius's hand. His wife, Creusa, follows through the night a few paces behind. Trailing, she gets lost. Aeneas never sees her again—except her ghost, who approaches him on his visit to the underworld.

He sets sail with a group of men, searching for a new home and nation. On the way, a storm wrecks his ship on the shore of Carthage, the land of Dido. Carthage was the enemy of Rome, connected in the minds of Virgil's readers with their other great enemy, Cleopatra, whom they'd only just defeated at Actium.

Deeply discouraged, Aeneas's men sulk in the woods. Aeneas's first act narrated in the epic is to declare his status with a hunt. He hikes to a crag from which he can survey the situation, and immediately discovers a herd of stags. He pulls out his bow and arrow, and doesn't quit shooting until he's taken down seven stags. He is leader, hunter, victor.

This version of Aeneas, as epic hunter, is interrupted in Carthage. As he is reconnoitering the wilderness, his mother comes upon him. His mother is none other than Venus herself. Aeneas is sharp, but he doesn't recognize his mother. Why? Because she's in disguise. Her knees are bare, her dress is gathered in a knot. She has a bow slung across her shoulder. She has appeared to her son in the guise of a hunter.

She is Venus *venatrix*. The pun is unmistakable, and vestiges of it linger for us in the play upon venery, the love of hunting, and venereal—an adjective now associated mostly with diseases. Venus often appears in the guise of a huntress. Ovid portrays her that way in his story of Venus and

Adonis, and Shakespeare, as we'll see, develops the connection with great wit and insight. Venus's prey is typically less macho than the hero's: she prefers, say, hares to boars, doves to stags. She hunts for lover's gifts. Venus as huntress: she reflects the long-standing conflict between Venus and Diana, goddesses of love and chastity, and is reflected also in the battles between Hippolytus and Dionysus and many others.[20]

Venus gives Aeneas a new prey: Dido. Lovely, strong, and passionate, Dido is the queen of Carthage, related to the Amazonians, and she carries herself like a huntress. When Aeneas enters the city and sees Dido for the first time, she is called "the arrowy one," reminiscent of Diana.

Immediately, at Venus's order, the predatory Cupid shoots Dido.

She is the wounded prey. Dido becomes the prototype for the classical world of love's hunted victim. Virgil describes her as pierced by an arrow, a *coniecta cierva*, a stricken doe. For the rest of her short life, she wanders the streets of Carthage in a rage of desire, like a wounded doe, with a "deadly arrow stuck deep in her flank."

Yet Dido herself becomes the huntress, in one of the most wonderful and famous and paradigmatic lovers' rendezvous in all literature. As Virgil puts it,

> *venatum Aeneas unaque miserrima Dido*
> *in nemus ire parant.* . . . (4.117–18)

Aeneas, he says, and the wretched Dido prepare a hunting trip into the forest. Hunting in classical myths always skirts the possibility of sex, especially when couples are involved.

The royal pair organize a huge hunting party for the whole court, a grand royal hunt in the Middle Eastern tradition.[21] Both metaphor and scene of love, hunting is a strategy for consummating Dido's passion. They have snares and nets, horses and hounds, hunting lances and other jangling weapons. Beaters are sent into the hills to drive game down to the level ground, where horsemen wait to kill them, and the lovers appear in hunting clothes. Dido wears Phoenician clothes, piped with gold braid. Her quiver is gold, her hair bound in a golden clasp. Aeneas looks like Apollo himself, wearing a wreath of gold and laurel in his flowing hair.

The hunt is in the mountains. They sally forth from the city gates and into the "trackless forests of game." Wild goats are in the crags, leaping down the slopes. Stags gallop over open ground in wooded glens. Aeneas's son, Ascanius, rides ahead, hoping for manly quarry. He looks for a frothing boar or a sandy mountain lion. He doesn't want any tame quarry.

Yet Aeneas is the true hunter here, and not of a boar or a mountain lion. This *venator amoris* finds a beast he can tame.

Venus deceives all the other gods, especially Juno, into thinking the pair are forming a love match. They agree to help her consummate the relationship. Venus contrives a storm.

When the thunder and lightning and dark clouds interrupt their hunt, the rich hunters in all their regalia scatter. Dido and Aeneas flee to a cave, their own sweet grotto. The grotto is to become an important feature of love and hunting in later ages, as it was for Actaeon too. Hunters discover the love grotto. It's the cave of love. Sex is rarely far away, in any hunt—a cloudburst, a short sally, a secret cave.

Theirs is the interrupted hunt: *Venatus interruptus.*

In the cave, Virgil says that Dido meditates on a furtive love: *furtivu amorem* (4.171). Love in the woods has grown furtive, stealthy, strategic. The royal hunt was a pretext for this other hunt, it turns out. The two are married hugger-mugger. It's not a true marriage, but Dido calls it a marriage. They have a ceremony, and that will serve her turn.

The double hunt—heroic and erotic—defines Aeneas's character and culture. He must choose. Soon Venus recalls her son to his larger pursuit, chastising him for forgetting that his destiny requires him to move on, to seek a new land. It is the symbol of the official view of love and desire in the Roman world: the erotic must be relegated to little more than an adventure, an excursion, a side trip. It is, really, a distraction from the main quest. Aeneas remembers his duty. He crushes his feelings for Dido, rises out of his sensuality, and with a renewed sense of national purpose vows to leave Carthage.

He abandons Dido. She builds a huge pyre from which, on top, she can see Aeneas's ship sailing from the harbor. As he leaves, she torches the pyre and dies of her own passion.

Aeneas is the hunter of his own destiny, the hunter after Rome, and the hunter after Turnus. Turnus is his adversary once Aeneas and his men arrive in Italy. Before Rome can be founded, Aeneas must defeat the native inhabitants—Turnus and his tribe. In an extended simile, Aeneas is likened to a *venator canis*, a hunting dog, and the doomed Turnus is his prey, the *cervum*, or stag (12.750 ff).[22]

The unfortunate Dido lost her love contest, and her loss is a symbol of the triumph of Rome over women in the battle for the hearts of men. Aeneas's stoic virtue triumphs over Dido's deep passion. Reason over emotion, discipline over pleasure, duty over relationship—these lessons are all contained in Aeneas's abandonment of the servile and cervine Dido. The erotic hunt was subsumed under the heroic hunt. Here is the main legacy of

Aeneas's founding of Rome. The male sense of destiny included the female within its sphere only as a diversion or a distraction from his larger mission. In the scheme and scope of the male hunt in the West, the erotic hunt was subordinated to the heroic.

The hunt was and is a way of escaping the complexities and trials of relationship. Aeneas taught all Western men, whether they've read *The Aeneid* or not, how to deal with their emotions. Ovid himself, actually, recommends hunting, literal hunting, as a cure for disappointed love. It is a *remedia amoris*, a remedy for love: "You might study the joys of hunting: Venus has often been beaten into a shameful retreat by Diana. It's a good opportunity to let your smart young dog chase the running hare, or leave your nets among the green ridges. You can scare the timid deer, or confront the boar with your thrusting spear. . . . With these hunting pleasures, you can unlearn love, but only by deceiving yourself."[23] Note the reference to the contests between Venus and Diana. For Ovid, a hunting trip gives the disappointed lover time to recover.

Does the literal hunt still function as a way to hold the erotic or the feminine at bay? It startles me to hear how vividly alive these structures of thought and feeling remain in us. The actual and the sexual hunt still trace strange intersections, and the hunt is a way of escaping the complexities of passion and desire, feeling and relationship. I have for many years been a member of a men's group which meets every week. We share our deepest feelings in this group, and know each other intimately. The purpose is to form bonds of truth and honesty, caring and support. The goal is to help ourselves see ourselves more clearly, and to experience parts of ourselves that have, for complex reasons, been exiled from us as individuals. It is never easy coming to see how we feel, how we experience, and, more importantly, how we might each experience ourselves more fully and more deeply.

Several of the men in this group are literally hunters. One night, I remember, one of the hunters talked about how he had changed. He is an avid hunter. He knows parts of the Cascade Range on the West Coast with an intimacy that any of his two previous wives would have envied. His current girlfriend, he said, was having certain problems. He was proud now of his ability to listen to her better, to be more present. In the past, he said, he would not have wanted to deal with his wife's problems or emotions. In the past, he said, if a wife told him of a problem, he'd head downstairs into his basement. There he had a machine that made bullets. He could load the shot into shells, packing them tight, for his guns. He'd go down to the machine and start packing shells. Give him a complex emotion, and he'd start making bullets, he said.

He learned to change, though the instincts to escape from feeling run deep and surface in many ways. I spent years of my own life trying to deny the tangle of my own emotions. I was never very successful at it. My emotions were too strong and powerful, and I finally had to face them. That turned out to be a great gift in disguise. But a kind of Virgilian ideal, the strength of Aeneas, was for many years an ideal for me. I remember copying out Aeneas's excuse to Dido on a small card and taping it to my desk. When he was telling her he was leaving, he said, *"Italiam non sponte sequor."* "I pursue Italy not of my own free will."

Many men have come a long way from the workaholic obsessions implicit in Aeneas's Roman hunt. I know that I have opened up to a rich inner life of emotion. Still, when the beasts of passion get restless, I can flee into my head, take refuge in work. I have never gone to the basement to make bullets. If I've ever chosen any weapons, I'd have to say my bullets have been words. I have loved language like a weapon, and I can retreat to a study instead of the hunting woods of Ovid or the bullet machine like my friend. We each of us have our own versions of the hunt to hold the beasts at bay. It's the macho preference of doing to feeling.

8

Language can be a weapon, and it can be a trap. In many ways, man the hunter has been trapped in his own language. Certainly, the language of desire is the invisible hunting net of our passions. The problems of masculinity are both more simple and more deeply complex than we have imagined. They are a matter of culture and consciousness, rooted in the social forces and imaginative sources that have shaped the contexts of our lives.

I know, in my own case, I never imagined myself as an erotic hunter. I never wanted to see myself in that light at all. Yet at one point in my adult life, I began to explore the terrain of my own desire. Like Ovid, I wanted to understand desire. I was, I think, driven by a desire I did not understand.

The language of hunting shapes much of our talk about sex and sexuality to this day. Men still are on the prowl, still act like wolves, look for the easy mark, find the fair game, declare open season on some women. The language is easily and infinitely expandable, confronting us at almost every turn in any conversation about sexual relations.

All men know what it's like, in a crowd, to spot a woman they think they can "score" with. I still hear this gamy language, and men even revel in it by themselves, when a whole menagerie of female-creature metaphors define men's sexual fantasies. You don't have to be a predator, I discovered, to be a hunter.

What is lacking in these myths, these models of desire, is a nuanced challenge to the violence of the desiring hunter. That challenge remains for us to discover still.

What is so remarkable, so conspicuous in the discussions and representations of sexuality in the ancient world, is that it is never told in terms of what we now consider love. Intimacy, emotional connection, love—these have a surprisingly small part of *Amor* in the classics. Desire is predatory because it portrays a relationship based not on connection but on lack, not on intimacy but on strategy. The conception of desire is based exclusively on bodily hunger—the hunter's hunger. And desire is given priority over emotional intimacy.

I only realized this accidentally. I had met Marlene in Europe, and though I was lonely, I was not looking to fall in love. An affair, perhaps. We traveled together throughout Europe, visiting some of the great hunting venues in the area. We visited the castle of Amboise, the site of the great hunting parties of François Premier in the Renaissance—a castle with hunting scenes carved in the capitals, celebrated in a poem by Richard Wilbur:

> Sometimes, as one can see
> Carved at Amboise in high relief, on the lintel stone
> Of the castle chapel, hunters have strangely come
> To a mild close of the chase, bending the knee
> Instead of the bow. . . .[24]

We visited Chenonceaux, the beautiful château over a river in the Loire Valley that was the home of Diane de Poitiers—the Diane who styled herself a Renaissance huntress, counterpart to the goddess Diana. Diane de Poitiers was portrayed in sculpture and paintings with stags and hounds, and loved to ride to hounds with François and her lover, his son, Henri, later king.[25] We also visited the Doñana in southern Spain, one of the great *cotos* or hunting preserves in all of the Iberian Peninsula. There we saw hundreds of wild boars and the elegant, spotted deer with the exquisitely palmated horns, the *dama*. This small deer was said to be favorite game of ladies of the Renaissance court, suitable for women's more tender natures.

Our traveling was a perfect image of our relationship, and of the restlessness of our desire itself. We were on the move, wandering, meeting in faraway places.

Without realizing it, I grew to love Marlene deeply. But we weren't able to bring our love home with us. We learned about desire, but didn't know how to make the transition to love. We could travel, but we could not come home. When we came home, the relationship inevitably fell apart, slowly, sadly. It crashed around us, and we were painfully helpless to stop it.

Still, it was that relationship more than anything that made it possible for me to begin to see something about myself. I had loved desire, but had not learned how to form a relationship. I had been trapped in a concept of desire I hadn't even realized possessed me. It seemed crucial, after that relationship, to begin to link desire to intimacy and permanence. I began to wonder what desire might be if it were linked not to a sense of lack, but to a sense of personal abundance. How, in other words, can desire be imagined so that it isn't based solely upon a kind of codependence—need and wound? I had always built desire upon the condition of its own transience, chase and move on. What would sexual desire look like if it were linked to emotions instead of the body, exclusively? Can desire be linked to love as well as lust? We don't commonly treat it so. Might other metaphors for desire begin to emerge besides the hunt and the game? I had been trapped in a language I hadn't even realized held me in its power.

I am reminded of another story in Ovid's *Metamorphoses*. It's the story of Venus and Mars. Venus is married to Vulcan, the Olympian blacksmith, blue-collar god in the Greek pantheon. Vulcan is also the son of Juno—wife of Jove, matron of the gods, the virago in the marriage relationship. Venus and Juno are eternal enemies. (Venus's son Aeneas was persecuted by Juno on his journeys, and Juno favored Dido.) Vulcan learns that his wife Venus is having an affair with Mars. He is shocked— illicit love may be more entertaining, but it is also more dangerous. He fashions a plot to capture them. The great smith forges at his fire a net (*retia*), a hunter's net so fine that it can hardly be seen. He hangs it from the ceiling of his bedroom, and tells his wife that he's going away for a stretch of time. The net is hung so cunningly that it will fall to the bed with even the slightest motion. While he's gone, the two lovers retire to the bed, where the net drops on them and captures them in each other's arms (4.170–193).

The two lovers are captured in the moment of their desire. The net falls upon them, forged of bronze. The desiring couple is the quarry that's caught. The word also is a net, a simple metaphor like hunting, and we are all captured in it. We are like the other gods, who come to see the love couple, Venus and Mars, captured like love quarry in the bronze net. They all laugh and snigger at the two gods caught in their own chains. But one of the gods is overheard to say that he would risk such public shame for the chance to sleep with Venus. This divine desire, bound up in hunting nets and caught in the act, is perhaps the secret fantasy in our hearts, that we have not yet dispelled.

5

THE GENTLES ARE AT THEIR GAME

[The duke] . . . that for the hunt is so desirous
And namely at the great harte in May
That in his bed there daweth him no day
That he nys [is not] clad and redy for to ride
With hunt and horne and houndes him besyde,
For in his huntyng hath he such delyte
That is all his ioye and appetytte
To been him selfe the great hartes bane.
For after Mars he serveth nowe Diane.
                    —Geoffrey Chaucer, "The Knight's Tale"[1]

Manhod I am therefore I me delytht,
To hunt and hawke, to nourishe up and fede,
The grayhound to the course, the hawke to the flyght,
And to bestryde a good and lustye stede.
These things become a very man in dede. . . .
                    —Sir Thomas More, "Manhod"[2]

A sport for Nobel Peeres, a sport for gentle bloods,
The paine I leave for servants such, as beat the bushie woods.
To make their masters sport. *Then let the Lords rejoyce,*
Let gentlemen behold the glee, and thereof the choice.
For my part (being one) I must needs say my minde,
That Hunting was ordained first, for Men of Noble Kind.
                    —George Gascoigne, *The Noble Art of Venerie*[3]

In the middle of a leafless wood outside of Toulouse, in the south of
France, I find myself staring at a deer with an aluminum crucifix on its
head. It is mounted behind an altar in the woods, under a rustic open-air
shed. Several of us have gathered amid the oaks and beeches to hear a

mass, celebrated by a priest in full robes. Of the many incongruous elements in this scene, the most startling is that of the trophy of a deer's head hung, like an almost surreal vision, as a kind of religious icon. It broods above us. Between its spreading nine-point antlers, someone has perched a crucifix, wrapped in crinkled aluminum foil that reflects the low November sun with a bright, chintzy glint.

It is as if the deer has been substituted for the body of Christ. As if the stag were a sacrificial stand-in.

I stand in the midst of a sizable group of people in this unlikely clearing in the woods to celebrate a Sunday service on behalf of hunters. Both the mass and the stag's head bearing a crucifix commemorate an ancient saint of the Catholic church, Saint Hubert. In the seventh century, Hubert had been an avid hunter. The story goes that, after chasing the most beautiful stag he had ever seen, it turned to face its persecutor. Between the stag's horns was the cross of Christ. "Why dost thou persecute me?" the stag asked. Saint Hubert converted to Christianity, soon rose to be a bishop of the Catholic church, and became the patron saint of hunters. He was an exceedingly popular figure in the Middle Ages. His conversion is depicted in the glorious stained glass of Chartres Cathedral from the early thirteenth century, as well as many paintings. Several orders of knights were founded in his name, and Saint Hubert's Abbey supported a famous kennel in the Ardennes where hundreds of hounds were raised. It was a popular place of pilgrimage.[4]

This miraculous, cruciferous stag is supposed to be invoked by the deer with the aluminum cross. It seems an anachronism in the woods.

This Sunday is November 3, still recognized as Saint Hubert's Day, the festival of the huntsman, and I am celebrating a mass in honor of hounds and hunters. We are in a national forest, Gresigne Forest Dominiale, with two teams of hunters. The hunt we are here to witness is itself a survival from the Middle Ages, and had in fact been developed in the mountains and forests of this region—a medieval relic. It's a form of the hunt that, through the course of several hundred years, from about the eleventh century to the seventeenth century, was the classic form of hunting, the preferred pastime of the aristocracy, the "prince's sport." Called the *grande vénerie ou chasse à courze de cerf*—the grand hunt or chase by coursing for the stag or hart—this style of hunting is directly descended from the hunting Chaucer describes as the favorite daily activity of Duke Theseus in *The Canterbury Tales* of 1400. Chaucer calls this the hunt "par force," which meant chasing a stag or hart, as they preferred then to call a male red deer, with hounds through the woods.

I have come with Emmanuel Ménoni, a balding biologist with bright eyes and an intelligent smile. His face beams with wit and earnestness. He studies the capercaillie, the big black grouse of the mountain forests in France and Spain, the grand cock of the woods, the supreme bird of the hunt in these regions. Emmanuel loves to hunt and lives in the mountains. He wants to be like his grandfather, a mountain man of the Alps. We smile at each other, self-conscious at this religious spectacle and a bit embarrassed.

"This hunt," he whispers, "is the hunt of lords and kings from before the revolution. Some say it's for the elite."

We have come to glimpse the patricians at play. Or, as one character puts it in Shakespeare's *Love's Labor's Lost*, as king and princess and cohorts go hunting and dallying in the forests of Navarre, "The gentles are at their game" (4.2.166).

"I know," I whisper back to Emmanuel. "I feel like I've gone backward about four or five centuries."

There are no kings at our mass in the woods, but it is an aristocratic scene. Emmanuel and I have parked his ancient Renault truck, painted proletariat gray, among Jaguars and Rolls-Royces along the sides of the dirt roads near the oaks. It is a brilliant, wealthy, animated assembly, reeking of money and style. There are two teams of hunters gathered, one team wearing impeccable red velvet hunt coats with silver buttons and elegant white cravats. The red velvet flares like a skirt down to their knees. Most of the men wear black riding hats, and the women wear black caps, bordered in gold, that remind me of the hats in George Stubbs's paintings of the gentry in the countryside. Their black leather boots, polished to a bright sheen, come all the way up above their knees. The other team is appointed in all respects the same, except that their velvet is hunter green. Slung around their necks and under one arm, many hunters carry a gleaming brass horn. They are impeccable, the men's hair cut perfectly, the women in elegant, understated makeup.

They are going to ride to the hunt with horses and hounds and horns. Several have their horses out and are sitting upon them, even as the service is being spoken. Two dogs, black-and-tan limiers, are leashed to two hunters right next to me as the priest recites the mass.

And then the weirdest thing happens. It makes both Emmanuel and me snigger. As the priest finishes wishing a good and successful hunt for the people gathered on this lovely morning, he prepares to offer a blessing. He does not bless any of us in the crowd. He does not bless the people who have celebrated the mass. Rather, he walks over to the two limiers standing near me, raises his hand above them, and makes the sign of the cross, repeating the benediction at the same time. Then he walks over to two mounted horses and repeats the spiritual gesture.

The animals are singularly unmoved by his ministrations. But a laugh ripples through the people. Then he blesses two horses near me. "They had a hard time," said Emmanuel to me, "finding a priest who would conduct this ceremony." Though it seems a bit ridiculous for the priest to bless hounds and horses, Emmanuel is enchanted by the dogs. The black-and-tan tricolor, or limier, was the classic French hunting dog, he told me, originally bred at Saint Hubert's Abbey in the Ardennes, and supplied to the kennels of the king. They aren't swift, but have a superb nose.[5]

After the beasts are blessed, anise-flavored bread is distributed among the crowd. This is not, I think, an official mass. This isn't really communion. Elegant ladies in hunting clothes pass baskets of bread, and it feels more like noblesse oblige to me.

Everything about the day and the hunt is orchestrated, within the constraints of a very democratic and secular age, to correspond as nearly as possible to the hunting ritual as it was followed by kings and princes from the Middle Ages. The medieval hunt was conducted according to elaborate ritual and carefully prescribed rules. Elegant hunting manuals emerged in the course of time to instruct the lesser nobility—and gentlemen—in the arts of hunting, and could be found first in French, and then in English, German, Spanish, and Portuguese; one manuscript was in Italian. The hunt was to begin with a "Gathering" or "Assembly" in the woods, a secular communion in some lovely green spot. The "Assembly" was not a mass. It was a meal, presided over by king or lord. Birds sang. It was a *locus amoenus*—a "pleasant place."

We had already eaten our meal, in a hunting chateau not far away, a lovely two-story house in stucco painted the caramel color of Cracker Jacks, where they kept the kennel just for the dogs, some fifty of them, for today's hunt. We had feasted before the mass, and as Emmanuel said, "*Ventre plein, chasse bien. Ventre creux, chasse jeux.*" The good hunt starts with good eating. The point of this hunt is not to get food. It is even more ritual than sport. It is a rule-bound activity, and you have to decipher its purposes in some terms other than the literal. Its purpose is something quite different from subsistence. In fact, if successful, and the hunters kill a *cerf*, only the dogs will eat it. Not the hunters.

This hunt, glorified in feudal manuals of sport, is its own text. It has to be read and interpreted. In *Troilus and Cressida*, Shakespeare refers to all the hunting manuals in the Middle Ages and the Renaissance. His hero, Hector, is about to duel with Achilles in front of Troy, but Achilles is studying him hard. Hector says to Achilles,

> O, like a book of sport thou'lt read me ov'r;
> But there's more in me than thou understand'st. (4.5.239–40)

The book of sport, as Hector suggests, was precisely this: a way of reading men. It became a rigorous way of knowing who they were. It prescribed an elaborate decorum of manners and language and behavior. The sport of the chase, and its rituals, located male identity within a hierarchy of social class. The hunt of Saint Hubert's mass, with its forested communion, made it perfectly clear: the hunt reinforces social values.

What this sport, what this chase, could not really explicate was the inner life of men.

It encoded two themes, both of them primarily social: the great man in the hunt could exercise social power, could take his place amid the nobility, could even rule; and hunting provided a whole set of class distinctions, through which society itself was ordered and composed. In short, you could know a man—his station and his status—by his methods of hunting and his knowledge of the aristocratic hunt. These two themes—the art of ruling and social class—could conflict, but conveniently they usually overlapped. The hunt as it developed in the Middle Ages drew upon elements of the ancient heroic hunt, but this grand chase was used for new and modern purposes. This hunt provided both a theory and a practice of government.

When the service for Saint Hubert's Day is over, I am ready and eager to proceed to the hunt. But there is yet more ceremony. A "forester"—in the Middle Ages and Renaissance, he was the king's "professional" hunter—had gone out the night before and early this morning, and had selected one stag in particular for the hounds to track and try to bring to bay. The hunters will track this deer, and this deer alone, which Shakespeare in *Cymbeline* refers to as "th' elected deer" (3.4.109). Then one man, the highest ranking probably, would try to kill the deer by hand. He is going to try it today, Emmanuel told me, in the old-fashioned way—with a sword. It is a dangerous feat, called "blading," in which the man approaches the bayed stag on foot, avoids the antlers of the desperate and usually charging stag, and kills it with a strike to the throat. Ghastly as it is likely to be, I am still excited by the prospect of seeing something so ancient and so, well, daring.

Before we can proceed to the hunt proper, we have an important additional rite to observe. It's carefully described in the manuals from the Middle Ages. All the hunters at this service gather around a central figure, noticeably different from the others in an olive trench coat and a Charles de Gaulle hat: the minister of agriculture. He is, in effect, Emmanuel's boss. All hunting in France is overseen by the Forestry Department, which is part of the Ministry of Agriculture. Next to him is an older man, an organizer of the hunt, with distinguished silver hair in short, elegant curls, aristocratically disheveled. He wears white gloves to hunt. These two men are at the center, surrounded by all the other hunters in red and green.

Several of the gathered hunters blow a hunting song on their gleaming brass horns.

From the side, a hunter steps out in hunter's khaki and sweater. He holds something in his hands, wrapped in green boughs. The forester has to make a formal presentation to the master of the hunt. It is in this capacity that the minister of agriculture is present. He is, essentially, a modern substitute for the king or high prince. The forester's job is to demonstrate to the lord of the hunt that the stag to be chased was "warrantable," that is, big and noble enough for the peers. In the Middle Ages, such a report involved an entire forester's science—of tracks, of rubbings in the woods, of bellowing, and of excrement. The climax of the forester's report is the presentation of the "fumes," as they were called in medieval English, or "fewmets." It is the presentation of the scat of the selected stag.

This science and ceremony is "how one great hart may be known" as one English hunting manual put it.

In this moment of scatological obeisance, this essentially anal observance, the meaning of this essential feudal hunt seems condensed. As a sport, the hunt was a social institution. As a ritual, the hunt was a political tool. In both cases, the hunt was a way of constructing men, teaching them how to find their places in society. For all its anachronistic feel, I stand watching the *grande vénerie* in the French woods, realizing that this hunt was how men learned their sense of place in society, and that sociological lesson is this hunt's chief legacy to us now.

Once the report is accepted by the minister of agriculture, the hunters all take to their horses. The hounds begin to bay and yelp, the scene grows animated and confused. Hunters blow their horns, playing the notes that meant they are to go in "quest" of the stag. And we, Emmanuel and I, pile into his proletariat-gray Renault, and rattle down the bumpy road to try to find a place where we might be lucky enough to see some lord of the realm blade a stag.

2

Even more than war, hunting was the crucible out of which medieval lords contrived to hammer the myths of monarchy. A kind of social propaganda, long before newspapers and mass media, hunting gave a pageantry to peacetime, and the early monarchs exploited the visual display in their hunting to control the minds of their subjects. It's not too much to say that through hunting, early monarchs contrived much of the centralization of the modern state, centralizing political power in the figure of the king. The hunt was nothing less than an instrument of statecraft, a form of diplomacy, and the sign of the health of the country. In addition to the pleasure the chase provided, it also located the health and vigor of the body politic in the physical body of the king.

The king became the "father of the game," and his hunting was quite literally the image of his patriarchy. For early modern kings, hunting was indispensable to their self-image and their techniques of governing. So obsessed were these rulers that, for example, Duke Johan Georg I, the Elector of Saxony, caught or shot during his reign between 1611 and 1655 the exact total of 116,906 animals. His son, Johan Georg II, between 1656 and 1680 killed 111,141 animals—about thirteen per day.[6]

For the Franks along the Rhine, a long tradition made hunting a mirror within which to view the power of the monarchy, and all game belonged to the king, literally. Hunting was the exclusive right of the king and nobles, and it impinged heavily upon the common people. Charlemagne (742–814) was both the great monarch of the Frankish empire and a passionate hunter. "By going hunting so frequently," writes Notker the Stammerer in his early biography of the great king, "and by exercising his mind and body with such unremitting zeal, he has acquired the habit of conquering everything under heaven."[7] The hunt and the monarch were virtually synonymous.

But Charlemagne's father, King Pepin, revealed the pragmatic philosophy upon which the royal addiction to hunting was based. It was more than the moral virtues that it taught of courage and hardiness, more than the conditioning of physical health, always adduced by hunters in defense of their sport. In his biography of Charlemagne, Notker tells a story to show how Pepin proved his worthiness to rule the empire.[8]

It seems King Pepin had discovered that his military advisers were speaking contemptuously of him behind his back. A man of action, he moved quickly to bring them into line again. According to Notker, Pepin ordered a bull of "fantastic size and ferocious attitude" to be set free in a large arena in the court. He then ordered a "savage lion" to be set upon the bull. The lion charged the bull, and with "tremendous fury" seized it by the neck and hurled the bull to the ground. The king looked at his gathered officers. "Now," he ordered them, "drag the lion off the bull, or else kill it on top of its enemy."

They were all dumbfounded and terrified: "They all looked at each other in terror, their hearts frozen with fear, and just managed to gasp out an answer. 'My Lord,' they muttered, 'there is no man on earth who would dare attempt such a thing.' " Pepin looked upon them with disgust and disdain.

He rose from his throne, drew his sword, and entered the arena. In a single vicious slash, he severed the lion's neck. With the élan of a trueborn king, he sheathed his sword and resumed his seat on the throne. "Do you think I am worthy to be your master?" he sneered at his commanders. "They fell to the ground as if they had been struck by thunder. 'Is there anyone so foolish that he would deny your right to rule over the whole of mankind?' they replied." Pepin, concludes Notker, had proved that he was "master over beasts and men."

In the exercise of this mastery, hunting was used both to seize and to enforce control over men and countries, and it was the propaganda by which, in its extravagant and ostentatious forays into the forests, royalty reaffirmed its prerogatives.

William the Conqueror, for instance, brought Frankish and Norman styles with him across the English Channel, and used hunting not only for his pleasure, but also for reducing the island country to his rule. After winning the Battle of Hastings in 1066, he established the hunt for the Plantagenet kings who followed him as the only true sport of kings. To do so, he seized land and suppressed the Anglo-Saxon traditions of hunting with nets and pits and hounds.

In Anglo-Saxon England, all men had been allowed to hunt, and their great lord of the animals, Cerunnos, the horned god figured in many pieces of art, is surrounded by animals. William made it the king's pleasure and prerogative to hunt. In seizing lands, he made over huge tracts of land into forest, converting what were once even villages and homesteads into areas for his hunting, evicting and dispossessing peasants and landholders alike.

The Anglo-Saxon Chronicle characterizes his inordinate appetite for the hunt as a central law of the land, a crux of social policy. William, for example, created both preserves and laws for the game:

> He made great protection for the game
> And imposed laws for the same,
> That who so slew hart or hind
> Should be made blind.

> He preserved the harts and boars
> And loved the stags as much
> As if he were their father.
> Moreover, for the hares did he decree that they should go free.
> But so fierce was he that he cared not for the rancour of them all,
> But they had to follow out the king's will entirely
> If they wished to live or hold their land,
> Property or estate, of his favour great.

He is said to have put five-sixths of the countryside of eastern England into forests for his hunting—Wessex, Kent, Essex, and East Anglia. It was a system of ownership and prerogative. The forests were for the king's pleasure alone, or at his franchise by any he alone might allow. His descendants, the Angevin kings, placed as much as one-third of the country of England into forest, which meant under the crown's ownership, to be used almost solely for royal sport.[9]

The hunt was a symbol of the well-ordered society, but even more, it was the vehicle through which that order could be maintained and regulated. Through the Forest Laws that were established to control these lands, the king owned all the game in the kingdom. Though the game all belonged to him, the hart particularly was the beast associated with the king.[10]

He could farm out his privileges, for money usually, and the system of forest laws which evolved reflected the feudal hierarchy which came to be associated with good social order, the king's privilege firmly lodged in the center. The descending privileges of the hunt were expressed through the categories of the forest, the chase, the park, and the warren. The king and his officers alone might hunt the forest; the chase and the park indicated areas that were unenclosed or enclosed, respectively, and could be hunted only on franchise from the king explicitly, usually by barons. The warren was also held on franchise of the king, but to a wider group of men.

In such a well-organized scheme, each division of the hunting lands had its own specific beasts which could be legally hunted there. The beasts of these categories varied from one theorist to the next, but were essentially these. In the forests, belonging solely to the king, were the beasts of venery: the hart (male red deer), the hind (female red deer), hare, boar, and wolf. The hart was uniquely regal, even more than the boar, which was considered manly but not necessarily regal to hunt. The beasts of the chase were those hunted by dispensation: buck (male fallow deer), doe (female fallow deer), fox, marten, roe. Beasts of the warren were also held by franchise, but were decidedly less stately, a kind of minor hunt: coney (rabbit), pheasant, and partridge.[11]

Whole armies of men, also, had to be organized to maintain the king's hunts, and the hunt was quite literally a microcosm of social order. The king or baron employed foresters, rangers, and woodsmen to maintain his forests. Chaucer's yeoman was a "forster," clad in "coat and hood of grene," well taught in "wode-craft." His job was to guard the "vert and venison," the trees and the harts. Similar employees included woodwards and verderers. A verderer, for example, was a judicial official whose duty was the care of the king's forest, its game and green growth or vert.

The king's estates for hunting were similarly huge. Gaston Phèbus, for example, was said to have 600 horses and 1,600 hounds, all maintained for his hunting pleasure. Valets of the kennel had to be trained, huntsmen taught their duties. Queen Elizabeth made her courtly favorite and furtive lover, the earl of Leicester, her first master of the buckhounds and her master of the horse—signs of his high station in her court and intimate place in her heart. One of his most famous gifts to her was a richly enameled crossbow, for hunting from stands in the forest, or, in the language of the hunt, from "trysting" places.[12]

Falconers were similarly required. When Edward III invaded France for the Battle of Crécy in 1346, he took with him 600 hounds and 130 falcons. Falcons were kept on aristocratic estates in "mews," huge spreads of cages, with professional falconers to feed, breed, and train the birds.

For all these positions, men needed to be trained, apprentices not merely in the hunt, but in the well-disposed order of feudal society. With its retinues of men and animals, its rules for hunting, and its carefully worked out social laws, hunting was its own little world, its minor kingdom, its social microcosm.

This society was centered upon the body of the king. The king needed to maintain his health, as a sign of the health of the state itself. King James I of England had a mania for the hunt. When he ascended to the throne in 1603, he escaped to his many hunting lodges as often as possible. His favorite was in Cambridgeshire, where he spent as much as a third of the year. The people might grumble, but he put the matter succinctly in defense of "his immoderate exercise of hunting." If people complained, he wrote, let them understand the importance of hunting to the king: "The Kinge . . . finds such felicitie in that hunting life, that he hath written to the counsaile [Privy Council], that yt is the only meanes to maintain his health, (which being the health and welfare of us all) he desires them to undertake the charge and burden of affaires, and to foresee that he be not interrupted nor troubled with too much business."[13] Sir Francis Bacon, James I's great lord chancellor and the philosopher who helped to institute the great reforms in scientific knowledge, put the theory of statecraft implicit in the hunt succinctly in 1614: "Forests, parks, chases, they are a noble portion of the King's prerogative; they are the verdure of the king, they are the first marks of honour and nobility, and the ornament of a flourishing kingdom."[14] Hunting was the mark of nobility in a man and greatness in a kingdom. That's why the poet William Somerville called the chase "The sport of kings, / The image of war without its guilt."

Nobles and kings throughout Europe made hunting an obsession, a passion that went much deeper than can be accounted for by the pleasure of killing animals or the need for physical exercise. The appetite for their addiction was too great to be explained by the joy of the woods or the pleasure of the chase. Its hold on their hearts and imaginations was too powerful not to have had sources deep in their social and personal psychologies. What was at stake was a certain image of the male, and the male body in action, as the center of social health and power. This powerful and active body was the pin upon which society depended, a notion perpetuated in the same way for us by movies of the boffed and bulked bodies of action heroes.

The French not only invented the rules of the royal sport, they executed it in its most refined incarnations. The French were, quite literally, at the top of their game. And so we can turn to them for a story to epitomize the way men, in the image of the king, insinuated themselves through hunting into the object which all gazed upon, the cynosure of court and culture.

François I ruled France between 1515 and 1547, the contemporary of Henry VIII in England, both great Renaissance princes. Of all the Valois kings, François fancied himself the greatest hunter (though his son, Charles X, 1550–74, wrote a treatise on hunting, *La Chasse Royale*). The great book on French hunting in the Renaissance, by Jacques de Foullioux, maintains the flattery posthumously and the cult of royalty in the hunt by calling François *"le père de veneurs,"* the father of hunters. As effectively as any king, he exploited the hunt as a form of social control as well, a form of display and propaganda.

Thus, the story is told of François in his contest with a "furious" and "raging" boar.

Most of the châteaus in the Loire Valley of France are glorified hunting lodges. François's favorite was at Amboise, along with Fountainbleau. He repaired to Amboise frequently to hunt, where there are relief sculptures of hunting scenes. On one such sojourn, he decided that he wanted to entertain—*récréer*—the ladies of the court. To do so, he sent his hunters into the forest around the château with nets and cords, ordering them to capture a *sanglier vivant*—a living boar. The hunters captured a young boar, four years of age, put it in a big trunk made of oak, and dragged the beast back to court.

Meanwhile, in the château, François had his tradesmen construct a large enclosure in the courtyard out of chests and trunks. About this arena, they built an elevated viewing gallery, which could be reached by four stairways.

François proposed a *"combat corp à corps"* with *"l'animal furieux"* in the presence of the entire court. It was to be a battle body to body, king and beast.

But the ladies of the court, including the queen, protested so strenuously at this idea, worried about the safety of the royal person, that they prevented the fight. Instead, the king devised a more harmless entertainment. He ordered mannequins to be made, which, when struck by the boar, would spin in pirouettes.

François gave a signal. The chest containing the boar was opened, and the beast came charging out, "villainous" and "bristling" and "furious," clacking his tusks. He rushed the mannequins angrily, and they spun in the air. But then he began to look for an escape from the enclosure in the courtyard, running about the arena, inspecting the edges. At one of the stairways, the boar noticed a break between two of the boxes that were used to make the wall.

With a violent crash, he burst through the barricade and rushed up one of the stairways into the gallery where the king sat. As the story is told,

> the boar without turning around, goes straight for where the king was. Five or six of his gentlemen try to put themselves between the beast and the king. The king would not put up with that. At the moment when the beast wants to attack him, from that good spear that he held in his fist, the king give the beast a thrust with his sharp point right through the chest. The boar is transpierced, mortally hit. He leaves the king, staggers back into the courtyard by another stairway, after making several steps, falls dead and stiff.[15]

The image of the chivalrous king, François had saved the queen and her ladies, whose joy it is reported was "boundless" that he had escaped his peril. *Le veneur intrépide* delivered the court from the fury of the beast, and won the admiration of all the ladies and gentlemen there gathered. How truthful the story is may be a matter of doubt. But the importance of the story lies precisely in its value as propaganda. The hunt gave life and meaning to feudal manners. This staged hunt, like the carefully scripted narrative, proved the manliness of the king and was the hunt that elevated his reputation on the throne.

In Europe of the Middle Ages, hunting became an elaborate game—the game of the game. Kings were masters of the game, in both senses. They mastered the animals, and they were masters in the game of hunting. Their codified hunts, and their elaborately staged displays, may strike us as utterly anachronistic, out of place, irrelevant. But the lesson is in the form, not the content. It was a lesson in hierarchy and social status. Like François at Amboise, the kings staged their hunts to enforce these lessons on a nearly daily basis—who's on top, and who's watching. Strip this game of its fancy ornaments, its highbrow theories, its elaborate rituals, and it becomes visible in a new way. It's about social power. It's not even about life and death. Killing the beast was another way to teach this central lesson: The game is about winners and losers.

Men learned their lessons well, because we still live with this legacy.

The hunt was a highly artificial game. But because the game was about life and death, it seemed so real. And because the game was so full of pageantry and pomp, it seemed so beautiful and dazzling. Who could see it was only a game?

3

Emmanuel and I climb into his gray Renault truck, which rattles ferociously on the dirt roads through the forest, and head into the leafless oak woods looking for an eminence from which to view the hunt. So are many other people, clumped along the roadsides, hoping to be lucky enough to glimpse the stag. Even better, we all hope to see the hunters on horse bring the stag to bay.

The sun slants through the gray trunks of the oak trees, and the floor of the forest is almost orange with the litter of fallen leaves. Emmanuel and I find a place on a small rise, with a nice view over blackberry brambles into the open woods. The hunting horns blast out their notes, ringing through the woods. There is an elaborate musical vocabulary for the hunt— different notes mean different stages of the hunt, from beginning to baying to blading the stag, as well as different instructions to the hounds.

The people on horses seem to slide through the forest in their vermilion and hunter green, hallooing their dogs to find the stag. They move before us like a strange parade through the woods. The elegance of the scene is striking, these beautiful people with their music and their cheers, their dogs and well-bred horses.

What was most striking about watching the hunters riding to horses and hounds was its careful decorum. This hunt was a school for manners, conducted with an elaborate civility. An easy example: even the calls the hunters used for their hounds were specified in the manuals from the Middle Ages. Hunters were to encourage their dogs with certain words, and reprimand them with other words. The "music" of the hounds gave great pleasure to hunters, signifying a joy in life, a lustiness in living. We can ourselves catch glimpses of the importance of the hunters' language of the hounds in our own words. "Halloo" is meant to cheer on the dogs, for example, as well as "so-ho." "Harrier" is drawn likewise from hunting language, as in a harrier aircraft or harrier hawk. When a dog harries the prey, or harasses it, that comes from a French word, *harer*, to incite dogs to a prey. The "hayrer" was also a breed of dog, according to the duke of York.[16]

But if there was a code to follow, it applied as much to the hunters as it did to anything intrinsic in the hunt itself. As a code, it dictated a behavior that was a mystery as much as a mastery—a mystery in the medieval sense that guilds, for example, taught mysteries to their members, and only the members would know the content of those mysteries. The forms and formulas of the hunt were themselves a mystery to the men in the know, an etiquette of virtuosity as well as virility. Like all such encoded or rule-bound behaviors, this code contained its own meanings. It governed behavior, constructed categories by which nature could be correlated with society, and it offered allegorical readings of the beasts themselves. The knowledge of the hunt was called, in the manuals, "skillful Trystram's [Tristan's] lore." This reputation derives from Sir Thomas Malory's *Le Morte Darthur*, in which Tristan's knowledge of hunting was said to contain the secret of all gentleness. Malory writes a panegyric of "Tristram":

> And after as he growed in might and strength he laboured ever in hunting and in hawking, so that never gentleman more, that ever we heard tell of. And as the book saith, he began good measure of blowing of beasts of venery and beasts of chase, and all manner of vermains; and all these terms we have yet of hawking and hunting. And therefore, the book of vencry, both for hunting and hawking, is called the book of Sir Tristan. Wherefore, as me seemeth, all gentlemen that bear old arms ought of right to honor Sir Tristram for the goodly terms that gentlemen have and use, and shall to the day of doom, that thereby in a manner all men of worship may dissever a gentleman from a yeoman, and from a yeoman a villain.[17]

The lore of Tristan teaches men how to know their place—not in nature, but in society.

The most beautiful exposition of the way in which hunting served as a kind of apprenticeship in courtly manhood lies in Gottfried von Strassburg's *Tristan and Isolde*.[18] This is probably the earliest and purest version of the tale—an adulterous love story between a knight and his lord's wife.

Following the convention set down in antiquity, Tristan announces his heroic status by his hunting. But he gives the hunt a uniquely medieval cast, because hunting for him has almost nothing to do with killing the beast. The meaning of the hunt for him, and his followers for several centuries, was precisely in the things that make it so strange to us: it made men gentle. It demonstrated how power was distributed among men, how it was articulated in a society.

A knight of King Mark, in Cornwall, Tristan comes to England quite by accident. He has actually been raised on the Continent, but was abducted at fourteen by Norwegian traders in hawks and falcons. When the traders land briefly in Cornwall, Tristan escapes.

As he is wandering in the woods, he happens upon a hunting party of King Mark. They are pursuing a stag, a hart of ten points on its antlers, signifying it is suitable for royal hunting. They had harried it for some distance. There is a great clamor as the men bring the deer to bay, and the horns sound the measures that mean the "mort" of the deer.

Yet the moment of the kill is passed over in the narrative. It merits only a subordinate clause, and is virtually meaningless. "Now, when the hart had been killed," writes Gottfried, "the one who was Huntsman-in-Chief laid it out on the grass on all fours like a boar."

This move of the huntsman reveals his boorishness. It is so offensive to Sir Tristan, still watching from the woods, that he can't forbear stepping forward and reprimanding the huntsman's barbarity, in a style so sweet that it can not give offense.

"Stop, in God's name," he blurts out. "What are you at? Whoever saw a hart broken up in such fashion?"

The huntsmen stops at the sight of the strange boy scolding them from the bushes. Because of his clothes and carriage, he seems noble, and they pay heed. Tristan undertakes to instruct these Cornish louts in the true manner of gutting a stag. His disquisition establishes the importance of method and propriety for connoisseurs of hunting. Tristan teaches only one stage of the hunt, what is called the "breakup" or "undoing" in hunting manuals. It exemplifies the sensibility that governs the entire hunt. The poem actually gives a set piece on the breaking up of a stag as it could be found in any number of hunting manuals. In the story, the breakup is told in such loving detail that it must of itself have brought great pleasure to Gottfried's readers, something of the way we love to see, over and over again, an instant replay of a great play in football, replete with color analysis. Or a favorite movie.

Hanging his coat upon a tree and smoothing down his hair, the young Tristan turns the hart onto its back. He cuts the hart open, from muzzle to pizzle, pulls out the breast from the backbone, and dismembers the stag—cutting it in quarters "according to the rules of the chase."

Next, he proceeds to the "*fourchie*." The Cornish hunters have no clue what this mystery is, so he teaches them with pleasure. He cuts a fork from a tree, and ties to it the pieces of the innards of the hart that would be especially reserved for the king himself. These include the pizzle and the "numbles" or the kidneys and the surrounding flesh. He wraps these onto the fork with the "net" from the intestines and decorates them with green foliage. The precise parts of the stag so tied to a fork varies among writers. In the breakup of the stag, each member of the hunting party is reserved a portion according to his station. In some manuals, the "numbles" are not given to the king, but to the poor, and are made into a pie, which is the origin of our phrase "humble pie."[19]

Now thoroughly impressed and awed by this young boy, the huntsmen watch Tristan as he teaches them how to conduct the "*curée*." It is the emotional climax in the woods. Tristan flays the stag and spreads the hide out on the ground, fur side up. Then he takes the head of the stag, which he has cut off, and places it at the top of the hide. The stag impersonates itself on the ground. Then he smears the hide with a precise recipe of the stag's guts, chopped up.

The *curée* is prepared. The hunter calls his hounds with a particular call on the horn, and gives them the stag. The *curée* is the hound's reward. So beautiful is this stage of the ceremony, it completely converts the huntsmen to Tristan's style. They insist on learning all the niceties.

In French, the *curée* was derived from the word *cuire*, which meant the hide of the deer. In English, the *curée* became the "quarry," which quickly became the generic word we still use for any prey.

But Tristan's mysteries are not yet exhausted, and what to me is the most compelling part of his hunting style is yet to be revealed. It does contain a secret, the secret of men in medieval and Renaissance society. The dismembered stag lies upon the ground. It remains for the men to transport it back to King Mark "in the approved manner." Again the huntsmen beg Tristan to educate them. He instructs each man to take up his portion and they carry these toward the castle, Tintagel, the same castle where it is thought King Arthur himself was born.

It is a splendid castle. As they approach its gates, Tristan orders the men into ranks. It is a stunning and mystical moment. "But ride two and two together," he instructs them,

and keep close beside one another, preserving the shape of the hart. Let the horns go ahead, the breast follow in their track, the ribs come after the fore-quarters. Then arrange for the hind-parts to follow on the ribs. After that, you should see to it that the quarry and the fourchie bring up the rear—such is true huntsmenship. And do not be in too great a hurry—ride in due order, one behind another.

They ride through the castle gates, the dismembered body of the hart reassembled into new, artificial shape.

For men, hunting was a way of knowing. In his dexterous social performance, Tristan's handling of the dissected deer seems as if it were a science. Which it was. He took the other men to school in the woods in Cornwall. He gave a sort of anatomy lesson of the deer, and it turned out to be an anatomy lesson in the body politic, too. The men quite literally found their place around the dissected and reassembled body of the stag—it taught them how to place themselves for their reentry into court and castle. It taught them their place.

Body parts, body politics, social bodies: the dismembered body became the vocabulary of social membership. The self was enacted in the externals of the body and strictly regulated, almost anal, social relations.

Society was built out of the deconstruction—the undoing—of the deer. For Tristan, his knowledge of hunting promotes him in King Mark's favor, and he rises to prominence. He becomes Mark's "Master Huntsman," and later his quarry turns out to be none other than the king's wife, Isolde.

Gottfried von Strassburg's treatise on the "undoing" of the stag, à la Tristan the hunter, might almost come straight from one of the manuals on hunting, so precise and detailed is it. The rituals are so lovingly told in *Tristan and Isolde*, and written up so frequently in the manuals or "books of sport," it's easy to see that the men reading them loved the rehearsal of the details for their own sake. They weren't written merely for the uninitiated. The hunting event captured something essential about their lives, offered a defining moment in men's lives for them, so that they never tired of reading and hearing about it.

4

Many men would read these "books of sport" in the Middle Ages and Renaissance to have the mysteries of the hunt explained to them. What's striking to the modern reader, going through them, is how little most of these books seem to have to do with hunting itself. They rarely take the reader into the woods, to give the sense of how one might actually stalk and catch a deer. They seem to the modern reader utterly alien in their ideas about hunting. But they teach something else: the vocabulary that creates out of the medieval hunt its own unique world.

Yet one book, and one manuscript really, transcends all the limitations of most of the medieval documents—*Le Livre de la Chasse*, or *The Book of the Hunt*. Its author is Gaston Phèbus, described by those who knew him as the paragon of his age, the Comte de Foix et Béarne in the Pyrenees, a princely knight celebrated at the end of the fourteenth century by no less a figure than the great chronicler of chivalry, Jean Froissart. Froissart left England to visit Gaston, and was so enchanted by the prince that he called him the embodiment of the chivalric idea. Gaston was surnamed "Phèbus" for the glowing golden hair that distinguished him, that made him brilliant as the sun. Phèbus means "brilliant," and makes a comparison with the shining Apollo Phoebus, the sun god. Gaston was a golden figure—Froissart says he was the most handsome knight he'd ever seen.[20]

In his prologue, Gaston says that he began his book on May 1, 1387. He died on a hot day in August 1391, after an arduous bear hunt in the forests near Pampeluna. He'd just finished reciting the book to scribes. Only thirty-nine or forty manuscripts of this *Le Livre de la Chasse* were produced, all for nobility like Ferdinand of Aragon. The original manuscript was dedicated to Gaston's friend, Philip the Bold, a prisoner in England of the interminable wars between France and England. But one manuscript is a pure treasure, one of the most prized possessions of the Bibliothèque Nationale in Paris: "Fr. ms. 616." This was originally produced about 1400, either for Charles VII himself or one of his princes. It came into the possession of François I, and as one of his favorite books, he took it with him on his invasion of Italy.

I have seen this manuscript in Paris. The director of the library and Gaston's modern editor, François Avril, brought the manuscript to me. As I turned its parchment Codex pages, it was impossible not to feel in the presence of a treasure. What distinguishes this manuscript is that it has eighty-eight exquisitely beautiful, brilliantly painted illustrations of all the beasts of the chase and venery, all the hounds used in the hunt, and all the techniques of the chase, from trapping to stalking to shooting the long bow to the noble *grand chasse à courze.*

I've turned the pages of this manuscript with a slow and lingering reverence. Marveling at their beauty, at the amazingly fresh and vivid colors and the loving portrayal of the animals and hunters and landscapes, it's impossible not to be drawn into the enthusiasm and the joy of the hunt that is captured in this book. The hunt was a way of life for these aristocratic men, and the exuberance and love lavished on this manuscript, as well as on the text itself, makes clear that for these nobles, hunting transcended technique and even sport. It had come to represent for them an entire view of life. Gaston says in his opening paragraph that there were three passions in his life: *les armes, l'amour, et la chasse.* The barking of the hounds filled their days with a lust, wild joy of life. The hunt as pictured in his book had come to represent the vigorous, chivalric life itself. In its sweetly innocent paintings, done in a fluid Gothic style, at once so delicate and so full of life, this manuscript realizes visually a new imaginative experience of hunting.

It's at about the same time that Chaucer was using hunting to convey this same worldly lustiness for life. Published in 1400, the *Canterbury Tales* describes a monk whose pleasure in hunting showed him for no man of God. He was a "manly man," Chaucer says satirically, "Of priking and of hunting . . . was al his lust."[21]

Most stunning about Gaston's manuscript are the eighty-eight hand-painted miniatures of various features of the hunt—the swirling rocks of mountains, the brilliant carmines of the flowers and hunters' robes, the cerulean hues of the backgrounds, the fields in rich greens, like the flesh of avocados. And the animals, quaint, vaguely realistic, but rendered with a warm charm that makes each all the more lovely. Stags bound away from hunters, rabbits run down roads into nets artfully set, and chamois cling to high rocky mountains.

Like the paintings, the book is largely realistic—full of the advice of an avid hunter. Gaston repeats some errors of natural history—that a stag may live to be hundreds of years old, for instance—but his true interest is a hunter's interest in animals—where they live, what their conspicuous habits are, how to catch them.

Gaston's text was translated into English, probably about 1406 or so—the exact date isn't known. It was written by Edward, the second duke of York, while he was in prison for treason. This man was a ferocious soldier, dying in the van of Henry V's troops at Agincourt in 1415. But his book, which he called *The Master of Game*, is the first great book on hunting in the English language. It was the duke of York who reported the *curée* as quarry. He describes the royal personages—king and queen—standing to watch for the "great hart" as it is driven to them by foresters in the "trysting" place.

The primary goal of the hunt and its manuals, though, was to provide a knowledge of feudal manliness. They provided a knowledge in language appropriate for a man of station. And they created a knowledge of nature. Nature itself, and the animals that were sought, reflected the culture that was chasing them.

For example, one of the great treatises in English, by Dame Juliana Barnes (or Berners), shows the mirror that nature held up to men. She wrote a rhyming primer to help all "gentyll persons" in *The Boke of St. Albans*, two treatises, one on hunting and one on hawking. It was published in 1486, and reprinted frequently for over a century.

She gives all would-be gentlemen the following sermon:

An Eagle for an Emperor
A Gerfalcon for a King
A Peregrine for an Earl
A Merlyon for a Lady
A Goshawk for a Yeoman
A Sparehawk for a Priest
A Muskyt for an holiwater clerk
A Kestril for a knave.[22]

Gyrfalcons, merlins, sparrow hawks, and muskets—the fierce little male sparrow hawks: the world of the hunt is an allegory of social class. There's a hawk for each order. Poor men might gain pleasure from the hunt by capturing hawks for their lords, she suggests. Our word "musket" derives from "muskyt."

The Scottish had their own variation on this personification of hawks and social class. The fifteenth-century *Book of Howlett* gives the eagle for emperor, erne for king, gyrfalcon for duke, falcon for earl marshal, goshawk for chieftains in war, sparrow hawk for knights.[23]

The hierarchies of an aristocratic age found their objective correlatives in the mirror of nature.

As the period wore on, later into the Renaissance, the manuals were produced less for the upper classes, and more for the rising middle classes. The older aristocracy held on to much of its power, of course, but it too was challenged. Its form of knowledge—hunting and hawking, with its training in war and weapons—was increasingly assailed by the learning in universities. Government became less about wielding feudal power, and more about civil administration by a new meritocracy, in large measure with differing values. The humanists increasingly challenged the hunt as the appropriate education the aristocracy's young men should receive, as not fitting them for civil service. The attack on hunting among the upper classes had begun, however, as early as 1159. John of Salisbury, in his influential *Policraticus*, attacked hunting as a sport, with all its elaborate preparations and rituals, as reducing men to bestiality. "In our day," he wrote satirically, "this knowledge [of hunting] constitutes the liberal studies of the higher class."[24]

Still, the appetite for knowledge about hunting as an accoutrement of class held on among the newer rising professionals. The manuals were pitched to their tastes—how to make a gentleman. The hunt was associated with a kind of social elitism. As an inveterate producer of manuals of all sorts put it, the hunt remained a part of a man's education. It remained, he wrote with a kind of nostalgia, *The Gentlemans Academie*.[25]

The satire of dramatist Ben Jonson suggests that hunting was its own education, at odds with the humanists' knowledge in books. Hunting was a language that all gentlemen should know, but by 1600 it had become the butt of satire, a foppish anachronism. One young fop decides he must know "the sciences of hunting and hawking," but he needs a book to master it. The boy defends himself to his angry uncle: "Nay, look now, you are angry, uncle; why you know, an' a man have not skill in the hunting and hawking languages nowadays, I'll not give a rush for him. They are more studied than the Greek or the Latin. He is for no Gallant's company without 'em."[26]

The manuals are full of a language we still use, lingering traces in our education in a certain form of civility: a herd of deer, a flight of pigeons, a brace of greyhounds, a couple of hounds, a litter of whelps, a covey of partridges, a flight of swallows, a swarm of bees, a flock of sheep, a host of men, a bevy of ladies. These all come from Dame Juliana Barnes for the various "company's of beestys and fowlys."[27] Men had to know the grammar and vocabulary of the hunt. It was a popularized version of self-cultivation to speak the language of the chase. Our books and videos of self-improvement are direct descendants of this genre.

The hunt created a certain social syntax: then as now, men could be known by the creatures they pursued. The chase defined a certain hierarchy of manliness. As Richard Blome wrote, stags were superior to hares in the chase, because "none but persons of Estate and Quality have the Privileges and Convenience of Forests, Chases, and Parks; but Men of lower Rank may sometimes divert themselves with the Hare."[28]

As I sit on the hummocks and roadsides in southwestern France, watching the velveted hunters pass among the gray oak trees, they have a certain dreamy quality to them. I am one of a large crowd of onlookers, all of us waiting patiently during a slow day, waiting to see if the two teams might catch the stag. There is no doubt that the scene is impressive, even beautiful in its way. It makes a pageant out of the woods, a visual spectacle, and there is always the sense that something exciting might happen at any minute. I find myself comparing what I am watching with the lovely images in the illuminated manuscript Français 616 of Gaston Phèbus's *Le Livre de Chasse* that I've seen. The vivid greens and reds of the hunters' outfits remind me of the sumptuous colors of the many miniature paintings in the manuscript. There is a high beauty, a reach of imagination, that connects nature and art, hunt and the manuscript. In literature, in ritual, and in the discipline of the "books of sport," hunting transcended its origins in nature. It became a high art, one of the defining features of European aristocratic culture. It was an elegant, extravagant artifice. The grammars and dictionaries of the hunt structured more than behavior. They gave men a way of being. Hunting was, both literally and figuratively, a way of articulating who they were. This was how men learned to express themselves as men.

Hunters stream through the woods, pursuing stags and boars, and ride straight into the imagination.

5

Each culture seems to see in the hunt an important set of images by which to undergird its sense of rightness. They seek in nature a kind of foundational image for themselves. And they turn to the hunt to give them the foundation they seek. It sanctions their view of the world and society. The late twentieth century used archaeology to justify its view of hunting. The ancient Greeks founded the hunt in the great heroic myths. The medieval mind created in the hunt a spiritual allegory.

The impulse to make beasts into spiritual symbols—to see allegories in animals—was fundamental to the medieval Christian mind, and while it seeped into romances, it also found its way into natural history. The hunt did not figure prominently in the Bible. The references are few, and the violence of the hunt did not make hunting narratives a congenial trope for Christian spirituality. The great hunters like Nimrod are typically associated with tyranny and sinfulness, and the hunt is frequently associated with a sinful struggle in the psyche of the individual in Christian tradition. In fact, all hunting was officially prohibited to the clergy, Chaucer's monk and Saint Hubert himself notwithstanding. From the Council of Agde in southern Gaul in 506, priests, bishops, and deacons were explicitly barred from keeping hounds and falcons. Other councils renewed the prohibition, a sign that the lust for hunting was irresistible among the spiritual princes. Hugo of Saint Victor, for example, writes, "The hart is a chaste and pure soul. The arrows are evil longings. The hunters are devils."[29]

From the few allusions to hunting in the Bible, however, a pervasive and well-perpetuated tradition of understanding both the hunt, and the animals in the hunt, developed. The animals of the hunt were, like other animals in the medieval bestiary, understood in largely allegorical terms. Nature was the text of God, and his truths could be read in nature. Nature was a rhetoric and grammar of the soul.

The principle source of this "method" of understanding the hunt can be traced to one of the earliest manuals of the hunt there is: *Les Livres du Roy Modus et de la Royne Ratio* (The Books of King Method and Queen Reason). The king gives the "methods" of the hunt, and the queen gives the underlying rationality of the creatures being hunted—she gives the meanings, the "moralizations and figures." The combination of political philosophy with theology codified a stratification in hunting and a divine sanction for discovering the same hierarchies in nature itself, among animals of the hunt—between high and low game. Classes of game could be moralized in social and "divine" terms.

The two great creatures of the hunt, in the medieval and Renaissance imagination, were the boar and the stag. The boar, for example, had a long association in Western thought with epic heroism. Something of that aura hangs over the treatment of the boar in the accounts of its hunting in Gaston Phèbus, whose book draws from *Roy Modus*. The queen, Ratio, though, explains that the stag and the boar are actually opposed. The hunt accounts for the division, the categorizing, of nature into good and bad, noble animals and vermin. In the words of the queen of ratio, of reason, there are five "sweet" and five "stinking" beasts, *"bestes douches"* and *"puans."*[30] The stinking beasts are also known as *"bestes noires,"* our *bêtes noires*.

The stag is the most eminent of sweet beasts, together with the roe deer, the daim (another cervid), and the hare. Among the stinking beasts, the boar was placed at the top, together with the other vermin—wolf, fox, bear, and otter. These categories were repeated long into the English tradition, and it was only much later, in the seventeenth century, that the fox was lifted into a noble creature to hunt, a pleasurable creature to hunt.

The boar had long been associated with Germanic peoples. In *Beowulf*, the ancient oral epic of the Saxons in England, the boar is a frequent image, the heraldic emblem of the warriors. The Old Norse word for boar also means "noble warrior" or "prince"—*jofurr*. It figures also in the *Nibelungenlied*, in the thirteenth century, contributing to the view of the boar as a kind of Germanic cult animal. And in the Christian tradition, the boar came to be associated with the defeat then of heathens—the Christian warrior triumphing over the pagan cults. In literary treatments, the boar was elevated to a quasi-draconian state, a monster more than an animal. It was linked with the devil itself, from a scriptural passage, Psalm 89: "Why hast thou then broken down her hedges [protecting the vines of the Lord] . . . ? The boar out of the wood doth waste it, and the lone beast doth devour it."

In Queen Ratio's exegesis, the boar is a figure then of the Antichrist. His evil properties are legion, including lechery, pride, anger, and a loving to wallow in the mud—that is, to bathe in the world's filth. That it is cross-toed signifies its deformation, like the vanity of men who follow fashion to extravagant lengths (shoes curling half a foot beyond the toes were highly fashionable then among the aristocracy). It makes sense, then, that Shakespeare's Richard III, as both a raging warrior and the devil incarnate, had the boar as both emblem and epithet: "Thou elvish-mark'd, abortive, rooting hog!" (*Richard III*, 1.3.227).

Yet if the boar was Antichrist, the great symbol in nature of Christ himself was the stag. Perhaps more than any other beast, the stag signifies the hunt itself. It was through the allegorization of the stag that medieval and Renaissance princes demonstrated their legitimacy, their lineage, if you will, as an agent of Christ. And they reconciled the conflicting demands of Caesar and Christ, political imperative and spiritual decree, through the magic of ritual and imagery. This is one great function of ritual and symbol—it transcends the contradictions of our lives and reconciles the paradoxes that beset us daily, holding them in harmonious suspension.

The boar could not come close to approaching the stag in its range of symbolic power and emotional resonance for men. With the quest of the stag, we move into a numinous world where the wild things of the forest have a special association with the wild things of the human heart. The sacred stag springs from Psalm 42:1, on the zeal of David to serve God. "As the hart panteth after the water brooks, so panteth my soul after thee, O God." The image of the thirsting deer at the brooks of the Lord was full of such deep religious intensity that it was the beginning for Saint John of the Cross in his mystical meditations on his endless longing for God.[31]

In the treatises on hunting and natural history, the stag became an emblem of Christian virtues. Queen Ratio gives the antlers as nature's reminder that we must observe the Ten Commandments. According to the queen, the perfect deer, the royal hart, has at least ten points. Such would be the hart chosen by the prince on a hunt, and it would be designated a "hart royal." Those ten points represent the Ten Commandments of the law "given to men by Jesus Christ."

This creature is capable of miracles, a sign that it is the most marvelous of all God's creatures. In an Elizabethan treatise on hunting, by George Turberville, the sacred nature of the stag or hart is revealed in its lore. The hart was able to cure itself of disease by eating a special herb, the dictamnum, possessed of miraculous powers of healing, an emblem of how men might heal themselves of evil. This herb could help stags evade hunters. When wounded, the stag would find this herb in the woods, and swallow it, making the arrow fall from its side.

Most important, the stag is himself a hunter, a figure of Christ as hunter after evil. The stag is the enemy of the serpent, Turberville claims. He will march directly up to the serpent's den in the woods. There, the hart or stag will force his breath into the hole of the den. The breath of the hart has such virtue that it will drive the coiled serpent out of its den. Then the hart kills the serpent with its feet, trampling and devouring it. The hart fulfills the prophecy of the Old Testament, that one will come to bruise the serpent that caused the fall.

The image of the hart as Christ found many literary manifestations. One of the most delicate pieces of literary natural history is in Malory's *Le Morte Darthur*. During a mass with Galahad, Percival, and others, a hart entered the church, transformed himself into a man, and then left through a window. A hermit interpreted the moving symbol to the astonished onlookers:

> And well ought our Lord be signified to an hart; for the hart when he is old waxeth young again in his white skin: right so cometh again our Lord from death to life, for he lost earthly flesh, that was the deadly flesh which he had taken in the womb of the blessed virgin Mary; and for that cause appeared our Lord as a white hart without a spot. . . . For wit ye well never erst might no knight know the truth, for, ofttimes or this, our Lord shewed him unto good men and unto good knights in the likeness of an hart.[32]

The hart was capable of perpetual rebirth, it was thought, a sign of its connection with Christ.

As a result, one of the hart's distinguishing characteristics was its longevity. Turberville reports, on the good authority of Gaston Phèbus, that a hart can easily live up to a hundred years. He even reports that one hart was captured, three hundred years after the death of Caesar, wearing a collar. The collar bore the engraved arms of Caesar, with the phrase, *Caesarus me fecit* ("Caesar made me").

Through this story, the ellision from spiritual to secular was made. The miraculous stag, capable of surprising revelations, could reveal none other than the pedigree of the prince as a man worthy to possess the stag of Caesar. Caesar's stag was a common enough myth in the Middle Ages and Renaissance. France's Charles VI was said to have captured a deer in 1381 with a collar that said, "Caesar gave this to me." Presumably, Caesar gave the deer to Charles, as well.

Of all the spiritual stories about the *cerf*, or stag, that explore the relationship between political power and spiritual longing, the one that moves me most powerfully is the story of Saint Hubert. It was also the most popular story of its sort in the Middle Ages and Renaissance. Actually, it's the story of Saint Eustace, who is the more ancient and probably the original of Saint Hubert's story. It was told frequently. Saint Alferic gives a version in Old English. The Genoese archbishop Jacobus de Voraigne wrote a Latin version in the thirteenth century that was widely read in his lives of the saints in *The Golden Legend*. In the vernacular, in France alone, fourteen versions were produced from the thirteenth century. The queen, Ratio, in *Roy Modus*, refers to Saint Eustace repeatedly, and the references provide her with the point of departure for her allegory of the stag.[33]

Saint Eustace's hunt is the story of the scared chase—a legend in which the worldly chase of soldiers and politicians is transformed into something more spiritual and pure. It is the story of the heroic hunter meeting with a god. Actaeon discovering Diana or Artemis in her grove is a similar story, widely told in the Middle Ages. Saint Eustace, though, meets with God himself in the form of a beautiful stag.

Saint Eustace was originally known as Placidus, a great hunter and archer. He was a master of soldiers under the Roman emperor Trajan. He loved to hunt with his soldiers, and one day while hunting, he came upon a herd of deer in which he saw a stag larger and more lovely than all the rest. The stag left the herd and bounded alone into the forest. While the soldiers pursued the other deer, Placidus gave chase to the lone stag at full speed. As he chased it with all his strength, the stag at last mounted a high rock. Placidus drew near, pondering how he might capture it. As he was admiring the great stag, he noticed that, between his horns, the stag bore a holy cross, gleaming brightly in the sun. On the cross was the effigy of Jesus Christ.

Jesus then spoke to Placidus, through the stag's mouth: "O Placidus, why dost thou pursue Me?"

The stag continued: "For thy sake I have appeared in this beast, for I am Christ, Whom thou unwitting adorest; thine alms-deeds have ascended before Me, and therefore am I come, that in this stag which thou didst hunt, I Myself might hunt thee!"

Overcome with fear, Placidus fell from his horse and lost his senses. When he awakened, after an hour, the stag was still with him. The stag told Placidus that he, Jesus, created all the creatures, and divided the light from the dark, and was crucified to save all humans. Placidus saw that he had been living in error, converted, and sought the stag's advice on how he should now conduct his life. The stag told him to return to the city and be baptized, taking the new name of Eustace. He followed the stag's instructions, and returned to the woods again the next day to hunt, where he again met the cruciferous, speaking stag. This time the stag warned him that the devil would fight against him severely. He must be prepared.

This surely happened. Eustace met with more tribulations than Job. His servants died of plague and he lost his wealth. With his family, he traveled to Egypt, where he lost both wife and children in a river and thought them dead. After years of trials, he was reunited with his wife and sons, only to be sentenced to death for not paying homage to the Roman gods by the new emperor Hadrian, who began to reign in about 120 and was perhaps the most famous of the Roman emperors for his hunting. A lion was released upon Eustace and his family in an arena. But the ferocious lion merely bowed its head meekly, as if to adore them as saints, and ran away. More ordeals followed, including a bronze bull within which the family was to be burned alive. They died, but miraculously were found within after three days, intact.

This is a compelling story of faith and spiritual strength. The stag serves as a visionary, quasi-divine creature, and has a long history in this capacity. It can be the sacred creature of Artemis, and has antecedents in both Indian and Buddhist literature.

As I watch the hunters chasing after a stag in the woods of the Gresigne Forest in southern France, I think about Saint Eustace and Saint Hubert. Through the centuries, the cult of Saint Hubert gradually displaced that of Saint Eustace. Saint Hubert became a bishop, and the patron of hunters. Saint Eustace was a martyr and visionary. The story of Saint Hubert had a more worldly lesson for a world growing increasingly sophisticated and suave. I sit on the hood of Emmanuel's gray Renault, watching hunters on thoroughbreds charge through the trees. I actually hope, if they bay the selected *cerf,* that I will be in position to see the death. But I know, as well, that my sympathies are with the stag. I hope it will escape.

I had entered into this book, this project, with an open mind about hunting. I had never hunted, and I did not expect that studying hunting would transform me into a hunter. But I was more than willing to give it the benefit of the doubt. Perhaps, I thought, there is something intrinsic in hunting that makes it a privileged activity. Perhaps there is some intrinsic and even biological drive in men that makes them, at some deep level, all hunters. That was the way I came into this project. But I know, as I watch this *grande chasse*, that what I want from animals is not their death. Why I always chase after them, why I am willing to travel to such far parts of the globe to see them, study them, be with them, is that I am always looking for some deeper revelation in their company.

The animal as a sort of divine or spiritual messenger is one of our great legacies from the Middle Ages and the Renaissance and the Christian tradition. The story of Saint Eustace speaks of a human longing to chase the elusive beast, to discover that the beast has things to teach that we had not grasped. The longing that informs the hunt is, in the story of Saint Eustace, lifted to a higher plane. It is lifted to a spiritual level.

For the Middle Ages, the lesson of Saint Eustace was not the pagan lesson of the hunter hunted—Actaeon's lesson. The hunter and the hunted are mutually dependent. You cannot have a hunted without a hunter. This model of the hunter creates the hunted, and they become reversible and interchangeable. Rather, the lesson for them was that when the hunter becomes the hunted, he identifies with the victim. This is the uniquely Christian contribution to the hunting motif as spiritual history. It offers the consolation of the hope for victim victorious.

6

Emmanuel and I watch the *grande chasse à courze de cerf* from various places through the entire day. By late afternoon, the sun has a sharp autumnal slant to it, and it is becoming clear that there is little likelihood the hunters are going to kill the beast. Apparently, we learn, it has fled early in the day to a copse of trees, thick and dense. When the hounds try to rouse it from its "harbor," considered in the manuals as a "ruse" by the notoriously clever stag, they discover that a boar is also in the thicket. The deer frustrates the hounds and hunters for the better part of the day.

About five in the afternoon, Emmanuel and I decide to walk down a small dirt road. We suddenly see a man gesticulating madly and yelling on the edge of the road.

Then the *cerf* steps calmly, slowly, out of the bushes and into the open road. We are all flabbergasted and, don't ask me why, all three of us— Emmanuel and I and the anonymous stranger—start running toward the stag. Strangely, it heads straight toward us. It betrays no sense of fear. We can hear dogs heading toward us, invisible in the bushes. Horns blast. The hunters are not far behind the *cerf*. This might be it. This might be the moment when the hunters bay and blade the deer.

It trots right up to us, no more than a few feet away, with an utterly uncanny sangfroid. It is not afraid of us. It has a complete indifference to us, as if it had not been the object of the chase for the entire day, as if it were totally unconcerned that for a large contingent with us, the destiny of this deer is death. It has been harried all day, and yet it merely walks within five feet of us, sharing a dirt road in the rural forest.

I am breathless. The *cerf* is huge—much bigger than I'd expected, much bigger than our white-tailed and mule deer in the United States. He is a huge elk more than a deer, and moves with a regal carriage and dignity. It is easy to see, with his broad spread of antlers—I am too excited to count the rack—and the aplomb of his head, looking down upon us in demure and dismissive regard, how he has come to be associated with royalty. It is easy to see how he could be a vehicle for divine instructions. I am staring at his long neck, in burnished fur, and erect head, and straight powerful muzzle.

Then, close behind, two dogs pop from the brush and come nipping at his heels. Still, he does not break into a run. He trots by us, very close. I follow, but can't keep up with his trot. He flashes his white tail at us and cuts off the road and up the hill, pursued by the dogs.

Two women hunters, both in green velvet, emerge from the woods on their horses. They see the *cerf* climbing the steep slope, and pursue by keeping to the road, which switchbacks up the same hill. They are by now disheveled and sweaty. They look altogether more harried and upset for their day of hunting than the *cerf*.

Emmanuel and I run back to the Renault and tear up the hill. We've glimpsed the *cerf*, and we are both ecstatic. You could hardly call it a vision, but it was a glimpse of something special. If the hunters kill it, I want to see it. But by now, my sympathies are with the *cerf*. We careen up the hill, to a large field at the top, just in time to see the *cerf*, far ahead of the hunters, lope through a field, jump a hedge, and run off into the agricultural areas surrounding the national forest.

Emmanuel and I turn around. We leave the forest and head back to the Pyrenees. Emmanuel is so excited, he's beaming. He wants to go hunting himself tomorrow. He tells me we can go to a forest reserve of a friend of his, and we'll really try to hunt a beautiful *cerf*. We drive over two hours back to his lovely, slate-roofed house on a steep hill in the Pyrenees. We get out of the car in the cold, clear darkness. Millions of stars light the clear sky. It is brisk and beautiful and I feel very alive. In my mind's eye, I can still see the *cerf* running away from us. I love the idea of the stag, as in Saint Hubert's and Saint Eustace's stories, beckoning us to some other journey, some other quest, some other vision. In our literal age, we have little habitat remaining for such magic deer as these two saints encountered. But their stories invite us to see beyond the literal hunt, to an allegorical quest.

I take a deep breath of cold air. Yes, I'll go hunting tomorrow. We'll get up early and climb deep into these mountains, to be at a peak at dawn, with red deer feeding. But for now, I am full of the stag that got away. I look up at the black sky filled with white stars. I think about the stag's white rump. I think about how the currents of an entire culture can come together in the single image of a deer. Or a chase. Or, for me, in this fleeting image of an animal. And I think about how an animal, like a deer that becomes magical, can lead us. I feel the sharp mountain air in Emmanuel's small Pyrenees village.

7

King John was particularly fond of falconry. Though he was more addicted to the prerogatives of the hunt than many of his royal predecessors, whose indulgence in the sport were themselves legendary, he excelled at falconry. He has come down to us as the model of the ineffectual English king whose barons humiliated him at Runnymede in 1215, forcing him to sign that first document in modern democracy, the Magna Carta. A principle complaint in the people's social unrest was his abuse of the Forest Laws—which had since the Norman Invasion of 1066 been a central source of social unrest in England.

When John extended the laws of the forest to small game—which thereby created additional grievances for poor men, for whom hawking was very popular—he incited the "loyal revolt" of the barons that led to his humiliation at Runnymede. His humiliation stands as an example of the way hunting lay at the center of class dissension in English and European history.

The fierce forest laws made it illegal for anyone to hunt in forest, park, or chase, and put most animals off limits to noble and peasant alike, and were a weapon in class struggle into the nineteenth century. The laws had been introduced to England from the Continent by William the Conqueror, when he invaded from Normandy in 1066, and were harsher than anything the Saxons had been accustomed to. Roman jurisprudence had argued that *ferae naturae*—wild animals—were ownerless property in the forests, and hence anyone could hunt them. William started from this premise but came to the opposite conclusion. He argued that no one within the royal forests could hunt but he and those he authorized. The laws afflicted the poor more than the rich and well-connected, but no one was exempt. Little is known about the laws, which were not codified under William. On the Continent, nobles commonly limited hunting rights of vassals without any legal sanction but their own decree. To hunt without permission was to poach. And much that is known about the laws derives from the protests against them, in England and on the Continent.

The penalties for poaching were notorious and brutal.

A "venison thief" might have his eyes gouged out or suffer amputation or castration. In the years following William the Conqueror, game laws came and went, but they remained strict and the object of detestation by country people. Under Henry I, for causing a beast to run without license until it panted, a freeman was fined ten shillings and a serf was scourged. If the beast was a royal stag, a freeman lost his freedom and a serf was outlawed.[34]

In the Magna Carta, the nobles made the reform of forest laws and hunting rights one of their principal demands. They wanted both forest and game more accessible to them, by king's warrant. They made King John "dis-afforest" all the lands that had been added to the royal forests for the last generation, and they made sure that no one would henceforth lose life or limb by breaking the forest laws.

Hunting was the nexus of contests between social classes.

This was the age of Robin Hood and his legendary band of outlaws in Sherwood Forest. The legend of Robin Hood was too important in the lays of the people not to reflect an important truth for the lower classes. Most people in England were in no position to force the king into legal concessions for game. Rather, for them, the forest laws drove them into lives as outlaws. For the peasants who had to make their lives near the great tracts of forests that had been set off limits to them, hunting itself served as a form of political protest. They were poachers.

Poaching was the hunting of the underclasses especially, though nobles and bishops would also hunt illegally if the opportunity presented itself. Poaching was a symbol of the injustice of the king's laws and a way of flouting authority. Noblemen like Sir Tristan might idealize the courtly hunt, and their submission to its rules and procedures. But this elitist form of hunting was supported by a vast social institution of repressive laws that formed another kind of political subjection. Gaston Phèbus speaks "unwillingly" and disdainfully of the hunting of common people. He prefers not to teach taking beasts unless it be "by nobleness and gentleness." The many artful traps and "gins," used by common people for catching game for the "pot," he calls a kind of "falseness": "I will speak no more of this chase," he says, dismissively, "for it is one pertaining to villains, to the common people, and to peasants."[35]

In many ways, the aristocrats' hunt was built on the suppression of common people's hunting—both in the political control of non-Christian heathens, and in enforcing class distinctions. What it also did was create another kind of hunting in their shadow, furtive and illegal, which made men outlaws.

To arbitrate the unending violations of the game laws, a vast legal system developed, the forest courts, which were habitually clogged. They typically imposed fines or prison sentences. But many poachers who were caught simply fled the law and lived, perpetually, in the forests. Those men of the forests were declared by the courts "outlaws"—let "him bear the wolf's head." It was a terrible sentence since it meant he could be killed with impunity, but these men often joined in bands, lived in the wild country, and made the forest their lives.[36]

The great symbol of the poacher as romantic outlaw, living in defiance of the king, was Robin Hood. By the mid-fourteenth century, his legend was already very popular. He and his "merry men" made Sherwood Forest their home, wore hunter green, and lived off poached venison. One of the earliest ballads of Robin Hood, "Littel Geste of Robyn Hood and His Meiny," shows how the other side of our political consciousness—the romanticization of the virtuous outlaw—was linked with the poacher in the woods, not so much rebelling against authority as mocking it.[37]

The Sheriff of Nottingham had gone out for a long hunting trip, and while he was gone, Little John broke into his house and plundered his pantry. He made off into Sherwood Forest with a nice collection of plates and cutlery.

When he got into the forest, Little John realized the Sheriff was likely to be nearby. Taking his leave of Robin Hood, he made his way through the woods to the place where the Sheriff was hunting. Seeing Little John in the woods, the Sheriff demanded to know what he was doing. "I have been in the forest," replied the monk,

> And a faire syght I can se:
> It was one of the fayrest syghtes
> That ever yet sawe I me.
>
> Yonder I sawe a right fare hart,
> His color is of grene:
> Seven score of dere upon a herd
> Be with him at bydene.

This is merely a ruse to lure the Sheriff into the outlaws' lair. Following Little John, the Sheriff suddenly finds himself face-to-face with his nemesis, Robin Hood himself.

The scene that follows is famous, and was immensely popular in the Middle Ages. The miserable Sheriff is humiliated by being forced to sit down to dinner with Robin and his band of poachers. The meal is, of course, poached venison, served on the Sheriff's own plate. In this fete in the greenwood, Robin Hood not only flouts the Sheriff at his own game, but achieves an inversion of social values that can make the outlaw into the hero.

The social symbolism of poaching became a pervasive part of medieval and Renaissance culture. Shakespeare uses hunters banished to the woods, in both *As You Like It* and *Cymbeline*, to comment on the injustice and corruption of court life. In both plays, true nobility is a matter of the spirit, not the affectations of the "envious court." And in their "velvet friends," the "poor sequest'red stag," the sophisticated courtiers in the Forest of Arden are able to moralize the spectacle of the chase in *As You Like It* into a commentary on the injustices of "usurpers, tyrants," and "fat and greasy citizens" (2.1.1–63).

Poaching has become a metaphor for crossing boundaries, and may have nothing to do with literal deer. Shakespeare, whose genius was that no part of the culture seemed beyond his imaginative reach, created a nocturnal poacher of other men's wives. Falstaff can defend his reprobate and thieving life by appealing to the virtues of the hunt, turning them on their head. He is a bandit, for example, in *Henry IV, Part 1*, willing to steal at the drop of a hat in the woods at night. But when accused of robbing and thieving, he calls himself a "squire of the night's body," one of "Diana's foresters, gentlemen of the shade." He steals under the countenance of the goddess of the hunt (1.2.21–29).

Falstaff is the great comic creator of masks, and when he appropriates the hunt as one of "Diana's foresters," he proves that hunting provided a mask for every layer and level of Renaissance men.

Shakespeare may himself have been a poacher. A very old story, probably apocryphal, has it that he was caught stealing deer from the park that belonged to Sir Thomas Lucy at Charlecoat, near Stratford. It was to avoid the bitterness of the prosecutions against him, as the story goes, that Shakespeare fled Stratford, as a young man, and journeyed to London, to become a great playwright.

If this is true, he may have used his plays to make his revenge on the unlucky Sir Thomas Lucy. One theory holds it that *The Merry Wives of Windsor* is his satiric revenge, for a very dim-witted gentleman named Shallow, with a coat of arms of quartered "luces," or louses(!), has come to town to prosecute Sir John Falstaff, whom Mister Slender claims has "beaten my men, kill'd my deer, and broke open my lodge."

Poacher Falstaff is, but he is the wittiest and most disgusting poacher in literature. He takes the idea of poaching—of crossing boundaries and stealing—to new metaphoric levels. When he poaches, he's after "does," not bucks. He wants the wives of Windsor. He tries every device possible to seduce them from their husbands, but they see straight through him. He is transparent, and the comedy is watching him be exposed. The wives abuse him triumphantly by getting him to dress up in the costume of a stag and meet them in Windsor Forest, one of the most popular venues for venery in England.

Falstaff gets himself up in the guise of a character called "Herne the Hunter," who was a "sometime keeper here in Windsor forest" (4.2.19). Herne the Hunter wore great ragged horns and cavorted with the animals of the forest, and he belongs in the category of folklore creatures of the English countryside. Falstaff puts a buck's head on his own head, and, disguised as a stag, he waits at a great oak in the forest for his rendezvous with the wives. The clock strikes midnight. As he says, Falstaff is feeling his grease. He's literally horny.

"Remember, Jove," he proclaims,

> thou wast a bull for Europa, love set on thy horns. O powerful love, that in some respects makes a beast a man; in some other, a man a beast. . . . When gods have hot backs, what shall poor men do? For me, I am here a Windsor stag, and the fattest, I think, i'th' forest. Send me a cool rut-time, Jove, or who can blame me to piss my tallow? Who comes here? My doe? . . . My doe with the black scut?

It's Mrs. Ford. She hails the hot and horny Falstaff: "Sir John? art thou there, my deer, my male deer?" (5.5.3–17).

The puns have flown thick in the woods. They've also grown raunchy. The scut of a deer, for example, is its rear end, and in Elizabethan English became slang for female genitals.

At that moment, the second wife arrives at the Windsor oak, and this stag thinks he's been transported to paradise. He feels like a "brib'd buck," a cut-up deer which poachers have had to do hastily, for fear of being caught. He promises his horns to their husbands. For the rest of them, well, each wife can have a haunch. "Am I a woodman," he chortles blissfully.

But the joke is on him. The poacher is nabbed. The whole village descends upon the mortified Falstaff, and they expose him as a beast and outlaw. And then, surrounded by fairies, he is forgiven and all can return to town.

Whether the appetite being fed was metaphoric or literal, sexual or gastronomic, poaching gave an entire society a language for identifying men in relation to social norms. They might be outlaws or rebels, romantics or deviants. The hunt, as both a social institution and a metaphor, pervaded society at all levels and gave men, in its various forms, a wide range of social masks out of which they might create their identities. But poaching in its various forms, literal and literary, proved that more people than just the king could use the forest for their playground and their politics.

8

I'd like to linger just a bit longer on Falstaff's disguise as Herne the Hunter. There's something more, and perhaps more interesting, going on in this scene of the fatman beneath an oak tree, wearing horns on his head, than I've so far suggested. The imagery draws on more than a nocturnal rendezvous in the woods, a clever prank by two merry wives. I've not read anywhere of an explanation for this "Herne the Hunter," except Shakespeare's own, earlier in the play, when he is described as "Sometime keeper here in Windsor forest" (4.4.30). In addition to a horny and cuckholdy Falstaff, I think the image of Herne with the horns on his head evokes another deep imaginative tradition in British folklore. I suspect that Herne, "keeper of the forest," glances not very indirectly at an ancient mythological Celtic figure—a god named Cernunnos, "the Horned One."[38]

Cernunnos was a Celtic god in pagan Britain, though he appears in various forms throughout Europe. Most famously, Cernunnos is portrayed in a relief sculpture on the Gundestrup cauldron in the National Museum of Copenhagen, though representations of a horned human figure appear in several places in England as well. On the Gundestrup cauldron, the human figure of the god sits cross-legged in the midst of several animals, natural and fantastic, and he is crowned by a splendid pair of antlers. His name literally translates as "the horned one." This Celtic god was sometimes conjoined in worship with Jupiter, who assumed the attribute of "Cernenus," a stag god. Cernunnos for the Celts was "the lord of the animals," and gets his powers over animals through the stag. When Cernunnos struck the stag on the head, the animal's bellows summoned all the creatures of the forest to the deity's presence—rams and wolves and fishes and even a snake with the head of a ram.

It is a brilliant conception, Cernunnos, and has often been compared to the Indian god Mohnejodaro, perhaps a prototype for the god Shiva in his aspect as Pashupati, "Lord of the Beasts." Certainly, the nearness of the name Cernunnos to Herne, the evocation of the "horned" god, the connection with Jupiter, and the connection with the British native lore of nature gods and fairies link Falstaff in this disguise as Herne with Cernunnos. Even as the lordly and officially sanctioned hunting styles prospered in England, the suppressed Celtic traditions survived in the native imagination of the lower classes. Perhaps he reappears here in the Falstaff disguise as a horned Herne, the image of a subversive, nocturnal desire.

If Herne is an evocation of Cernunnos, he is reduced in Falstaff's comedy to disguise for a sexual poacher. Still, there is redemptive power in the forest scene, as the fairies ring the horrified Falstaff and forgive him. Whether as Herne the Hunter or as Cernunnos, there is the evocation of another set of values for the hunter, connected to spirit and imagination and forest. Like Robin Hood, an alternative tradition persists in the people's imaginations and narratives, marginal and shadowy and able to emerge only outside the city. Cernunnos and Herne have more in common than the phonetics of their names and the horns on their heads. As mythic hunters and human stags, they are both nearly forgotten versions of a deep desire to believe in a keeper of the forests and a lord of the animals. They are repositories of a deep, suppressed, and nearly forgotten sense of the interconnections between spirits of humans and animals, where the deity has a human face and animal attributes. Through Cernunnos and Herne the Hunter, we glimpse an intimate and emotional connection to nature, one in which we have to venture outside the current boundaries of our lives to discover any more.

9

Emmanuel lives in a five-hundred-year-old house on a mountainside in the central Pyrenees. That night, after coursing a *cerf*, we gather around a table in the kitchen, with his wife Catherine and two children, to eat dinner. We eat food from the immediate region—a stuffed duck, a local *fromage de bragos*, sweet lettuce. We discuss why it is that men hunt. Every male over sixteen in southern France, says Emmanuel, is a hunter. "In the Pyrenees, all the hunters are male. Perhaps one or two in a thousand hunters is a female."

In France as in Spain, hunting is deeply associated with being a man. Then Emmanuel tells us about a friend of his who prefers hunting to being with women. This friend, a hunter, prefers his dogs to women. He likes their smell better than perfume. "My friend," says Emmanuel with a slightly embarrassed glance at his wife, "says it is more difficult to train a wife than it is to train a dog."

Catherine shifts in her chair, looks ominously at Emmanuel, who laughs.

"A wife takes at least ten years to train, my friend thinks," Emmanuel says. "A good dog takes only two years."

In the Renaissance in Europe, though, women frequently hunted. They had "chases" particularly suited to them—fallow deer, for example, the lovely small dappled deer with the palmate, spreading horns. They were frequent falconers, riding out of the castle to fling birds at herons and cranes. In *Don Quixote*, the idealistic knight errant deduces one woman is *una gran señora* and a duchess, because she carries a falcon on her wrist. Diane de Poitiers, in France, cultivated an entire mythology around herself as *la Diane chassereuse*, the modern goddess or queen of the hunt, a new Diana. Her beautiful image as huntress is commemorated in a statue in the Musée du Louvre, by Jean Goujon, called *Diana and the Stag*. Queen Elizabeth of England used hunting as part of the cult of the Virgin Queen, reminiscent of the goddess of chastity and the hunt, as well. One of her courtiers and playwrights, John Lyly, describes a courtly hunt while she took a progress through the English countryside in August 1591. The queen hid in a stand within a bower and, presented a crossbow by a girl dressed as a "nymph," "her Majesty shot at the Deere" driven toward her.[39]

Women hunted avidly in the Renaissance, proving at once that the hunt is not intrinsically about masculinity, and that in the Renaissance it was seen as a royal and aristocratic prerogative. Class complicated gender distinctions.

The next morning Emmanuel and I get up long before dawn. We're after a *cerf*, and to find one, we're climbing a mountain on the other side of the valley.

Driving through the predawn darkness, we see several groups of men gathered in their military greens. They are teams of French hunters, gathering for their Sunday hunt for *sanglier*, the boar. We're on our way to meet Jean Paul Lardos, a close friend of Emmanuel.

Jean Paul is an avid, fanatical hunter. He lives in a house in the country, near Montrejeau, where he owns five falcons, including three peregrine falcons. He also has several ferrets, which he uses to hunt rabbits, sending them down the rabbit holes as Gaston had said peasants might do. He built towers amid the trees on a ridge near his house, where he hides during migrations to shoot at the huge flocks of pigeons that fly into his tree, attracted by the pigeon decoys he ties to branches.

We are meeting Jean Paul because he bought the right to hunt in a section of forest on the mountain. In France, you can buy the right from the government to hunt on a section of forest. Several hunters usually band together to pay the price, because it's expensive. Jean Paul and nine other hunting friends pay two hundred thousand francs per year for the right to hunt on this section of mountain forest we are about to hunt. They can renew this lease for up to twelve years, and for that they can hunt anything on the mountain—*isard*, roe deer, *cerf*, boar, partridge.

As Emmanuel and I wait in the dark at a trailhead, he says to me, "This is for rich hunters." It's the modern version of the feudal franchise system in Europe.

On his biologist's salary, with a family to support, Emmanuel can't afford this kind of hunting. We are Jean Paul's guests. According to Emmanuel, there are class tensions in southern France because many people cannot afford this kind of hunting. The issue of status and class persists, reflected in the hunt. Emmanuel says that some men in each village, for example, have very many dogs. And the man with the most dogs is the one the others will vote for in elections for mayor.

You don't have to be a Marxist to feel the undercurrent of class and money in the way these men are arrayed in their hunting styles. Even Emmanuel finds people who hunt only for food, and not out of some passion for the hunt, somehow declassé.

We meet Jean Paul at the forest, and we begin hiking before sunrise. The trail is wet and rocky up the mountain. We step on shiny, slippery chunks of slate, almost silvery even in the dark from the water—it's this slate that is split to make the beautiful steep slate roofs on the houses in the region. We hike among beech trees in the dark, lining the trail.

Emmanuel hikes like an *isard*, the "mountain goat" of the Pyrenees. I tell him he must have an *isard* for a grandfather. He laughs. "I have two dreams," he says. "One is to move to northern Canada and be a trapper. The other is to have cows and to live in the Alps. I want to be a mountain man, as my grandfather was. I love wildlife and the land, and now I know that I am a lucky man. Many people in France are very *triste*, bent over by their lives. But I live here in the mountains and am lucky to be with animals."

Jean Paul moves up the trail like a man in charge. With his black beard and longish, slightly rakish hair, he vaguely reminds me of a country gentleman. He could easily have been one of the *veneurs et chevaliers* of the Pyrenees, with Gaston Phébus, not far from here. He doesn't speak English, and I don't speak French. But we both speak Spanish, it turns out, and begin to chat away like old friends. He tells me he loves falconry more than any other kind of hunting. "*La cetrería*," he says, "*es la caza más bella.*" Falconry is the most beautiful hunt. We make arrangements to take falcons out at a later time.

A gray dawn spreads across the black silhouettes of the mountains as we emerge from the forest into an alpine clearing. There are flecks of white snow here and there, and gray calcite rocks protruding from the mountain itself, like bones. We are ringed by high and bulging crests. On the top of one of the crests, against the dour clouds, are the silhouettes of five roe deer, dainty and shy. They're like miniature deer with tiny antlers on their heads.

Jean Paul signals us to be quiet now. He leads us up a very steep slope to our left, so steep we crawl on all fours up it. Near the top, Jean Paul says to me, "You must avoid all noise now."

We all peer over the edge, very cautiously. In the meadow, several *cerfs* are grazing in the thick gray light. They don't notice us. One is a large male. I crouch beneath the crest, and Emmanuel lies flat against the mountain, feet widely spread apart. He slithers up so that he can see the *cerfs*. A nod from Jean Paul confirms—he gets to shoot.

He aims his rifle slowly, carefully.

All is tenseness and apprehension, and then when the rifle explodes, it's as if the morning does too. The whole range of mountains around us echoes when he finally fires, and Emmanuel bolts out of his belly crawl at the same instant. We all leap to our feet and over the ridge, into the meadow, with him. Only the large stag remains in the meadow, and he's running. Downslope. His huge rack of antlers jerking. I'm not even sure if Emmanuel has hit him.

I don't know if Emmanuel is sure or not either. We run toward the fleeing stag, afraid to let him get out of sight. He leaps with incredible agility and power over a blackened, fallen tree. Emmanuel stops, lifts his rifle frantically to his shoulder, and tries to get in another shot before the stag disappears down a steep drop among the trees.

Before he fires, the *cerf* crumples to the ground after his magnificent leap over the down tree.

He falls next to a patch of snow. We fairly fly toward him, down the hill. The forest burned not long ago, and several charred stumps loom against the gray sky. The momentum of his leap has twisted the *cerf* onto his back, his antlers dug into the earth under his head, his gray chin lifted upward, in tortured contortions.

When we get there, he's not yet dead. His large, wide ears are still twitching, and his mouth is bleeding. I watch his dark brown eyes slowly lose their luster and shine, and go to the dull gray hue of death. With one final groan, he dies. More blood spews from his mouth.

Emmanuel is ecstatic. He hugs Jean Paul, who is also beaming. "It is my first *cerf*," Emmanuel says.

I'm startled by that comment, since I know he is such a passionate hunter. But I say nothing, and I guess that it is still very difficult to get access to hunt a *cerf*. To commemorate his success, I take his picture behind the body of the deer—the modern ritual of the postmortem. Men in these photos define themselves by the beast they have captured, the way Tristan returned with the hide of the deer, singing his way into the castle.

Emmanuel goes to an evergreen tree, cuts a bough, and places it in the bloody mouth of the *cerf*. "I learned this from my grandfather," he says. "It's a way to respect the animal you've killed. My grandfather would also drink the blood of the animal after he killed it. He said it gives force."

We don't drink its blood. The men gut the deer. The first thing they do is cut off its testicles, *les couilles*, a traditional European feature of the gutting of a deer. François I himself, the Renaissance king, is described on one "unsuccessful" hunt returning to the château with fourteen testicles, not so much a trophy as a testimony to the hunter's manly power, appropriated from the animal.[40] The hunt was disappointing to him, because he wanted more deer.

We had hiked for at least two hours to reach this mountain meadow and kill this deer. Now we have to haul the deer out. Jean Paul and Emmanuel tie the animal up with ropes, and we drag it down the mountainside. When we get back down to the truck, Emmanuel loads the *cerf* in his Renault and drives off.

I ride with Jean Paul to his country house, where we later meet Emmanuel. We spend the gorgeous November afternoon eating a dinner of venison and taking Jean Paul's hawks out to hunt.

After dark, we drive back to Emmanuel's mountain house. But it turns out that the *cerf* is no longer in the truck. I ask him what has happened with the deer. "I took it to a restaurant in Montrejeau," he says. "I sold it."

I am suddenly disillusioned. I had thought that Emmanuel was becoming a mountain man, connecting with his grandfather's way of life in the high mountains. Yet this hunt has turned into a commercial venture.

"I sold it to help Jean Paul pay for the expenses of buying the rights to hunt that land," Emmanuel explains. The deer went for twenty-two francs per kilo.

Now, as in the Renaissance, hunting the *cerf* is a kind of privilege, and Emmanuel feels privileged by this day's hunt. We pull up to his house, and his two dogs race to the car, barking and yelping. Their tails are wagging furiously. The sky is dark again, and millions of stars are like a swath of bright bloom across the black depths of space. The mountain air is sharp, cutting. As we get out of the Renault, Catherine and the two kids come out of their beautiful old house and stand on the front porch. Its slate roof rises to an angular peak, pointing toward the brilliant stars in the clear night sky.

As we walk up to the house, Emmanuel gives her a plastic bag. In it is the liver of the deer.

She goes inside. Emmanuel and I linger outside for a moment, with the dogs.

"Emmanuel," I say, "I know you love animals. And I know you have a passion for the hunt. Can you tell me, why is it you want to kill something you love?"

Emmanuel is a very thoughtful, honest man. The question interests him. He ponders it silently under the stars for some time. We pet the dogs and feel the bracing November air. Emmanuel gets a bemused look on his face.

"That is the great contradiction of the hunter," he says. "I don't really know. Perhaps it's only a perversion." Then we go into his sixteenth-century house.

6

THE SHOT AND DANGER
OF DESIRE

When night dogs run, all sorts of deer are chas'd.

—Shakespeare, *The Merry Wives of Windsor*, 5.5.238

Curio: Will you go hunt, my lord?
Duke: What, Curio?
Curio: The hart.
Duke: Why, so I do, the noblest that I have.
O, when mine eyes did see Olivia first,
Methought she purg'd the air of pestilence!
That instant was I turn'd into a hart,
And my desires, like fell and cruel hounds,
E'er since pursue me.

—Shakespeare, *Twelfth Night*, 1.1.16–22

Manhood entered the modern world artfully camouflaged in hunter green. The hunter looked so natural, no one realized he'd invented the costume. It's a trick of the mind: dressed up as a hunter in green, men disguised themselves from themselves in an artificial cryspis. We forgot—and forget—the artificiality of the hunter, and of the notions of masculinity he supports. Men became somehow invisible. They became hidden from themselves. We looked so natural, in our mind's eye, roaming the woods in green, we forgot we invented this figure. The ritualized hunt was a way of rendering conventions invisible, of giving them a natural habitat.

This is the hunter in our heads.

But there's another hunter we carry inside of us, as well. He's more deeply embedded in modern notions of manhood, and more closely linked to modern notions of male identity. He lives in a thicket that's more dense and shadowy than any found in nature. And the creatures he chases have proved both more vulnerable and more elusive.

He is the hunter in the heart.

In the Middle Ages and the Renaissance, this erotic hunter took on a new prominence in men's emotional lives. The love hunt was inherited from the classical Romans and Greeks, but it was transformed as it was transplanted. For the ancients, the hunt as a metaphor for love was confined largely to sex itself. Desire was understood as largely male—men were the pursuers, women the pursued. Orion had a monstrous appetite, Artemis was chaste. Sexual desire in men was imagined as uncontrollable, sweeping everything before it and seeking immediate gratification. Desire might be primordial, in the figure of Dionysus, but it was also somehow external to men, an alien and powerful force that wreaked havoc on men and gods alike. It was a power that could come upon a man, and it was irresistible. What it was not, however, was an integral part of male identity. As Ovid's erotic hunters make clear, the love hunt was illicit, marginal, and shadowy. Female erotic hunters like Venus were largely a threat to this model of masculinity. If anything, the love hunt took men away from the epic hunt— or, their "true" masculine calling.

At least, it took men away from identity as we think of it now. Ovid's erotic hunters seduce and abandon, or are themselves destroyed by their love. Sex may be irresistible, but it was somehow unmanly, and a lecherous Jove looks somehow a bit ridiculous chasing wood nymphs. Better to retire to the mountains and live chaste. The true man was not a lover, but a man on a mission, easily figured as a hunt. Identity came not from the erotic, but from the heroic hunt.

It remained for the Middle Ages and the Renaissance to really develop the idea that desire might be creative as well as destructive, and that the dangers and pains of love were themselves somehow ennobling, somehow exquisitely part of longing. It remained for this period to bequeath to us the notion that desire itself—first chaste desire, but also in time more overtly sexual desire—might teach us the secrets of our identities.[1] In time, the erotic hunter of the Middle Ages and the Renaissance served to guide men into the labyrinths of our inner lives—desire became the secret of the self. The chivalric spirit transformed the erotic hunt. The erotic hunters of the Middle Ages and the Renaissance dedicated their lives and their souls to the chase of desire. In the quest to master its secrets and dangers, they gave themselves over to it entirely. It held for them the mysteries of experience, and they were willing to die for desire.

In the "shot and danger of desire," as Shakespeare put it in *Hamlet*, one could begin to unravel the reasons for one's life. Increasingly, the erotic hunt promised to reveal the secrets of that inner life. It's a hunt we haven't been able to abandon, since we still look to desire to tell us, under the shams and conventions and artifices of our mundane lives, who we really are. What makes us burn most brightly.

From the lovely tenderness of the Gawain poet to the elegant baroque intricacies of Andrew Marvell, the erotic hunt didn't just convey its lovers to the social margins. It conveyed them to an inner landscape that seemed to reveal truth—the truth of the tempted soul. It conveyed them to the wilderness of a psyche beset with duty and temptation, exquisite joys and scarcely endurable pains.

Michael Foucault, the French philosopher, argues that during the Middle Ages sex and our experience of sexuality changed. During the classical period in Greece, he claims in his *History of Sexuality*, sex and desire were largely a matter of morals and behavior. It was concerned with a question of who was master and who was submissive, a concern that orchestrated postures in sexuality into ethical concerns: who's on top, who's below. Who's penetrated.

But under Christianity, he argues, sexuality became more complex. Sexuality in general, and sexual acts in particular, became as it were the secret of our identities. Associated not simply with behaviors to be regulated, but with sin itself, sexuality itself became central in understanding who we are as individuals. For the self-scrutinizing monastic, concerned with the purity of his soul, eager to make himself ready for God, sexual desires like a wilderness of demons were rigorously examined. And confessed. It's a commonplace that the precursor to the psychologist's couch was the priest's confessional. Sex is the truth revealed in both of these private places.

As Foucault asserts, "In a Christian morality of sexual behavior, the ethical substance was to be defined . . . by a domain of desires that lie hidden among the mysteries of the heart, and by a set of acts that are carefully specified as to their form and their conditions." The result: "The development of a hermeneutics of desire together with procedures of self-decipherment."[2]

That is to say, sexual desire became central to self-understanding. The interior hunt was not an allegory of mastery, but a journey to secret dreams and fantasies. Tell me what you want, I'll tell you who you are. It is the secret in which, when revealed, we discover ourselves.

The paradoxical upshot of this new role for desire in the psychology of masculinity was that, both for single men and married, masculine identity came to be defined also in terms of their emotional investments in women. It's a tipsy emotional balance, built upon a fearful psychological contradiction: the more that men discover their identities in heterosexual desire, the more vulnerable they are to their feelings. The more vulnerable they are to the women.

According to one scholar, in the Middle Ages and Renaissance, despite the importance of the hunt for the great princes, the erotic hunt displaced the epic hunt in literature.[3] And male identities, she might have added. The tensions between the two hunts, and two ways of being a man, did not disappear. But a new way of imagining manliness was emerging, in relation to desire and women. And so the contradictions between these two hunts, the epic and the erotic, became a source of male anxiety. The manly thing was the epic hunt—for boars and harts. Since it involved "feelings" and women, the erotic hunt was viewed as more "effeminate," but no less poetic and powerful. It was the hunt for hares and harts.

Tensions, however, remained between the two types of hunts, as between two ways of being male.

Consider the mystical hunt of love—it leads to disaster, at the hands of a kingly hunter.

Consider what happened to the father of the hunt for princes, Tristan. He became a hunter after love. He pursued the faint scent of his desire into deeper troubles. We've already seen in the last chapter how Sir Tristram's knowledge of formal hunting etiquette elevates his status as a man in the court of Mark. Yet, ironically, it is Tristan who will become the prey—the prey of Mark, who hunts him down later. Tristan becomes the hunted quarry in the story. He is the quarry because he falls in love with Mark's bride, Isolde, whom the author, Gottfried von Strassburg, calls "Love's falcon."[4] In true courtly fashion, the knight falls in love with the lord's queen—and love is identified as illicit, dangerous, and for all the idealism in it, deadly. It is the stuff of the hunter and hunted. In Virgil, Aeneas moves from the erotic hunt back to the epic hunt. In *Tristan*, the hero moves from the epic hunt to the erotic hunt. It defines the new and deepening emotional resonances of manhood.

Tristan falls in love with Isolde on the boat that brings her to Cornwall to meet Mark. They are, as the poet says, caught upon Love's "limned twig," setting snares for each other in covert lurking places. The two clandestine lovers become thoroughly enmeshed—trapped and snared—in their love. And though they try to conceal the love from Mark, he is suspicious, and he himself weaves his own nets, lays his own traps, for the pair, "Love's huntsmen." When he finally catches them, he exposes them publicly; and then, unable to put them to death, he banishes them together from his court.

Together, the lovers leave Mark. Tristan leads them to a cave he had discovered in a "savage mountainside" during one of his many hunting excursions. The cave is a magical place. It was once inhabited by giants, but now is barred by bronze doors. Inscribed across the cave are the words: "The Cave of Lovers." It's a cave of the imagination and sweet desire.

Tristan and Isolde move into this exquisite cave. It consciously echoes the cave of Aeneas and Dido. Except that it is their home and destiny, whereas Aeneas's cave was a digression. A crown of gold, surrounded by beautiful gems, adorns the center of the vault. The floor is of smooth marble, "green as grass." In the center of the cave, "there was a bed cut from a slab of crystal, broad, high, well raised from the ground, and engraved along its sides with letters, announcing the bed was dedicated to the Goddess of Love."[5]

They live for some time in this wild retreat. Their feast is love. Their goal is their desire. They are sufficient to their desire. Few people, says Gottfried, are lucky enough to see this cave. He has heard reports of it. Some have tracked the wild game through remote wildernesses and woodland streams, but their toils are not crowned with success. Gottfried says he found the cave, saw the doors, even tried the lever. He saw the bed of crystal and danced there "a few times." But he was never to have "my repose on it." This is of course not a literal place—it's an allegory. "The sun-giving windows" in the cave "have often sent their rays into my heart," says Gottfried in this touching autobiographical aside. "I have known the cave since I was eleven, yet I never set foot in Cornwall."[6]

This cave is the lover's heart, and it's a new destination for men.

But Mark, the lovers' lord, is deeply sorrowful. To relieve his melancholy, he goes out hunting. And his hounds unharbor a strange stag in a herd, maned like a horse, big, white, with undersize horns. The hunters follow this strange white stag through the morning, and it leads them straight to the Cave of Lovers.

This is the new prey—*le cerf d'amour.* The mystical, almost spiritual stag of love. It leads them to Tristan and Isolde, lying in the crystal bed. This white stag escapes Mark, and is attainable only by such beautiful lovers as the pair in the cave. It marks a new ideal, a charmed ideal of the hunt, and of manhood itself. But it is not attainable by ordinary hunters like Mark. It is the marvelous creature that exists, not in nature, but in the heart and the imagination of love. It is the creature that leads men into themselves. We have pursued this stag into that other beautiful wilderness of the psyche.

This new chase is not simply about domination. There are new complexities here. The erotic chase now portrays desire as a goal, as a destiny, as a way of life. While illicit, as it often was in the ancient world, it is now charmed, idealized, housed in a golden cave with gems and marble and crystal. And hunting marks out this inner territory as a natural habitat for men. It takes us into the habitat of desire and love. But for all its beauty, it is marked by new complexities, new masculine scripts and codes, new psychological tensions. The lover Tristan is pursued by his lord Mark. This marks the conflict between what are now two ideals.

The erotic chase became pervasive in language. The puns on hunting and sex are endless in medieval and Renaissance England—heart/hart, dear/deer, chaste/chase. Chaucer punned on hart/heart/hurt, too, with "herte" being the past tense of "hurt." Many hunted animals were figured in the venereal lexicon, and Shakespeare's language harries these creatures mercilessly. Hares had long been associated with Venus, probably because they were considered notoriously lecherous and able to change sexes at will.[7] To chase a hare means something quite specifically sexual, usually female: "Her love is not the hare that I do hunt," says one Shakespearean character in *As You Like It* (4.3.18). The hare could also represent specific sexual parts, male or female. Chaucer's "General Prologue" to *The Canterbury Tales* combines puns on hare and "pricking" or riding in discussing the lechery of the monk: "Of pricking and of hunting for the hare / Was all his lust" (191–92). Mercutio in *Romeo and Juliet* describes the nurse as an "old hare hoar," punning on whore. And since she is old, the nurse as hare is not good meat—the pun on hair, meat, female genitalia, and whore combine in a joke about "hair pie" (2.4.134–39)—which is a slang expression still in use. "To raise a hare" means something quite specifically male, to have an erection. In *Troilus and Cressida*, for example, Shakespeare's character Pandarus sings an obscene hunting song about "Love's bow" which "Shoots buck and doe." Its wound, he says, "tickles the sore," and the "lovers cry, O ho, they die!" (3.1.116–20).

One of the most pervasive puns was "to die," slang for an orgasm. Shakespeare in *The Winter's Tale* refers to an orgasm as the "mort o' th' deer" (1.2.118)—the death of the deer, the lovers' cries of sexual passion suggesting hunters crying "soho," also.

But the abounding linguistic turns are merely surface traces of the paradoxes of sexual desire that were explored in more profound ways in extended narrative and verse. The point is, hunting took men deeper into themselves. It was the vehicle for psychic exploration, and even more important, emotional self-discovery. Men could easily slip between hunting and sex, one minute loving hunters, and the next hunting lovers. The question for us out of this venatic sexual wilderness, is to what extent the hunt shaped the landscape of love—how fully and in what ways did hunters define the natural habitat of sex? And also, to what extent have we inherited these hunters' notions of sexuality? Is desire, like Cupid himself, for us a predator? Do we see the gardens of love through the eyes of hunters, also?

As important, hunting became an image to understand the tensions in desire. The imagery led men into a new sense of the demonic in desire. The very thing that we pursue is the thing that is so dangerous. The hunt gave us a sense of the paradox and mystery of desire. The hunt mapped for us the wilderness of desire—it defined the geography of our psyches.

It took us not only into the beautiful caves of lovers, but into the snares of the unconscious.

We need to call this hunter forth, let him speak, see what the lay of the land is like. Here's how Shakespeare summarizes this habitat of the heart. Lust is itself a hunting, and a mark of our tortured, guilty psyches:

> Th' expense of spirit in a waste of shame
> Is lust in action; and till action, lust
> Is perjur'd, murd'rous, bloody, full of blame,
> Savage, extreme, rude, cruel, not to trust,
> Enjoy'd no sooner, but despised straight,
> Past reason hunted, and no sooner had,
> Past reason hated, as a swallow'd bait
> On purpose laid to make the taker mad:
> Mad in pursuit, and in possession so,
> Had, having, and in quest to have extreme,
> A bliss in proof, and prov'd, a very woe,
> Before, a joy propos'd, behind a dream.
> > All this the world well knows, yet none knows well
> > To shun this heaven that leads men to this hell.
> > > (Sonnet 129)

Despised in the minute of orgasm. Yet, past reason hunted. The pursuit of a dream. A bait that, swallowed, makes us mad. A heaven that leads to hell. Such are the contradictions that come to define male desire. It's through their eyes, male hunters' eyes, that we came to see human desire as an endless process of longing, death, regret, and obsessive pursuit. It's a remarkable world these hunters opened up, where ecstasy seems so closely tied to horror. And men learned to chase a compulsive and tortured sexual desire. Yet one thing remained constant. Hunters had somehow naturalized the compulsive male chase as the story of sex. Hunters took men to the borders of their natural experience, someplace between tame and wild, and there they discovered the body of sex in the body of nature.

Through these particular distortions of longing and power, we created the natural habitat of sex.

2

It's almost a commonplace, now, to observe that the state of nature is a reflection of the state of our own souls. The nature we see is the nature of our inner lives.

What's also true is that we have used nature to construct our souls. Through our inventions of nature, we simultaneously invent our selves. In our versions of nature—in the themes we focus on, in the images we adore, in the particular facts we accept as representative, in the kinds of knowledge we take as "real"—in these representations of nature, we mark out the limits of our imaginations and our hearts. Nature is a text. In both its real and its imaginary forms, in both its external and its internal manifestations, we see in nature a syntax of our selves. It is a code, and deciphering the code shows us where we're at.

That's what we mean when we say that, always and everywhere, nature invites us to be what we are.

In the Middle Ages and the Renaissance, a redefined hunting actually changed the interior landscape itself. And it changed men's relationship to themselves. It marked out our tensions and our ambivalences, our longings and vacillations, our temptations and our resistances. The metaphor of hunting was psychologized, and in the process erotic hunters moved through this space, experiencing it in new ways. They discovered the joys and torments of a new, highly self-conscious relationship to themselves.

Take Shakespeare, who in so many ways reflects, explores, and creates many of the new emotional possibilities for men. The hunt carries men and women alike to the frontier zones, but the frontier is not merely of experience in nature. This frontier, though, has a psychological edge. We move to the boundaries of a man's emotional capacities. In his plays, hunting is frequently used to describe love and self-discovery. Shakespeare likes to explore psychological boundaries, and uses costume and hunting to do so. In *As You Like It*, lovers go to the forest, women dress in male disguise—Rosalind as a young boar hunter, with her "boar spear on my thigh." In the woods, she'll take part in stag hunts and hare hunts. But the stag hunt, you might say, becomes a drag hunt—the real interest is less in heroics than in the self explored under the postures of conventional roles, conventional clothes.

The hunt as a language and a costume becomes a way for Shakespeare to explore the definitions of the self, only increasingly now it has become linked to desire.

No story reflects the use of erotic hunting for psychological exploration more than Shakespeare's adaptation of "Venus and Adonis."[8] In this poem, roles are again reversed: the goddess is the hunter, and the young male is the hunter-hunted.

When the theaters of London had to be closed because of the plague in 1592, the young Shakespeare probably wrote this short erotic poem about two hunters in love. In his lifetime, the poem was the most popular piece he wrote. He called it the "first heir of my invention," which was either an exaggeration or a mistake, and dedicated it to the playboy earl of Southampton. At least nine editions appeared before Shakespeare died in 1616. Many conservative modern critics have been embarrassed by the immodesty of the poem. But not his more worldly and aristocratic contemporary readers. Shakespeare turned to Ovid for his lessons in love and sensuality, but as was always the case when Shakespeare borrowed from a source, he took his teacher to school.

In Shakespeare's version of the famous story, Venus is a forty-something huntress with a taste for young boys. And "rose-cheeked Adonis" is not much of a hero, at least in epic terms, as he was in other versions of the story, or in the paintings of the story by the Italian masters like Titian, Veronese, or Carracci, all of whom produced virile images of Adonis, rising to the hunt, or lounging in the arms of the Queen of Love. In Shakespeare, he's a barely pubescent boy, pretty and delicate and easily manhandled by the amorous Amazon who loves him.

This poem articulates the tensions between hunting and love, manliness and effeminacy, and it plays with them in witty and sophisticated ways. The boyish Adonis aspires to manliness—"Hunting he love'd, and love he laugh'd to scorn" (4). There is a question in this coming-of-age story about what would make a man. Adonis has two choices. The boar hunt—the epic hunt, the hard hunt, the manly hunt. Or, as Venus recommends, the hunt for the hare—the erotic hunt, the soft hunt, the more "effeminate" hunt.

Shakespeare takes us down some new, eccentric paths in the garden of love. The situation—aged huntress loving a resistant and adolescent hunter—becomes a study in the psychology of sexuality—both of female appetite and male fear of sexuality.

In Shakespeare's poem, a purple sunrise comes to the dewy Garden of Adonis. Mounted on horseback, the young Adonis hies himself to the chase. His cheeks are rosy—he's more beautiful than the nymphs of the countryside. He's a "tender boy," almost effeminate in being a "Stain to all nymphs, more lovely than a man" (9). He's even more beautiful than Venus herself. His ambition is to hunt the "toothy boar," symbol of manliness. All this recalls the ancient motif of hunting as a form of the rejection of love—hearkening to Pentheus and Hippolytus in the classics. The epic hunt marks out a psychological territory apart from love, a manliness that disdains love. Shakespeare takes us beyond this easy dichotomy, though. He may have come centuries before Freud, but Shakespeare, like him, is a master at exploring the expressed and hidden feelings in the human heart. Shakespeare uses Adonis the erstwhile hunter as a study in the dynamics of identity and sexual fear. In Shakespeare's story, we're exploring the shadowlands of the psyche.[9]

Plus, Shakespeare clearly revels in the exploration of this relation between horny goddess and prissy hunter, clearly delights in the scene and its possibilities. Venus is "sick-thoughted," and it's the soft hunt of love she's after. She makes straight for Adonis, who's on his horse. She promises Adonis "A thousand honey secrets" if he'll get off his horse. He refuses, and she pulls him down on top of her—"O, how quick is love!" (38).

It is the Queen of Love who is active, aggressive, pursuing. She inverts the standard clichés of the passive female, and it's she who uses predatory language for her desire.

She pounces upon him like a predator—"governing him in strength, but not in lust." She feeds upon him as an "empty eagle," shaking her wings, devouring all she can of his flesh, kissing his cheek, his brow, his chin. Perched above the tumbled and panting Adonis, Venus "feedeth on the steam, as on a prey" (63). Wrapped by her arms, Adonis is a bird "in a tangled net."

He loathes her lust, and denounces it. He is virtuous, even prudish. Her "time-beguiling sport" is to him shameful. His marble coolness only fuels her lust. In the most famous passage of the poem—often quoted and alluded to in the Renaissance—she tries to seduce him in hunting language, witty and nearly irresistible, even to the prudish and standoffish Adonis. She embraces him in her arms, locks her "lily fingers one in one," and makes an invitation that even the effete Adonis can barely resist:

> "Fondling," she saith, "since I have hemm'd thee here
> Within the circuit of this ivory pale,
> I'll be the park, and thou shalt be my deer:
> Feed where thou wilt, on mountain or in dale;
> Graze on my lips, and if those hills be dry,
> Stray lower, where the pleasant fountains lie.

"Within this limit is relief enough,
Sweet bottom grass and high delightful plain,
Round rising hillocks, brakes obscure and rough,
To shelter thee from tempest and from rain:
    Then be my deer, since I am such a park,
    No dog shall rouse thee, though a thousand bark."

At this Adonis smiles as in disdain,
That in each cheek appears a pretty dimple,
Love made those hollows, if himself were slain. . . . (231–43)

The lexicon of venery provides the goddess with the imagery of seduction—the "pale" or fence of her arms, enclosing a park where the deer
Adonis can find "relief" or pasture to feed. The body of nature is the body
of love's desire, and all the erogenous zones of the female body are contained within the limit, the ivory pale, of this hunt.

The habitat of sex is the female body.

Even more than that, Shakespeare seems to delight in the way Adonis
smiles. His cheeks dimple with a smile, home for Cupid—a very pretty
"conceit" of the sort Renaissance courtiers delighted in. Shakespeare's interest is in the dynamics of desire between two people.

And within the psyche of a single male—Adonis. He scorns her. He
flees her. There is something unmanly about his refusal to love: "Thou art
no man," says Venus, "though of a man's complexion" (215).

The psychology of sex—the terrain Shakespeare enters with these
hunters—is a terra incognita from which there's no easy return. Despite
the "honey secrets" and witty "grazing," it's also a frightening world for
Adonis. That's a main point in the poem: the venereal and the venatic
male are neither of them what they appear.

Shakespeare moves into psychic shadows. What is Adonis afraid of?
Venus, yes, but also himself. The great irony is that, for all his aspiration to
conventional manliness through the boar hunt, he's at least pre-sexual and
probably impotent.

At one point, Venus pulls the prim and prudish boy onto her as she
falls on her back. She grows excited. Even he seems ready to go, trading
horse for goddess. But as Shakespeare says,

All is imaginary she doth prove,
He will not manage her, although he mount her,
    Than worse than Tantalus' is her annoy,
    To clip [embrace] Elysium and to lack her joy. (597–600)

Adonis is impotent, and he's had enough. Tomorrow, he suddenly announces to her, he'll hunt the boar.

He abandons her. The next morning, she awakes to the sounds of baying dogs, and her fantasy runs rampant, imagining her beautiful Adonis dead. She rushes to the scene of the boar hunt, and nearly passes out at what she sees. Adonis lies dead and mangled in the woods, killed by the "foul, grim and urchin-snouted boar."

Adonis's encounter with the boar has, in Venus's eyes, erotic suggestiveness. The boar, she imagines, had "thought to kiss him, and hath kill'd him so":

> " 'Tis true, 'tis true, thus was Adonis slain:
> He ran upon the boar with his sharp spear,
> Who did not whet his teeth at him again,
> But by a kiss thought to persuade him there;
>   And nousling in his flank, the loving swine
>   Sheath'd unaware the tusk in his soft groin.
>
> "Had I been tooth'd like him, I must confess,
> With kissing him I should have kill'd him first,
> But he is dead, and never did he bless
> My youth with his, the more I am accurs'd."
>   With this she falleth in the place she stood,
>   And stains her face with his congealed blood. (1111–21)

In an unmistakably erotic description, the boar "sheaths" his tusk, "nuzzles" his "tooth" into the "soft groin" of the boyish Adonis. The Roman Ovid has, in the Elizabethan Shakespeare, become strangely Greek. The homoerotic pleasures of the hunt lend a whole new meaning to Adonis's reluctance to love Venus. And it is given the cast of the fear of women, a sense that their sexuality might be, like the Queen of Love Venus, aggressive and oppressive and predatory.

Venus can only envy the boar.

Venus flies off to mourn her lost love, and prophesies that from now on love will be sweet in the beginning, but unsavory in the end. It will be "Ne'er settled equally," and always be "fickle, false, and full of fraud" (1140).

In our post-Freudian age, we're perhaps cynical about a landscape shot through with desire. But Shakespeare and the Renaissance introduced us to this terrain, in which each psychic trail is redolent of some lingering dream. In this labyrinth of desire, a garden of sudden turns, sex and death become our central mystery, our greatest preoccupation. The wound of the boar might stand for the wound that we cannot separate now, in our imaginations, from desire itself. The boar might have kissed him, but he killed him first. We are likely to be drawn, unconsciously and inexorably, to exactly that desire that lies near one of our deepest wounds. The hunting scene has left us with the pose of Venus above the mangled body of her youthful lover, the iconology of an erotics of exquisite pain. Her face is "stained" with his "congealed blood."[10]

In his comedies, sonnets, and longer narrative poems, Shakespeare focuses on the study of desire, and the drive toward identity, as the critic Northrop Frye has argued, is often erotic.[11] In Ovid, Love was a god, universal and absolute, depersonalized and static, emotionally simple and morally predictable. It is essentially one thing, settling alike upon Apollo as well as Jove, heroes and shepherds with its strength. In Shakespeare, and the Renaissance, Eros is concrete and individualized, dynamic and emotionally complex, even suspenseful.[12] It is precisely in these eccentricities of desire that we discover the uniqueness of character, the secrets of our selves. For Ovid, the *magister amoris*, Eros meant essentially one thing—a story of hunting culminating in domination or its reversal. In Shakespeare, seduction has grown more complex, a twisting narrative of push and pull, a negotiation. The distribution of power between the two lovers is much of the erotic element, and the key to the psychology of each lover is how he or she is placed in the dynamics of power and desire.

The hunter as an erotic figure has followed a strange new trail into the psyche, pursuing a fantastic beast. There is no longer one hunter's story. Each hunter has his or her own trail through the garden of sexual fantasy.

3

Another sexual fantasy. This one is my own. It describes a stage in my own erotic and sometimes erratic odyssey toward self-realization. And it suggests how these cultural stages—like the one described by Shakespeare's "Venus and Adonis"—condition our own personal psychic evolution.

Like so many men in this late part of the twentieth century, my own genuine search for self began in earnest with divorce. Divorce and failed relationships seem to be the catastrophes that spur many men's personal awakenings. My own divorce propelled me into the whole world of single life—and forced me to scrutinize carefully who I was, what I wanted, what my relations, physical and emotional, were like. When I began to look beneath the received conventions, behind the easy postures and standard roles men can so easily fall into, I began to examine what my imagination was really like.

I remember dating one woman shortly after the divorce. Sarah was a masseuse. She was an expert in jin shin jyutsu, an Asiatic form of massage, using very light touch on various spots on the body. The idea is that these most delicate of touches will loosen energy paths. And you can get grounded in your body.

Sarah and I traveled to Mexico together, and stayed on the beach in the Baja. I was full of wild energy, feeling emotionally wounded and free after the divorce. One evening, Sarah offered to give me a jin shin jyutsu massage. I agreed, and was lucky enough to get several over our week in Mexico. They were wonderful. Frequently, she would barely touch me, not even touch me. I would relax into the experience. And my imagination would begin to take over. I moved into a magical place, partway between dream and sleep. And the images would begin to flow through my mind, vivid and clear and rich.

As Sarah moved her fingertips over points on my body—forehead and heart, pelvis and wrist—I began to picture myself on a beach. With me were three other men, all close friends. We were holding hands and dancing wildly in a circle. And I was screaming on the beach, "No one can touch me! No one can touch me!"

And we whirled like dervishes under a darkened sky.

The ironies here are thick. There I was, in my fantasy: wanting to be free and wild and untouchable. Untouchable. And yet the fantasy was produced under the gentle touch of Sarah.

Like Adonis, I wanted to run wild with the hounds, metaphorically speaking. At the time, this inner image of myself felt powerful, independent, and liberating. I wanted to be with men, away from women and the wounds of love. I look back on that time now in my life, and I can see that I was free but afraid. I did not want to be vulnerable and hurt.

One psychological function of the hunting metaphor for sexuality and intimacy is that it allows men to simultaneously act upon the need for human closeness and maintain some distance. The hunt, as sexual and courtly game, does what any game between people does—it allows a certain form of closeness, while preserving emotional distance. All of this is unstated and indirect—the emotional needs and fears remain implicit. In my own case, I loved being with a woman, but not really involved. I was passionate, but my very emotional nakedness was a sort of shield. I have had to move beyond this state for my own emotional growth.

The hunting metaphor gives men a way of confining closeness to sex— it marks a boundary for them between sex and emotions. It gives the illusion of control—a control that can so easily be upset, and that is always threatened. Hence, the ongoing anxiety. Men legitimate, as it were, regular excursions into an emotional wilderness, without allowing their emotions to get too deeply invested.

This is one of the laws of desire, one which every hunter knows in his heart: in desire, always make sure that you're not the one who gets hurt.

That fantasy marks an important psychic stage for me. I have had to come a long way from there. I have had to learn enormous amounts about myself, about trust, and about connecting desire, not just to the body, but also to the heart. This is the difficult transition from desire to love, from physical to emotional intimacy.

<h1 style="text-align:center">4</h1>

If medieval France was the birthplace of courtly love, Italy seems to have been its nursery. Medieval and Renaissance Italy is a kind of imaginative locus for the greatest loves—the Florentine Dante in his love for Beatrice, and, in literature, Romeo and Juliet. Another love, that of the Italian Francis Petrarch for the Frenchwoman Laura, transformed the emotional history of men.

She was a married woman, in all probability, if she truly existed. We don't know who she was. The poet never revealed her real identity. He says only that he first saw her in Avignon, in the Church of Saint Claire, on the sixth of April, 1327. It was in the morning. Twenty-one years later, on the exact same date, in 1348, she died. "A light was withdrawn from our day," said the poet, Francis Petrarch, of the woman he loved deeply, but always from afar. It was a relationship that was never consummated, never realized in life. It was lived entirely through the poetry that Petrarch wrote of her—the "scattered rhymes" that were the wailing of his heart.[13]

He called her Laura, a fictitious name, a pun on the "laurel" that was Apollo's symbol of poetic fame. In the *Rime*, Petrarch wrote 317 sonnets, 29 *canzones*, 7 ballads, and 4 madrigals largely to her beauty and her ennobling effect on his soul. Though he neither invented the sonnet form nor the type of courtly love he wrote of in his poetry, he made the sonnet the genre of love for countless courtiers over the next three centuries, and courtly love the ideal of love for equally long. (Indeed, when those two lovely youths later meet at the masked ball in the Capulets' house, that warm evening in Verona, Romeo and Juliet speak of their budding love, they even speak to each other in the Petrarchan language of love—a famous sonnet spoken in dialogue.)

Petrarch's most famous sonnet describes his love as the quest for the most beautiful and elusive of all creatures in the forest. He is a hunter who does not seem to hunt, driven by "Amor" or Cupid to "follow the wild beast that I adore."[14]

His "hunt" is an emotional discipline, and the hunter learns to forgo his lust for the magical creature of his desire.

> A pure white doe in an emerald glade
> Appeared to me, with two antlers of gold,
> Between two streams, under a laurel's shade,
> At sunrise, in the season's bitter cold.
>
> Her sight was so suavely merciless
> That I left work to follow her at leisure,
> Like the miser who looking for his treasure
> Sweetens with that delight his bitterness.
>
> Around her neck "Do not touch me"
> Was written with topaz and diamond stone,
> "My Caesar's will has been to make me free."
>
> Already toward noon had climbed the sun,
> My weary eyes were not sated to see,
> When I fell in the stream and she was gone.
>   (Petrarch, *Rime* 190)

Una candida cerva—this creature has moved out of mythology and the hunting manuals of the time. She is a fabulous creature in the bestiary of the heart, and is drawn from hunting lore. The white doe is a combination of Diana's deer and Caesar's deer, and she is off-limits to hunters. Many magic deer populate the history of Europe, and since the ancients, deer have been associated with metaphors of love.[15]

This doe has other near mythological relatives, not the least of which is the white unicorn that hunters pursued throughout Europe, which because of its purity could be captured only by a virgin, in whose lap the pursued unicorn would rest its head. Petrarch can see the white deer, but he cannot touch her. He is not really hunting, and he would love to gaze on her forever, his desire stuck in his eyes, a voyeur really, but a voyeur who has made looking into a high art. She escapes, he's devoted, and when she flees, he falls comically in the stream.

The Petrarchan posture is a transforming conception in the history of desire. The sonnet was powerful as a way of giving immediate expression to the desire of the self and its ambitions. Petrarch gave us an ideal posture for loving—perfect, chaste, impossible, painful. Love is the exquisite suffering of the noble heart. In his idealization of chaste desire and an even more chaste woman, Petrarch created images of the unattainable as the goal of love. What's important to note about this love is that it created a new form of masculinity. Desire itself became the way the new and more modern male could express himself, could actually create himself in the intensity of his feeling. It is the condition of this incarnation of masculine identity.[16]

The play of desire became embodied in elaborate courtship games. The contradictions in this desire were handed down in the clichés of courtly love—the icy fire of Petrarchan love. Yet, not the least of the contradictions, the real discipline and aesthetic of Petrarchan love, was that sexual desire must always be chaste, and that pleasure was inextricably laced with pain. Death was the true culmination of love. It might be said that Diana, goddess of the hunt and chastity, has been sexualized.

Petrarch did not invent this love. Closely related to courtly love, idealization of Eros began a century and a half earlier, sometime between 1174 and 1186. At least, that's when it was codified in a handbook, a manual for lovers, called *The Art of Courtly Love*; and even here, the author places hunting at the center of men's desire. In the prologue, Andreas Capellanus, the author, calls love "this kind of hunting." And when he describes where this love comes from, he says the rules were discovered in the mouths of two hunting dogs that a knight found when he captured a "hawk on a golden perch" in the heart of King Arthur's castle. And this hawk, this bird of love, enables him magically to win the hand of his mistress, who had disdained him until this moment. Courtly love is related to the chivalric quest of the knight-errant, pursuing and killing the dangerous beast for his mistress—it is the tale of Saint George slaying the dragon, which was repeated over and over and over again in many guises.

Something new had entered the hearts of European men. They were being trained in a new way of feeling, a way that inaugurated a new aesthetic of the self for men in relationship to their feelings and to others. The game of love acquired certain rules, certain proprieties—men learned how to conduct themselves, in this idealized world of courtly love, with a new elegance. This new hunt elevated courtly dalliance itself into an art form, a code for proper courtly behavior. Sir Thomas Wyatt in England loves with his sonnets, using the metaphors of the hunt. "They flee from me who sometime did me seek," he laments, "with naked foot stalking in my chamber." Wyatt reminisces about a sweet encounter with this deer, when she loved him back. She took him in her arms, "long and small," and kissed him: "Dear heart," she says, with a double cynegetic pun, "how like you this?"[17]

Jean Ronsard and Edmund Spenser and Andrew Marvell, Jean Passerat and Du Bellay—for these and many other poets the hunt (especially for deer) became a well-established metaphor for an idealized romanticism and a code of conduct. It was a discourse of the new man's desire. It taught men how to sublimate illicit sexual feeling into socially appropriate forms—idealization of the mistress rendered loving safe.[18]

In Shakespeare's romantic comedies, from first to last, men are smitten with this posture in desire, and the women undertake a sexual education of their men. They must be more or less systematically educated in how to feel.

These men often learn to approach love in the guise of hunters. *Love's Labor's Lost*, one of Shakespeare's very early comedies, already contains most of the elements of his great comedies that come later in the 1590s. Never as popular, because more cumbersome and less delightful in its wit and story as the great comedies, *Love's Labor's Lost* nevertheless shows Shakespeare actually working out the forms of love that will inevitably be associated with his drama—great romantic love. What can pass unnoticed, because we take it so largely for granted, is that as the men are being educated in the nature of women and love, we in the audience have been educated. Modern scholarship has focused on how Shakespeare actually worked out in his drama ways of loving between men and women, and made the drama both a reflection of and an education in new cultural standards for love, to new imaginative models of desire.[19]

In *Love's Labor's Lost*, the King of Navarre and three of his courtiers vow in the opening scene to withdraw from society and the world and pledge themselves to an intellectual life. They'll even renounce women. Though the courtiers hold back at first, they give in to the king, and promise. No sooner have they done so, than the Princess of France arrives with three ladies-in-waiting, and they put the men's silly pledge to the test. As the clown in the play—often the spokesperson for homely, not to say comic, truths—puts it, "Such is the simplicity of man to hearken after the flesh" (1.1.216).

The men turn into foolish lovers almost immediately. As in other great Shakespearean comedies, the resistance of men to love is a prelude to a major fall.

After only one encounter with the women, one of the men laments that he has already "turn'd sonnet."

In *Love's Labor's Lost*, the courtship moves through a masked party and culminates in a hunting scene in the woods. The Princess of France proves the best hunter, and it's clear throughout—in puns as well as banter between men and women—that the real hunting going on here is between the sexes. The princess is not only fair game, she is a fair shot as well. She hunts only for reputation and convention, in reality pitying the "poor deer." The dialogue makes clear she is both idealized and feared. She says,

> But come, the bow: now mercy goes to kill,
> And shooting well is then accounted ill. . . .
> And out of question so it is sometimes:
> Glory grows guilty of detested crimes,
> When for fame's sake, for praise, an outward part,
> We bend to that the working of the heart;
> As I for praise alone now seek to spill
> The poor deer's blood, that my heart means no ill.

To which her male servant replies:

> Do not curst wives hold that self-sovereignty
> Only for praise's sake, when they strive to be
> Lords o'er their lords?
>
> (4.1.24–38)

The movement goes double in this elaborate emotional and sexual game: the more the female is idealized, the more her power is feared. This is, in the words of the play, "sport by sport o'erthrown."[20]

One theory holds is that this scene, perhaps written in 1592, was modeled on Queen Elizabeth. A passionate hunter, often spending every other day in the field, the virgin queen had immense powers—she could both shoot and dominate her men. She customarily spent her summers on "progresses" through her realm, staying at country estates of her nobility, who "entertained" in lavish and opulent extravagances. The hunting of the Princess of France may have been inspired by an account of the "Queenes Maiestie in Progresse, at Cowdray in Sussex, by . . . Lord Montacute" in 1591. With a "great traine," the queen arrived on a Saturday, August 14, and was royally entertained with banquets and allegorical productions. On Monday, with nymphs singing to her of "chast desires," her "Maiestie shot at the deere." She saw sixteen bucks "pulled down with Greyhoundes."[21]

Elizabeth was simultaneously the idealized and feared, chaste and loving woman—much like Diana in antiquity. She was the inaccessible object of male desire, longed for and feared. The entertainment, like Shakespeare's play, was an elaborate courtship game that elicits and controls men's desire. It's a contradictory set of ideas, very hard to deal with psychologically. Women were actually given power and control of men's desire in this idealization of desire,[22] a control which leaves men emotionally very vulnerable.

Where there was this idealized, disciplined desire, lust and terror were often trailing in its wake. When these hunters engaged their virtuous lovers, they were in for some of the surprises, some of the dark secrets of love. It is part of the structure of this controlled desire that fearful beasts await them in the night. Both in courtship and in marriage, neither unruly sexual energy nor fear of betrayal could be contained by the ideals. In fact, the more both courtship and marriage were idealized, the more susceptible men became to their own sexual fears. The flip side of this ideal was another demonic sexual hunt.

Men feared the new incarnation of Actaeon—the horned man, or, the cuckold. The betrayed husband is a perfect figure of a new erotic hunter, in whom we can explore the dark side of this new erotic ideal.

5

When Actaeon, the hunter who was turned into a stag when he glimpsed the naked Diana bathing with her nymphs, entered the worlds of Petrarch and Shakespeare, he changed from a hunter to a pathetic, betrayed husband. The image of this hunter underwent one of those cultural transformations in which myths register changing social values and personal consciousness. Petrarch's Actaeon, like the figure of Actaeon evoked by Falstaff at the end of *The Merry Wives of Windsor*, is a cuckold. He is an animal figure—made a beast by his ungovernable desire. He is a man wearing stag's horns—the victim of the sexual hunt.[23]

Through the cuckold, the hunt became associated with the newly emerging social institution—romantic love culminating in marriage. The demonic hunt, inherited from Pentheus and Dionysus in antiquity, took on a distinctly modern cast. Still associated with sexual appetite, it embodied all men's fears about their wives' sexuality, on which so much of their own masculinity had come to depend with the increasing role of eros in modern identity.

The most influential and important study of English Renaissance sexuality continues to be that done by Lawrence Stone, *The Family, Sex and Marriage in England, 1500–1800.*[24] Though his conclusions have been debated and qualified, the main points of his argument remain solid. He demonstrates that important shifts have taken place in the importance and meaning of the family in modern social life. During the period, Stone shows that a shift gradually took place, leading away from the arranged marriages, based on property alliances, of the medieval aristocracy, to an emphasis on the married couple in a more isolated nuclear family. These changes were accompanied by a corresponding shift away from the official idealization in the medieval monastic praise of celibacy and virginity to the Renaissance and Protestant glorification of "holy matrimony." The change is not absolute and sudden, but one of ideals and prestige, of emphasis and degree.

The result of this change is that, not only in the Petrarchan idealization of women and chaste desire, but in marriage itself as a social institution, men found their identities more closely tied to their women—wives and daughters particularly—than felt comfortable. It is the great psychological irony of this highly patriarchal period, when men argued strenuously for their preeminence, that as fathers and rulers men conceded their private and emotional identities as men to women. Marriage was a way of bringing order and coherence to sexual chaos and the apparent bestial horrors of sexual desire. It's a widely accepted principle concerning Shakespeare's plays that he establishes marriage as the great goal of desire, and symbol of social coherence.[25] The conflict between the men and women in Shakespeare's plays, for instance, drives directly to the question of the man's identity. Their power as men was grounded in their ability to control their women at home, which is often in doubt. As Coppélia Kahn puts it, "Shakespeare's works reflect and voice a masculine anxiety about the uses of patriarchal power over women, specifically about men's control over women's sexuality, which arises from this disparity between men's social dominance and their peculiar emotional vulnerability to women."[26]

The most concrete fear men have of women, in Shakespeare, is receiving "the horns." One critic has argued that the horns, like the female tongue, is the phallus displaced, to locations where it doesn't belong.[27] The great anxiety suffered by men, the anxiety that finds obsessive reiteration throughout the period, is the fear of being cuckolded. It appears to have been imagined, by the men of the time, as a virtual plague. Michel de Montaigne, the great French philosopher of the sixteenth century, speaks thus of the common plight of cuckoldry for married men:

I know a hundred Cuckolds. . . . Seest thou not how many honest men, even in thy presence, are spoken of and touched with this reproach? . . . For no man is spared. And even Ladies will scoffe and prattle of it. And what do they now adaies more willingly flout at, then at any well composed and peaceable marriage? There is none of you all but hath made one Cuckold or another. . . .[28]

This common affliction of men—another intersection between hunters, beasts, and erotics—is found throughout Shakespeare, and is the main worry men have about marriage. So powerful is the fear of the cuckold's horns, it keeps them from marrying. The early comedy *Love's Labor's Lost* ends with a song between Winter and Spring, between the owl and the "cuckoo." The comedies may culminate in marriage, but that does not dispell the fear of their women's sexuality:

> When daisies pied, and violets blue,
> And lady-smocks all silver white,
> And cuckoo-buds of yellow hue,
> Do paint the meadows with delight,
> The cuckoo then on every tree
> Mocks married men; for thus sings he,
>   "Cuckoo;
> Cuckoo; cuckoo"—O word of fear,
> Unpleasing to married ear!
>   (5.2.894–902)

According to the OED, the word *cuckold* for a betrayed husband finds its earliest use about 1250, in a poem called "The Owl and the Nightingale." The word is thought to come from the cuckoo bird, famous in natural history—especially Renaissance lore—as the bird which lays its eggs in another species' nest, to have its young raised by false parents. The switch is that the cuckold is not the male seducer moving from one nest to another, but the victim who may unwittingly raise another man's child.

This is a uniquely male fear. It is something that happens to husbands, not wives.

If the wife remains faithful to her husband, she tacitly validates his virility. If she does not, she calls his sexual prowess into question. He winds up with highly visible horns on his head, the object of mockery by the entire community. These are the emblems of shame—phallic symbols, signs of the male's impugned and debased virility, as surely as the stag's horns certify the masculinity of the great hunter who takes down a ten-point buck. The men in Shakespeare's comedies know this, and it is the reiterated obsession with them. Once he's betrothed to Beatrice and reconciled to the marriage he has so strenuously resisted, Benedick in *Much Ado about Nothing* summarizes his resignation to marriage and the phallic fears he suffers in a single joke, his last comment on the marriage in the play: "There is no staff more reverent than one tipp'd with horn" (5.4.123–24).[29]

Cuckoldry is a central preoccupation of the men in the Renaissance and in Shakespeare's drama. Like Benedick in *Much Ado*, the men in the comedies resist marriage because they are afraid of being cuckolded—of being, as is said early on in the play, "horn-mad" (1.1.270). As the movement of the comedies is toward marriage, the men must allay their fears, and often in the plays what was once terror becomes a comic praise of the inevitable horns of the married man. At the end of *As You Like It*, for example, the exiled men in the forest return to camp from a successful hunting foray. The men give the hunter who killed the deer the "leather skin and horns to wear," and "sing him home":

> Take thou no scorn to wear the horn,
> It was a crest ere thou wast born,
> Thy father's father wore it,
> And thy father bore it.
> The horn, the horn, the lusty horn
> Is not a thing to laugh to scorn.
>   (4.2.13–18)

The "lusty horn" is a visible symbol of male virility—in hunting and in cuckoldry.

The family is one of Shakespeare's central themes, and male anxiety about women's sexuality—that "chaste treasure," in Laertes's phrase to Ophelia—becomes the center of several of his most powerful tragedies. It is not in Shakespeare the actuality of betrayal he worries about. It is the male fantasy of betrayal that is his theme. It is the way in which cuckoldry has become one of the central fixations of male identity that he explores—the demon under the pretty face of Cupid.

Hamlet's primary anxiety, even more horrible and certainly prior to his knowledge that his father was killed, is the revolting idea that his mother slept with Claudius, his uncle, whom he loathes as a goatlike "satyr." *Othello* though is the main document in Shakespeare's obsession with the theme of women's appetites. As he falls into Iago's well-designed trap, Othello loads his speech with hunting images:

> If I do prove her haggard,
> Though that her jesses were my dear heart strings,
> I'ld whistle her off, and let her down the wind
> To prey at fortune. . . .
>   I am abus'd, and my relief
> Must be to loathe her. O curse of marriage!
> That we can call these delicate creatures ours,
> And not their appetites! I had rather be a toad
> And live upon the vapor of a dungeon
> Than keep a corner in the thing I love
> For others' uses. Yet 'tis the plague of great ones. . . .
> Even then this forked plague is fated to us
> When we do quicken. Look where she comes.
>   (3.3.260–77)

The haggard is a female falcon taken as an adult from the wild, and notoriously difficult to tame for falconry. The "forked plague" is, of course, the cuckold's horns.

They are common among men. At least that's what Iago claims. The plague is a mental torture, the most horrible anxiety for a man. Iago pesters the sore in Othello's mind with vicious pleasure:

> *Oth.* A horned man's a monster and a beast.
> *Iago.* There's many a beast then in a populous city. . . .
>   Good sir, be a man;
> Think every bearded fellow that's but yok'd
> May draw with you. There's millions now alive
> That nightly lie in those unproper beds
> Which they dare swear peculiar; your case is better.
> O, 'tis the spite of hell, the fiend's arch-mock,
> To lip a wanton in a secure couch,
> And to suppose her chaste! . . .
>   Marry, patience,
> Or I shall say y' are all in all in spleen,
> And nothing of a man.
>   (4.1.62–88)

"Nothing of a man": Iago elides the horrible fantasy of being cuckolded with emasculation. Othello is losing his manliness in his passion.[30]

The drive toward male identity in Shakespeare is pocked and patterned by sexual issues. These in turn are associated with the control of women. Bachelors and married men alike cringe under Othello's terror—that they cannot control women's sexuality. Wherever the cuckold appears in Shakespeare—whether in the wife Adriana in *The Comedy of Errors*, to the wives in *Merry Wives*, to women at the end of *The Merchant of Venice*, to the false accusations made against Hero in *Much Ado*, to Leontes's tortured imaginations that his wife is pregnant by his best friend in *The Winter's Tale*—the virulent men attack women who are true and honest. It is the dark side of the male imagination—the connections between male identity and male desire—that Shakespeare anatomizes in penetrating ways.

Men's investment in women's sexuality cuts across generations as well as genders. One of the men's preoccupations in Shakespeare's plays is if the father can know his own child. This worry ranges from jokes and asides to its culminating horrors and anguish in *The Winter's Tale*, where Leontes believes his children are not his own. "My brows," he moans, and turns to his son Mamillius. "Art thou my boy?" (1.2.119)

It doesn't require a Shakespeare or a Montaigne to tell us how murderous jealousy can be. We have only to read the papers—O.J. Simpson comes to mind—or search our own hearts and experience to know the pain of sexual betrayal. At the same time, Montaigne posed a question that we would be smart to consider: what if "we not be lesse Cuckoldes if we lesse feared to be so? according to womens conditions: whom inhibition inciteth, and restraint inviteth."[31] He wonders, that is, if somehow men don't make themselves the greater victim as the cuckold by their very fears. He suggests that there might be some other way in which men might love and desire in heterosexual relationships that would make them less susceptible to the thing they fear so much. The point here is that cuckoldry—the fear of betrayal—is part of the structure of desire as it was experienced, and invented, during the Renaissance.

Men learned to locate women and desire, not merely in the center of their hearts, but in the center of their identities. She became, for heterosexual love, central in the intimate emotions of the male. As Shakespeare suggests in his plays, it's the woman who teaches men, guides men, tutors men in what it means to feel. Most men today I'm sure would recognize just this—in intimate relationships, in relationships involving intimate feelings, they turn to women, not other men.

But the very emphasis placed upon desire and sexuality and women made men vulnerable, and afraid. They turn to the woman for closeness and an affirmation of their virility, but must hedge their fears with distance also. That distance can be established by the idealization of women and virginity among bachelors, and the control of wives by married men. But their appetite must be controlled. Or the result is the cuckold's "hunt." Sex has become an artifact in the male imagination.

It's easy to see, in this psychology of desire, how the hunt as an image would be so apt. Not only can it express both the ideal and grotesque dimensions of this erotic imagination, but it is deployed as a sort of erotic strategy. In its finely tuned modulations, in its sudden reversals of tone and meaning, it can both inflame desire and lay bare the worst nightmares of betrayal. It defines both the light and the dark, the ideal and the transgression. The language of the hunt gave to men a great if dubious psychological gift—it gave them a way to express a new need for intimacy, and simultaneously a strategy for asserting distance and control. The cuckold was born out of the complexities of this new erotic hunt. A new beast of prey, he took his place in the unnatural history of sex.

6

What seems to be clear is that hunting is a language that establishes boundaries between the hunter and the hunted. The boundaries shift in different periods and cultures, and the two elements that the boundaries establish—identity and relationship—shift with the changing of the boundaries. But in establishing boundaries, what is marked out is the me and the not-me. The hunter establishes what is the Other, and how he will relate to it. Women, animals, and nature itself can figure easily into the category of the Other—the enemy that men desire.

Hunting gives men strategies for approaching what they fear. And it set boundaries on how close they could imagine themselves being with the objects of their hunts. It gives them manly identities and sexual personae. But it limits their ability at identification. By making nature and women into the prey, into the enemy, into the object of suspicion, he set boundaries on his own emotional life.

We have inherited the hunter's vocabulary for understanding the male heart. Can it be much of a surprise, in this context, that men find it difficult to understand their own emotional urgings and needs? That they are more comfortable speaking in terms of physical than emotional intimacy? And that they'd rather not discuss physical intimacy, but boast of sexual athleticism, even if it means lying?

What has happened is that, in laying down the boundaries of these erotic hunters, men lost touch not only with nature and women, but with their own emotionality. We have, I think, displaced our emotional life onto women and beasts—they are a language we use for intimate emotions and sexual feelings. They provide the language of the "effeminate" feelings and the "bestial"' instincts. Can it be much of a surprise that men are only now learning to take charge of understanding their own emotional and psychological depths. That men find their own emotional range so constricted—to success, to scoring, to being in control?

Emotions, though, are not forces simply to control. They are simply to be experienced, as well, and in the process they lose much of their mystery—and, in the case of the feelings men most want to control, their terror. The animal and the female suggest the inner territory that we need to reclaim for ourselves, for they carry the burden of our own personal dissociations. We can begin to renew ourselves, and expand our emotional capacities, by expanding our boundaries and by approaching the margins cautiously, but not armed for battle. We can begin to search in ourselves for the feelings we tried to disown and distance. In reclaiming our own emotional lives and taking responsibility ourselves for our own sexuality, perhaps we can begin to understand ourselves more fully in terms of ourselves. We can begin to experience our own emotions, as truly and as genuinely as possible.

Only then, I think, will men begin to have more genuine relationships, since they will bring more genuine selves into the bargain.

This, it seems, is what many men are looking for in our own troubled age: a larger experience of themselves and a greater emotional intimacy with the world they inhabit and the people who share their lives.

Each of us has to sort out, either intentionally or unconsciously, how personal experience and private psychology intersect with cultural heritage. Our cultural heritage—this hunter with so many disguises—sets boundaries on how we experience ourselves. Our own emotions, even, come to us in language and images that culture has shaped. And our own most formative experiences also have shaped the way we experience our experiences, if you will. It's our job to know ourselves by knowing how we feel. We grow by leaving behind what no longer serves us well.

In my own case, over a decade of being single during the age of AIDS has constituted much of my education in masculine desire. Before a painful divorce, I'd been married for fourteen years. During this, my single decade, I came to be pretty experienced. But what I've realized is how sophisticated I can be about desire and longing, and how little I know about what it means to love.

The great poet Theodore Roethke has said that the body moves, though slowly, through desire, "we come to something without knowing why." Slowly, in that labyrinth of the soul, I've come to realize what it is I'm looking for.

The picture of one's heart's desire emerges slowly, coming often in fragments and pieces, over time. For me, it came in traveling, often to very remote places, always searching for something, searching for some part of myself that I felt I had lost.

I could not usually tell you what it was I was looking for. I loved being surprised by what I would encounter—encounters where, in the far reaches of geography and imagination, I would feel myself merge with place and moment, and feel myself burn brighter, eager always for more, growing incandescent. What I did not know at first, what I can now see and even cherish, is that I was following desire more deeply into myself.

It is, finally, only our experiences that we have, and in these experiences, we are invited to seek out ourselves. We are seized and transformed by the images that we did not know we sought.

Something similar is true in relationships. We discover ourselves in them, and through them we learn what we are looking for. In a number of relationships, I learned a little from each about who I am, how I relate, and what I need to learn.

One experience, in a particular relationship, epitomizes for me one of these transforming moments.

I had been traveling through Europe with a friend from London. Rachel and I had known each other for some time, had met when I was teaching once in London. There had always been a charge between us— something hot and exciting. As she said, she knew the minute we met that our relationship would be "dangerous." And now, some years later, we decided to travel together and see what might be possible.

We agreed on southern Spain. In Granada. Andalusia seemed to both of us a romantic land of long sunlit days, and exotic Moorish palaces, and bizarre birds like the hoopoe. Together, we chased our desires through fantasies we created.

One night, in a hotel room, we staged an impromptu performance of *Hamlet*. She was a playwright and actress, and I was her apprentice to the stage. We each took different parts. Rachel assigned them. She did most of them. I got bit parts, Osric, for example, and Rosencrantz and Guildenstern. Scene by scene, she enacted a frenetic parody of the play, with a whole acting troupe's worth of English accents, racing through scenes. It was comic and hysterical, and I was laughing like a madman watching her tear through the lines.

And she wanted to play a game. You have a choice between two possibilities, she said one day in the car, and you must choose one. Which would you rather be: lips or tongue?

Apple or snake?

Safe or sorry?

At night, we loved to wander the dark streets of medieval European towns. I loved kissing her under lamplights.

In Granada, one cool morning we visited a compelling exhibition in the old part of town of medieval techniques of torture. In shocked disbelief, we gaped at metal devices of torture and social control; "bridles" to stop the tongues of shrews, chastity belts to prevent wives' cuckolding jealous husbands, and "breast rippers" for witches and women condemned of "libidinous acts" were among the many on display.[32]

When we emerged from the exhibition, Rachel saw the gorgeous bird we were hoping to see, the hoopoe. It flew right by the door of the exhibition building, over the fence, and disappeared into the thick trees of a wooded ravine. We sprinted behind it, up a trail through the ravine. The trail led uphill, slowly climbing above the treetops, giving a view down upon the ravine and the trees. Before long, I could see the birds, beautiful creatures, about the size of a crow, with orangish pink bodies and broad wings, strikingly patterned black and white, like a zebra.

A light rain began to fall on us. On the other side of the river, across from us, we could see where gypsies had made their homes in the caves on the hill.

For many years I had wanted to see a hoopoe, one of the most beautiful creatures in Europe. They are named after their call, a deep and resonant hooping that floated through the woods that afternoon. I hoped to see them perched, as well, or up close. In addition to their softly stunning plumage, they have a crest on their heads that they can raise up, also patterned in a bold black and white. Their beak too is long and curved. They are at once elegant and clownish in appearance, beautiful and, with crest up, wildly madcap.

In medieval bestiaries—those ancient encyclopedias of spiritual meanings in the guise of animal lore—the showy hoopoes were symbols of caring and nurturing, "doing mutual kindnesses to each other," as the bestiary translated by T. H. White puts it.[33] It is a magical moment when insight is accompanied by a sense of emotional resonance, when head and heart come together, when we step into alignment with ourselves, the world, and each other. In that ravine, I was full of caring for bird and place and person.

At some point, a thunderstorm drenched us, but it didn't matter. All afternoon we chased hoopoes through the ravine, with gypsies on the far hill, soaked by a thunderstorm.

The feeling was like planets orbiting into alignment, exerting an irresistible gravitational pull. My body was pulled and tugged by forces beyond it, pulling me outside of myself. We have lost an intimacy that we're trying to rediscover, and the ability to feel closeness with nature, with others, and with ourselves are the same. At moments like this one, with Rachel and the hoopoes and the ravine, I feel the pain of what I have missed, an ache that rises up inside me. Men have forgotten that they are defined by what they are connected to, not only by what they can control. Open up, and boom! Love: it's inside you, and you are everything you love.

Love is not a general and impersonal state. Nor is it an irresistible god, however young and waggish and playful. Those are conceptions that have helped men understand their own experience. Love is a capacity people develop. People learn to love, and they come to believe in their own ability to love by loving in specific relationships, in specific places, with specific people. Perhaps, in the history of masculinity, this capacity to love was somehow transferred in men's emotional lives onto women, the "*candida cerva*." Perhaps, as well, men never really learned to experience love from the inside. It has always seemed somehow alien in the way it's been conceived—external and alien.

Whatever the exact explanation, men's distance from their own emotions is not something that can be explained away by genetics or an appeal to nature. Men can learn to experience themselves more deeply, and to reclaim their own emotional lives as their own, internal and personal. My own over the last few years has been just this process of moving more deeply into my own emotional capacity, opening it up, experiencing it more fully. It takes work for men, so stereotypically categorized as reasonable and active, so stereotypically imagined as distant from their own emotions, to move through the walls that they've erected between themselves and their feelings. Their own metaphors, their own ways of conceptualizing masculinity, are one of the most tenacious of those walls, because they make the task itself seem impossible. But it's not.

I remember being in the ravine with hoopoes flying beneath me. I rose and fell, in and out of myself, past convention and all its confirming ways. I would rise into something larger than myself, and fall back into a larger self. This capacity to love is cultivated by rising past boundaries, like birds rising out of the trees. And then we settle back, having gotten a better view of the landscape.

With centuries of history and conditioning, in which men have used metaphors like the hunt to mark the boundaries between themselves and their feelings, they have marked off a large part of themselves as alien from themselves. The other that we imagine outside of ourselves is the other inside, looking back at us. And it's time to begin to recapture this part of our own experience, or perhaps to claim it as ours for the first time.

The path forward is marked for each person by a unique intersection of cultural heritage and personal experience, by the shadows of history and autobiography.

That particular relationship with Rachel careened joyfully and riotously through a number of towns in Europe, and through a wide range of feelings. It also careened into a sad and difficult good-bye. Lust, love, and loss—the three L's of relationships. Yet each relationship offers the chance to work out an emotional issue, to address an emotional stage that has to be dealt with, at least if your eyes and heart are open. Each can mark a step forward, offering what needs to be learned at that stage. Rachel had given me a great gift—an image of what I was after. In the Spanish ravine, chasing hoopoes in a thunderstorm, I felt one of those arrivals that serve, through time, as guideposts in the long journey to self-discovery.

7

"THAT MASTER CREATION ... INDEPENDENT MANHOOD"

"From my boyhood upwards I have been taxed by the facetious with shooting-madness, and truly a most delightful mania I have ever found it."
—William Cornwallis Harris, *Wild Sports of Southern Africa*[1]

... he had seen men come of age before and it always moved him. It was not a matter of their twenty-first birthday. It had taken a strange chance of hunting, a sudden precipitation into action without opportunity for worrying beforehand, to bring this about with Macomber. ... Look at the beggar now, Wilson thought. It's that some of them stay little boys so long, Wilson thought. Sometimes all their lives. Their figures stay so boyish when they're fifty. The great American boy-men. Damned strange people. Damned strange fellow. Probably meant the end of cuckoldry now. Well, that would be a damned good thing. ... Be a damned fine eater now. He'd seen it in the war work the same way. More of a change than any loss of virginity. Fear gone like an operation. Something else grew in its place. Main thing a man had. Made him into a man. Women knew it too. No bloody fear.
—Ernest Hemingway, "The Short Happy Life of Francis Macomber"[2]

There is nothing understated or demure about anyone in the van. The woman next to me has dyed her long hair a flaming vermilion, spiced with cayenne orange. She sits next to a guy from Yorkshire, his very pale face flushed pink, two rings in his nose, and very long dreadlocks, streaked in peacock blue and cadmium yellow. Smiling, I crowd into the van, jostling shoulders with a crew of students from the University of Nottingham. They all wear thrift-store army jackets, and their hair is either cropped military short, or is an artificial riot of intensely dyed colors. They carry enough metal in nose rings and pierced ears to open a small jewelry store. It's a postpunk gang, fitted for harassment and sedition.

We're heading into the heart of eighteenth-century, pastoral England. A fine mist hangs over the muddy December fields, and filtered sun hovers amid the branches of the leafless oaks in the idyllic fields of Leicestershire. The famous Quorn hounds are hunting today, and this group of "hunt saboteurs" is out to ruin their day.

We watch the velvet-suited hunters assemble in a field adjacent to the town of Knowlton. They're elegant in their beautiful red jackets, white cravats, and breeches. Tail-wagging hounds chivy impatiently at the feet of perfectly groomed thoroughbred horses. Two men carry long whips, to control the hounds—they're the "whippers-in." The master of foxhounds wears a black top hat, and his hands, in white gloves, work the reins of his bay horse nervously. He eyes the van, and us inside it, suspiciously, as we idle slowly past the assembling hunters—in England, to hunt means to ride to hounds after foxes. To hunt pheasant, for example, is called "shooting." The contrast between them and us—aristocrats and punk students—could not be more striking. Or more comical. Here is a society tearing at its own hierarchical seams, so carefully cultivated over the last several centuries, and what it is extruding is anger and distrust.

They try to ignore us, and head off to hounds. We careen after them in the van, and when the hounds hightail it across an open field, we pile out of the van and tear off after them on foot. I'm wearing rubber Wellingtons, and I run along with the saboteurs, laughing from time to time like crazy. There are the hounds heading to a stand of beeches in the far distance. An elegant party of hunters sits idly on their horses, on a far hill, waiting for the hounds to flush a fox. And here we come, in hot pursuit, this motley crew schlepping and screaming through the muddy English fields.

The Quorn pack has an ancient and distinguished pedigree. They are the original foxhounds, first bred in the Midlands by one Hugo Meynell (it rhymes poetically with kennel). He's the reputed "father of foxhunting." In 1753, he acquired Quorndon Hall, and began breeding hounds fast enough to keep up with the speedy red fox. As a result, he elevated foxhunting—disdained as vermin chasing by Elizabethan nobles—into a fast-paced, hard-riding chase. Ideally suited to the chase, Leicestershire's expansive open fields soon became the heartland of the sport. It grew prodigiously. By 1775 Meynell was famous throughout England. Quorn, and Leicestershire, became synonymous with foxhunting.

Nigel, the Yorkshire student, tells me that the Quorn is still a favorite pack of the royal family. Until an unhappy recent event, when members of the hunt were filmed for TV in the unsporting act of digging a fox from a hole and killing it, Prince Charles was a member. But foxhunting remains the last truly aristocratic survivor of the medieval trilogy of hunting, hawking, and tournaments.

We have been chasing the hunters and their hounds around all morning in the van and on foot without much noticeable effect when, pursuing them as two riders and hounds pursue a fox into a thick stand of oak and beech, we spot Harry Cross running through the field. He seems to have materialized out of nowhere. The saboteurs really hit their stride when the legendary Harry Cross shows up on the scene. He's enormously fit, and I'm told that he runs after hounds and foxes all day, virtually seven days a week. He's just there, and then he runs with the hounds right *into* the woods. The rest of us ditch the van once again and make a mad dash across the field. The thick mud on my boots is like blocks of concrete, but I slog doggedly on.

I'm laughing, actually, as I arrive next to one of the saboteurs on the edge of the copse. Horsemen have begun to gather not far from us, waiting on their horses for the fox to be roused from its covert.

As the saboteurs gather together, they begin to halloo. Nigel has a hunting horn, and he blows hard. He imitates the notes that would call the dogs in. Others blow horns, too, and the rest yell hunting calls at the dogs. The idea is to confuse the dogs, to call them off the fox.

Compared to the stately if slightly anxious poise of the hunters, we make a cacophonous crew. I'm thinking, This is Ken Kesey's Merry Pranksters versus Anthony Trollope.

Then we begin milling around the hunters on their horses. Some of the saboteurs talk with them. Urge them to leave the hunt. "We're just trying to stop things from being killed," a student, head shaved, dressed in proletariat gray, explains. His audience is a woman, who's got a very maternal worry on her face about her barely-teenage daughter beside her.

Sometimes, these confrontations have erupted in violence. The saboteurs claim they've been beaten up by the hunters. But today everything is quite peaceful.

I approach one horseman, who seems to be doing some foxhunting of a different sort, hanging back with a very pretty, aristocratic-looking woman. He's wearing tweeds, the casual hunting look, not the more formal red velvet. When I approach, he volunteers that he's a horse trainer, and he's giving her lessons on jumping fences. I ask him why he hunts fox.

"It's part of rural England," he replies. "If people don't like it, they should stay in the towns."

Nigel hears this response, and gets furious. "I'm from the country, the heart of Sherwood Forest," he spews. "And I resent being told to stay in the town. Most of these hunters are doctors, lawyers, rich people from towns. Let 'em stay there."

In its heyday, in the early nineteenth century, a mystique had come to hang about this sport. It was a national institution, replacing the deer chase and the hare chase as the preferred rural hunt. A myth surrounded it. It was the sport of the upper classes, like that archetypal country Tory and fox-hunter, Squire Western in Joseph Fielding's *Tom Jones*. It was simultaneously associated with the landed aristocracy and with a kind of social democracy—at once the sport of gentlemen and open to all out in the country. The hunting field was the meeting place for all the social classes. James II hunted fox, and one Sir Richard was reputed to have spent one-third of a million pounds on foxhunting; on the other end of the spectrum, in the nineteenth century a dustman grew famous riding to hounds beside the upper crust, who made something of a mascot of him. The hunting mythos pervades the great eighteenth-century novel, *Tom Jones*. Tom Jones himself is praised for "his great love of hunting," and the fox-hunt itself characterized as "rough and masculine [in] Nature." As it grew in popularity and prestige, its apologists found in foxhunting the cradle of all the hardy and manly virtues that increasingly came to be associated with country life. As cities grew, the country became the seat of all manner of nostalgia and ideology. The English countryside came more and more to be thought of as the source of those very qualities that made England the owner of empire. Manliness and nationalism—they were equated with foxes and the sweet loveliness of hedgerows to be jumped.

It was this manly British foxhunter who was the spectral and mythological presence that accounted for British prestige throughout the world. He drew his vigor and health from the English countryside, as well as his moral spine. And he was regularly contrasted with city-dwelling, effeminate foreigners. One famous sportsman, the journalist R. S. Surtees, opened his book on hunting with the observation: "I respect hunting in whatever shape it appears: it is a manly and a wholesome exercise, and seems by nature designed to be the amusement of the Briton." It's a theme that was to be repeated throughout the next two centuries, with variations: the country breeds hardy, ruddy-cheeked men; the city, effete and effeminate Bond Street men. Or Frenchmen.[3]

From their vantage high in the saddles, the hunters in red must see the saboteurs as a ragtag proof of the decline of the British Empire. Surely, we appear to them the rabble that gives the lie to the theory of the harmony of the classes in the English countryside. But the sport of the squires had been a point of class conflict in the English countryside under the succession of two dozen Game Laws from 1671 to 1831, by which the country squires contrived to maintain property requirements for hunting, and thus support their own privilege. The laws were more restrictive, and the punishments more severe, than they had been in five hundred years. Poaching intensified as a form of protest, and intellectuals like Thomas Carlyle and William Cobbett made hunting the focus of an entire social system's injustice. The fury against landowners was habitually linked with foxhunting. Poaching was succeeded by more explicit protests, as the *Edinburgh Review* noted early in the nineteenth century: "an internecine war between gamekeepers and marauders of game;—the whole country flung into brawls and convulsions, for the unjust and exorbitant pleasures of country gentlemen."[4]

In the rapidly changing world of the eighteenth and nineteenth centuries, hunting adapted its forms and rationales. Its association with manliness was not lost, but transformed. Manliness, like hunting, took new guises, called forth by new social needs and justifications, always contested. The connection with manliness and nationality became new and much more important parts of the new myth and new ideals of the modern hunter. Still, as the industrial world created greater challenges to men's self-confidence and complacency, the conservative morality of foxhunting proved suggestive but ultimately inadequate to meet the demands of the new, more mobile and bourgeois society being born. Foxhunting was too domestic, too tame finally for the massive energies being released by capitalism, science, and global conquest. The British foxhunter exported his ideals around the globe, and, as I'll show, they found their most powerful incarnation in the figure who transformed and then embodied manhood in the nineteenth century—that figure of imperial grandeur, the big-game hunter. Manhood graduated from the country club to the global stage. The lion hunter replaced the foxhunter as the emblem of British glory.

Nigel does not buy any of the high rhetoric by which its champions defend the foxhunt. He has a sardonic description: "Just an aristocratic upper-class dogfight—dogs versus fox-canines."

As I talk to the trainer, a hullabaloo rises down the muddy path from where we're standing. The fox has been chased from cover and has raced right in front of the standing saboteurs and mounted horsemen. The hounds are now behind him in full cry. We go screaming after the whole pack—first fox, then hounds, then horses, then saboteurs. It must make quite a sight in the quiet English countryside.

That afternoon we see three foxes given one sort of "run" or another. The worst abuses we take are the sneers of the top-hatted master of foxhounds. We manage to thoroughly disrupt his day: no foxes taken, and no run undisturbed.

The most memorable moment comes late in the afternoon. The sun is going down, with golden shafts of light pouring across the quaint country-side, bathing the stuccoed and thatched houses in the soft light of winter. The air is cold—ice is forming on ponds in the fields. We are in the van, patrolling the roads, on the lookout for the hunters, whom we've lost. As the air thickens with heavy wetness, we spot the horses far across a softly undulating field. They're at full gallop.

The driver of the van hits the gas, and we fly toward a spot, up the country road, where it appears the fox will cross. The van whines, going al-together too fast, leaning through sharp turns. This is the most danger I've felt all day. Suddenly, we see the red fox running for his life across the green grass. I see the fox first. He's headed right toward us. There's barely time to make out details—a flash of fur, black tip, touch of white. Was that the tail I saw?

The driver slams on the brakes. We skid. The fox bolts onto the black-top road just in front of us. We skid to a stop and watch the fox disappear into the field on the other side. Here come the hunters. Meanwhile, the van is stopped in the middle of their way, horn blasting, and all the saboteurs cheering in wild joy.

Horsepower versus horses, dyed red hair versus Tory red coats: a post-modern vanguard in a postindustrial age, harassing the guardians of a preindustrial culture. It's impossible not to see the social symbolism in the saboteurs' efforts to save the fox. In saving foxes, the student-saboteurs want to subvert a national icon at this far and declining end of the British Empire.

2

"Are you enjoying our safari?" Louis asks me, puffing on his pipe and lean-ing against a glacial rock, dumped here thousands of years ago. He smiles amiably and breathes heavily. He's exhausted. His fleshy face is a cheerful, exercised pink. We've hardly started to hunt.

"It is very dangerous, no, this hunt for the *isard*?"

Louis laughs outright, speaking in English, his eyes alive with wry charm and irrepressible delight. Louis, a pilot with Air France, is in his af-fluent fifties. In pursuit of the agile *isard*, he's lugging through the high mountains a frame that's not so much out of shape as it is addicted to bour-geois, worldly pleasures—he got that well-fed smile behind a table, not hunting.

"For a very old hunter like me," Louis says in tones dripping with cool French irony, "the *isard* is very strenuous."

He pauses. Puffs on his pipe.

"You see the effects of too much pipe smoking." Louis exudes a very engaging sang-froid. "And too much whiskey. Well, maybe not too much whiskey."

In the knapsack he carries on his back, he's fully prepared for the day: at least four different pâtés, several fine cheeses, bread, and a Beaujolais nouveau premier, just in yesterday. Behind us, the sprawling views from the open mountain peaks reveal a few oaks, junipers with red berries, rocks purple with lichens, and melting fields of snow under a warm November sun. We look down upon the Cerdagne country, and the Vallie du Carol, with its tiny village of Carol. The mountains, in the Pyrenees, are called the Soulane du Carol. *Soulane* means they have a sunny exposure, and the sky is a soft blue, like larkspurs.

The *isard* graze on the high slopes. It's the local name for the chamois, a goatlike animal that's a symbol of these mountains themselves, one of the first creatures of the hunt in Europe. Men take pride in their trophies of the *isard*—its upright horns, rounded backward like oversize fishhooks, identify the men who take them as men of the mountains. Though the shrinking globe, high-powered rifles, and easy transportation have made the *isard* less of a hunter's challenge, in the nineteenth century it was a prized creature, object of expeditions and safaris into the Alps and Pyrenees. Lord Byron evokes the *isard* in the wild wanderings of his hero Manfred, and makes the creature a symbol of the hero's romantic quest. I've seen drawings of them in prehistoric caves—Las Chimineas, for example, in the mountains of Spain. They are creatures of the highest elevations, their faces framed in a dramatic V by two black swaths.

Occasionally, they glance toward us, in complacent and grass-chewing stares.

We've been stalking this group of *isard* for hours, and it's beginning to look like they might elude us. This late in the season, they are wary. Nevertheless, the genial Louis is delighted with himself and the scenery.

"In all things," he says expansively, "it is a pleasure to hunt the *isard*. My colleagues at work must have a lunch meeting today in the office. But for me, the life is here."

Louis's entire rhetoric of the hunt adopts the arguments of the big-game hunters of the nineteenth century, and the way they used the hunt to reinvent manhood for a tired and overworked age. Far-flung safaris and treks into national wildernesses gave men their escape from the soft lives of the city, and gave them the chance to be real men in the primitive wilds. Manhood faced a crisis, men thought. And they made the hunt into a new ethical imperative, one of the primary expressions of a new social agenda.

This new hunter was very much a self-conscious creation of men worried about their futures. In the cities of an industrializing Europe and America, men lost their bearings, grew dispirited as stockbrokers, clerks, and scriveners like Bartleby. The figure of the wilderness hunter promised to redeem the effete city-bred man who'd lost his way.

Unlike anytime before, hunting was explicitly adduced as the agency of self-generation for men. It was a program and an ideology for the re-creation of manliness. Hunting would redeem men from the very world they were busy creating at home in the cities.

As the great safaris to far continents offered men an escape from the mundane lives and routine jobs of the city, the hunt also reflected the values and the psychology of the society that was evolving. If it seemed to offer men an alternative lifestyle to emerging capitalism, it also promised to teach them the very values they would need to rise to the top of that new jungle which they were learning to regard with such anxiety and ambivalence—the city.

This new hunt, at once imperial and nationalistic, enabled men to link their own identities with the identity of the nation—the new hero became the lone male, making his independent way in the wilderness. Connecting science with ethics and politics, nature became a school, offering tender young men the rough tutorials they needed for success in the world. It would fit them for any job in the city. It offered an apprenticeship for politician and entrepreneur alike. Nature, and its allied sciences, would be the mistress of those virile nations that emerged to rule the world, and what it taught them was the discipline of violence and blood.

The big-game hunter, embarked upon a two-hundred-year career, became an enduring cultural type. As Hemingway was to make explicit, when the new hunter went into the woods, the one beast he really sought was his own lost masculinity.

Consider the remarkably successful Boy Scouts. This organization was invented in 1908 by R. S. S. Baden-Powell, an English army officer and voracious hunter. It was quickly imported into the United States as the Woodcraft Movement of Ernest Thompson Seton. In his fabulously successful *Scouting for Boys*, one of the best-sellers of the twentieth century, Baden-Powell proposed a program of training for boys that would save them from the emasculating pressures of modern society. To solve the "boy problem," Baden-Powell urged training in frontier lore:

> These are the frontiersmen of all parts of the Empire. The "trappers" of North America, hunters of Central Africa, the British pioneers, explorers, and missionaries over Asia and all the wild parts of the world, the

bushmen and drovers of Australia, the constabulary of North-West
Canada and of South Africa—all these are peace scouts, real *men* in
every sense of the word, and thoroughly up on scout craft, i.e., they understand living in jungles, and they can find their way anywhere, are
able to read meaning from the smallest signs and foot tracks; they know
how to look after their health when far away from any doctors, are
strong and plucky, and ready to face any danger, and always keen to
help each other. They are accustomed to take their lives in their hands,
and to fling them down without hesitation if they can help their country
by doing so.[5]

Hunting offered the promise of becoming "real *men*," a phrase that in itself
carries the irony of the project that these theorists of the new masculinity
undertook. The phrase, like the emerging cult of masculinity that it reflected and helped create, is a sign of the self-consciousness of this new
program and the notions of virility it espoused.

Baden-Powell developed most of his notions about boy scouts from the
scouting troops he'd seen during the siege of Mafeking during the Boer
War in South Africa, in 1899–1900. The idea was that boys could be organized so that they did deeds useful to themselves and to the empire. The
frontiersman and the backwoodsman were Baden-Powell's models, and
their moral worth is acquired through "contact with Nature."

Baden-Powell traces the genealogy of this new hunter to all the earlier
"scouts" in English history. His progenitors ranged from the chivalric
knights like Richard Coeur de Lion, to adventurers like Sir Walter
Raleigh, to Frederick Selous in modern times, who created the Selous
Scouts in South Africa. The man to emulate is the heroic hunter, trained in
animals' names and calls, in stalking, and in spooring, as well as other
frontier lore. For modern boys, Baden-Powell offers Rudyard Kipling's
character, Kim, who taught the lesson "that boys should be trained to manliness and not be allowed to drift into being poor spirited wasters who can
only look on at men's work."[6]

The manly ethic of scouting placed energetic action above reflection,
vigor above sentiment, toughness above softness, "pluck" above cowardliness, duty against ease, guilelessness against subtlety, technology against
beastliness. And King George above all: "Almost every race, every kind of
man, black, white, or yellow, in the world furnishes subjects of King
George V." In America, Ernest Thompson Seton founded the Boy Scouts
of America in 1910, and in four years had one hundred thousand members.
By 1917, the number had tripled. As this extremely popular nature writer
put it in his introduction, "*manhood*, not *scholarship*, is the first aim of ed-

ucation" (his italics). The Boy Scouts were also called the "American Knights in Buckskin."[7]

This crisis in masculinity had been brewing throughout the century, and we continue to live in its shadow. In many ways, the current men's movement reflects the same concerns and themes as the spokesmen for masculinity between 1860 and 1920.

As a contemporary writer about the Boy Scouts of America put it, the scouts offered men "an organized effort to make big men of little boys . . . to aid in the development of that master creation, high principled, clean and clear thinking, independent manhood."[8]

"That master creation . . . independent manhood": at the end of the century, this man was a hunter. Men like Theodore Roosevelt, an icon of American manhood for millions of men, turned to the hunter for a way out of modern "degeneracy." Men like Buffalo Bill Cody offered models from the Western frontier—now vanished but appearing on stage in Chicago and London—of the unrestrained glories of uncompromised maleness. Earlier versions of manhood in the United States had stressed men's spiritual nature, or the more passive and social virtues, like benevolence and piety. But the change that took place with the image of the hunter over the century, and coalesced in the Boy Scout and the buckskinned hunter, stressed physical courage and a focus on the self-made man.

This hunter was partly a reaction to the industrialization of modern society. The "nonmasculine" and sedentary jobs increased in number. They were "brain work," and insulted masculine self-identity. Clerical workers and salespeople and government employees increased between 1880 and 1910 from 756,000 to 5.6 million. Plus, women dominated the upbringing of boys more and more, as well as controlling their education in school. Combine this with the close of the frontier, which Frederick Jackson Turner proclaimed in his famous essay in 1893, and men suffered this nagging sense of a vanishing virility. Of impotence and emasculation.[9]

The frontier was gone, and with it, many worried that manhood was gone, too.

The theorists of masculinity understood the problems they were facing in a number of ways. They thought of the conditions as "overcivilization." They thought of it as the "Europeanization" of American culture. But mostly, men thought of their plight in terms of the "feminization" of culture.[10]

Men were being raised by strong-willed Victorian women who demanded new jobs, new voting rights, and new access to male power. And these new women threw a sociosexual wrench into men's identities. In Henry James's novel of 1886, *The Bostonians*, the male protagonist Basil

Ransom defines the underlying sexual anxiety that gripped the men of the age, "the most damnable feminisation":

> The whole generation is womanized, the masculine tone is passing out of the world; it's a feminine, a nervous, hysterical, chattering, canting age, an age of hollow phrases and false delicacy and exaggerated solicitudes and coddled sensibilities, which if we don't soon look out, will usher in the reign of mediocrity, of the feeblest and flattest and the most pretentious that has ever been. The masculine character . . . that is what I want to preserve, or rather, as I may say, to recover; and I must tell you that I don't in the least care what becomes of you ladies while I make the attempt![11]

The modern hunter was the front line of defense against the woman within.

The embodiment of this exaggerated concern with masculinity, and an important spokesman in the process of reifying sex roles into ideologies, was Theodore Roosevelt. His life was transformed when he stepped off the train in North Dakota in 1883, after a horrible bout of asthma and a severe political disappointment in New York, to go buffalo hunting on the plains. He discovered the frontier and the men of the West. Their lives, especially of hunting, he identified with the manly virtues necessary for great men and great races. The hunter and cowboy "does not have an overwrought fear of shedding blood," Roosevelt writes. "He possesses, in fact, few of the emasculated, milk-and-water moralities admired by the pseudo-philanthropists; but he does possess, to a very high degree, the stern, manly qualities that are invaluable to a nation."[12] Roosevelt was a national hero to millions of men who saw in his vigor, his courage, and his direct rhetoric the salvation of masculine identity from the threats of an artificial economy and an overly feminized culture.

The trip to the Dakotas transformed Roosevelt's life and imagination. His bold manliness was the antidote men craved. Perhaps it was the antidote to his own sense of being a sissy, of conquering female weakness represented by his own "neurasthenia." Roosevelt's famous speech to a Chicago men's club at the end of the century on "The Strenuous Life" praised the man with "iron in his blood," who "does not shrink from danger, from hardship, or from bitter toil, and who out of these wins the splendid ultimate triumph." He borrowed the idea of the Rough Rider from the shows of that famous Great Plains hunter and scout, Buffalo Bill. His entire persona was part of a nation's renewed quest for masculine fulfillment, rescuing the American male from the threat of too much femininity.

Theodore Roosevelt was on the National Council of the Boy Scouts. This organization gave men a way to reassert control over boys. And it wasn't boys, any longer, that men were distinguished from. It was from women. The word "sissy," for example, had formerly meant a little sister. At the beginning of this century, it defined a new creature—the effeminate boy.[13]

In England, Baden-Powell also feared that men had slipped into effeminacy: "Every boy ought to learn to shoot and obey orders," Baden-Powell intoned in the beginning in *Scouting*, "else he is no more good when a war breaks out than an old woman."[14] The cure to weakness was the rough classroom of nature.

When the frontier died, the hunter was reborn in men's imagination and literature, and the new myth of the hunter overwhelmed all sense of fact. Owen Wister dedicated his novel *The Virginian* (1902) to Theodore Roosevelt. From Jack London and *The Call of the Wild* (1903) to Edgar Rice Burroughs and his first Tarzan books (1912), boys entered manhood and the twentieth century with aggressive virile fantasies of the wild, all-male life.

As both species and gender, man triumphed in the nineteenth century, according to Baden-Powell and Roosevelt and countless other hunting men, because he was willing to shoot, and more important, because he was willing to kill. Great men made great nations, and hunting taught the lessons of mastery, closely connected to national pride. It was this skill that made the Euro-American men, in the phrase from the pioneer in big-game hunting, Gordon Cumming, "the white lords of creation."[15]

Traditional manhood had undergone a crisis, and the hunter emerged to rescue the male from this female captivity. The hunting male became the embodiment, not of class as for the medieval aristocrat or en-classical squire. Rather, the white male body came to stand for race, species, and gender. The physical prowess of the hunter was idolized. His special knowledge was violence. Violence became a kind of science, a discipline, an ethic. Predatory competition and Social Darwinism were the melancholy laws of nature, and both were thought to be synonymous with manliness.[16]

"The Great White Hunter" is the legacy of these global wanderers. I still know men who refer to themselves by this phrase after hunting, say, elk. I have students who use it in describing a formative hunting trip with their fathers in a college essay. Usually, men are slightly self-conscious and even furtive when they use it, aware of the vaguely racist overtones, but the language and the masculine image have endured for several generations of middle-class and upper-class men. My friend Louis, the jovial French hunter, is invoking this tradition when he asks me, through his laughter, how I like our "safari." His irony is appropriate, since there's nothing even vaguely dangerous or heroic or even really adventurous about this day in the mountains. Still, the word is a lens for this experience. You don't have to hunt the far-flung corners of the world to imagine yourself pursuing big game like the forefathers in Africa and Asia.

Louis was just taking a day off work to chase *isard* in the mountains. He's huffing and puffing and hanging back, and by midday, I've begun to doubt that he'll even get to fire his rifle. But Louis would still have a trick or two to show me today. I shouldn't have underestimated my delightful hedonist hunter.

3

With Louis and me is a guide, Alain, and a biologist, Claude. To hunt in the French Pyrenees, you must have a state-employed guide with you who actually chooses for you the particular creature you will kill. This is part of the biological management of the hunt. Today, Alain says we are to try to choose a young male. Sometime after noon, Alain and Claude select an *isard* that looks promising, and we creep across the rocks and grasses to try to get close enough for Louis to get a shot. This proves trickier than you might expect. The chosen isard eyes us impassively as we slink toward him, and with several others in his loose herd, he frequently turns a white rump to us and ambles with blithe disregard a bit farther off. It's as if, in his confidence, he's almost taunting us.

We creep up a large rock that shields us from several *isard*, grazing almost directly across from us, on the other side of a shallow cut in the mountain's flank—a small group of six *isard*, and of those, one stands exposed against the blue sky on a huge rock outcropping.

Louis downplays the importance of the kill, but I know it matters to him. "The first shot," he says to me, "is for you."

Alain signals for Claude and me to wait behind the rock. He and Louis slither on their bellies toward the *isard*. Louis is well equipped—he has a very expensive Austrian Manchliner rifle with four-power Swarovski scope—the best ballistics and optics. But he has to get within about 120 yards for a good shot.

At about 80 yards, Louis and Alain confer briefly. Louis takes aim, and his shot echoes across the ravine. He misses. The *isard* leaps like a goat from the rock. Claude, next to me, laughs aloud at Louis. A second shot. I can't see the *isard* anymore. Claude guffaws. "He missed it, not once, but twice," he says to me.

Louis and Alain are jumping across the scree by now, and soon they wave us over too. Louis is standing above an *isard*, his face shimmering with pride.

"Sorry about the first shot, old man," he says as we catch up. "It was for you"—he's speaking to me now. "But it was stress. I was too excited. Plus, I was too winded."

Manhood continues to be carried in the quality of a shot, as well as the price of the rifle. Louis handles the pressure with a self-deprecating and garrulous wit.

"Oh, in all things it is a pleasure," he goes on in his own not-quite-grammatical English. "A good shot, you know, makes a very definite sound. It is more satisfying than any orgasm."

He continues to banter amiably while he cuts off the testicles of the *isard*, his trophy.

Soon we are picnicking in the sun. The *isard* lies next to us, and we have spread out a blanket on the dry ground, amid the lichen-covered rocks. Louis pulls out his Beaujolais Nouveau Patrich Chubot and his pâtés. Chaffinches and partridges fly around us. The scene is magnificent and I feel quite literally above and apart from mundane life that creeps its petty pace in the villages below.

Then and there, I decide that I will hunt for something myself. When I return to the United States, I am going to hunt for deer. And I will try to kill one. There's something about hunting—about killing—that's a mystery to outsiders, opaque as steel.

I tell Louis that he has inspired me to try hunting myself. He lifts a cheerful toast to me with his superb wine. The sun is slanting now, winter and late afternoon. It skitters over the old rocks, and they flash green with lichen and light. In his own little flare of national fervor, Louis gives a perfect big-game hunters' spin to the day.

"When you go home, and hunt for your own deer," he says with an ingratiating smile, proudly, "you can remember this day and this *isard*. And you can tell your friends that French hunters are the best."

4

In 1860, England's Prince Alfred, later the duke of Edinburgh, hunted in South Africa. In the Orange Free State, a huge safari was organized on his behalf. Natives circled as many as twenty-five thousand animals and drove them toward the waiting prince. According to estimates, as many as six thousand animals were shot on that single day, and several natives were trampled to death by the charge of a terrified herd of Burchell's zebras.[17]

I find myself coming back to this story over and over, wondering what kind of culture could sanction killing on such a vast scale in a single day. And what kind of mentality. The nineteenth century glorified the figure of the hunter as never before. He took on a new force as a nexus of uniquely modern social issues—he became a showman, a politician, an ideologist, a social reformer. In an era obsessed with global expansion and global exploitation, the hunter was both the vanguard of empire and one of its chief apologists. The country squire gave way to a new image, one that was to become a primary metaphor for a conservative version of manhood.

The two excellent examples of the big-game hunter are Roualeyn Gordon Cumming and Frederick Courtenay Selous. Though not the first great white hunter, Cumming pioneered the "African myth" for big-game hunters, reveling in the persona of an unbridled and profligate killer in a paradise of game. By the time Selous arrived in Capetown a generation later, the game was nearly gone, and he adapted by transforming himself from a commercial ivory-hunter to a highly self-conscious naturalist-hunter. Both fashioned from their hunting exploits a personal myth that made them heroes for their generations of Victorian men at home. At the heart of all their activities—cutting across and unifying the themes of scientific exploration and global conquest and manly ethics—was the great law of nature these hunters discerned and disseminated: the regrettable, inexorable, and exhilarating law of violence.

Roualeyn Gordon Cumming was perhaps the most celebrated English hunter of the century. Two recent studies highlight Cumming as a paradigmatic figure of the great hunter—Harriet Ritvo's *The Animal Estate* and John MacKenzie's *The Empire of Nature.*[18] He cultivated a reputation in England through his extremely popular two-volume narrative of his hunting expeditions, *Five Years in a Hunter's Life in the Interior of South Africa*, as well as through his spectacular exhibition of trophies and his lectures, including the display in the Crystal Palace of the Great Exhibition of 1851. He advertised himself as "The Lion Hunter," and traveled the country for eight years with trophies and "curiosities" that filled nine wagons. In 1856, he fueled his fame with a shorter version of his exploits, called more dramatically *The Lion Hunter in Africa.* His contemporaries were suitably awestruck by his presence and his stories, styling him "the greatest hunter of modern times." He had a thoroughly modern knack for publicity, and the entrepreneurial energy that made him a success as a showman embodied the capitalist ideals of the age. He seems to have created, or at least marketed, the myth of the great lion hunter, shaping both the hunter's and the male imagination for several generations. As explorer of Africa and creator of the hunting myth, he liked to fancy that he "pioneered the way which others have since followed."[19]

He was a hunter from his youth in Scotland, he says, where he claims he grew weary "of hunting in a country where the game was strictly preserved, and where the continual presence of keepers and foresters took away half the charm of the chase. . . ." Rather, he longed "for the freedom of nature and the life of the wild hunter—so far preferable to that of the mere sportsman. . . ." He joined the army as a way of getting abroad, landing in Capetown as a rifleman in 1843. He quit the army to have more time for hunting in the interior.

In his Highland kilt and gray stalking cap, he was a colorful and distinctive figure on his five expeditions through the South African veld. He journeyed inland with a huge entourage, a quasi-military operation involving oxen, horses, massive Cape wagons, and Hottentot servants—the expeditions enacted a microcosm of the empire itself. What he found in the hinterlands was a fabled world. The Scotsman abroad encountered a prodigal nature, full of noble and rare species, a vast and teeming preserve of game. It was a nature seemingly waiting upon the hunter who would take possession of it. "To endeavor to form any idea of the amount of antelopes which I that day beheld were vain," Cumming writes of their astonishing numbers in migration, "but I have, nevertheless, no hesitation in stating that some hundreds of thousands of springboks were that morning within the compass of my vision." Cumming says of his hunting springbok: "Each morning and evening, we rode out and hunted springboks, killing as many as we could bring home."[20]

Shooting virtually every day, Cumming says he enjoyed "a glad feeling of unrestrained freedom" in Africa unlike any other period of his life. It isn't an exaggeration to say he was a prodigy of slaughter, chasing everything that came within his sights—and it was for his virtuosity in killing that he was famous. He killed ostriches and elephants, giraffes and wildebeests, hartebeests and boars, rhinoceroses and hippopotamuses, lions and leopards. His bag included some twenty-six species of antelopes: elands and springbok, blesbok and koodoo, steinbok and duyker, among many many others. With a particular fervor he pursued the gemsbok or oryx, a particularly beautiful antelope with long, straight horns, "which is supposed to have given rise to the fable of the unicorn."[21] He shot quaggas, a lovely zebra species, with glee. The quagga would be extinct within two decades. His hunting produced a trophy collection of a vast number of species that achieved gigantic proportions.

His encounters with lions, though, made him famous, and became the stuff of mythology. Killing a lion summarized the distinguishing character-istics of the perfect English hero: "A recklessness of death, perfect cool-ness and self-possession, an acquaintance with the disposition and manners of lions, and a tolerable knowledge of the use of the rifle."[22]

The lion was the animal par excellence for big-game hunters, "the justly celebrated king of beasts." For Englishmen, it had inevitable national associations—a national and imperial icon. Two lions rampant rise on ei-ther side of the heraldry of the royal device. Two lions guard the base of that pillar to the empire, Nelson's Column in Trafalgar Square. In his vivid encounters with lions, Cumming fashioned the "overpoweringly exciting pastime of hunting" into the paradigmatic test of modern manhood. The lone male defeated the king of the jungle by superior intelligence, cool, and technology. His story of a lion hunt is an existential confrontation with death itself.

Mad to hunt a lion, Cumming had been scouring an area through tor-rential storms for a few days, riding in a vicinity where he suspected from the wariness of game that a lion was hiding. When he finally sighted her, he writes, "Spurring my good and lively steed, and shouting to my men to fol-low, I flew across the plain, and, being fortunately mounted on Colesberg, the flower of my stud, I gained upon her [the lioness] at every stride. This to me was a joyful moment, and I at once made up my mind that she or I must die."[23] She had an "imposing appearance" at a broad and level *vlei,* a swampy watering hole. But Cumming pursued her implacably. She turned to growl at him—"deep-drawn, murderous growls." This she did in a futile attempt to intimidate him.

Cumming dismounted and approached her. He had his "boy" Kleinboy with one rifle, and his friend Stofolus with another. The lion, he says, put them in a "precious stew," and his men had faces of "a ghastly paleness." He had "a painful feeling that I could place no reliance on them."

In the climactic moment, the lion approached within sixty yards of the men, and kept advancing. Cumming shot, and the ball struck her in the chest, "upon which she charged with an appalling roar, and in the twinkling of an eye she was in the midst of us."

Stofolus's rifle exploded in his hand. Kleinboy "danced about like a duck in a gale." The lioness leaped upon Colesberg, Cumming's horse, and cut his ribs and haunches with her "horrid teeth and claws." But Cumming remained the picture of cool in the midst of the colonial chaos: "I was very cool and steady, and did not feel in the least degree nervous, having fortu-nately great confidence in my own shooting; but I must confess, when the whole affair was over, I felt that it was a very awful situation, and attended with extreme peril, as I had no friend with me on whom I could rely."[24] The natives could be counted upon to flee. The great hunter had only himself to depend upon in the moment of crisis.

The scene is contrived to show the cowardliness of other nations, including the natives—illustrative of the superiority of the British as men and as hunters. Cumming wrote with unmitigated racism of the natives who accompanied him into the wilds, and he frequently beat them mercilessly. For readers, this heavily dramatized account with the lion must have offered a vicarious reenactment of imperial conquest itself.

It is this solitary encounter with the beast that the big-game hunters delighted to tell, and that the safaris themselves were structured to produce. This lion was within a "few paces" of Cumming when he dropped her dead on the plain. He was cool in the encounter, but lingered grotesquely over her death throes. "In the struggles of death she half turned on her back, and stretched her neck and fore arms convulsively, when she fell back to her former position; her mighty arms hung powerless by her side, her lower jaw fell, blood streamed from her mouth, and she expired."[25] He took a macabre pleasure in violence and death. These hunters liked the death throes of their prey. In such highly dramatized and quasi-allegorical encounters, the cool of the solitary man in the wilderness contrasts with the bloody savagery of the beast. As Ritvo shows, the hunter dominated the natural world by virtue of his willingness to indulge in a delight with raw power and naked violence—which "underlay the serene majesty of empire."[26]

Even in the abundance of Africa, the game could not sustain such wholesale slaughter as Cumming and others like him inflicted on it. By 1872, when Frederick Courtenay Selous arrived in South Africa, barely a generation later, the game was nearly done.

Selous was an enormously popular figure, the product and personification of the African myth for later generations of Victorians. As Cumming had fired his imagination as a boy with his vivid stories of terrorizing lions, so Selous was the model for countless British boys coming of age. He was a celebrated hero. Selous was the original of the popular Allan Quartermain in H. Rider Haggard's books for boys. His lecture tours sold out, and his tales of encounters with lions were greeted with cheers. Unlike Cumming and Buffalo Bill, he tried to eschew the more flamboyant antics of the hunter showmen—he resisted demonstrating lion kills, for instance. But he carried with him mounted trophies on his lectures to enhance his prestige and authority. His biography was written by J. G. Millais, painter and hunter and son of the famous Pre-Raphaelite painter John Millais. According to Millais, "Thus when he spoke either in public or private life, he spoke direct from his heart and experience, and Men recognized the Man."[27]

Later in his hunting career, Selous was guide to such men as Theodore Roosevelt and the Baron Lionel Rothschild. Roosevelt said Selous was the embodiment of a manly country: "It is well for any country to produce men of such a type; and if there are enough of them the nation need fear no decadence."[28]

His three most popular books were *A Hunter's Wanderings in Africa* (1881), *Travel and Adventure in South-East Africa* (1893), and *African Nature Notes and Reminiscences* (1908). He included a proud tally of his kills during the 1870s in an appendix at the end of *A Hunter's Wanderings*, for which he took some severe criticism. Over three years, the number of game animals—excluding elephants—was 548 to Selous alone. As an elephant hunter, his skill was prodigious. Between 1872 and 1874, Selous shipped one hundred thousand pounds of ivory out of Matabeleland. At about 50 pounds per animal, this "white gold" was the equivalent of over two thousand animals. Much of it may have been traded ivory. Selous and other hunters regularly blamed the natives, whom they supplied with guns, for the loss of wildlife in Africa, but Europe's appetite for ivory (for billiard balls and piano keys, among other things) was the real cause.[29]

When his widow donated his own private collection of trophies and animals to the British Museum, an exquisite collection containing the finest specimens of several extremely rare species, there were over five hundred animals, including nineteen lions.

It was tales of risk and violence that the public clamored to hear, and Selous obliged them. In Victorian fashion, his terrifying tales of dangerous adventures and hairbreadth escapes were always suitably adorned with the proper moral. He was the daring white male, alone and making his way in a dangerous world. "I had time to realise the full horror of my position," he says of one harrowing encounter with natives. "A solitary Englishman, alone in Central Africa, in the middle of a hostile country, without blankets or anything else but what he stood in, with a rifle and four cartridges."[30]

Selous was also known as the greatest lion hunter of all time. He tried to decline the honor. In a predatory century, his total of thirty-one lions lay far below the two hundred plus of others. But he made of the kills the perfectly tailored stories out of which myths are fashioned. His most popular lion-hunting tale, from *Travel and Adventure in South-East Africa*, illustrates both the requisites of heroism in a dark African night, and the insight of the naturalist-hunter into the Darwinian laws of nature.[31]

At four o'clock in the morning, Selous awakened to the rending bellows of an ox in its death throes. The cries echoed from hill to hill across the African valley. Selous's Kaffir, for whom he had great disdain, whispered to the hunter, "Shumba, shumba." Lions were busy among the cattle doing their "butcher's work," and Selous listened to them "crunching bones" as they ate.

As the beneficent surrogate for the empire, Selous roused himself from his sleeping blankets to take vengeance on the marauding lions. The dawn was rising red against the hills. The lions, as many as five of them, were long gone by this time, but, suspecting they might return, he determined to make himself "master of the situation." His impulse was to kill these lions—"to come to terms with them." It was, he felt, a "strong and natural" desire, since he had to protect his property of Kaffirs, cattle, and horses. "A party of five lions," he says in characteristic English understatement that drips with heroic cool, "was dangerous neighbors."

As he meditated on the scene, it was the inevitable Darwinian moral that he called to mind, linking a scientific fact everywhere verified by these hunters with a moment of English patriotism. It is "Mr. A. R. Wallace," Darwin's competitor in the development of the theory of natural selection and evolution, that Selous thought of:

> I would that that distinguished naturalist, Mr. A. R. Wallace, could hear the piteous cries of an ox being slowly bitten to death by lions, or of a donkey being vivisected by hyaenas. Such cries are terrible to listen to, and revealing, as they but surely do, the frenzy of fear and agony of a dying brute, are a powerful appeal against the cold cruelty of nature's inexorable laws.

The cold cruelty of nature. It is the "inexorable laws" of nature that these hunters find throughout nature. It is the imperative of their lives, a projection of their cult of masculinity and the cult of virility among nations. Selous often thinks of Darwin, as here with Wallace, in conjunction with the patriotic impulse. He even names one of the mountains he discovers in his travels Mount Darwin, "after that illustrious Englishman whose far-reaching theories—logical conclusions based upon an enormous mass of incontrovertible facts—have revolutionized modern thought. . . ."[32]

Violence is the imperative of these hunters' lives. Their comments on nature are entangled skeins of insight and projection, reason and rationalization. Here is the self-justification for Social Darwinism—in the cult of masculinity and the competition among nations. Their urge to kill, as Selous said, was "strong and natural," and to the fittest go the evolutionary spoils. It must have justified their own killing, because they never challenged the circularity of their own thinking: that they focused on the killing in nature because they were themselves such killers. These hunters imagined themselves the avengers of the weak, whose "piteous cries" are raised with such futility against a Darwinian nature suffused with violence.

This lion-hunting adventure makes the connections between hunting, Darwinian zoology, and empire explicit. At one point, as a lion charged him, Selous remembered Edwin Landseer's lions at the base of Nelson's Column in London. Landseer was the great Victorian wildlife painter—a hunter who romanticized animals and often portrayed the hunting of animals with glorified and exaggerated violence. (See "The Otter Hunt," "Last Run of the Season," "Return from the Stag Hunt," "The Drive," "The Hunting of Chevy Chase.") Selous also named his favorite horse Nelson, after the great admiral commemorated at Trafalgar Square.

Selous decided to build a small hut from branches, lay bait, and wait for the lions through the night.

When night returned, Selous entered the hut with rifles and blankets. The moon was barely a silver crescent, and the hut was down in a valley where a thick mist hung heavily on him. As a result, he couldn't see a thing through the pall of night.

Very quickly, Selous made out a "dark shadow" with a "noiseless tread" looming over the carcass. He could not see well, despite his intense alertness. He thought it was a lion, from "the boldness of the beast" and the way it held its head low. As he was thinking, two more "misty forms" loomed on his right, coming toward the hut. A "dark something" on the right padded directly up to the flimsy hut, standing within three yards of the concealed man. Selous pointed his gun at the creature.

He fired, and the report of the rifle was "instantly dwarfed and drowned by the terrific roaring grunts of the lion, wounded unto death indeed. . . ."

But then, a second lion approached, and gave a "gentle shake" to the hut of sticks. The lion ripped one of the branches off the hut.

The lion clearly could push its way inside his hut. Selous took "instant action." He pushed the muzzle of his rifle between the poles and fired:

> Once more, and for the third time that night, the report of the rifle was answered by the most terrific grunting roars it is possible to conceive, uttered, as they were, within six feet of [my] ears. I am sorry I had not a phonograph with me in order to preserve these powerful expressions of the feelings of a wounded lion. Suddenly released in a London drawing room, I feel sure they could not fail to produce a very marked effect. Well, the expanding Medford bullet, received at such close quarters, must have given the lion a very nasty jar. I fancy that it fell over. . . .

Lions were a male target, as a playful 1908 account of two women hunting in Africa had made clear.[33] The male hunter was engaged in what was tantamount to hand-to-hand combat with five lions, yet he thought of London and its drawing-room culture of ladies and lords—dramatizing by juxtaposition his own vigorous courage and manhood. He was very self-conscious of his experience as a story, shaping his own role in his imagination for the people in London. He was the hunter wrestling with beasts, and he knows this story will itself have "a very marked effect."

Not only was Selous the very image of understated cool and perfect manly action, but his story also illustrated the superiority of humanity to the beasts. Through the night, two more lions arrived to feed on the carcass, but the darkness—like holding "one's head in a basin of ink and endeavor[ing] to read the future of Mashunaland"—was too intense to allow a shot. While one of the three wounded lions groaned in the agonies of a slow death nearby, the other lions continued feeding. "These groans and moans had no effect on the lions at the carcass," Selous reflected.

> They ate away the whole time, undisturbed by the thought of their two
> dead comrades lying stiff and stark within a few yards of them, or by the
> piteous moans of the remaining member of their family which was evi-
> dently in a dying condition. Truly they possessed two requisites of ter-
> restrial happiness—a good appetite and no conscience.[34]

Though told ironically, these lions offer an object lesson for predatory businessmen in that other Darwinian jungle—the city.

This was Selous's last great lion adventure, and it is told as a culminating story to his great contribution to the empire—what for him was the crown of his career. He led the British forces into the interior to claim Rhodesia (now Zimbabwe), preempting any Portuguese claim. He served as scout, charting the route, and it was one of his proudest achievements. In 1890, he scouted for the military expedition that built the road into the interior to Salisbury, making possible the occupation and colonization of the country. The dream of gold in the hills inspired the forces, along with the glory of service to country. It meant that Selous had to betray his old friend, the native chief LoBengula, who first allowed him to hunt elephants in that country, nearly twenty years earlier. Selous felt no remorse.

The explorations of hunting helped to give England a claim to "Rhodesia," and his expedition was another of the adventures that contribute to the manliness of the race:

Such undertakings as the expedition to and occupation of Mashunaland cannot but foster the love of adventure and enterprise, and tend to keep our national spirit young and vigourous. Like an individual, a nation must in time grow old and decay; and when once the love of adventure is so far dead within the breasts of young Englishmen that tales of dangers and difficulties successfully overcome no longer fire their blood, and induce a large percentage of them to give up ease and comfort at home and seek their fortunes in wild and distant lands, then will the decadence of England have set in. As a nation we are probably already past our prime; but that we still possess a vast fund of vigour and energy there can be no doubt.[35]

The decadence he fears is represented by the "effeminate and luxurious Portuguese."

John MacKenzie argues that natural history should not be understood as an abstract body of truth and knowledge, but as part of cultural behavior. It needs to be set in a "sociological framework," he says:

The study of natural history in this period has surely to be placed in an imperial context. In fact taxonomies never entirely conceal the human social and cultural relationships that lie behind them. This can be readily seen in examining the connections between hunting, hunters and natural history displays in the late nineteenth and early twentieth centuries. Classification meant killing, and the collection of specimens for scholarly examination and public display involved killing on a large scale. The viewer of the resulting zoological exhibits . . . [was] aware in one way or another of the justificatory ideas implicit in these activities, above all the curiosity, classificatory power and destructive capacity of the hunter in the service of a scientific knowledge that epitomised Western man's command of a global natural world. That command was, of course, "race"-specific. It was the preserve of Europeans and Americans. . . .[36]

One need not agree with all these conclusions to realize that hunting was deeply implicated in national and personal identities for men. The Darwinian lesson of the age—"nature red in tooth and claw"—dyed men's self-concepts in blood.

It's hard not to be horrified now, when reading the tales of these empire-building hunters. The scale of the destruction is far too great to be accounted for by a simple love of freedom and sport, and it seems more than a century-long cultural aberration. The game on several continents—

Africa, Asia, and North America—was nearly exterminated by hunting. One must look more deeply to understand these hunters. They themselves said it: they were acting upon profound combinations of psychological and cultural forces.

The violence of the hunter was the law of nature and of nations. In his flimsy hut, surrounded by a profound African darkness, with roaring lions just feet away, Selous is the imperial and Darwinian hero. He crosses the line from civilization to savagery, and his own tough-minded violence is in his mind his entrance into nature, enabling him to face it on what he imagines to be nature's own terms. He is the self-appointed guard, for the drawing rooms of London, at the entrance to a bloody nature. Through his violence, he reduces nature to control. And he brings it to terms for lords and ladies back home. He orders nature, converting it to a catalog of museum pieces. Nature was a darkness, and the hunter was the man on the edge, locked in a blind battle for supremacy.

The night of lions has an eerie Freudian feel, a story of the Victorian age locked in a blind battle with the frightening beast just outside the hut. Selous offered to men back home a bracing ethics of death.

5

Selous apparently enjoyed being photographed. As a young man he posed in hunting costume, bearded and muscular, with a rifle and a native assegai or spear, seated on animal skins as if enthroned. He's the image of fitness, the ideal physical specimen. For the Darwinian, the hunter was the embodiment and the agent of sexual selection. The heads of the perfect males, mounted on the wall, are the reflected image of the hunter himself. The antlers and horns—and the search for the biggest and most perfectly endowed males of the species—signified the hunter's indirect obsession with eugenics and genetics. They are the signs of the great male. The male body is its own trophy—Selous's photograph is its own trophy—and to the strongest go the spoils.

The trophy is the way male dominance is given corporeal substance. Dead animals don't speak. But they can be read, and then their message is: This space is male space—women beware—and the fittest male gets, not only the biggest trophy in the woods, but the most winsome female. The trophy defines the male body—image of transcendent virility—and the boundaries between the sexes.

The head of the animal mounted on the wall floats as it were in space. It is the disembodied but tangible image of masculinity, presiding over male gathering places—hardware stores and barbershops, garages and dens, barns and lawyers' offices—with a speechless and, despite its glassy eyes, frightening benediction. Trophies on the wall are the gargoyles of the cult of masculinity.

They protect the spaces reserved for men—the "den" after all is the male "preserve." The language of the trophy room is the language of the hunt, imported into daily life of men in the city. The trophy is the response to an age afraid of an endangered masculinity.

The trophy identifies a kind of defensive masculinity. The trophy is a mask of aggression, hiding all men's fears. The head of the buck, with glass eyes and mouth slightly ajar, is the gargoyle at the gate—it's often mounted above doors and windows and other female architectural symbols. It's the beast whose image is used to frighten away the unbelievers, to announce the perils involved in entry to the space. It frightens away all who are not men—all who are not fit to enter the male sanctum. For boys, the trophy announces the rite of passage to manhood. The trophy alienates women—it simply chases them away. The trophy marks the castle walls. It is the ideal image of men's fear of the female. More accurately, it marks their fear of the female in them. It is the symbol of male fear of feminization.

We don't know when trophies began to be really popular. In the eighteenth century, according to John MacKenzie, the clubs and libraries of men were largely innocent of dead animals. But in the nineteenth century in England men used souvenirs of the hunt as part of the architecture of business, clubs, and home to create uniquely male spaces. The relation between hunting and sexual segregation, MacKenzie writes, was expressed in such crazes as the specifically male sanctums of the smoking room and the billiard room, decorated with furs and heads, even the hooves of elephants for umbrella stands. All men could bask in the reflected glory of the hunt. Partly the architecture and decoration were a self-conscious attempt to re-create the feel of the great hunting lodges of medieval lords like Charlemagne and the English kings. But the trophy itself was the most portable and condensed expression of an aggressive and frightened masculinity in the home and city. The skins of animals, especially great cats, began to appear on floors and walls. Some private collections, like Selous's, were huge, involving a wide range of individual species. Edwin Landseer, the wildlife painter, had thirty pairs of stags' heads and antlers, bulls' horns, rams' heads, a wild boar's head, the skeleton of a deerhound, a bison, tiger skins, and a stuffed swan.[37]

The ideal trophy was an adult male animal, the largest and most perfect physical specimen available. By upholstering their own male sanctums with stuffed animals, men could reproduce masculinity for themselves. Without women.

The phallic gun was reproductive. The bullet was semen and seed. Together, they quite literally re-created a masculine image, like the photograph.

The trophy enforces what Stuart Marks, in his study of hunting in South Carolina, *Southern Hunting in Black and White*, calls the "masculine mystique."[38] He argues that the styles of hunting and the meaning of hunting are grounded in history, class, race, and gender; these things are not timeless universals operating in a cultural void. For the men he interviewed, buck hunting is different from coon hunting. "The buck hunter," he writes, "is the epitome of the masculine mystique." Buck hunting means autonomy, freedom, and status.

The horned heads on the walls and barns announce this message to all the world.

A trophy is not simply the souvenir of a hunting trip. Put it on the wall, and you mark the divide between male and female space, physical as well as psychological.

It's a magical boundary, and the boundary is inviolable. According to Marks, southern buck hunters learned their "masculine mystique" by hunting with their fathers at an impressionable age, and this mystique has a "semisacred quality." Failing to live up to the norms in the ideal is to start a "slide down the slippery slopes toward feminization." Trophies herald from the wall the sacred male space—the trophy aggressively imported into the domestic space of the woman's home, carving out of daily life a private male world. According to Marks, "The vivid images of men's stories, the obscenities and violence, the ethnic and racial jokes, and the lewd sexual fantasies exemplify a masculine world and a deep-seated dependence on women."

The roles and rules of masculinity are established with a hostility and aggressiveness that convert the boundaries and relations between the sexes into a skirmish, its own strange hunt. One blunt hunter whom Marks interviewed put it with unvarnished male aggression: "It's the politics of cunt and hunt."[39]

The phallic rifle hanging above the female hearth.

In this space, associated with Darwin and fathers and historical origins, gender roles become reified, fossilized even. Huge psychic investments are being defended in the preserves of male egos. It's the aggressiveness with which the hunt is used to ward off the female that's most fascinating. The exclusion is violent, angry, frightened. Jack London is the prophet of modern male atavism, of predatory men returning to the bestial. *The Sea-Wolf,* for example, is a long Darwinian parable on men in a boat. They are animals in their maleness, seal hunters who procreate themselves in their hunting, part of that pseudosexual daily "grind":

a company of celibates, grinding harshly against one another and growing daily more calloused from the grinding. It seems to me impossible
sometimes that they ever had mothers. It would seem to me they are a
half-brute, half-human species, a race apart, wherein there is no such
thing as sex; that they are hatched out of the sun like turtle eggs, or receive life in some similar and sordid fashion. . . .[40]

Before his conversion, Jack London's narrator is called " 'Sissy' Van Weyden." The male world of the boat, like Melville's *Pequod*, does not need
women. Van Weyden is reborn into true manhood on this boat of men, fa-
thered by the hunters. The bourgeois equivalent of this self-creation is the
photograph of the male with his dead animal. He rises above, even out of
the creature, in a miracle of autogenesis. The photograph is the self in the
making. It documents the male miracle.

In Hemingway's "The Short Happy Life of Francis Macomber," the
animosities between the genders are marked by the hunt and ironically in-
verted. Macomber is a coward and alcoholic, but shortly after arriving at
manhood through the killing of an elephant, his wife shoots him in disgust
and vengeance. The boundary between the sexes is firm, and while women
can be hunters, if they are, they must be feared.

6

Perhaps the best story to illustrate the ways in which this imperial and
Darwinian hunt intersects gender roles comes from R. S. S. Baden-Powell,
the founder of the Boy Scouts and apologist of modern masculinity. His
story unconsciously displays a remarkable truth about this attitude toward
women and gender relations, confusing women as "prize" and trophy of
the hunt.

The story is told in his volume on hunting throughout the empire,
called *Sport in War*, published in 1900.[41] The story's phallic nature is trum-
peted in the title, "The Ordeal of the Spear." It is a story in which sexual selection meets sexual hostility. It is a story in which Darwin meets Freud on
the hunting field in India.

Baden-Powell, like many of the military hunters in this century, was
used to making the equation between hunting for animals in far away continents and hunting down the human inhabitant. He wrote of hunting "wild
beasts of the human kind," and of "this man-hunting [which] afforded us
plenty of excitement and novel experience."[42] Conquering natives in their
native lands was, in this language, sport. But these gentlemen rarely de-

scended to woman-hunting with the spears. That remains an unconscious part of their hunting.

In the shade of a "mango tope," or grove, in India, Baden-Powell says, a camp had been pitched for a pig-sticking meet. Pig sticking was the name of one of the most popular forms of imperial diversion—men on horses ride for a wild boar, to see who among them might be the first to draw blood, and so win the prize of first blood. Women did not actually hunt. But they did watch.

An American woman, Miss Edna Clay, was among the socialites who had come out to the jungle to witness this men's entertainment. She had been wintering in the area with her mother, and like many, she found the social cheerfulness of a military outpost more agreeable than the Continental watering places that formed the habitat of so many other wandering Americans.

But in the drizzle of this pre-Christmas day, Miss Edna Clay was depressed and restless. When her mother inquired why she seemed too distracted, Miss Edna Clay announced that she would not be leaving India with her family. "I have been a fool," she said.

"I have allowed myself to fall in love."

Her mother laid aside her glasses, and beaming, asked to hear more.

There were two eligible bachelors in camp. One was named Jack Austin, whom her mother preferred. He was young, and dashing, and "Lord Ravensham's heir." He was called among his friends "the Devil"—cheery, lighthearted, ready for any game going. The other was Major Calvert, a dark and handsome man, but older and taciturn. His friends called him the "Deep C"—a keen sportsman but quiet by disposition.

In choosing between the Devil and the Deep C, Miss Edna Clay had fallen for the Deep C. She tells her mother that she fell in love with the Deep C when she heard "the sad sorrowful little story of his life." As with Desdemona, his travails bred a kindness and a sympathy in her.

As this conversation was progressing, the two gentlemen in question were themselves sitting in their bachelor's tent, and the topic rather naturally fell to a consideration of Miss Edna Clay herself.

As they talked, it emerged that each of them had been quietly entertaining the thought of proposing to the American woman. Once they discovered this, they felt in a fine dilemma—"a queer hat," as the Devil put it. For how could they maintain their gentlemanly code with each other, and still resolve the question, who might be allowed to propose to the lady?

They considered letting Miss Edna Clay decide, but knew that that could only make her uncomfortable. Far more gentlemanly to resolve this matter between themselves, between two men.

So they hit upon the "ordeal of the spear." They would have a pig-sticking contest. The man who drew first blood was the winner, and in the contest between these two soldiers, the one drawing first blood would also win Miss Edna Clay.

The next day, the men were out on the beat early. The women, Miss Clay among them, appeared sometime after the beaters had begun to stir among the bushes, rousing the boars that would provide the day's sport. The women rode in howdahs, the elegant cabins perched atop the elephants' backs.

The contest for the pig was joined, the men charging on their horses after a fine old boar that wove and dodged and evaded. It was a neck-and-neck race between the two men, lasting for the better part of the morning. But as the race for first blood neared its climax, the boar made straight for a tree jungle not far distant, its only chance of escape. At that moment, Miss Edna Clay appeared from among the trees. She had an excellent view of the chase—"though little she [knew] how much its issue may affect her own future."

The Deep C closed in upon the pig, and was about to stab him, when his horse "pecked" at the crucial moment. The Devil swooped in on his horse, seized the advantage, and drove his spear in the boar's flank. It was not a good thrust, but it counted as a first. At that moment, he looked up to see Miss Edna Clay, who was a spectator of the game. The "magnitude of what he had won, in winning the first spear, caused him to vent his lungs in a piercing hoot of exultation."

Once the boar was properly dispatched, a native with a terrified face came running hurriedly toward them. In a few moments, they were standing beside the body as it lay on a charpoy, a kind of native cot. She looked almost as if she were resting after a bout of tennis, according to Baden-Powell:

> Her white frock and gay silk were fresh and scarcely disheveled; but there was an awkward uprightness about the small brown shoes; her form seemed flattened down into the cot, and the unnatural sternness about the waxen face, with its half-closed eyes and parted lips, showed that Edna Clay was dead.
>
> Her elephant, frightened at the final rush and turmoil of the race, had turned and fled among the trees, to the instant destruction of the howdah and its occupant.[43]

The story is true. Included at the end of the story is a photograph, a memento mori one might say, but looking exactly like the photographs of hunters standing above their trophies. In some frighteningly literal way, the contest among men was the Darwinian contest, along with the Freudian sublimation of sexual energies into the boar chase. But by one of those psychic twists that has its own inexorable logic, the prize they ran for was not the boar, but the lady.

With the natives slightly behind them, the two men stand above her, their left hands in their coat pockets, elbows akimbo in the stance of a British gentleman at his awkward ease. Their safari hats are in their right hands, leaning against the cot on which the lady is stretched out. And they contemplate her with a melancholy that is not expressed in the story—the body of the woman laid out so beautifully, so quietly, so daintily submissive beneath them.

The men's impassive expressions, heads turned slightly from the camera, reveal emotion only indirectly. All is implicit. Beneath the surface of the hunt, there is this lurking and unconscious hostility to the desired female. She is the accidental victim of their violence, and it's not clear if the sexual contest is between the two men or between the men and the woman.

In the photograph, it's as if she is resting after her "ordeal of the spear." She is not the prize, but the hunter's literal trophy after all. She might symbolize the role these men unconsciously wished for the married woman. In the order of nature, she's learned her place. As trophy, she is a generic woman, achieving in a way the melancholy destiny men secretly wished for her sex—the perfectly passive female, spread out beneath their feet, no longer able to come between them.

7

Here are two very different responses to the paradigm of modern manhood as articulated by big-game hunters. One, by the great twentieth-century British poet, W. H. Auden. The other, by an American writer, Roy Blount, Jr.

W. H. Auden frequently commented in poetry on the traditions handed down to his generation by the great hunters of England. In 1933, he very succinctly pulled together several of the themes of the hunters—violence, science, and empire:

> Beneath the hot incurious sun,
>> Past stronger beasts and fairer
> He picks his way, a living gun,
>> With gun and lens and bible,
>> A militant enquirer . . .
> Whose family have taught him

> To set against the large and dumb,
>   The timeless and the rooted,
>   His money and his time.
> And ruled by dead men never met,
>   By pious guess deluded,
> Upon the stool of madness set
>   Or stool of desolation,
> Sits murderous and clear-headed. . . .[44]

Ruled by "dead men never met," the modern man is a living figure of speech, a synecdoche, "a living gun." He embodies his violence. With his gun and lens and Bible—empire, science, and missionary zeal—he is mad in ways he does not know—"murderous and clear-headed" rationality.

Roy Blount reasserts the images of masculinity the hunters bequeathed, and like them, he does it defiantly, aggressively, reveling in his defensiveness. In his column for the *Men's Journal*, Blount describes his irrational but primal urge for prime beef.[45]

Blount admits that his craving for meat is not healthy. But some need impels him to eat it. He's the modern defensive male, insisting on clogging his veins with cholesterol, out of atavistic need. "I knew in my heart, and my arteries, I should get over this atavistic craving. But how? Repress it? That would be unmanly."

What he does instead is go on his own hunt for the perfect steak. It takes him to the domain of true and real men, to a fiercely holy temple of primitive virility:

> A day or two later I went down to the meat market in lower Manhattan to check out a bar called Hogs and Heifers. A sign on the door said, NEVER MIND THE DOG—BEWARE OF THE OWNER. The decor featured a boar's head, a stuffed owl, a stuffed turtle, a bull's head, a cow skull, a small alligator skin, a nine-and-a-half-foot mako shark, a stuffed duck suspended from the ceiling by a stiff wire so that it bobbed continually in the breeze of the overhead fan and the head of either an elk or a deer—I couldn't be sure which, because the animal's face was obscured by several dozen brassieres suspended from its antlers. At another point on the wall a number of neckties hung from a hook. I got the idea that this was not a good place to enter wearing a bra or a tie or carrying a pet.

Under the sightless gaze of dead animals, men can reinhabit a utopian world, unproblematized by sex and social responsibility, bras and ties. Man has become a species apart.

8

I turn uphill and step directly in a pile of bear poop.

"Damn," Willy grunts. "Bear. If you see a bear, shoot it."

"Do you have a license for bear?" I look at him as we head up the steep hill, leaving the logging road and skirting the side of a narrow clear-cut in the forest, a tangled swath of stumps and slash.

"Don't worry," Willy shoots back at me. "If you shoot a bear, I'll get a license."

Pause. Then, afterthought: "If you see a coyote, shoot it too."

He laughs. I laugh. It's funny that spirit in hunters, and men, that makes them hate laws and restraints, a love almost of anarchy. It's very male. It's the same impulse that made Cumming leave Scotland to look for "the freedom of nature . . . of the Far West." That made Roosevelt call hunters, in their "wild, free, reckless lives . . . the arch-type of freedom."[46]

Even Edward Abbey, the great environmental writer, made his wild hero, Hayduke, a militarist and a hunter. He's in love with the wild spaces of the southwestern desert, passionate in his commitment to the tonic of violence, and a lover of the anarchic freedom he found in the American West.[47]

Yet Willy is not an American by birth. He's from Germany, where he grew up hunting. He prefers hunting in America because it's less restrictive than in modern Germany, where elaborate training in guns and game must be completed before one can have a license. Willy is blond and ebullient, strong and in fine physical shape. He owns his own construction firm, but hunting is his grand passion. It's visceral and sexual. "I've hunted all over the world," he says to me with a smile when I ask him about his background.

"Mouflon rams in France. Pussy in Spain."

With us is Scott. He couldn't be more different from Willy. They're good friends, hunting buddies, an odd couple of hunting: Willy as the wild Oscar, Scott as the neat-freak Felix. He's thin and keeps his dark hair very clean cut. He's an accountant for the state government in Washington. His hunting clothes are clean and even pressed. He carries all his gear neatly stowed and folded, each in its place: knives, gloves, boots. His new Dodge pickup has recently been polished to an apple red shine, and we knock mud off our boots before setting them in back, on plastic. He doesn't talk about hunting much, he tells me, because he doesn't like the judgments people make now.

He tells me about when he first learned to hunt, with his dad and his uncles in Oregon, and how exciting it was to kill his first deer. But he didn't like it, either. The deer died slowly. It made him cry.

Scott could be a Boy Scout.

As many men told me, killing an animal has to do with possessing the animal, compromising it. And with power. But what mystery is it, in the human and male psyche, that is expressed in the urge to hunt and kill? Clearly, there are immense cultural forces carried in the act of hunting, giving men as it were an identity and a vocation, a way of imagining themselves in the world. Scott, for example, kept hunting because it was closely associated with his family—a uniquely American, frontier-generated mythos for the hunt, as we'll see.

But what about the psychology of killing? It seems to me that I could understand this dimension of the hunt—this heart of the hunt—only by actually hunting something myself.

In the crook of my arm, loaded, I carry a borrowed Winchester. What gauge? Ballistics is one of the definitive mysteries of conventional modern hunters. But I forget the minute Scott tells me. I've never slung a rifle before, except a BB gun. I never killed anything, except a robin, one Sunday morning as a kid after finishing my paper route. I have never personally killed an animal since.

Willy and Scott and I have driven down a bumpy logging road in the Cascade Mountains, just outside the boundary of Mount Rainier National Park. It is a glorious October day, high Indian summer, thick sun pouring like syrup through the evergreen forest, glowing on the brown grass of the open slopes. I've been hunting for deer for two days.

If I see one, I am going to try to shoot it. I share the hunterly notion that every excursion into the forest can be a trip into the far reaches of the self. The hunger for experience, not theory, urges me forward.

The power of the hunt is that it can take abstract ideas about manhood, whole systems of social value and personal ethics, and convert them into concrete action. It embeds ideas in stories. In the process, the story becomes a script—a language written for us that we follow. Social identities generate the need for self-confirming action.

Manhood is not, finally, a theory. It's the shape we give to individual lives. It's the shape we give to our experience. Or more accurately, manhood is one of many pressures impinging upon our experience, shaping our consciousness and our bodies. It's part of the language we grow up with, and we take it in, a network of words. And between our lives and our words, our bodies and our ideas, we fashion the trajectory of our lives. We fashion a story for ourselves, always being revised, always subject to change and redirection.

There's a sort of social physics to the shape of our lives. The vector of my life—its direction and intensity—veers between words and flesh.

I'm surprised as we hike at how much I want to see and shoot a deer. I can feel a certain fierceness in me, and hunger. It's as though, in the image of the deer, a great cathexis of energy has taken place. The image of the deer becomes a locus of energy. Part of me is fixed in the image. I feel some quickened sense of vitality, some urgency within, which is attached to the image of a black-tailed deer stepping at any instant from the forest. Ortega y Gasset calls the hunter "the alert man": "There is a universal vibration. Things that before were inert and flaccid have suddenly grown nerves, and they gesticulate, announce, foretell. . . . Now everything is imminent and at any instant any figure of the countryside can become—as if by magic—the hunter's prey."[48]

As the three of us hunt, we decide our strategy will be to hike up this steep slope in the mountain foothills. Loggers have clear-cut a wide swath up the hill. Willy hikes among the big trees on the left. Scott works the middle of the cut. I tromp through the thick brush and younger firs on the right. We're trying to flush a deer.

I work the margin alone with my thoughts. What is clear to me is that the mystique of hunting—always perplexing to people who don't hunt—can only be fully understood from the inside. It can only be done by doing it. And the only way to hunt, really, is to be looking to kill.

All hunting that does not involve at least the possibility of killing is purely—merely, I might say—metaphorical. To be truly hunting, you have to be willing to kill. And when you use the metaphor of hunting, you are always evoking the ethos of killing and possessing.

As we hike up the hill, no deer emerge to disturb my alertness or my thoughts. I am alone with myself. I climb over the slash of the clear-cut and poke into the forest. The bouncing songs of winter wrens drift through the branches. I feel an intense focus on the possibility of a deer. I want to kill one. It is a very goal-directed desire.

Men rarely kill only for meat or survival. Whenever men—and women too—participate in the hunt, they are inevitably acting out some mythic story that they carry, already, in their heads. They are always in the grip of symbol and metaphor—useful for all cultures in the way they help to shape reality and reflect that reality back to us in manageable, meaningful ways. One value of metaphor—of human language generally—is its ability to restructure reality and shape our characters. It's only one of the many paradoxes about hunting that it is an activity that imagines itself about flesh and blood and physical realities, and yet has been overwhelmed by words, symbol, fantasy.

The confrontation that takes place in the woods is always, in some measure, not between the man and an animal, but, if he is alert to the inner hunt as well as the outer, between the man and his myths. Men are always preceded into the forest by their fantasies.

The animals of the hunt are the invisible and silent partner in men's history, the shadow history of men, the unacknowledged partner in male identity. Who can imagine how many animals have been killed for sport? The beasts have not only subsidized civilization's growth—usually killed, even slaughtered, in the name of civilization—but they have underwritten the story of manhood.

The beast is a concept used by men to make possible both a psychology of personal identity and a history of exploitation—men project onto animals their own darknesses, and then kill the animal for its symbolic value. The animal is bestiality, emotion, instinct, body, aggression, mindlessness, freedom, and sex. The hunt enabled an expression of the Victorian ambivalence to animals and animality. Man the hunter could imagine himself a beast, the master beast in the Darwinian struggle for life. In psychological terms, they fought the beast within and made themselves masters of their impulses.[49]

In its various ways, the beast is not a creature, but a social category, a repository and an allegory for our fantasies of the dark sides of our nature. The beast is a way of thinking. The beast is part of the syntax of male psychology: Man is the subject, and the animal is predicate or direct object. In the history of manhood, the beast is the primary antagonist in the politics of male identity.

The literal animal is the victim of our symbolic quests—the scapegoat for men's strange inability to inhabit their own lives, their own bodies, their own emotions.

Yet, in that catchall category of the Other, which men create to hunt, a category which includes women and races and animals, only the animal cannot speak for itself. Surely that's what makes it the perfect victim. The value of hunting as a metaphor of social relations and social meanings is that, unlike humans, animals cannot talk back. They cannot contradict the hunter.

Men as hunters have defined themselves in a bewildering array of postures and positions around the beast. And those postures change, through culture and history, as the symbolic beast changes. It is a complex and shifting arrangement of symbols, attitudes, and meanings. Shift the symbolic content of the beast, and a new posture of man to animal results. A new hunt is invented. A new meaning to manhood occurs. What is constant is that in the West we have made trophies, not totems, out of animals. Direct objects, not predicates.

But it isn't simply dominance men get from the imagery of hunting. There's another payoff. Roualeyn Gordon Cumming in South Africa gives a clue to it. He describes chasing a herd of oryx, or gemsbok, which many consider one of the most beautiful of the antelopes in Africa. "Burning with anxiety," Cumming says, he had come upon a herd of ash-colored bucks, giving chase to them. They were the beautiful oryx, or gemsbok. Choosing a female with "uncommonly fine long horns," he knocked her over with two bullets in the shoulder. Such a chase taxed his physical resources. "My thirst was intense," he writes, "and, the gemsbok having a fine breast of milk, I milked her into my mouth, and obtained a drink of the sweetest beverage I ever tasted."[50] The great white hunter milking a beautiful dead antelope directly into his mouth: Male freedom seems to be defined with an almost sadistic, quasi-sexual pleasure. Cumming is posed with the beautiful female gemsbok—he's being fed. It's a perverse image of nurturing.

Hunters are sustained by the animals they have killed. The dying animal allows the hunter to invent himself, all the while thinking that he is autonomous. It's a feat of psychological magic—the occult side of male rationality. The creatures which supported him, which gave his psyche its mode and momentum, were invisible, silent, dead.

He thought he had accomplished the greatest trick of all, this hunter—a life without obligations. Like a head without a body, like a trophy on a wall. Disembodied consciousness, unattached, uncluttered by sentiments.

One more story from Frederick Courtenay Selous. While hunting elephants, he describes more than once just what the hunting ethic of these big-game hunters demanded of their emotions. Selous was hunting a beautiful cow elephant, which he shot as she charged him. She hit the ground, but was not dead. As Selous approached, she "reared her lofty head once more, and gazed reproachfully at me with her large soft dark eyes." For a moment, Selous regretted every shot he'd fired at her. He actually wished every bullet "unfired" that had laid low "this beautiful and inoffensive creature." Instead, "stifling all remorseful feelings," he fired another bullet into her head, and killed her.[51]

More clearly than in any other story I've read, Selous describes the psychodrama of the hunt. He is created as a man-the-hunter in the strategic management of his emotions. It's a psychic ecology he describes in stifling his feelings, as much as an ecology of predator and prey in a Darwinian nature. What he did to animals described what he had to do to his own emo-

tions. In the hunt, we have the visible traces of a deeply rooted consciousness, a way of relating not only to others, but also to the self.

All the clear-headed and clean-living strength of the male hunter—that
northern European stock, that northern cool: hygienics and eugenics. The
dark side of the big-game hunter's program for creating men in their image
was simultaneously to create, in the process of stifling his feelings and remorse, a dark side of himself. He created an inner wilderness of controlled
emotions and stifled feelings, a whole ecology of the unconscious. It seems
clear to me that Selous's dead elephant cow is the image of his suppressed
empathy. And he stands as a type, defining the way the hunter in killing
makes the animals into the images that stand at the gate of a blank spot in
the soul.

Something like these sentiments are working their way through my
consciousness as I'm hunting on Mount Rainier for a deer. But they aren't
thoughts, yet. They're still feelings, or intuitions, that are not yet fully rea-
soned or articulated.

On the other side of the cut, Willy is motioning for me to look up the
hill. I look upward. The crest of the hill bulges outward, over the clear-cut,
with huge Douglas fir trees rising behind it. I can't see any animals at first.

I look harder.

I see the head of something emerge over the crest. Then another. And
another. Another. Four cervids. My heart races. My muscles tighten. I quit
breathing. I try to stay cool, collected, prepared.

Is this to be my chance?

Looking quizzically over to Willy, I ready the rifle, holding it in two
hands. I want to do this right, and I'm excited as hell inside. But Willy is
smiling and gesticulating. I can't yell over to him, and his gestures confuse me.

I look back up, and realize why he's smiling.

Four big-eared elk are peering down at us, over the crest of the hill,
watching us approach. All cows. They have a passive, disinterested look in
their black-eyed, long-nosed faces. Cunning faces, with nostrils quivering
and flappy lips. They have a funny kind of curious indifference to us, a
vague aloofness, exaggerated no doubt by my own heavy-breathing struggles to climb this stumpy hill.

I think to myself, Those are big deer. Then I think, too bad elk season
has passed.

At the same instant, I know I am not going to shoot a deer. We've been
hunting for two days, and I will spend another day after this one looking
for deer. But I know I won't see one. I know it with a certainty that comes

from inside, when outer and inner worlds seem to correspond perfectly to each other.

The elk turn around, and they flash their asses at us, big cream-colored patches, targets to taunt three panting hunters. They saunter off in casual disregard.

And I can feel something shift inside me. I lose all interest in killing. Strangely, I don't care if men hunt. And I'll keep hunting all day and all of the next day, too, with Willy and Scott. It's not the real hunter in the field I care about. I actually enjoy the vitality of many hunters. It's the hunter within I'm interested in, and what he's done to us in the name of manhood.

The larger issue is whether men can begin to take responsibility for their own feelings, their own dramas, their own metaphors. Men need to begin to take responsibility for the way they have imagined themselves, and the way Others have been impressed into duty, into parts, in this psychodrama made real, scripts they didn't write.

The elk have vanished from the crest of the hill, and with them my interest in literalizing a fantasy. I have no need to act out some private drama.

When I reach the top of the crest, Mount Rainier is visible across the valley of the White River. There are no elk on the hill, though Willy and Scott and I see traces of them—tracks and scat. A flock of hundreds of red crossbills swoops out of the silent evergreens—pretty red alpine finches with perfect Darwinian bills that look like calipers, for pinching nut meat from pinecones. They're a pink cloud, an avian cumulus in the trees.

The mountain in the autumn sun is superb. Dazzling. Sun on snow. And everything is changed, I've passed through some unseen door in the day. There are other sources of power available to us, but we need to learn to recognize them, nurture them, and, when the moment is there, let them in.

I let Mount Rainier's power, its almost tangible physical presence, take me—a perfectly noncarnivorous rush of landscape and love. I take it in deeply. There is power that does not depend on opponents and victims. I am sustained by the power of moments like these—by mountains and birds and disappearing elk, and by all the connections that I've been smart enough to nurture.

8

THE LONG HUNT

The ancient amusement of shooting the Christmas turkey, is one of the few sports that the settlers of a new country seldom or never neglect to observe. It was connected with the daily practices of a people, who often laid aside the axe or the sithe, to seize the rifle, as the deer glided through the forests they were felling, or the bear entered their rough meadows, to scent the air of a clearing, and to scan, with a look of sagacity, the progress of the invader.

—James Fenimore Cooper, *The Pioneers*[1]

In my own mind, there is something singularly American about the rifle. It seems to belong to us culturally, whether we like it or not. At least, the rifle seems to have been born in America, home-grown and star-spangled, although it wasn't; German and Austrian huntsmen were carrying rifles by 1600. . . . In my mind, too, I see the rifle more as the hunter's tool than the soldier's, though for a while in America the hunter and the soldier were one and the same. Our first and perhaps finest contribution to the world of arms, the graceful, sharpshooting Kentucky long rifle, was so named not because of its place of manufacture, which happened to be Pennsylvania, but because it was the preferred weapon of the Kentucky hunters who helped Andrew Jackson whip the British in 1815 in New Orleans.

—John Mitchell, *The Hunt*[2]

You couldn't find anything in the three-room log cabin in the mountains that would remind you of the romanticism of the American frontier. Especially not its owner. Tom has a defiant smirk under his scruffy blond beard, and his biceps bulge under a black T-shirt. He's got a bony face and sharp features. It all combines into an effect of vague menace. He reminds me of a blond Doberman.

He tries to bluff us with sneers and attitude, but the show is halfhearted. We're here to bust him, and after a brief confrontation, Tom's machismo quickly collapses into a sad and pathetic confession. From bull to bleating calf.

I'm relieved. You never know in a bust, and Tom's neighbors had already told us that they don't trust him, that they have to keep an eye on him. "He's kinda crazy," one neighbor told us. "He just gets out there and shoots. He doesn't care what he shoots at."

We've driven through a glorious sunset over winter wheat in eastern Oregon to be at Tom's cabin just at dark. It was a short drive up Route 1, outside of Pendleton, into the Wallowa Mountains. We hoped to catch Tom just getting home from work at the nearby meat cannery, but when we arrived, the cabin was dark. No one home.

We sat shivering in the car, the three wildlife agents and I, listening to Game Three of the World Series and waiting.

When Tom's Mustang pulled up, he was with his wife, Dawn Marie, and his twenty-month-old baby girl, dressed in a pink sleeper. Jeff Williams, the agent in charge of wildlife violations in this part of the state for the Oregon State Patrol, serves Tom a search warrant in the dark. We're here to search for illegal game. The laws are very specific. One tag, one elk. Tom was reported to have taken four or five this season.

We follow the family into the cabin. The little girl is scared, wide-eyed, clinging. Dawn Marie is nervous. She turns on the TV immediately and apologizes for the incredible mess in the cabin. She begins to straighten the place up. It's a futile gesture, and the first impression is devastating anyway. This is anything but "Little House on the Prairie." It's hard to believe that anyone could live in this squalor. The loop pile carpet is littered with the unvacuumed detritus of who-knows-how-many days. Dirty clothes spew from the bedroom and spill through the living room floor. Plastic toys in garish colors—green, purple, yellow—litter the carpet, along with several dolls.

On the dinette, the leftovers from several days' worth of out-of-the-can meals. Dirty pots half full of pork and beans and Kraft macaroni and cheese, plates cluttering every counter and appliance top, including the top of the refrigerator. Someone's been eating mushrooms and Skippy peanut butter.

While the other agents begin to search, Jeff questions Tom about his hunting. Jeff is not belligerent in the least. Jeff is shorter than Tom, and he's wearing a blue police jumpsuit with a shiny badge that makes him look, well, boyish somehow. Hardly intimidating. He simply asks Tom about the rack, or the meat, from "the four-by-four elk."

The numbers indicate the number of prongs on each of the elk's horns or antlers.

Tom lies. "I don't know."

Jeff searches his face carefully. "Okay then, where's the spike?"

A spike is a young bull just getting its first horns.

A guilty smile flickers in the corners of Tom's mouth. He sneaks a glance at Dawn Marie, who glowers at him. His jaw juts forward. He realizes, with that question, that Jeff already knows the whole story. I watch him almost visibly implode.

"It's here," he confesses. The game is up. He looks whipped.

"You want to talk to me now?" Jeff asks.

Tom shrugs his shoulders. "I don't care." And, humiliated in front of his wife and baby, he begins to spill the truth.

The drama is over, though the squalid little cabin still reeks with tension. While Jeff interrogates Tom, I can't take my eyes off the paneled walls of the small living room. They have clearly been decorated by Tom, not Dawn Marie, in a crowded but decidedly geometric disposition. Several big drawings of the heads of dogs are symmetrically placed on the wall above the TV. He's got a bow above the wood stove. Beside it, a quiver full of arrows hangs slightly askew. A rack from a deer is centered just above the bow, and has pheasant feathers decorating the tines. Four plaques on the wall form a square around the bow and rack, trophies from bow-shooting contests. A couple of photographs of Tom and his brother with fish and game they've bagged, and four bows and ribbons (in blue, white, and yellow: more awards for his ability with the bow) complete the wall and give it a splash of color.

In the bedroom, hanging above the bed, is a handgun, a .44 pistol. As I walk in there, Tom breaks off his confession with Jeff and warns me and the other agents: "Be careful with the .44 on the wall. I keep it loaded at all times."

He's boasting. But it's an ominous boast to me—the bed seems such an intimate place for a loaded gun.

Male aesthetics: Tom's made his family's house into a shrine to his own passion for hunting.

It's a testament, as well, to what amounts to an addiction to killing.

Tom is a poacher, and the trade in illegal wildlife in the United States is big business. According to the wildlife agent I'm with, Jeff Williams, one man in the Pendleton, Oregon, area was making two hundred thousand dollars per year trafficking in illegal bobcat pelts. In 1993, about thirty thousand grizzly and black bears were poached inside the national parks and forest for trade purposes. The business in illegal wildlife in the country exceeds $200 million per year, and is growing.[3]

Still, unlike Tom, most hunters in the United States hunt more or less legally. As of 1991, of the United States population 16 years of age or older, 14 percent of the males and 1 percent of the females hunted. Of the 14.1 million hunters in 1991, 92 percent were male, and 8 percent were female. These hunters exert an influence out of proportion to their numbers, not only on our thinking about masculinity and our relations with nature, but in the way our natural lands are managed.

The number of men who hunt is also declining, also indicating how rapidly this sport is changing. Dedicated hunters worry that recruitment for their sport is declining—the country is increasingly urban, and more and more families are fatherless. This is a sport that is handed down from elder male to younger in family traditions, uncle or father to young boy. During the 1980s, the number of hunters in the country declined about 3.5 million, and in Washington State, for example, the number of deer tags sold in 1979 was 250,000, but in 1993 it was 200,000. It's a common appeal among hunters that hunting is deeply ingrained in their genes and even in their blood, and that they can't be expected to change several million years' worth of evolution in a single lifetime. The declining numbers of hunters in the United States weaken that argument.

Like Tom, most avid hunters in the United States are young, between eighteen and thirty-four. As men age, they tend to enjoy the woods and companionship and time away as much if not more than the actual hunting. Certainly, the need to kill an animal declines with age. In a given year, hunters will legally kill about 200 million animals in the United States. Deer are the preferred game of men, but the number also includes about 50 million mourning doves, 28 million quail, 22 million squirrels, and 102,000 elk.

Hunters spend a lot of money in pursuit of their game. The amount spent in 1991 was $12.3 billion by all hunters. Like Tom, most argue that getting meat is an important reason for hunting, but in terms of economics, they are only supplementing their diets through their sport. As with Tom, hunters would find it cheaper per pound to buy their meat from a butcher, given the amounts they spend on weapons and motels and transportation and clothes. The average hunter in 1991 spent $896, whether he got an animal or not. And this does not include special equipment like boats and campers and cabins and trail bikes.

Hunting is also primarily a rural sport in America. The Montana Department of Fish, Wildlife, and Sports claims that 47 percent of all adult males hunt. They say that 7 percent of the females "participate." Like Tom's wife, Dawn Marie, hunts with her husband. But like her, most women who hunt are not real vigorous in pursuing the sport.[4]

Nor are most men, really. The vast majority never stray too far from the road. They make camp around their truck, drink beer with their buddies, and if they shoot, it's usually where it's not too far away from the truck. They want to cut down on the work involved in dragging a carcass back to the road. I've been out with several hunters who hunt deer from the road, and watched one man shoot a young deer using the truck as a support for aiming. It's fair to say that these men are usually decent people, what you'd call good guys, though they'll sometimes shoot at things they shouldn't.

The number of women hunting seems to be rising. It's becoming more fashionable for women to hunt. It's in line with the entrance of women into many formerly male sanctums. Most feminists dislike hunting; but a few seem to think that, in the imagination and the art of hunting, as opposed to the killing, women are in fact even better suited to hunting than men. "Like a woman," writes one of them, "hunting won't sit down and be just one thing."[5]

Anyway, a lot of men hunt, and a few women. And a lot of women love the men who hunt.

Whatever else it is, the autumn ritual in the woods with guns continues to be an exercise in being a man. Its role in the life of American manhood derives from something other than the number of hunters in the woods. It derives from the history of hunters in our woods—from the frontier.

It's hard to know why someone like Tom has killed four elk in one season—whether it's for protein as he claims, or profit, or passion. When Jeff and I bust him, not one of the elk in his possession is legal. He has the remains of four in his house, and as it turns out, he doesn't even have a tag for one of them, and one would be the legal maximum. Tom swears to us he did it because he needs the meat. "Last year," he says, "we ran out of meat. So this year I wanted to make sure we didn't run out."

It seems like a lame excuse. If he needed meat, he could easily have bought many many steaks with the money he's spent on his hunting equipment—guns and rifles and bows and arrows. And besides, that's hardly an excuse to take *four* illegal elk. While we're searching Tom's house, Jeff tells me that there's a big illegal business in elk. It's part of what he calls "the commercialization of wildlife." You can take an elk "cape," the salted hide, and sell it to a taxidermist for anywhere between five thousand to seven thousand dollars.

I have to ask what someone would want with an elk cape.

The animals were "good Boone-and-Crockett quality," he told me. That means that by the standards of the big-time trophy hunters in the country, members of the Boone and Crockett Club, a marketable animal would have to be a prize specimen. If it were, the taxidermist will mount it, add antlers, and sell it. "Has to be prime, a 'number one' animal, and then it's major money," Jeff says.

Who would want such an animal that they didn't shoot themselves?

"Lots of people buy trophies," Jeff has said. "A lot of professionals like to put 'em in their offices, or in hunting lodges. All's I know," he says, "there's a clientele, and people seem to be able to find 'em. Here, the average for a fully mounted elk is about two thousand dollars."

Did Tom intend to sell the antlers and cape?

Probably not. He seems decidedly small-time. And he doesn't seem to be into money. We go into his basement and locate a beautiful rack. Tom only rises out of his defeated depression twice during the bust. Once is over this rack. He tells us how he shot the animal, and he grows nearly lyrical in his excitement. He shot it with his bow and a carbon-tipped arrow. "The carbon arrow penetrated the elk's heart," he says. "The carbon arrow is the best way to go."

He loves the kill, and there is a whole aesthetics associated with the animal's death. Soon, Tom is telling us about how he killed a bear this year, too.

And the other time is when we confiscate his bow and arrow. Jeff takes it off the wall and lets Tom hold it for a moment. Tom positively dotes. It's a Martin 400 "Firecat" Pro-Series 4000 compound bow. It is painted in camouflage. It has wood grips and is counterbalanced. The arrows are Easton Graphite #3-39/440 Superlite #3000, with black-and-gray fletching.

This is what Tom loves. The weapons and the kill. That bow is worth about one thousand dollars—top of the line, Jeff tells me.

It's hard not to feel saddened. He spends that much money on a bow and arrows, and he makes his wife and baby daughter live in a shabby cabin.

And then he loses the bow and arrows. They're confiscated, along with all the antlers, the cape, and sixty-six packages of frozen elk steaks they'd wrapped and put away.

We leave him and his family standing on the porch in the sharp mountain air. Tom is worried about his bow. His wife is pissed at him. She's scowling, since they got cited and lost all their meat. She's also embarrassed. It's very likely they'll get none of it back, depending on what happens when they go to court.

In the truck on the way back to the state patrol headquarters, Jeff tells me he thinks Tom did it because "guys like that just wanna kill. Maybe it's that a big rack proves how manly they are. These guys love bugling in the elk, and when it comes in, they shoot 'em. They wanna do what they wanna do."

Jeff stops to reflect. "People out here are used to killing," he says. "But what they don't like is wasting what they kill. They'll sometimes exceed their bag limits, but they turn on waste like gangbusters. Ninety-two percent of the guys out here hunting are tremendous people. But what hits the papers? Some guy selling thirty elk out of his tavern in Meachem. Joe Sportsman doesn't get the credit he deserves."

A silence falls over the cab of the truck as we head back to town with booty of our own, spoils of our bust. Every culture is defined by its criminals as well as its heroes. They define the norms, highlight the boundaries. The wheat fields around Pendleton are dark and broodingly still. In my mind, I see Tom and his family, standing on the porch of their mountain cabin.

Tom seems a sorry case. He loves to kill, and he loves his weapons. The woods to him mean a kind of freedom and lawlessness. He loves the hunt more than his family. Is this what the frontiersman has become—a sad parody, a caricature even, of the quintessential American hero? Or is Tom what the frontiersman really looked like, the reality under the myth—a mountain man stripped of the glory of empire and cause of national expansion, on the far coast of the continent, where destiny and frontier both reached their limit?

2

I'm looking at a crinkled old black-and-white picture of myself, from when I was about six years old. I'm wearing jeans and a vest. The gun and holster are slung in what strikes me now as very stylish, very rakish angles, low off my right hip, and tied with a big string around my thigh to keep the gun from flopping all over. On my head is the true emblem of the outfit, my "coonskin cap," at a careless little-boy angle. It's no cheap imitation coonskin cap, either, it's made of real fur. Under the cap, my face looks so young, so incredibly and impossibly cherubic.

Yes, that's me. It's hard to believe. So many changes ago, for me and the country. I was a boy, like 10 million other little boys in the fifties, in the costume of a mythic American man. I grew up in a suburb of Seattle that, back then, still felt rural enough to simulate a frontier. I still vividly remember my dad trapping "mountain beaver" in our yard and hanging them on the clothesline.

In the photo, I'm in front of two huge rocks in my backyard—bigger than I was. Sometimes, my sister and I straddled those big rocks and pretended they were horses to ride. Mostly, the rocks served as a gate on our half-acre property between the green-grass yard and the uncleared woods, and we'd pass between them into a wilderness of childhood adventures, sometimes playing "Lewis-and-Clark," exploring, building forts in trees and in deep holes in the ground, and often camping out at night.

In the picture, I'm stalking along the frontier, looking for bear and "injuns," singing Davy Crockett's theme song, à la Fess Parker and Walt Disney from the mid-fifties, "King of the Wild Frontier."

Lately, I've revisited Crockett's legend, through his own words and the comments of others about him. This much later in my life, and with all that both our culture and men have gone through in the last forty years, Davy Crockett's frontier strut has lost its boyish innocence for me, and is the occasion for my wondering about the way boys become men—the historical making, if you will, of manhood in America.

In his coarse and boastful autobiography, written like a self-serving stump speech for a backwoods politician, Crockett describes one year of hunting bear down the Mississippi, with his eight large dogs, one of which was named Andrew Jackson. In a story told in almost loud tavern idioms, Crockett zooms in upon one very large bear, "a screamer." Out of his interminable accounts of animals killed, this bear fight can stand as a paradigm of the American frontier hunter.[6]

Crockett says he had been hunting all day, and had already killed one bear. As he was heading back to camp, his dogs made a new "warm start," and he decided to follow them. Night was coming on, and he was compelled to walk very slowly through the thick vines and brambles of the "harricane," falling as he describes it over logs and into the cracks of earthquakes. He waded a very cold creek. From their barking, he was convinced the dogs must have treed their new bear. Climbing steep hills, missing his dogs, turning to find them again, he discovered they had treed a bear in a forked poplar.

It appeared to him merely a lump, "not plain enough to shoot." So at last he decided to "shoot by guess, and kill him." He fired away. The bear didn't fall. He only "clomb" higher in the poplar. Davy fired again. Same result. He prepared to fire a third time, but realized the bear had fallen and was now "among my dogs, and they were fighting all around me."

"So I took out my knife," he says with a frontiersman's resolution, "and stood, determined, if he should get hold of me, to defend myself in the best way I could."

But the bear showed no interest in Crockett. Instead, it kept fighting with the hunter's pack of dogs. So Davy aimed his rifle blindly in the dark and fired at the bear. No luck. He only hit it in the haunches. The bear crawled into one of the cracks made by an earthquake. Davy grabbed a pole, determined to punch the bear awhile with that. But the bear would not come out.

Davy crawled into the crack after him, virtually confronting the beast in its den:

> So I got down, and my dogs got in before him and kept his head towards them, till I got along easily up to him; and placing my hand on his rump, felt for his shoulder, just behind which I intended to stick him. I made a lounge [*sic*] with my long knife, and fortunately stuck him right through the heart; at which he just sank down, and I crawled out in a hurry.

That night Crockett kept his thighs "wondrously warm" by shinnying up and down the bear tree, hundreds of times. Crockett's close combats give him a certain quasi-bestial potency himself, and often suggest barely concealed hints of a certain violent, heated sexuality.[7]

Plus, Davy Crockett keeps score. He boasts that in that one year alone, he killed 105 bears.

Out of such tall tales, Americans gave a uniquely national cast to the hunter-hero myth. Out of the legends around a hunter-hero like Crockett, they made sense out of their own national experience on this wild continent. At the same time, such legends as Crockett's created a masculine landscape, "enmasculating" the landscape, if I can invent a word. They gave a particular male shape to their understanding of the wilderness. And for all the obsessive fighting and exploring an external wilderness, there is something narcissistic in these men, perpetually on their own private journeys, perpetually asserting and recreating personal identity.

In the "myth of the frontier," the wilderness offered a land of unlimited opportunity for the strong, self-reliant man. He is first and foremost an individual, alone and ambitious, willing like Crockett to abandon wife and family for "long hunts" and even for a suicidal last stand in Texas. He's the man on the move, looking for the next big creature, the next promised land, always restless, seeking that ultimate hunt which, as in the case of Ahab, will enable him to transcend himself, his insatiable hunger, the circumstances of his own life, even history itself.

Bred out of the actual experience of men, the myth of the hunter in the American imagination became the vehicle for shaping and simplifying the national experience of a growing country, and it made men masters of themselves, a continent, and history. It became the original and central organizing metaphor for how the male can not merely prove himself, but create himself in the woods. It is the myth of the self-made man in the woods, the mythic genesis of American manhood. Like Crockett's many legends, the myth of the hunter came to have a life of its own in the popular imagination, a strange mix of homage and exaggeration, including the invention of very strange fictional characters modeled on Crockett, one of whom was called, comically, "Nimrod Wildfire."

There are various kinds of hunters, as we know, and various kinds of masculinities. And I've been reading another hunter-writer, who puts another spin on American men who hunt.

John Mitchell in 1980 published a thoughtful overview of hunting in America, with the modestly grand title, *The Hunt.* He's more inclined to an ethical view of hunting than Davy Crockett, is more a revisionist of hunting, and he makes an odd contrast with Davy Crockett's grandiloquence. He writes for *Audubon* magazine, and subscribes more or less explicitly to the less violent, more sporting and ethical school of hunting, with the machismo factor tamped way down low.

What's striking about Mitchell's survey of hunting and the American hunter's psyche in 1980 is that, like hunters in conversation, he's on the defensive. From opening day hunting in northern Michigan, to the hunt of exotic species on a Texas farm, to natives on a subsistence hunt in Alaska, the panorama is filled with disoriented hunters, looking constantly over their shoulders.

Compared with the brash and unabashed boastfulness of Crockett, and even of Roosevelt, the tone seems odd in the mouths of hunters. The sport hunter, in Mitchell's pages, is a man of sense and sensibility. He's rational and responsible. And he's plagued by doubts, much like the conventional American white man of today. All the complicated emotional baggage is handled more or less sotto voce, as if men hope that by not saying anything too loudly, they won't have to deal with what frightens them.

The cause of this defensiveness and self-doubt is very clear—hunters feel besieged by the sense that they are creatures of bloodlust, bent on violence. The broad question at stake is, To what extent are hunters in some way responsible for, and related to, the violence in modern America?

Although Mitchell acknowledges the rifle as a quintessential American artifact, even if we didn't invent it, he wants to disclaim any relationship between hunters and violence. And the reason for that, as becomes clear, is that he wants to distance American masculinity itself from the impeachment of violence.

Mitchell raises the issue of social violence—of hunting for humans, of predatory crime—against the backdrop of the most legendary act of violence, perhaps, in this century. He's come to Texas, a hunter's heaven, and

he's in Dallas. He makes a de rigueur pass by the Texas Schoolbook De-
pository, where Lee Harvey Oswald used his rifle to shoot President
Kennedy. And as Mitchell cruises the vicinity, he hears on the radio that
somewhere in the area, a sniper is loose "once again." Kennedy's ghost
hovers in the area. And the sniper is using a "deer rifle."

That gives Mitchell pause. "A *deer* rifle." He pauses to consider
"snipers with deer rifles":

> Over the years, I resisted making straight connections between the gun
> and the hunting issues. I believed that the two could be viewed apart and
> separate, with few loose threads. I knew that some anti-hunters favored
> stringent gun controls and that a few anti-gunners favored curbs on the
> chase. But for myself, I could not see even a looping link between the
> urban mugger's zip gun and the outdoorsman deep in December woods;
> or, for that matter, between the assassin of a President and a rifle that in
> other hands happens to be used to assassinate deer. Reasonable people
> assure me the issues are best viewed apart, and kept that way. But as I
> noted before, not everyone is reasonable.[8]

Even if a deer rifle does the killing, he says, there's no connection.

You might call the question of violence in hunting, and violence in
American men, "the hunting question." By the metaphor of manliness, men
are hunters. But reasonable men know that urban killers and wilderness
killers are two separate phenomena because the links between them would
have to be "looping" and not immediately visible.

This seems to me a bit like making men in a certain image—of the
hunter—and then trying to disavow responsibility for the implications of
that image.

That disavowal takes the form of ethics and an imperative of rational
restraint. The good hunter is not a knuckle-walking, redneck "hog-hunter."
He is something much more respectable, and just as this more respectable
hunter disavows any relation with his more slovenly cousins in the field, he
disavows any relation with his gun-toting cousins in the streets.

Yet, just as men use deer rifles to kill other men, so men use Uzis in the
field to shoot down deer.

The "hunting question" is not one of direct cause and effect, of obvious
causal links, clear and apparent. There is a much deeper logic at work. I
want to look at precisely those murky links, those "looping" links that lie in
the subliminal region of the psyche, and, if it exists, in the national ideology of manhood. What is the relationship between Mitchell's hunter and
Crockett's hunter?

Mitchell's disavowal of any connection between hunting and violence in America doesn't wash. The connection lies in the myth of the American hunter, which in turn was the crucible out of which was created the American male. The connection between hunting in the field and hunting in the streets is made through the hunter within. And through the wilderness within.

And in his secret heart, the hunter knows it. That's why he's defensive. Because, lurking under the modern male, with his well-polished postures and his gleaming, well-adjusted rhetoric, all clean and crisp like an Eddie Bauer outfit, the hunter suspects there lies something savage and bloodthirsty.

Even Mitchell is uneasy. His doubts betray him. There is a sense among hunters that they are imperiled. That the antihunters have them surrounded. And even more, that they are imperiled from within. It's a gentle doubt in Mitchell, but it's enough to destabilize the fantasy of the well-adjusted middle-class male secure in his cabin or living room.

Mitchell opens his book in a comfortable cabin, in northern Michigan, built by his father.

Mitchell is going hunting the next day. But it's late night, and he's compelled by a strong and graphic image: the moose on the wall above the fireplace. His father had shot that moose long ago, in 1922, in New Brunswick. The trophy is lit on this autumn night by a flickering fire, flashing across the brown marble of the moose's "make-believe eyes." And Mitchell seems haunted: "Wherever I moved, the eyes seemed to follow. I spoke to the moose. I said, Moose, why do you watch me? Why do you look so sad when it no longer hurts?"

The beast can be shot, but it can't quite be laid to rest.

No wonder Mitchell says, a short few pages later to a woman, "Trying to explain hunting to non-hunters is like trying to explain sex to a eunuch."[9]

This is the gentlest of doubts, and Mitchell never lets his questions gain too much emotional force. Sentiment is kept under firm control. But the book itself, and Mitchell's venatic peregrinations all over the country, are an effort to make the moose quit following him with his eyes. To allay the guilt of his father, really, for having shot him. To make the demon of the moose—and all the prolific carcasses in American history—finally shut up. For they're all still in the hearts of men, all the dead beasts.

Mitchell knows it: he's haunted by his father's trophy. He's haunted by the dead animals that follow him in flickering firelight. This is the anxiety hunters in this century have not put to rest—it's what I'd call a uniquely modern hunter's complex.

The haunted hunter is suffering from guilt, deep and even national guilt. It's even guilt handed down from the fathers. The male tries to allay this guilt by bracketing it, by controlling his anxiety. He makes distinctions: He's not like a slob-hunter. He takes refuge in categories.

But the walls of rationality don't fully work. There is the lingering sense that, however strong this new and ethical hunter may be, however justified, the animals are slipping away. What's really vanishing is the whole world in which American men can prove themselves without this guilt. After trying to placate the moose on the wall, Mitchell ponders his father, who killed the moose. He derived from that other time, when the frontier was still alive but vanishing fast, a time of horse and bugles and even, says Mitchell, General Custer. The last of the bison in Kansas died in the month his father was born. Passenger pigeons in great flights still passed over Kentucky when he was a boy. This whole frontier heritage from the father rests in the accusing marble eyes of the moose.

Mitchell's unspoken, unacknowledged real question is, What is his relation to that frontier heritage? How are American fathers and sons, American men, responsible for their own history?

The frontier still has not been entirely won over from the beasts and the natives, who are restless outside.

The sense is that American men are being watched, so to speak, by the empty eyes of dead animals. These are the animals that were killed by the quintessential American men—the frontiersmen. In one sense, Mitchell is distilling one of the central American conflicts in the image of the male—the settler versus the hunter. The cabin fire versus the campfire. Mitchell versus Davy Crockett.

But more, in the defensive and haunted note of Mitchell's book, the crack in the male armor is betrayed, the mask drops for a moment, and we glimpse beneath the usually studied composure and competence of the thoughtful male. And he's haunted by the ghosts of his father's victims, linked to the victims of patriarchy itself. These worries flicker across his consciousness, but are perceived only in the inscrutable face of the moose. In these night complexes, the masks of masculinity begin to fray and falter.

These two images define the polarities in the male heart: Davy Crockett, hunter-explorer grinning in front of a pile of 105 dead bears; and John Mitchell, a cabin man, soft-spoken and thoughtful, interrogating his father's silent victims. He's trying to keep the doubts at bay.

Men have been doing a lot of push-ups in the last few decades to get themselves fit again, a lot of mental muscle-building. They've been doing a lot of hyperventilating too, after all these internal calisthenics to redeem the tarnished image of manhood. What is always also true about the American man is that he may have been born on the frontier, but he was born an old man. He feels he is always about to disappear. Despite his bluster, he's always fragile underneath.

Scratch the surface of the complex shimmer and shine, sandpaper the gleam of all those tightly balanced modern accommodations to middle-class life that the American male has made. There's a mandatory pose for upward mobility: hardworking, ambitious, but cooperative and agreeable. Sociable and competent. But just underneath the bright eyes and bushy tail lurks—

Norman Mailer.

Mailer, whose voice seems so very, well, male. Mailer—whose superlative form is "malest." Mailer, whose prose feeds on, erupts from, glories in, the male's violent dreams, exploits the hunter's complex as it informs American manhood. For him, the hunt is explanatory. For him, the hunt is the metaphor that explains the murder, say, of Sharon Tate in Southern California and the impetus for war that got us into Vietnam.

In his 1967 novel, *Why Are We in Vietnam?*, a bear hunt in Alaska defines the structure of the American male psyche. The book has nothing to do with the war explicitly. But the hunt is the expression of the American male's love of violence and competition, released from social restraints on the final frontier, Alaska. In an exculpatory preface that was added in 1977, Mailer links the violence in language and action in the novel with the murder of Sharon Tate in the summer of 1969. These are deep truths, he claims, somewhat mysteriously. There is no logical explanation for the way in which, writing to touch the depths of the violence in the male soul, he has drawn connections between crime and war and killing grizzlies. Writing is an occult force, he says, and the truths that emerge seem to come from "some invisible finger."

The torrent of prose in the book dramatizes the motions and motives of the mentality that lead us into war and into murder. And fucking. Corporate "big ass men" with Washington big ass connections go to Alaska to hunt "grizzer":

> They are not hunter-fighter-fuckers for nothing, no, nor with enclaves of high ability in karate, football, sports car, motorcycle, surfboard, and certain notions of the dance, as well as genius inquiries in electronics and applied existentialism without having to snoop here and there for powers, which they get from crime, closet fucking, potential overturn of incest since Tex is almost not above trying to get Hallie Jethroe [his father's wife] in one closet fuck this very night, plus ghoul surgery on corpses which is demonological you may be shit-and-sure, and derives from their encounter with all the human shit and natural depth of their

Moe Henry hunt [for grizzer] two year ago. So back to Alaska where the
boys got their power.[10]

Hunter-fighter-fucker: explicitly male power, which is bestial and even demonic in its origins, derives directly from this quasi-epical and wild hunting on the modern frontier of Alaska, and is the origin of both American
success and American tragedies like Vietnam.

The game is not only linked to the father, but in some sense it is the
American male's god, in a way unlike any other nation. There is this contradiction within the American male, between his longing for home and his
urge to wander, between the pioneer and the scout, the settler and the wilderness hunter, the village and the virgin land. Convention and subversion,
commitment and freedom. Between a nation of horny bastards and a nation
of devoted fathers. Between the father in the cabin in northern Michigan,
like Mitchell, or the frontiersman always on the move, like Davy Crockett.

What's not clear, in the telepathic depths of the male soul, is which
comes first: the atavistic pulse of a tribal chant, or the solemn benediction
of the old hunter-patriarchs.

What unifies both these types of American male—the trailblazer and
the pioneer—is that they were conceived as hunters. Across the continent,
we have pursued the beast like a curse and a hope, and often not sure
which.

The American myth of the hunt provided the materials out of which the
primary myths of the American male could be molded into coherent
shapes. As the single unifying myth of the American male, the hunter has
set the limits to what we have imagined ourselves able to be.

The American hunter gave us our symbolic origins, our foundation as a
hunt culture. Through him, we learned to articulate ourselves to ourselves.
Within the symbolic fields he pioneered, in his various guises, we can trace
the fault lines that divide us and define us.

3

American literature begins with a hunt. A deer hunt on Christmas Eve is
the opening scene and the first chapter of the first truly American novel. It
forms the opening chapter of our literature, when a buckskinned, skulking,
and blue-eyed hunter named Leatherstocking steps from behind a pine at
dusk and says nothing, but begins his almost wordless stalk through history
and psyche as the first distinctively American male, the first fully realized
American hero.

The first American is not really a Puritan, Thanksgiving notwithstanding. He's not really a Christian with starched collar and blunderbuss. And he's not a Thomas Jefferson, the Fourth of July notwithstanding, with his intellect and his words. He's a hunter with a Kentucky long rifle and a long knife, and he's gone more or less native. And he first comes to us fighting with a judge over the carcass of a Christmas deer.

In literature, our first hero is named Nathaniel Bumppo, but he comes into his own by abandoning this name and the quasi-feudal, European-based culture of New England, and heading for the woods. He's still called Natty Bumppo from time to time—as in "Natural Bumpkin." But we meet him when he's already got his hunter's name, for the clothes he wears on the frontier of New York: "Leatherstocking."

But for an American male, he can't have a name that smacks so much of, well, hosiery. The pun is probably important—the pun is on "Leatherstalking"—but it's too understated. Plus, he's just beginning his evolution, and will go through several increasingly "savage," increasingly deadly names before landing on the one that seems most true to his identity—Deerslayer and Hawkeye.

The male is the one who gets to name himself—and that privilege, the privilege of naming himself—comes largely from deeds. Already, this first hunter sees himself as the last true hunter, an old man at seventy, moving along a retreating frontier, slinking through margins, someplace between the sublime and the subliminal.

And he announces America as a hunt culture.

America has a special relationship to and idea of the hunt. America is a hunt culture.

Postrevolutionary Americans were obsessed with defining America—an American hero and a uniquely American way of life.[11] The anxiety over identity is also an interminable drama for us. Natty keeps it up, and we're always wondering who we are. It's the narcissism, perhaps, of a rebellious and orphaned child, obsessed with a search for identity that lasts a lifetime. We entered into ourselves, and embarked upon our unique path across space and time, continents and centuries, along paths scouted by Leatherstocking, the prototypical hunter-hero.

But when we first see him, the contest of the hunter is not with a deer, really, but with another hunter. It's the contest at our origins between the settler and the woodsman, plotted along the margins of town and forest, between Christian and pagan.

James Fenimore Cooper had already written two novels by 1823, when he published *The Pioneers*. But with this one, a romance set in a fictionalized version of his own hometown, Cooperstown, Cooper inaugurates the myth of the vanishing America and American.

The novel opens upon a sleigh passing through snowy winter woods—a quintessential American scene. It is Christmas Eve—the heart of the Christian calendar, the holiday which marks the center of Puritan town life. Judge Temple and his daughter, Elizabeth, are heading home for a Christmas fireside and a Christmas feast in Templeton, the town the judge has established in the frontier of New York State, his own little "temple" in the wilderness. The mountain and forest provide "innumerable vistas," but they have a dark and evergreen melancholy to them, and the lofty pines sway above the snow with a dull, plaintive sound.

The judge hears howling in the woods from the hounds of Leatherstocking. They must have startled some game, he says as he pulls the sleigh to a stop. Ahead, in the snow, he notices deer tracks. The judge grabs his "double-barrelled fowling piece" from the luggage in the sleigh, as "the light bounding noise of an animal plunging through the woods was heard, and a fine buck darts into the path a short distance ahead of him."

The judge aims and fires at the buck. But it dashes forward undaunted and apparently unhurt. The judge fires again. No effect.

His daughter is "unconsciously rejoicing in the escape of the buck," when

> a sharp, quick sound struck her ear, quite different from the full, round report of her father's gun, but still sufficiently distinct to be known as the concussion produced by fire-arms. At the same instant that she heard this unexpected report, the buck sprang from the snow, to a great height in the air, and directly a second discharge, similar in sound to the first, followed, when the animal came to the earth, falling headlong, and rolling over on the crust with its own velocity. A loud shout was given by the unseen marksman, and a couple of men instantly appeared from behind the trunks of the pines, where they had evidently placed themselves in expectation of the passage of the deer.[12]

The marksman is unseen and unnamed, but out steps the "nattily" costumed Leatherstocking, in buckskin breeches and moccasins, carrying always his rifle.

If the first act in the first American novel is the killing of the deer, the real drama is over possession of the deer. And the history of the country is suggested in this battle over the deer's carcass—between possession and dispossession. The judge claims the right of ownership, but Natty claims

the right of the best shot. Natty loses the battle, is pushed sulking and re-
gretful even further into the margins and shadows.

All Natty can do, besides shoot the heads off the poor birds in the
Christmas turkey shoot, is complain about the settlers. And ridicule them
as unmanly. He mocks the judge's rifle, ridiculing it as more appropriate to
pheasants in the swamps than a noble buck or a bear in the woods. For that,
you need a "long rifle."

In some ways, the question comes down to how the American man is
going to dress—in buckskin like Natty, or in furs and robes, like the judge.
Right from the start, the woods are the refuge of the disaffected male, con-
ceptualized as laconic, surly, manly—winning any shooting contest, but
losing the war for the frontier to the settlers.

But Cooper's heart is clearly with Natty Bumppo. The forests are
falling, the game vanishing, and the way of life he loves is doomed. And if
the first shot once determined a man's merit, that has passed to something
more subtle, and more insidious. "No, no, I never expected to live forever,"
Leatherstocking tells a minister later that evening,

> but I see, times be altering in these mountains from what they was thirty
> years ago, or for that matter, ten years. But might makes right, and the
> law is stronger than an old man, whether he is one that has much larn-
> ing, or only one like me, that is better now at standing at the passes than
> in following the hounds, as I once used to could.[13]

Even when we first meet him, the American hunter is an old man, subversive but growing impotent, carping ineffectually at the onslaught of
civilization.

The question is not simply who shot the deer. That alone doesn't deter-
mine who gets the deer. As the hunters bicker over the body of the slain animal, we have a classic image: who succeeds in American culture, who has
preeminence and power, is a question of how the deer is divvied. The male
creates himself, justifies himself, by his hunting.

For Natty, the rifle is the law, as a German immigrant puts it: "Ter rifle
is petter as ter law!"[14]

The judge gets the meat, and in the end of the novel, the hunter
Leatherstocking is sentenced to a fine and imprisonment for violating the
game laws. The judge was the winner in history, as settlements advanced
and his towns and laws spread across the continent.

The question is, however, to what extent can the frontier hunter, the
Leatherstocking figure, absolve himself from the guilt of the settlers in destroying the wilderness. Can this hunter—the progenitor of American man-

hood and maleness—absolve himself from the obscene and wanton violence through which Americans settled the wilderness? Or is he the father
of a violence built into the male, twisted into his heart from a life on the
frontier? Is the American male the son of the forest, or the despoiler of the
forest?

Cooper wants to affirm the innocence of the hunter, but it's clear that
he's not so sure.

Natty's comments on the "wasty ways" of the settlers in the famous
mass slaughter of passenger pigeons in chapter 22 are an indictment of the
settlers' wanton abandon. The "heavens were alive with pigeons," Cooper
writes, and the woods overrun with sportsmen armed with rifles, sticks,
crossbows, whatever. The townspeople exercise their civilized ingenuity in
a wholesale slaughter:

> So prodigious was the number of birds, that the scattering fire of the
> guns, with the hurling of missiles, and the cries of the boys, had no other
> effect than to break off small flocks from the immense masses that con-
> tinued to dart along the valley, as if the whole of the feathered tribe were
> pouring through that one pass. None pretended to collect the game,
> which lay scattered over the fields in such profusion, as to cover the
> very ground with the fluttering victims.[15]

Leatherstocking moves among the "execution" as a "silent, uneasy spectator," but finally blurts out in disgust, "This comes of settling the country!"

Such hunts finally destroyed the passenger pigeon, which is now extinct, and stand as the pattern of American settlement. Leatherstocking tries
to hold himself apart from the violence of the frontier, but can't. The six
bird species which have gone extinct in North America since 1600 were all
decimated by hunters.[16]

Leatherstocking is an almost miraculous American concept of manhood, the original Lone Ranger, the virtuous outlaw, the stranger. This is
his métier, controlling his passions, maintaining a manly chastity in the
woods. All desire is reduced to a deadly, disciplined aim. In the last novel
of the Leatherstocking "saga," *The Deerslayer* (1841), Cooper again opens
with a hunting scene. Leatherstocking is shown now as a young man in the
woods, just coming to manhood. He is with Hurry Harry, a reckless hunter,
vaguely like Crockett. Cooper is at pains to distinguish Deerslayer from the
slob hunter, Hurry Harry. "Fall to, lad," says Hurry when they kill the deer,
"and prove your manhood on this poor devil of a doe. . . ."

And the idealized Leatherstocking gives this hunter a lesson: "Nay,
nay, Hurry, there's little manhood in killing a doe, and that too out of sea-

son, though there might be some in bringing down a painter [panther] or catamount [mountain lion]."[17]

Leatherstocking is that strange American amalgam—the saint with a gun. Cooper wants his hero to have nothing to do with a Hurry Harry, a slob hunter who looks a bit too much like Davy Crockett's brand of tall tales and bragging slaughter: the hunter as frontier clown.

In *The Deerslayer*, Cooper's last essay into the Leatherstocking legend, Natty opens the novel not so much rescuing as protecting two young but not very attractive women in the woods. The point of this novel will be to study the lone hunter when a female loves him. The scene is a lake in the deep woods, where Cooper can delve into liminal and subliminal issues of the forest hunter's psyche, like sexuality and violence.

The main theme is hunterly identity. In this novel, he's metamorphosed into the more manly title of Deerslayer—better than Leatherstocking—for his exploits with the rifle in slaying deer. Deerslayer lives halfway between whites like Hurry Harry and the natives. To the slob Hurry Harry, he says, "They call me Deerslayer, I'll own; and perhaps I desarve the name, in the way of understanding the creatur's habits, as well as for sartainty of aim; but they can't accuse me of killing an animal when there's no occasion for the meat or for the skin. I may be a slayer, but I'm no slaughterer."[18]

Presumably, like the slaughterer Hurry Harry himself. It's a nice distinction, but it doesn't hold up.

Not long after this, he encounters his first Indian, who is "on the trail for mortal men, not for beaver or deer." It turns out that one of them is snooping around the cabin in the woods, and his practice as hunter proves good service in hunting the Indian, who in being pursued becomes a "creatur" and a "riptyle." But though Leatherstocking proves "his gifts are white," he takes a new identity now, the benediction of the dying Indian, who in his final breaths gives Natty, in honor of killing a man, the "more manly title" he has earned: "Hawkeye."[19]

In Natty's quasi-religious quest for a manly identity through hunting, he can't always sustain the poses his stoic self-control demands.

As hunter, he is a killer, dignify it how he will with religious words like "slayer." His favorite rifle is called "Killdeer," with a wrenching pun on the bird species that does the wounded wing act to protect its young, and the act of killing. His one "never-failing companion," Deerslayer loves his rifle more than anything, with its fine bore, excellent metal, and "perfection of details." The rifle makes him "King of the Woods." Without a rifle, he says, a man in the woods is merely a miserable trapper, or "a forlorn broom and basketmaker, at the best." The rifle is his guarantee of hunterly manhood. And—it was given to him by Hurry Harry himself, whose "vigorous manhood" and "constitutional recklessness" are so explicitly contrasted to Natty.[20]

As if to underscore the point, hardly has Deerslayer gotten his new and perfect rifle—hardly has he protested that he never kills except for food or clothing—hardly has he wrapped himself firmly in his noble words, and with "laughing and delighted eyes," he shoots an eagle from the sky— merely to see if "Killdeer isn't Killeagle, too!"

It's a shameful act, and Deerslayer feels the force of his hypocrisy. "What a thing is power!" he sermonizes, "and what a thing it is to have it and not know how to use it!"[21]

Natty's logical categories—slayer versus slaughterer—aren't proof against his impulses. His fine distinctions begin to bleed at the boundaries. The frontiersman is finally not much better than either the settlers or the slobs. There is this violence in his heart, expressed through his rifle.

Natty wants to see himself as separate from the settlers and the slob hunters, both, but he can't. The essential irony and paradox of his position, Cooper reiterates constantly, is that he makes the way for the American culture that destroys the wilderness—cutting trees, depleting lakes, destroying the deer. In the American advance across the continent, the hunter is in the vanguard. Leatherstocking is the manly figure, the man in leather. But he's already an anachronism the minute he steps into the forest and onto the page, blazing a trail for his own vanishing. He's looking for elbow room, and Leatherstocking actually sets the pattern of all Westerns when, in the final paragraph of his first novel, he has to leave again, and he moves into the forest. And he creates an American cliché, as Cooper describes him disappearing into the "setting sun."

4

Cooper's Leatherstocking appeared during a renaissance in the popularity of the hunter among the urban elite. Frank Forester (the pseudonym for the Englishman-turned-guru of the American wilds, Henry William Herbert) led the fashion, taking citified men to the Hudson River to get wild, to exercise their manly heritage. But the rough-skinned and wild-living frontiersmen were not always popular. It took two centuries for Leatherstocking to stride into the American scene as a hero. Earlier, he had been viewed with alarm and concern—a rough-living, godless man of the woods who abjured society for a lonely pagan wildness.

Frontiersmen were slovenly men, and even Cooper is at pains to state that he realizes that Leatherstocking is quite different from the mass of frontiersmen. He's a new ideal. As William Byrd observed in 1822, frontiersmen were anything but chaste. They slept naked in their blankets, in the smoke of their fires, to keep the dew off. They loved bear meat, which made them "a little too rampant." All the married men who ate bear were soon fathers when they returned home. It's not, he said, "a very proper dyet for saints."[22]

American individualism was born out of the conflict in our history between civilization and the wilderness. The man who stamped the template for all subsequent generations of the loner in the woods as hero was Daniel Boone.[23]

He did it by allying the skills of a woodsman with the ambitions of a society laying claim to the land in the wilderness: by putting the skills of the frontiersman, in other words, into the service of empire. He was the man in Manifest Destiny: the game hunter as land hunter. And he seems to have been a genuinely admirable man, unlike much of the riffraff on the frontier.

In the legends that grew up around Daniel Boone, his dual roles as frontiersman and settler, hunter and landgrabber, competed in an uneasy truce within a single almost mythic figure.

The story of his greatest long hunt, scouting the way across the Cumberland Mountains and exploring the entire wilderness state of Kentucky, a true hunter's paradise, illustrates his love of the wilderness. It suggests that new element the American hunter gave to the long history of the hunting myth in male thinking: he was a true son of the forest.

Before Boone, settlements had hugged the eastern seaboard. The Allegheny Mountains blocked the way west, an unknown territory "haunted" by Indians. A "Warrior's Path" led over the mountains, but it was not until Daniel Boone and a party of four—including his brother Squire—passed along a "hunter's trace" and connected with the Warrior's Path that the secret of Kentucky was opened to whites. He moved through the Cumberland Gap in 1770, one of the great achievements in American history, on what amounted to a frontiersman's "long hunt": those extended absences from wife and family that could last months and years.

While Boone and his party were hunting in Kentucky, they were robbed by Indians. Two of the party were killed. Boone and his brother kept hunting. After a year, Squire Boone agreed to take what small profits they had accumulated in furs back to the Yadkin Valley in North Carolina, to furnish the families.

But Daniel Boone chose to stay on in Kentucky.

He loved the absolute solitude of the forest. As a boy, he had hunted and roamed the woods endlessly, getting his first rifle when he was thirteen. But this stay in Kentucky was exceptional even for Boone. According to his first biographer, John Filson, he had no bread, no salt, no sugar, no horse, no dog. He spent another entire year alone in the wilderness of Kentucky, exploring, hunting. He was hundreds of miles from family and home and other settlers. Alone.[24]

He was happy. When another group of long hunters stumbled upon Boone toward the end of his sojourn in Kentucky, they found Daniel Boone lying flat on his back on a deerskin, completely alone and singing to himself. Other tales tell of him sitting alone in the woods, by a fire, singing to his queer-faced dogs.[25]

Out of tales like this, Daniel Boone emerged as the son of the forest. The myth was cemented when, in 1778, he was kidnapped by Shawnee Indians at a salt lick not far from Boonesborough. He spent five months with the Indians. He was wildly famous on the frontier, and the Indians knew him by reputation. They were overjoyed to have captured the great hunter himself, and the chief of the tribe, Blackfish, took him into his family. Daniel Boone was adopted by the chief himself. In Filson's account, Boone says he "was adopted, accordin [sic] to their custom, into a family where I became a son, and had a great share in the affection of my new parents, brothers, sisters, and friends. I was exceedingly familiar and friendly with them, always appearing chearful [sic] and satisfied as possible, and they put great confidence in me."[26] He received a new name, Sheltowee, or Big Turtle. He won a new father—an Indian father—and became an adopted son of the forest. His hair was plucked out, leaving only a tuft, and he was taken to the river, naked, and washed and rubbed to take all of his white blood out. Then he was painted, head and face: he was a Shawnee brave.

A foster child to the natives, son of the Indians, the story adds something entirely new in the Western imagination, a unique achievement in the American mind. Tutored by natives, this white hunter learns to identify with nature as well as conquer it.

For Daniel Boone did not stay with the Indians, though he stayed much longer than he had to. For the frontiersman is also white, and he never forsakes this other side of the great myth—his allegiance to white culture remains, transformed but intact.

In Daniel Boone, this allegiance is defined by his role as Indian hunter and empire builder. Without this, he surely could not have morphed into heroic legend. The most succinct way this motif was expressed, the most sensational example out of many that defined Boone as champion of white values, was the rescue of his kidnapped daughter.

His spunky daughter Jemima was abducted by Indians. It's a new version of the American captivity tale, and the rescue of the white female by

the heroic hunter—in this case, benevolent father—is the American heroic
story in its purest form.[27]

On Sunday, July 7, 1776, Jemima Boone and two other girls relaxed
after their Bible reading by canoeing on the Kentucky River. Jemima
Boone had apparently cut her foot on cut canes, and wanted to soak the
wound. Jemima and Fanny Callaway were fourteen, and Betsey Callaway
was sixteen. But this was a marriageable age, and all were either engaged
or beseiged by suitors. The young women floated on the river, and their
desultory drift brought them to the cane on the far shore. Near shore, they
tried futilely to pull themselves back to the river, when several Indians
sprang from the cane and stole them away.

These three girls were difficult prisoners. They did everything in their
power to slow their captors' speed as they made through the trails toward
Ohio. The girls broke twigs, dug the heels of their shoes into the soft dirt,
fell off their horse as if they were terrible riders, and lagged back like a
heavy weight. Betsey Callaway even ripped bits of her clothes and dropped
them on the trail, including a linen handkerchief with "Callaway" written
on it. All this was to leave evidence for the party of Daniel Boone and others who would come tracking them along the wilderness trails.

Boone tracked the Indians who had his daughter across the Ohio River,
guessing several times by intuition of Indian ways where they'd go and
what they'd do. He caught up with the Indians not far from Blue Licks. The
idea was to surprise the Indians as they cooked a buffalo. The Shawnees
and Cherokees apparently thought they had outdistanced the hunter. In
camp, they had laid their weapons aside, even the sentry they posted. The
whites snuck up on the camp, within thirty yards, when they were spotted.
After a brief exchange of volleys, the girls jumped up and screamed for
happiness. Several Indians were shot, two died of their wounds, and the
rest fled. The "poor little heart-broken girls" were saved by the hunters.

This incident raised Boone's fame for prowess and bravery throughout the frontier even higher than before. It became the basis for Cooper's
story in *The Last of the Mohicans*, when Cora and Alice are abducted by
Magua of the Six Nations. The young white virgin becomes the threatened
symbol of the civilization, rescued by the old white hunter.

The theme of defending the innocent—especially young girls—is one
of our preferred motifs. Politicians cast military operations in this language
(as, say, the invasion of Grenada). News media cast the stories of disasters
in this language, focusing on the search for survivors. And movies exploit
this trope as if it were inexhaustible, a favorite plot.

One of the essential functions of all myths is to reconcile emotional
contradictions. Richard Slotkin argues persuasively that the myth of Daniel

Boone as hunter enabled the American mind to hold two contradictory impulses together—not so much reconciled, as accommodated. The first: the Puritan notion of the wilderness as a howling and Indian-infested image of hell. The second: the more frontier notion, more uniquely American, of the beauty in wilderness, the attraction to the wilderness, the sense of the wilderness as a place of spiritual exaltation.[28]

Each view required a different response. The wilderness as terror demanded that the demons—whether beast or Indian—be exorcised. The wilderness was redeemed for culture.

The wilderness as spiritual cradle, source of wisdom and wonder and sustenance, demanded an initiation.

The hunter was crucial in both scenarios. He either destroyed the beast, or he identified with it. Regardless, he was assuming its powers, as he was the agent in establishing the always mobile boundaries between human and beast, culture and wilderness, town and forest.

He reconciles in his two narratives the difference between two ways of being in the wilderness: domination and intimacy. White stoicism and weapons, and Indian woodcraft.

Daniel Boone's fame was marshaled by various writers to serve different mythical purposes: John Filson employed it for attracting land buyers; Timothy Flint, as a symbol of empire and expansion; and Theodore Roosevelt, in the ideology of masterful manliness in the wilderness.

What interests me are the dual purposes of the hunter, which make such uncomfortable and strange bedfellows: the frontiersman who loves the "long hunt" even more than home, is adopted by an Indian chief, and embodies a new intimacy with wilderness and the wild; and the settler who is the agent and vanguard of the culture. The one moves through a hunter's paradise; the other, through a "dark and bloody ground."

And these dual impulses are not really between hunter and settler, though they obviously take that form. They are the dual impulses within an individual hunter. They mark his psyche, his personal internal migrations across the boundaries between human and animal.

The legends of Daniel Boone, and the stories of Leatherstocking, became the template for subsequent American heroes, from Davy Crockett to Kit Carson to Buffalo Bill Cody. For Theodore Roosevelt, Boone the hunter gave a morality of masterful manliness on the frontier. American hunters became the key to American history, the builders of the nation, those who flee from settlements. In *The Wilderness Hunter*, Roosevelt elevated these "untamable souls" from myth to ideology. Davy Crockett the tall-tale teller becomes "honest, fearless Davy Crockett." Daniel Boone was the "archetype of the American hunter . . ." leading his bands of backwoods riflemen to settle the beautiful country of Kentucky. . . . Boone and his fellow hunters were the heralds of the oncoming civilization, the pioneers of the conquest of the wilderness which has at last been practically achieved in our day."[29] The hunter was a nation builder, a man whose flight from cities made him, paradoxically, the herald of the civilization just behind him.

Roosevelt perpetuated the role of the manly, idealized hunter, moving between settlement and forest. In his day, as the frontier closed, he pursued the "wild warfare waged against wild nature" with an incredible fervor.[30] While resuscitating the wilderness hunter as a model for the strenuous life, Roosevelt helped develop the sportsmen's code in hunting, a system of ethical restraint that was an attempt by eastern patrician elite hunters, as well as European hunters abroad, to curb the excesses of the past century in their activities. While the reaction against hunting was strong enough to cause many to recoil from the sport, Roosevelt and others repackaged it in the form of the hunter-naturalist. In such organizations as the Boone and Crockett Club, of which Roosevelt was a charter member in 1887, such hunters worked to preserve habitat and their "manly sport with rifle."

And while they officially blamed the "market hunter" for the loss of buffalo and passenger pigeon, great auk and Labrador duck, privately they acknowledged that their own excesses as hunters were partly responsible. The clubs were formed at least partly to curb their own impulses through the sporting code, as well as to promote the new conservation ethic. This new sporting and conservation ethic enabled them to distinguish themselves from "slob hunters" and "game-butchers" and the "big-bag" hunters, as they referred to them—even though Roosevelt himself often boasted of the numbers he'd bagged.

And they prided themselves on the superiority of their natural insight, their tougher version of nature, in contrast to men like Ernest Thompson Seton, who renounced hunting. According to Roosevelt, Seton and his "School of Nature" taught only sissylike lessons. Those types, Roosevelt said disdainfully, were "nature fakers."[31]

Both in its advocacy of hunting as the most proper way to view nature, and in its work to save nature for the sport of hunting, the "hunter-naturalists" perpetuated the boundary between civil and wild that was generated by the first frontiersmen-hunters, displacing blame where possible on the slobs and the commercial hunters.

The hunter hero resides at the heart of American culture. Before Walt Disney in our century lifted Davy Crockett back to prominence, the more philosophical and laconic Boone embodied the frontiersman. But his death—indigestion from sweet potatoes—is less glorious than Crockett's heroic end at the Alamo. Still, Boone was made into 165 episodes of a TV series, starring Fess Parker.

Melville's Ahab abandons the rationalized version of the myth and pursues a demonic hunt for the white whale, the great metaphysical principle of the silent evil of the universe, through all the seas of the world. The hunting story is the great national epic, the epic of the tortured American consciousness. Thoreau knows the "savage" impulse at Walden, and a distant descendant of Thoreau's, Annie Dillard, likens her spiritual quest at Tinker Creek to the frontiersman mode: "I am an explorer, then, and I am also a stalker, or the instrument of the hunt itself. . . . I am the arrow shaft, . . . and this book is the straying trail of blood."[32]

D. H. Lawrence calls Leatherstocking a "killer": "But you have there the myth of the essential white America. All the other stuff, the love, the democracy, the floundering into lust, is a sort of by-play. The essential American soul is hard, isolate, stoic, and a killer. It has never yet melted. . . . And this, for America, is Deerslayer."[33]

Annette Kolodny argues in *The Lay of the Land* that the masculine hero is attracted to the land and the game as if they were a woman. And then he violates this feminized landscape. It is according to her the basic pattern in the American pastoral impulse—attraction, rape, and expiation. Richard Slotkin views the hunter-hero myth as the central metaphor of the American experience. It gave the American male the perpetual hope that there was a new land, and new animal, a new self—and he would rise again from the violence of the slain animal, a new self. David Leverenz suggests that the man-beast, a class-conscious hero, operates to salvage American masculinity not simply from impotence, but humiliation.

Every metaphor is determinative—it shapes not simply how we see reality, but it structures the kinds of responses that are available to us in action. The metaphor of the hunter and the captive has led us to conceptualize our relation to the wilderness in terms of an adversary, for all our love of its beauty and potential. Probably, the early continent offered our forebears other options besides the complex of motifs that slowly emerged in the hunter myth. What if they had not imagined that these hunters needed to exploit the land they fell in love with in spite of themselves?

But finally, the hunter is alone. Deerslayer's loneliness drives him away from love and a relationship with a woman. He is doomed to wander, "into the setting sun," like the classic American hero that he defines, because he is finally an old and impotent figure.

A saint with a gun: contradictions are too difficult to sustain, even for heroes like Leatherstocking, who can be irritatingly smug. Of course there is violence at the heart of this hero. His legacy in the twentieth century is the whole interminable breed of violent Western heroes, all of whom hope that through violence they can summon yet one last time an imperiled manhood.

A man who can use violence and not be tainted by it—that's the paradox of the American myth of the hunter. Leatherstocking's dead eagle is a reminder that the impulse is never fully restrained. This impulse marks the hunter's soul, the male's soul, which he struggles so mightily to deny and deflect.

The game as spoil and the land despoiled—the savaged landscape which the hunter opened up is also the image of a deeply troubled mind. He's restless, always moving. There is some unresolved motion in him— and it is unresolvable by the terms of the violence that impels him and keeps his desire fresh. He must always search for the new frontier, the new beast, the next thing to kill. In the woods, the original frontiersman doesn't have a horse. He doesn't have a friend, really. Not even a dog. Not another living thing. Certainly not a woman. He has only his rifle and his wits.

Still, there is something wonderful and attractive about the mythic frontiersman. I can't not like him, wild and melancholy and hopelessly displaced. He can be pompous and prim in his heroic mode, but there is that sulky sad side to him, which strangely redeems him. The settlers seem phlegmatic and complacent. The hunter is unsettled by the violence on the frontier, by his own violence. His discontent links him to his emotions, to his deeper self, and to a subversive impulse. He doesn't really like the settlements he serves.

He tries to be steady, but he's not very stable. From the moment we first genuinely meet him, he's always slightly illegal, in trouble, on the run.

With his skill in the service of national destiny, he hopes he can expiate the guilt that keeps him moving. The American soul—so restless and ambitious, driven as much as it is inspired. Always hoping the next valley is the paradise, the Eden in the wilderness. Because where he's just been, the game is already gone. The paths he found in the wilderness had become highways within a generation. He cannot escape the paradox, though he always believes that maybe he can transcend his own life. His restlessness, heading into the sunset alone, is a strange desire: the hunter is in flight, as much as he is in pursuit of a dream.

We now are haunted by the hunter myth of the fathers. Idealization is its own form of denial, and idealization was a way of justifying the violence on the advancing borders of the West. There is an ethic woven into the heart of what it means to be an American male, justified by the demands of life in the wilderness. Now we find ourselves surrounded by "last

frontiers," signifying loss as well as evoking a whole set of postures and attitudes. The idealized frontiersman, though, can't quite atone, and on the
last frontier, he's always on the way out. The savaged landscape is the tortured mind. Its violence eats us now from within, and makes us doubt.

Leatherstocking is the last frontiersman, even as we see him for the
first time.

It has been a long hunt indeed.

Once, conditions favored the hunter enough to make him legendary.
But that time passed with the frontier. Still, we continue to construct our
selves, and the future, out of the fabric of a past that never truly existed.

Now, in our cities, the metaphor of the hunter, with his restlessness and
his violence, has turned inward. The new hunter made *us* the prey.

5

Before proceeding to the modern urban hunter—predatory criminals and
sexual predators—I'll offer a brief exhibition of the hunter in the twentieth century. His credentials remain strong. At least, the myth of the frontier hunter continues to define the American male mystique in fiction and
movies. Two southerners straddle their hunters across the internal frontier, between ethics and atavism, patriarchal tradition and a survivalist's
primitivism.

William Faulkner's "The Bear" details the coming of age of a boy.
"Delta Autumn" understands the ways in which the legacy of the hunter's
violence, in the manhood of the South, has destroyed its own legacy. In
"Delta Autumn," the old man Ike McCaslin reflects over a hunting fire on
the legacy of men hunting:

> "God created man and He created the world for him to live in and I
> reckon He created the kind of world He would have wanted to live in
> if He had been a man—the ground to walk on, the big woods, the trees
> and the water, and the game to live in it. And maybe He didn't put the
> desire to hunt and kill game in man but I reckon He knew it was going
> to be there, that man was going to teach it to himself. . . . He put them
> both here: man and the game he would follow and kill, foreknowing it.
> I believe He said, 'So be it.' I reckon He even foreknew the end. But
> He said, 'I will give him his chance. I will give him warning and fore-
> knowledge too, along with the desire to follow and the power to slay.
> The woods and the fields he ravages and the game he devastates will

be the consequence and the signature of his crime and guilt, and his punishment.' "[34]

Faulkner's fictional and personal accounts of men hunting dramatize the struggle to forge a new and viable masculine role from the story of white southern masculinity to which he was heir. And his meditation on hunting swerves into regret, a sustained sense of the loss that has been wrought on the land by the "power to slay."

James Dickey celebrates the atavistic violence of the hunt. In *Deliverance*, sex, manhood, and violence merge in their ride down the wild river that will soon be dammed and flooded. It's another psychic lake for middle-class men with nightmares in the depths of their souls. The narrator, a paper-pushing adman named Ed, comes to the realization that Deerslayer resists with all his might, in spite of himself. Their bow-hunting trip down the river in northern Georgia turns into a hellish nightmare. Lewis is the macho man, played in the movie version by Burt Reynolds, a bow hunter who's made a pagan religion out of his well-muscled body. Bobby is a porcine insurance salesman. In the backwoods, the frontiersmen or mountain men they discover are not Noble Savages, but Genetic Defects. And rapists. In the movie, Bobby is played by Ned Beatty, and the scene of him being raped is unforgettable, squealing like a pig in the woods, obscene and pink and humiliated.

Later, Ed goes hunting for a mountain man who's still stalking them down the river, the man who raped Bobby. It's a fantasy of man against the wilderness, a struggle for survival. "I'll make a circle inland," he says, "very quiet, and look for him like I'm some kind of an animal. What kind? It doesn't matter, as long as I'm quiet and deadly. I could be a snake. Maybe I can kill him in his sleep. . . . I could see myself killing. . . . I wanted to kill him exactly as Lewis had killed the other man. . . . It was the same state of mind I had when I had hunted the deer in the fog."[35] The southern businessman discovers that under the declining routine of his life is the disturbing but invigorating truth. He touches the beast within, to learn he is a killer.

In addition to the heroics of the cool and steady great white hunter, manhood veers between these inherited versions and revisions of the civil and the wild—between a melancholy but manly struggle with the traditions of the culture, and a more or less sadistic fantasy of the bourgeois adman that, under the surface, there prowls an anarchic freedom and demonic desire.

6

Usually, the hunter is a man of technique. The hunter takes his time. He does what he does for art. He places himself, for the sake of sport, in a contest that pits two more or less equal parties. Hunter pursues game, and relies on art and patience to redeem him.

A predator, on the other hand, is greedy. He's moved by hunger. His appetite is rapacious, and if he stalks, there's always the sense of urgency. The rules of the predator are defined only by cunning and power. He's not after redemption of guilt, but indulgence of desire. The predator pursues prey.

As the hunter has receded in social prominence in this century, his aggressiveness coming as much from a besieged mentality as from anything innate, the predator has taken center stage. He's the darling of our imaginations, the star of the show, the guest in our homes every evening on Geraldo Rivera. He's the rapist, murderer, the midnight stalker. He's also the run-of-the-mill, anonymous urban criminal.

The predator has emerged full force on the modern scene. Sometimes he's still called a hunter, but the usage is always exploiting the connotations of the predator that are often latent in the word *hunter*. We have a phrase now that defines a social phenomenon that suggests that, in the evolution of the hunter, we've been going through a frightening mutation: sexual predator and predatory criminal.

In a hunting culture, predators take the metaphor in a perversely literal way. They hunt humans.

I'm not sure when this phrase was first coined. Shakespeare uses the concept of predator and prey in considering rape—as in "The Rape of Lucrece." It's hard to tell where the boundary is between literal and metaphorical, but in Shakespeare, the idea seems metaphorical, just as Orion's rape is mythical (though the stories surely depict some kind of contemporary reality to rape). But the idea now has become eerily literal. The *OED* says that the idea of predation ("addicted to, or living by, plunder") has "in modern use sometimes applied to the criminal classes of the great cities."[36]

The definition makes absolutely no mention of sexual predation. But it's a very common phrase, used in law to regulate sexual offenders, on the lips of everyone. The sexual predator is part of a whole social category, messy, hard to define, very poorly understood, a mystery to professionals and laypeople alike: rapists, mass murderers, serial killers (often associated with rape), wife beaters, stalkers.

These are the venal sins. But they have spawned a whole tribe of what you might call menial sins also, sexual harrassment being the most notable.

We now have a phenomenon. It's no longer mythic, but part of the postmodern cityscape. It's a sort of social pathology, and in many ways it seems to define for us, like AIDS and condoms and *Fatal Attraction*, our sexual ethos.

It's probably feminism, more than anything else, that has changed our perception of sexual crime and the gendered nature of crime. According to James Messerschmidt, in a recent book called *Masculinities and Crime*, criminologists have long recognized that the vast majority of crime—by arrest, conviction, and victim data—is committed by men and boys: 90 percent of the violent crimes in the United States. Gender has long been known as the key variable in the study of crime.[37]

Increasingly, the ability to explain the role of gender in crime is becoming the litmus test of the discipline, its central theoretical focus.

Sexual violence stalks us with a new import. It's the stalker, now, the sexual predator, who defines in the popular imagination the notions of male sexuality: Alongside the sentimentalism of *The Bridges of Madison County* and the sexual fear in *Fatal Attraction*, Anthony Hopkins in *Silence of the Lambs* defines a new and chilling male image.

He is in our most intimate places, this hunter—in our bedrooms and living rooms. He's peering in our windows. Sneaking through the dark spaces in our lives. Watching. Stalking. The sexual psychopath, the sexual stalker, haunts our lives in a way that suggests he is our own creation.

Culturally speaking, the sexual predator seems to be the terrifying culmination of the myth of the sexual hunter. He's an aberration, and an ethical monster. But he's more than that, also. He also bears a strange relation to a hunt culture. He's the logical conclusion of a long metaphorical tradition in which the sexual male is defined by his possessiveness and power—the language and rituals of the sexual hunt. In many ways, the sexual predator bears the shameful image of a culture whose winner is a heroic hunter, the capitalist with the most bucks, the one who knows how to "go for the jugular."

The sexual predator has been on the records for several centuries, but his modus operandi and his pervasiveness as a cultural phenomenon have changed. He emerges in full force in our century, a figure of late capitalist culture, with all its uncertain and destabilized mores.

We're obsessed with this figure, and not simply as a criminal and pervert. He's the hero in movies, often rivaling the star if not stealing the show. We establish a strangely intimate relationship with him, just as Jody Foster's character, Clarice Starling, becomes "friends" with Anthony Hopkins's Hannibal Lecter in *Silence of the Lambs*. It's not simply because we've got a job to do, another predator to catch, a trail to follow. It's because we have some weird undeniable relationship with this man, this cannibal. This Jeffrey Dahmer on the screen who might at any moment, perhaps, rise up *beside* us.

Or perhaps, *inside* us. That's too frightening to dwell upon, and so hardly ever stated. But why else can a movie like *Pulp Fiction* have such campy, popular appeal, with its everyday comic banter between two hit men bumbling through their day, like the rest of us? They see their "work" as "employment," and they're just doing their everyday jobs, making a living by making a killing.

There is a strange aura of paternal affection and benediction in the phone call Anthony Hopkins makes to Jody Foster, at the end of *Silence of the Lambs*, after he's escaped, to announce he's begun his career of hunting all over again. He moves on, wandering through the world. Through the eyes of the grotesque predator, we sneak peeks into windows where the shades are normally drawn, and see into the shadows of our lives.

The trial of O.J. Simpson was so sensational, not merely because of the crimes committed—the slashed throat of his ex-wife, the mutilated body of the male visitor. But Simpson's case tweaks the mind to meditate on the paradox that seems so difficult to imagine, but so "right" in that deeper and illogical sense of identity: He combines in one man both celebrity and shame, honor and horror.

He's the outsider who got in, and now he's inside out. We stare at him, whether he's guilty or innocent, and try to image this paradox: the sweet "Juice" gone bad, the epitome of the affable American hero, turned savage. The perfect man divided against himself, and splitting open with all his violent secrets of abuse and jealousy and maybe even murder laid bare before the world.

We've come to fear that any man, Everyman, might be a Senator Packwood waiting to happen. Predator has displaced hunter. The hard-won balance between beast and human has been upset, and the beast seems to have taken over—as in the story of our times, *Dr. Jekyll and Mr. Hyde*. The American hero of the frontier showed that the man gained by becoming quasi-bestial. In wrestling the bear, Davy Crockett absorbed the bear's power. These new unheroes tease us with glimpses of the monstrous desires we fear are latent in any man, at least any man raised in our hunting culture.

According to Elliot Leyton, the serial killer and mass murderer are criminals unique to our times. His detailed case studies in *Compulsive Killers: The Story of Modern Multiple Murder* argue that these serial murderers are not simply rapists and murderers. Although they are usually rapists, he claims they can't be dismissed as mere psychopaths and perverts. He argues for "the fundamentally social nature of their creation and the deep social meaning of their acts."[38] He calls the paperback edition of his study *Hunting Humans*. Hunting humans has become something more than a metaphor in the men he studies. There is a frightening way in which they have confused the image with the fact. With varying degrees of explicitness, Leyton says, multiple murderers see themselves as soldiers, as pirates, as hunters, and as manly avengers.

And they achieve that elusive wreath in our media culture, lasting fame, the final achievement for these "enterprising" men. He wants to know why does "modern America produce proportionately so many more of these 'freaks' than any other industrial nation?"[39]

He argues that they cannot be dismissed as "merely insane," because they don't display readily identifiable clinical symptoms. And he vigorously contradicts genetic theories for the violence of some men, fingering the suspicious XYY chromosome as an unsubstantiated claim. "Indeed," he writes, "the only reasonable conclusion that has come out of the biological approach is sociobiologist Edward O. Wilson's observation that there is no evidence whatever for any universal aggressive instinct (as had been previously posited by ethologists such as Lorenz and Ardrey), and that human 'behavior patterns do not conform to any general innate restrictions.' "[40] It's a social phenomenon linked to our particular century, indeed, our lifetimes. The Marquis de Sade and Jack the Ripper were fairly unique, and linked with particular social classes in their crimes. The modern rapist murderer is linked to the United States, according to Leyton.

Before the 1960s, the serial or multiple murderer was an anomaly in this century, maybe one per decade. By the 1980s, there was a new mass murderer every month. Their names are familiar to us; from David Berkowitz (the "Son of Sam") and Ted Bundy to Wesley Allen Dodd and Jeffrey Dahmer, they keep coming.

> The uncomfortable conclusion reached in this book is that there will be undoubtedly more. . . . I shall try to show . . . they can be fully understood as representing the logical extension of many of the central themes of our culture—of worldly ambition, of success and failure, and of manly avenging violence. Although they take several forms—the serial killer whose murders provide both revenge and a lifelong celebrity

career ... they can only be accurately and objectively perceived as prime embodiment of their civilization, not twisted derangement.[41]

Predation provides these men with a way to distill the themes of their lives into coherent identities and narratives.

Sex is not the prime motive for these men, any more than it is in rape, but it is usually an essential part of the business.

Edwin Kemperer, for example, used his hunting skills frequently in his brief but brutal career as a killer. He told his grandmother he was going to use his .22 to hunt rabbits, then in a conscious act, sighted the rifle on his grandmother's head and fired. Thus began his hunting for girls around Santa Cruz, California. He would take their decapitated bodies back to his room and put them on his bed like trophies, or store them in his closet to remove occasionally and admire. He once stopped his car to look at the woman he'd killed and stuffed in his trunk, "admiring my catch like a fisherman." And in language that grotesquely parodies the way hunters sometimes talk about their relationship to animals they eat, Kemperer said he ate portions of some victims in a macaroni casserole so "they could be part of me." He used his Buck knife to dismember some of the bodies, and he disguised the burial places with techniques he'd learned as a Boy Scout. He loved John Wayne, belonged to the NRA, sported a buckskin jacket, and kept score. Nor was he stupid. His IQ was 136. Including his mother and her best friend, he killed eight people.[42]

Ted Bundy preyed on middle-class women around Seattle. He took women as "possessions," and speaking of himself in the third-person singular, he considered his search for victims as hunting trips:

> "What happened was this entity inside him was not capable of being controlled any longer, at least not for any considerable period of time. It began to try to justify itself, create rationalizations for what it was doing. Perhaps to satisfy the rational, normal part of the individual. One element that came into play was anger, hostility. But I don't think that was an overriding emotion when he'd go out hunting, or however you want to describe it. On most occasions it was a high degree of anticipation, of excitement, or arousal. It was an adventuristic kind of thing. . . . He should have recognized that what really fascinated him was the hunt, the adventure of searching out his victims. And to a degree, possessing them physically."[43]

Bundy seemed to enjoy or derive some psychological rush from the cat-and-mouse game with the police, too. He left notes to the officers stalking him, enjoying the game from both sides, hunter and hunted. The body count for this young Republican campaign worker was twenty women.[44]

The examples could be multiplied endlessly. We're all familiar with them. The hunting of humans pervades our daily lives, in newspapers about the latest killer and rapist on the block, in neighborhood panic about sex offenders moving in after they've been released, in the controversial "sexual predator" law in Washington State, which makes it legal to imprison sex offenders indefinitely.

Carl Panzram offers a final quotation worth attending to. He's from another time, executed on September 5, 1930. He revels in the description of his crimes, as if his language were itself an act of violence. And it is: both crime and confession are statements made to public audiences.

He wrote from jail:

> We do each other as we are done by. I have done as I was taught to do. I am no different than any other. . . . I have murdered 21 human beings, I have committed thousands of burglaries, robberies, larcenies, arsons, and last but not least I have committed sodomy on more than 1,000 male human beings. For all of these things I am not in the least bit sorry. I have no conscience so that does not worry me. I don't believe in man, God nor Devil. I hate the whole damned human race including myself.
>
> If you or anyone else will take the trouble and have the intelligence or patience to follow and examine every one of my crimes, you will find that I have consistently followed one idea through all of my life. I preyed upon the weak, the harmless and the unsuspecting.
> This lesson I was taught by others: might makes right.[45]

He holds a twisted mirror, in which we see reflected back the fundamental law of a Social Darwinist. He's the sociosexual predator in the city jungle.

Leyton connects the multiple murderer directly with industrial capitalism, with its increasing sense of personal and spiritual insecurity, and a cultural milieu in which for the last century and a half Americans have glorified violence as an appropriate response to manly frustration. These criminals, he concludes, are the creation and the creatures of their culture.

For these men, hunting humans is not simply an expression of masculinity. Their violence is a way of creating masculine identity. They create themselves in the commission of the rape and murder. Out of impotent or frustrated circumstance, they create a sense of a personal myth, ironically, a life-romance. Leyton says that the data force him to conclude that "becoming a deviant is not a matter of personal or social pathology, social disorganization, deprivation, broken homes, viciousness, bad company or chance but a *negotiated passage to a possible identity* [his italics]."

These men are seizing the opportunities they see to fashion "a personal self-identity."[46]

People are not only the things they do. Their inmost part, their most intimate and secret part, is their soul. Every individual understands himself not simply as events, but as biography—his life is the meaning that he gives to the events of his life. A person creates a personal myth out of the materials at hand. In America, the male has available to him the myth of the hunter with all the key elements: The hunter is a stranger, lawless, struggling against a disenfranchising and destructive culture in which might makes right, and he takes his identity through acts of violence, hoping out of them to create a personal myth, a path to personal glory and power.

The sexual predator takes these historical elements of the male myth in America, and creates out of them something remarkable, something unique in history. He creates out of them an identity and, in a media culture, a personal fame.

There is a perverse logic to these men's lives. They are not senseless, though they seem crazy. Nor are they the automata of social institutions. They find creativity in violence.

Additionally, in this murky and troubling region of the psyche, sexual desire and even rape are closely allied in the mind with hunting. Radical feminists have for a long time viewed rape as a pathology of masculine self-definition. And in perhaps the most influential piece of feminist nature writing, Susan Griffin in *Woman and Nature: The Roaring Inside Her* links violence toward nature, and violence toward women, to a male mentality. In a chapter called "His Power," she describes in her lyrical allegorical style the hunt as the way he "captures her wildness":

> She has captured his heart. . . . He is fighting for his life. He faces annihilation in her, he says. He is losing himself to her, he says. Now, he must conquer her wildness, he says, he must tame her before she drives him wild, he says. (Once catching their prey [a hare], they step on her back, breaking it, and they call this "dancing on the hare.") Once he wins her over, . . . her voice is now soothing to him. Her eyes no longer blaze, but look on serenely. When he calls to her, she gives herself to him. Her ferocity lies under him. (The body of the great whale is strapped with explosives.) Now nothing of the old beast remains in her. (Eastern Bison, extinct 1825; Spectacled Cormorant, extinct 1852; Cape Lion, extinct 1865; Bonin Night Heron, extinct 1889; Barbary Lion, extinct 1922;

Great Auk, extinct 1944 [*sic*].) And he can trust her wholly with himself. So he is blazing when he enters her, and she is consumed.[47]

This is more than a metaphor for Griffin. It's a figure of speech that's become a nightmare reality: man as predator, woman as prey.

Theorists discuss rape in terms of hunting, recognizing that what is at stake is power, not sexuality. Andrée Collard links the hunt and rape:

> Hunting is the *modus operandi* of patriarchal societies on all levels of life. However innocuous the language may sound, it reveals a cultural mentality so accustomed to predation that it horrifies only when it threatens to kill us all, as with nuclear weapons. Underlying all this hunting is a mechanism that identifies/names prey, stalks it, competes for it, and is intent on getting the first shot at it. This is blatantly done when the prey is named woman, animal, or land. . . .
>
> Nature has been blamed for being either seductive (and dangerous) or indifferent to man. Siren-like, she beckons and invites hooks and guns in the same way women are said to lure men and ask for rape. Or, like the cold, uncaring "bitch," nature does not respond to man's plight and must therefore be punished. Seduction and indifference are in the mind of the beholder who projects them in order to rationalize his acts and the rationalization works because the culture approves it. We know that women want to be raped as much as deer and lions want to be shot and the earth, sea, and skies are asking to be gouged, polluted, and probed.[48]

For her, hunting is rape, and there is justification in the original stories of Orion to bolster her assertion.

Certainly, hunters understand the connection between sex and hunting. What is implicit in the analogy, always, is the gruesome way that violence becomes eroticized. Hunters talk erotically of the animal:

> "It becomes a love object. There's tremendous sexuality in this. I don't mean the parlor sexuality of the psychoanalyst who sees the gun as a phallic symbol, but sexuality in the sense of wanting something deeply, in the sense of eros. All quests, all desires are ultimately the same, don't you think?"[49]

Sex and death are linked when the hunting metaphor shapes men's desires.

In many ways, the sexual predator is the climax of this study of the history of the hunt as a masculine metaphor. The sexual predator—whatever his crime of choice, whatever his depredation—appears strangely incomprehensible. He's a horror and a monster.

But, look at the language. It's the trail of the hunter—sexual predator. We can stalk him in the language we use to describe him, in the language he uses to describe himself. His words are his tracks, left for us to follow.

This view of the predator, taken in historical and cultural perspective, gives him a genealogy and a history.

Yet hunters try to deny the family resemblance. And why not keep this perverse predator in the closet? This is not to say that hunters are responsible for this psychopathic predator. But the predator is an indictment of the hunt as the vehicle for creating masculinity. More than that, he's an indictment of the cultural icons of masculinity that hunting has produced.

The sexual predator and predatory criminal are rattling bones in the closet. His very murders are a vocabulary to us, and the lexicon is the hunt. The hunt's legacy to manhood is this terrifying amalgam of honor and horror, virility and violence. As Hamlet said, "For murder, though it have no tongue, will speak with most miraculous organ."

7

I met Janna in a twelve-step group, ACOA: Adult Children of Alcoholics. Perhaps I should have guessed from the tattoos and the broken nose, the big hair and the tight clothes. But I suspected nothing. We hardly spoke for months. But slowly, we began to talk, and I enjoyed her spirited, no-bullshit, rebellious nature.

We slowly became friends. And my reward was the trust that developed. And slowly, she shared some of her stories, and she opened a window for me on a world I could hardly conceive—the grisly underground world of the sex industry, where the objectification of the body and the commercialization of sex make predators out of everyone.

Janna was thirty-three when we met, street-smart and street-marked. It had been fourteen years since she'd kicked heroin and alcohol—with the help of AA and NA—and now she was ready to try to come to terms with the deeper wounds. Behind the suspicious dark eyes and the spirited, cynical laughter, there was a little girl who'd stopped growing up at about the same time she started heavy drugs and prostitution—when she was about thirteen. Now, she was looking for a safe place to begin growing emotionally again.

She had been a prostitute for about eight years. She'd run way from home in Boise, Idaho, for the first time at thirteen. It was not that she was abused at home, but her mother and her stepfather ignored her completely. She fled to Alabama, where she intended to live with her father in a trailer. He would take her with him out to country bars. She'd dance with men there, and then her father would call her names—slut, bitch, tramp.

One night, her father's best friend gave her a ride in his pickup, pulled into a dark spot, and pulled a knife on her. "Yer gonna like this," he threatened, putting the knife to her throat.

When she told her dad that his best friend had raped her, he promised to beat the shit out of him, but did nothing. Betrayed and distrustful, she ran away again. This time, she hitchhiked to Atlanta. Along the way, a guy picked her up. With a female friend who was tricking, he taught her how to make money, "no matter what happened to her."

And so she started turning tricks and doing drugs. Her first trick was a young kid, a virgin and a Christian, at least according to her. They were both terrified, and she laughs telling about it now.

For over eight years, Janna lived by sex, drugs, and violence. She was "on the game"—a prostitute. The hour of the wolf is, in French, dusk or dawn, the time when prostitutes emerge. Socrates calls whores sexual hunters. A whore, a hare. Now, the prostitute is, in a way, both sexual prey and predator.

She worked in strip bars, and she liked it, she said. She liked the power she had over men with her naked body. And when she tricked, she wanted to take every penny a john had. "If he left with any money at all," she said, "I felt like I'd failed. I wanted to be the best. More than once, I had my pimp beat the crap out of a john who'd tried to stiff me."

She saw all kinds of men, too, she said. All kinds. Professionals. Laborers. All classes.

She doesn't talk like a helpless victim. The metaphor that comes up most in her talk is "disease." She talks in recovery terms now, about how unhealthy the sex industry is.

When she got to Atlanta, she says she went straight to Peach Tree Avenue, and as she talks, she slips into the present tense. She is only thirteen or fourteen at this point. She goes to a strip joint and massage parlor and tries to get in. But they won't let her in. They say she is too young.

"But I really want this," she said. "My cousin was with me. She was nineteen. She gives up and goes home or something. I don't know. I never see her again. But not me. I'm totally determined to get in this place." She paused. Something about the intensely focused refusal to play victim was frightening to hear, the self-destructive tenacity.

"I get this way," she said, looking to see if I was shocked.

Janna picks out a man at the door of the strip joint and massage parlor.

She knows just what he is. A pimp. She goes up to him, and looks him straight on. "Can you get me in this place?" she asks him.

He stares at her, checks her out. "I really want to do this." She's convincing him! "To get into this place. I want to know if you can help me. What can I do to get in there?"

She stayed with this pimp for nine months. He was violent, she said, but loved her. Still, when she was finally fed up with his beatings and control, and finally tried to leave, he came after her in the streets, smiling.

"That smile meant big trouble," Janna said. "Had his hands behind his back. He pulls a gun out and tells me to go with him, through a bar, to his place in back."

Janna said she knew that he intended to kill her. So, as they were walking through the bar, she turned on him. She started screaming at him. "If you're gonna kill me, you're gonna hafta do it here."

She was yelling in public, in front of all these people in the bar.

He got furious, and started beating her right there in the middle of the bar. Some big guys jumped him and pulled him off, telling her to run away as fast as possible. She ran out, and got her favorite cabdriver (she cultivated good relationships with a few cabdrivers) to get her out of the city. She heard later that one of the men who helped her was shot and killed in the bar brawl.

Janna said she had to develop instincts and intuitions for self-preservation. Plus, she wanted to kill herself anyway, so low was her self-esteem.

"I didn't believe anyone in the world cared for me," she told me. "No one at all. I totally tried to destroy myself, and I always went for the very worst."

Her wrists are slashed with huge scars. She had meant business. And she doesn't try to pretend she was always the victim. She'd provoke fights, she said.

She ran away from her pimp in Atlanta, hitchhiked across the country, and by sixteen, she was working the streets of Los Angeles. She took a new pimp and worked Sunset Boulevard.

"You have to have good instincts to work the street." It's obviously a dangerous way to make a buck. In the nineteenth century, the few serial killers there were specialized in prostitutes and blue-collar women. Now, most serial killers hit the sons and daughters of the middle class. As the social class of the killers has fallen, the social origins of the victims has largely been rising.[50] But prostitution is obviously still very dangerous. In Washington State, for example, the Green River Killer abducted and killed more than forty young prostitutes from the strip near the airport.

"Between the police and perverts," Janna said to me with a smile, "you've *gotta* have good instincts. I got so I could read some guy good on first glances—but still I got busted three times."

One night, a guy pulled up in a car and offered a pile of money "for hardly anything." She checked the man out, hesitated a moment, and decided he's okay. It was about 3:00 A.M.

She slid into his car.

He drove her off the Strip and down an alley. He stopped the car, turned off the engine, and reached in his pocket. But he didn't pull out a wad of money. Instead, he pulled out a knife. He came across the seat at her before she could get out of the car, and pushed the knife in her face. This was the second time Janna has had a knife pulled on her.

He demanded sex. This was rape, though prostitutes never have any sympathy in this regard with the law. Prostitutes are still considered, in some sense, fair game.

While he was on top of her, Janna was sure he was going to kill her.

"Then, what he did was, while he's still on top of me, he tells me to give *him* all *my* money." Janna stressed the words "him" and "my," and laughed nervously at how ridiculous this sounded now.

She lied. She told him she didn't have any money.

"Why I lied, I don't know," she said to me. "Except, at that point in my life, I was suicidal anyway."

And her eyes went vacant as she said this to me. I wondered just where she had gone, in her mind, for those few and distant seconds.

"He grabbed my purse, and told me if I'm lying to 'im, he's gonna kill me."

She had over a hundred dollars in her purse. He grabbed it, ripped through it, and found the money.

"I really thought he was gonna kill me," she said. But he didn't.

For some reason, he just pushed her out of the car and drove away.

Janna was very lucky. She went to the police immediately. She figured they wouldn't care that she'd been raped, but she thought they should know some john is pulling knives on hookers. When she told them what he looked like, they said he matched the description of a man they were looking for on Sunset Strip. He'd already killed ten other women.

Janna quit hooking at twenty-one. Turning down that last trick, she said, was really hard. All that money for one trick. Instead, she went to work in a doughnut shop. She never glamorized the life she had led, as she told it to me, and she didn't play the victim, though she'd been terribly battered. If anything, her rhetoric was pitched to shock my suburban sensibilities.

She finally quit, she said, because she wanted to get clean. And because she knew, if she didn't, she'd soon be dead. And because, as she said, she always had a heart.

In the world of pimps and prostitutes and perverts, it's predator against predator. It's the urban wilderness, reduced to bare bones. It's a very male world of commerce and consumption—people who exist for one another only as bodies and dollar bills. And no matter how you cut it, the women are the prey.

In the political economy of a society modeled on the hunter, the battle can sometimes be reduced to that most basic of equations: who's the predator and who's the prey. I find myself often thinking of Janna, and her struggle to create a role for herself when these seem the only two choices—predator or prey.

The world Janna inhabited for so long, and had such trouble escaping, seems particularly brutal and abusive. In a culture built upon hunting—in a hunting culture—predation and rape are more than metaphors. They are the hunter's values stripped of the aura of social glamour and heroic success, wearing a demonic sneer.

Though she hasn't used drugs or turned a trick in fourteen years, Janna's still fascinated with all the voluminous pulp we produce on murder, the literature on serial killers and sex addicts and, especially, the Green River Killer. After running away from an abusive childhood at thirteen, she's come a long way, and it's still a hard road home.

8

"The only reason I trap wolves," Jim is saying, "is to finance a lifestyle."

A woolly haze of altocumulus clouds scuds across the autumn sky, and the darkness inside the cabin, with its two tiny windows, seems to get thicker. Jim is a trapper in Alaska, and in addition to wolves, he traps lynxes, martens, foxes. His gaunt features and reserved manner are softened by gentle gestures as he moves smoothly through the shadows of the cabin, getting me a cup of coffee.

Jim built this cabin himself: a log cabin with a sod roof. It's strategically positioned on a high, spruce-covered ridge, and spruce grouse strut frequently into view. This frontier homestead enjoys a spectacular view of what seems like the whole open plain of the interior of Alaska. You can only get to Jim's cabin by bush plane, about fifty miles out of Fairbanks, with a close southern view of the fierce beauty of the Alaska Range.

Like most hunters and trappers, Jim seems reluctant to open up to a stranger about what he does for a living. Especially, he is taciturn about his trapping of wolves for the government, part of the state-sponsored wolf control program which has generated so much international controversy. But we're in no hurry here. We have the sweep and reach of space and time, and tomorrow we're going to check his traplines and scout for wolves.

It's one of the great sadnesses, and absurdities too, that the questions about hunting dissolve so regularly into personal attacks and personal justifications. Hunters are portrayed as either bloodthirsty slobs or rational ecologists; antihunters, emotional fanatics or sensitive advocates for animals' lives and rights. These are unfortunate categories, since they make abstractions out of people. I've spent time with many fine hunters, sensitive and warm and hospitable, and with animal defenders who were cruel to people. And I've seen almost rabid hunters and deeply empathic antihunters. But between the rationalizations of hunters and the moralizing of antihunters, there can often be little to choose from. What transcends both these categories, it seems to me, is an interest in life, both human and animal—a genuine interest in and empathy for how all earth's creatures try to work out their lives in this world.

For Jim, trapping and hunting are a way of life, and not an occasional recreation. He's living in a state that calls itself the "last frontier," with no apologies to outer space. Under his reticence, Jim has a warm heart and a depth of soul that is the direct result of his own struggle to find his way and maintain a connection with the land.

He'd banged around the Lower Forty-eight for several years, got in trouble, and figured he'd better try to find some better way of living. He tried fishing in southeast Alaska, but hated the downtime and the drunkenness in fishing villages, where he spent too much of his money. So when he heard through an acquaintance about this homestead, he tried it, and committed himself to making it work. Now he lives here with his sometime girlfriend. She's much younger than Jim, in her twenties. She reminds me of the old hippie chicks. She comes for extended visits and then leaves. Also with him is his son, also in his twenties. He sleeps in a tent about a hundred yards apart from the cabin.

It's high autumn, with a bracing cold in the nighttime air. The next morning, when we leave to check the trapline, Jim's girlfriend leaves too. She heads back for Portland. We hike up a creek into the foothills of the mountains. As a wolf trapper, Jim's no stranger to the controversy that swirls around him. The fierce battle over wolves and wolf control in Alaska recapitulates, in modern terms, the historical dilemmas we've inherited from our frontier heritage. What should be our relationship to this frontier: exploitation or identification? In Alaska, hunters and wolves are locked in a battle over the wildlife resources in this state so full of seemingly inexhaustible resources. Who should have more right to a moose, a wolf or a hunter?

But on this hike, I'm more interested in how Jim's way of life shapes his emotional life. The question is not how men structure relationships, how they channel the dynamics of their identity, and what they are and are not able to feel. What can a man feel, and what language does a man give to the feelings he does feel? How does an internal emotional politics relate to the politics of relationships, interpersonal and interspecies?

We hike ten miles up a creek, over ridges and increasingly high plateaus that seem to bow before the absolutely superb mountains. One morning, we walk along one of these plateaus in a warm fall sun. We sit for a long time on the ridge, watching the lowlands below us for wolves. The wind is sharp, cold, abrasive. The sun is cleansing. The mountains behind us are a fiercely brilliant white against the distant blue of the open sky. There is a raw scrubbed brilliance on the face of things. Below us, autumn is torching the blueberry bushes, their incendiary colors of muted, burnt reds and scorched siennas lighting up my pyromantic heart.

A grizzly bear is feeding on the blueberries, shaggy and golden amid the red bushes.

I'm so happy, I feel like I'm being shaken clean in the wind and sun.

Jim points to a small herd of caribou that have appeared on the plateau just behind us. They are browsing on the lichens and grasses. A peregrine falcon tilts and feints above them on the wind, its sharply pointed wings bent backwards like scythes, a predatory beauty.

That's when Jim and I both notice another animal sneak over the ridge and skirt the periphery of the caribou herd. Engrossed in their grazing, the caribou don't notice the animal. Its legs are short, and it has shaggy fur, burnished with a golden tinge. It looks vaguely like a small grizzly bear, except that, as it runs along the ridge, it looks more like a low, shaggy carpet.

"Wolverine," Jim whispers to me.

I put my scope on it. A wolverine is the largest weasel in North America, famous for its fury. It has golden stripes down its back, and is scurrying along the herd, running more than stalking. Suddenly, it breaks into a run, a charge really, straight for one of the small caribou at the edge of the group. As if of one mind, the caribou seem all to spot the charging wolverine at once, and break into frantic flight. The wolverine races alongside of the small caribou, and surprisingly, is almost as big as the prey. It's trying to get a bite into its neck, and even rises up to try to knock the caribou over at one point. But the wolverine fails, and the herd escapes without losing any members.

The wolverine runs around in circles on the ridge, driven by a kind of frustrated, slowly receding predatory energy. Then it slips out of sight over the far side of the hill.

It was a thrilling sight, full of drama and excitement—the mountains, the bear, the caribou, the wolverine's failed chase. It summarizes a certain aesthetics of predation, and it definitely elevates our feelings. There is something absolutely, undeniably vivifying about the predatory scene, something that lifts the senses and stirs the soul. It focuses my energy and Jim's, and we come vividly alive in the presence of these creatures.

There's no doubt that Jim loves the land and the animals that live on the land, as he does. That sense of love, that sense of identification and a wilderness aesthetic, has always been a redemptive feature in the American soul, a sign of a wild and home-grown American spirituality.

In many ways, the predatory scene defines wildness for us. As a hunterly culture, we have a special affinity for such images. To dramatize nature, to make it especially appealing to the tastes of an American public, the Discovery Channel often produces its shows to dramatize the hunter and the hunted; snakes and sharks and big predatory cats, among others, have a special appeal. We easily convert such scenes into an American morality play—the allegory of the strong and the weak. The hunter, more than the shepherd or the settler, taught Americans how to love nature, how to see in nature images of our spiritual destiny. Even in the beautiful landscape, there is a latent violence ready to emerge, the predator's spectacle.

One more image defines another side of the hunterly view of the wild.

When we come back to Jim's homestead cabin, Jim's son has killed a black bear near the cabin. He shot it and butchered it, keeping the hide and the meat. He cut off the head and discarded it in the weeds beside the path at the edge of the clearing around the cabin. There's nothing unusual about this. No one comments on the bear's head at the edge of the clearing and the forest. It goes unremarked, though it's very visible from the path. But later, by myself, as I'm walking by, I stop and look at it.

By any standards, it's really quite grotesque. Hacked at the neck, it's been cast into the weeds, where it rolled on the back of its head and came to a rest. There's blood and grizzle and bone showing. The eyes have a glazed emptiness, a death's stare at the wide sky.

The mouth is slightly ajar.

I stare at it, and I can't avoid the conclusion that there's some unmistakable relationship between beauty and brutality in our aesthetics. Images of violence lie all around us in our lives, though this one is particularly conspicuous at the cabin. But in our own homes, violence surrounds as an art form, even. Our movies have raised images of violence to a high art. The screen-filling, colorful explosion and the high-speed chase are obligatory features of action movies, and done with incredible investments of money and talent. And football is both violent and combative as a sport. According to the anthropologist R. G. Snipes, warlike people are most likely to use their leisure for combative events.[51]

The bear's head struck me as a kind of warning and a strange, presiding spirit. It certainly wasn't a trophy, though Western hunters are more likely to find trophies than totems in animals. The head was really only garbage, a kind of detritus on the margins of the settlement in the woods. But it seemed definitely a message. It reminded me of the decapitated heads of traitors, hung on spikes from the walls of medieval cities.

Of course, I think of Davy Crockett and the piles of bears he boasted of killing as he tamed the wild frontier. And of the dead, staring eyes of John Mitchell's moose in *The Hunt*, watching him silently. Mitchell tries to interrogate that moose, to ask why he keeps watching him even after he's dead. But I'm not interested in guilt or anxiety as I look at this bear's head in the grass. It was an image of violence on the margins of our lives, all the more remarkable because it seems so inevitable and unremarkable. The heads of traitors on the city walls always meant something—they testified to the power of the ruler within the walls. And that's what this bear suddenly seemed to symbolize to me. And it spoke to some violent wilderness within, too.

The decapitated bear's head stands at the boundary, marking the passage between home and hills, through which only the hunter can teach us to pass. The death's head marks the passage between wildness and civilization, and violence is the secret of the passage that we made. And that makes violence the secret of both the wilderness of nature, and the wilderness within men. The bear's head is also a mask—for both nature and manhood as we've come to know them.

Man is the master, the pioneer, and, if he could only learn to see it, the maker of this boundary. Interrogate all the dead and decapitated creatures you want. The bear's eyes are open but dead. He says absolutely nothing. All the answers lie in us.

9

THAT STRANGER MAN

Songs are thoughts which are sung out with the breath when people let themselves be moved by a great force, and ordinary speech no longer suffices.

A person is moved like an ice-floe which drifts with the current. His thoughts are driven by a flowing force when he feels joy, when he feels fear, when he feels sorrow. Thoughts can surge in on him, causing him to gasp for breath, and making his heart beat faster. Something like a softening of the weather will keep him thawed. And then it will happen that we, who always think of ourselves as small, will feel even smaller. And we will hesitate before using words. But it will happen that the words we need will come of themselves—

When the words that we need shoot up of themselves—we have a new song.

—Orpingalik, "Eskimo Song"[1]

As both a child and as an adult, I've lived amid carnage. Most of it's been emotional carnage, but some of it's been physical. Much, though not all, has been inflicted by men. Damaged bodies, damaged souls: they're part of our inheritance from a hunting culture, passed down for several millennia, largely by men. The weapon and the wound: you can't worship one, as hunters have the spear and the gun, and not inherit the other. You can't imagine hunting as a warfare against nature, in the making of men, and not make wreckage.

Most men are not hunters. I'm not a hunter. But we live in a hunt culture, and its values are ingrained in us in the heroic images and the daily language through which we come to adult consciousness. So near to us are these images, this language, that they've grown largely invisible. We look through the hunting language, and the values in it—to a world that seems reality, unaware of the particular cast the filter of hunting imparts from us to the lives of animals and men. And we look inward, through the language of the hunter, and see looking back out at us a violent man. And we take him for the natural man.

It is the magic of the hunting metaphor that it reflects two ways at once, inward and outward, making it hard to find any place outside of it, where we can see it, alone. It's hard to get a place outside of the metaphor, where we can begin to imagine life—and ourselves—without its influence.

We live inside of hunting. And we live, daily, with its consequences.

I genuinely began this study with an open mind about hunting as a metaphor, eager to see where it would take me. It was a trail and a hunt of my own, to see especially where the codes of heroism and the imperatives of desire would lead me. I wanted to see what happened when one of the most important images in our thinking about human origins and human values was treated as a metaphor that men invented, and viewed from the point of view of gender.

I did not know the game I was pursuing. And I did not know the woods it would take me through. It led me also through parts of myself, dimensions of my own psyche that have been shaped by the hunter. I've come out of the woods with a larger view of the way men have been shaped by forces I hadn't realized had been at work. This study has been part of a long process of thinking about creating new ways for men to be and relate.

Change is a process, and we work slowly toward new lives, following desires and dreams and careful self-scrutiny. Change can also be erratic, as we run sometimes toward new ideas, and sometimes stumble. But we do change, and learn new ways of feeling and being. I feel new things stirring in me now, new capabilities emotionally, partly through this study of the male as hunter, and through learning to see how they were engendered in men.

We move down through layers, to touch the heart, and come back up, riding its currents, to some rich new vision.

2

Despite its apologists, ancient and modern, hunting is not so much an ethic as it is an ethos. It is much more a body of images and ideas, a field of contradictions and strong invisible forces, than it is a rational logic. This, of course, is its appeal and its power. It is image and metaphor, symbol and myth—and it appeals to the human need for meaning, not the need for a system of conduct, which is largely ethics. It wraps men in meaning, gives them crisp images by which they can know their own experience, mold their own experience, find themselves an identity and a destiny.

Hunting has taken as many different forms as there are periods and cultures. But its deepest promise for men is not meat, but a kind of psychic and social packaging. Hunting may well have first been discovered in the woods. It may well have originally been a tangible, literal reality—something men did. But it became something that men lifted out of nature, elevated, accorded a special status. And then reaffirmed in their forays into the woods. Hunting was cultivated in the heart.

That does not diminish the power of hunting in men's lives, though it does alter its status. As an image, hunting lies beyond the easy reach of logic, beyond the bickerings of hunters and antihunters. Sons may hate killing their first deer, but they learn to hunt because it's associated with Dad and family: this is the deep emotional level that hunting occupies. It is explicitly about the way fathers teach sons to be men. Like warfare, the hunt has seemed to offer men a way to feel like men.

It's a powerful appeal, and the hunt has always been associated with power, public and private, external and internal. It offers men access to a way of being that is powerful, and a way of relating that confers power. But the carnage it inflicts, the wounds and the wreckage, is not always apparent. Masculine bloodlines can be invisible. Hunting encodes for men two kinds of power, each associated with a different way of being male in American culture.

In the first type, hunting is an image of overt power. When the hunt is told as a narrative, this means a hunt which focuses on the most dramatic moments of the chase—usually, the kill, but also the suspense of the chase or the contest with the beast. There is always some element of menace and danger—crucial to true American heroes, and to their historical prototypes in the West. The goal is to defeat the beast. Whether it's heroic and triumphant or demonic and subversive, rationalized repression or emotional release, its mode of power is domination.

The triumphant male is his own justification, like Apollo, and the tragic male is his own consolation, like Pentheus.

Its heroes are Orion and Charlemagne, Gordon Cumming and Theodore Roosevelt, Davy Crockett and Jack London and all the men who kneel to unadulterated power.

The other hunt offers an image of covert power, more subtle in its deployment and manipulations. This is not the heroic or the violent hunter, but the responsible hunter. This man believes in patience and persistence, stalking and waiting in the tree stand. His justification in the hunt is technique and style and an ethical integrity. He has trimmed the abuses of his sport, and curtails the excesses in an ethos of restraint. For him, hunting is less an expression of self than a discipline. The goal is to tame the beast.

Whether through a sporting code or the stewardship of nature, this hunting's mode of power is control and management.

Its heroes are Xenophon as hunter and Tristan as lover, Frederick Courtenay Selous and R. S. S. Baden-Powell in their dedication to boys and empire, Daniel Boone and Deerslayer, and, as patriarch of American conservation, Theodore Roosevelt.

It's the difference between naked power and an apparently benign fatherliness. One is obvious, visible, and, while not easily expunged, at least easily fingered. The other is much more difficult to see. Its power is invisible, and its effects more insinuating since it looks so healthy. The effects can be seen in two very different sorts of modern fathers—one is more directly abusive, and the other simply withholds his love until the child, son or daughter, behaves.

It's the difference, say, between those two icons of modern fatherhood, the alcoholic father in a rage and the absent father who, either physically or emotionally, is a stranger to his feelings.

I've seen the effects of both kinds of fathers on their children, and know the damage they can do to that child's heart and soul. Enough damage to take a lifetime to repair.

Men have paid a huge price for either kind of power. They have deployed it against others—enemies, rivals, animals, women. It is through this power that men feel themselves existing. Hunting traces, not so much a state of being, as it does a dynamic through which a man may come into existence. It is how, in the sweep of events, he can locate himself, and, psychologically speaking, make himself real. That's what the process of acquiring an identity means—not that, literally, one doesn't exist. But psychologically, one's existence becomes clear and validated. For the hunter, this can only happen by killing or possessing an Other. Ortega y Gasset makes this point very clearly: "One does not hunt to kill, necessarily. But one kills to have hunted. And the goal of hunting is not the kill. The goal of hunting is *to take possession, dead or alive, of some other being* . . . [italics in original]." Nor does the hunter have to be successful: "The beauty of hunting lies in the fact that it is always problematic." No matter how sporting, Ortega y Gasset says, hunting "is not pure gentlemanliness," because the "venatic relationship" in the West involves just this "essential inequality between the prey and the hunter."[2]

As one hunter said, "Killing is the orgasm of hunting."

By taking another, or, as one hunter put it to me who no longer cared to kill animals, by "compromising" the animal, the hunter gains control over it. The animal, and the parts of others or the self that it must necessarily symbolize, are either killed or managed. They are made inferior. And in some sense, the hunter exists in that moment as the Other disappears. Identity is founded on an adversarial relationship, negotiated in power, in which the hunter is validated and the prey disappears.

As a model for intimacy, this is both dangerous and limited. Identity is created only through adversarial dynamics. I am defined by what I oppose, and how I oppose it. I am defined by the enemy I choose. I am defined by the beast I oppose. One has to wonder what the price of this dynamic is for the person who loses touch with whole parts of himself and the world because of the terms of his interaction. What happens is that he creates blank spots, blindnesses, and abysses of feeling he cannot enter. He becomes a stranger to himself, and despite some forms of involvement, a stranger to the world.

The hunter/stranger—he realizes himself as the beast vanishes. Dispossessed through possession.

Perhaps this helps us understand why so few men know themselves emotionally. The hunter, as Ortega y Gasset says, spills blood. The intimacy of the hunter is blood. Hunters dwell upon blood as one of the chief symbols of manliness: they speak of blood ties, and bloodlines, and bloodlust. Blood is the great human mystery, flowing inside of us, in our veins and arteries. Of all our fluids, blood is one of our most private, more so than our sexual fluids. The young hunter becomes a man when, from the entrails of the prey, he is "blooded" by an older male. This is a terrible model of intimacy—the private spilled—and publicly displayed as spectacle. The internal is violated. The price for male strength has been intimacy.

And the hunter, historically, usually chooses as his male foil the man who explores these more inner and private realms. This is the realm men need to recover and redefine. It has been vilified by men as effeminate and soft. But it takes its own kinds of heroes, its own kinds of strength, to explore the mysteries within.

As a model of existence, the hunter has proved problematic enough in the West when applied to animals. I resist moralizing on this point—but 60 million slaughtered buffalo continue to make a statement. Hunters have in many ways cleaned up their act, and I don't begrudge them their autumn fun if it's legal.

But what I want to emphasize here is that, as metaphor, the price men have paid is in self-knowledge and intimacy. There are mysteries here, still available to them.

The price men have paid for their power, in whatever guise, is this distance from themselves. They are strangers. The hunter/stranger, the weapon and the wound. These are the two sides of hunter.

Scratch the surface of a complacent conventionality, and there's a deep hunger in men for experiencing themselves at deeper levels than they've so far been taught. There's a deep desire to learn more about the stranger inside themselves. I know I've been searching all my life for men who could move into this part of themselves. They've been hard to find, which is why I think men usually turn to women for emotional support and closeness. Few men know how to talk about their deeper lives. It's very hard to find this ability in other men, who are usually stuck either in action or thinking, in their bodies or in their heads.

I know the damage men can do. I've felt it, and I've wanted to do damage myself.

I have felt like a stranger. I've felt most alive in faraway and remote places, among rare wildlife. I've loved wandering, following a kind of rootless desire, driven by my own sense of wounds, my own angers. I always thought I was chasing something—a hunter in the soul. And in many respects I was. But I was also in flight. The hunter in mythical terms, the hunter inside, is also always the hunted. The two depend upon each other.

Until recently, I think men understood their sense of loss and isolation, their sense of themselves as a stranger, as a metaphysical condition. It's only been in the last twenty years that we've been able to see the role of gender in our lives. I understand how difficult it is to reconnect with emotions. It's hard, in a culture that's spent several millennia trying to make the emotional disappear, to begin to call it back into existence. To make it reappear. As much as I value emotional presence and honesty, I have begun to realize just how distant I can be from myself. In my most intimate self, I'm fragile, wounded. It is this wounded and fragile self—the vulnerability of the flaccid penis, if you will—that men have avoided at all costs. We are most proud of the penis in its erect state. Man is the erect predator.

But the men I admire most are the men who have been searching for new ways of being masculine. Frequently, the men who have to lead us are the ones who have suffered the wounds. The hunters—the victors—are less likely to see the blanks in their own vision, until, like Actaeon, they are torn by their own hounds.

Every one, every man, has to follow his own path through, and out of, this cultural hunt. Every man has to come to terms with his emotional modes and capabilities himself, and I know that a discussion of "the hunter" only traces outlines, only maps a general field of analysis. There are many hunters, and many masculinities. Plus, there's often something vaguely embarrassing about men talking about their struggles and pains, since the white male has largely benefited from "the hunt." But the path to emotional genuineness is difficult and scary. It begins by facing yourself directly. It proceeds by means of the emotional courage required to experience yourself as you really are, under the proper postures. This is the more frightening wilderness, and in poets the hunt has often figured in an excursion into these marginal parts of the self.

3

For most of the month, I'd been waiting for a telephone call from Ed Shavings, a Chupik Eskimo born in a sod hut in 1923 on Nunivak Island. Nunivak is a hunkering, treeless island of abraded volcanic rock, battered during its long winters by the brutal storms that fall upon it out of the Bering Sea. It's about thirty miles from the mainland of Alaska, off the Yukon-Kuskokwim Delta, across the fast and dangerous currents of Etolin Strait. Ed now lives in the only village on Nunivak, Mekoryuk, on the north shore, at the mouth of the eponymous river whose name means, with native realism and wit, "the place of mosquitoes."

Ed had said he'd call me when the sea ice that froze the island and blocked the harbor began its spring breakup. As the ice opens into chunks and drifts in Etolin Strait, the big bull walruses would begin their spring migration from Round Island, down by the Aleutians, through the Bering Sea, up to their summering grounds in the Chukchi Sea. Usually, they pass by Nunivak, through the Etolin Strait, about the middle to the end of May. But this year, spring is late in Alaska, and Nunivak stays wrapped under cold and fog and the ice off shore seems never to break.

When the ice breaks, I'm going to join Ed on his native subsistence hunt for walruses off Nunivak Island.

During this same month, a close friend of mine at home, Eric Miller, has been dying. He has been following his own slow, inevitable migration toward a terrible death. For sixteen months, I have been a "buddy" to Eric, volunteering for the local AIDS foundation, and we fear, though it is never clear, that this might be Eric's last illness.

I volunteer because I want to offer something, to give something, to someone who might genuinely need it. What I hadn't known, but vaguely suspected going into this volunteer assignment, was how much Eric would give to me.

Eric is African-American. He's six foot eight, an imposing man, even with the cane he needs since the stroke that crippled his leg and led him to the doctor and the diagnosis, which wasn't really a surprise to Eric, that he is HIV positive. That was about four years before I met Eric, and he'd already progressed to full-blown AIDS.

We are about the same age. In his early twenties, a couple of decades earlier, Eric had been an excellent athlete. He loved basketball, and had made the free-agent camp for the Atlanta Hawks. But for some reason, maybe the pressure, he'd sabotaged himself, quitting unaccountably, and leaving camp before finding out if he could make the team. I've done similar things myself.

Eric is verbally imposing as well. He's a talker, and he can be incredibly eloquent in his street idioms. "Once a junkie," he once told me, "always a junkie. This ol' junkie ass don't know no different."

He has an immense charisma, and can dominate any social scene with his combination of words, blunt wit, and physical attitude. He has eloquent long arms and fingers, expressive limbs and digits, that he uses as a kind of vocabulary along with his talking, a powerful body language, that adds to his presence.

Mostly, I listen.

Slowly, over the months, Eric has told me about his life. It's a life unlike mine in almost every respect. He's lived in a very dark world of drugs and dealing, easy sex-for-drugs, and always ready cash.

But after he was diagnosed with AIDS, Eric dedicated himself to Jesus and God. I won't try to characterize his religious spirit, except to say that it was personal, energetic, and deeply felt. His faith helped him become clean and chaste. And more important, his commitment to God helps sustain him through the last years of his life. I am watching a man right his life as he prepares to die. I think what moves me most is watching Eric come to terms with his life, his disease, and his impending death, and to try to do it in a way that is full of integrity. Some people with AIDS, for example, want no extraordinary methods used to keep them alive beyond a certain point. But Eric wants to live as absolutely long as possible. He carries a great fund of life inside him, and he never acts the part of the victim.

As he has gotten sicker, and is in more pain, he has grown angry and more difficult. But he never gets bitter, and he never shows self-pity.

At one point, he said to me that he had never had a white male as a friend before. He didn't have many male friends in general, he said. Male relationships for him involved the usual mix of rivalry and camaraderie, playfulness and emotional mistrust.

He told me he thought God had sent me to him at this point in his life. I was honored by his trust.

But during this May, he gets really sick. He's hospitalized, runs an extraordinary fever, hallucinates, and is incoherent. From his bed, he can only fitfully recognize me. "Are you taking a helicopter today?" he asks once, apropos of nothing.

But Eric hasn't lost a lot of weight, and I hope that he'll recover.

He doesn't. He dies the day I get the call from Ed Shavings to go north and hunt walruses. I leave the next morning.

4

When I get to Nunivak Island, it's a Sunday, and I am sad and lonely. The ground on the island is muddy, and the long light of the subarctic evening slants onto the island in a tentative, fragile loveliness. The wooden houses on the island are an unpainted, faded gray, beaten by uncountable storms. Herring hangs out to dry in the wind on driftwood racks outside the houses, silver-skinned fish that gleam and shine in the slanting sunlight. Even though the ice is breaking up, the wind has suddenly shifted from the north, and all the ice in the Bering Sea seems to be driven in a jumbled mass against the shore, stretching in an angled architecture of frozen white for as far out to sea as my eye can look.

We're going nowhere until the wind shifts southerly and this ice is blown away. It's far too dangerous out there now.

Something in me feels similarly impacted. I have grieved for Eric. But I still feel full of something waiting to break loose.

It's Sunday evening, and Ed invites me to go to his church. I am feeling aimless and adrift, and go for a walk instead, trying to let the feelings inside have their time and their place. I walk out to the edge of the island, outside of town, and find myself—where else?—at the island cemetery. It overlooks the vast and endless scope of the sea. A dark line of clouds hangs ominously on the northern horizon. The weather seems to be coming from the north, not the south.

Eric is on my mind.

I go to church, after the cemetery. I'm not sure why, but I like the invitation. I walk to the burnt-red, steepled church on the other side of town, overlooking the harbor on the river. Only about a hundred families live in Mekoryuk, and the river, despite its name, is slow and lovely.

I open the door of the church—Evangelical Covenant—to find the service has begun. All eyes turn to look at me, the only white currently in town, and their faces are filled with beaming curiosity and friendliness. I slip into a back pew, as discreetly and inconspicuously as I can, while four women finish a hymn they're singing.

When the women finish, the minister stands up, looks out over the congregation, and begins speaking. He's very robust, and strides across the altar area as he speaks, using both English and Chupik, bilingual and self-translating. He tells a story about a time, long ago, when he was a young man. He'd been on nearby Triangle Island, and there were many many salmonberries. But he only had one bucket. He's a poor man, he says, born in a dirt house. But in those days he had sealskin boots, he says, with the hair off them. He filled his boots with salmonberries. And always, he says, he's been given enough, even if he was born poor.

As he finishes this brief story, and is about to plow into a longer discourse, he stops in midsentence. He looks out in the congregation.

"We have a visitor this evening," he booms out, looking straight at me. I feel myself blush faintly. "I wonder if he'll tell us, who is that stranger man?"

5

Perhaps the most gratifying feature of the hunt, as it's being resuscitated recently, is that hunters are trying to repair the damage that has been written into the Western terms of the hunt. White men have begun to recognize themselves as the stranger men, and are trying to imagine new forms of intimacy. Some hunters have turned to native and primitive traditions to find a wisdom that we can learn from. We're searching for a wisdom that can lead us deeper into nature, humanity, and the spirit that holds them together.

There is a strong feeling of estrangement in men.

William Carlos Williams writes that the turn to native cultures has always been one of the saving gestures of the American white man, the frontiersman who was part of the destruction of game and native cultures in his march across the continent. "He turned back to the Indians," writes Williams about the hero Sam Houston; "it is the saving gesture—but it is a gesture of despair."[3]

Those white men who are interested in matters of the soul, who refuse to reduce their lives to the terms of the stock market and the number of frequent flier miles on their business account, those men are searching for new ways of being. This impulse defines one of the important spiritual developments of our times—seeking the wisdom of tribal peoples.

I wasn't sure what I'd find in coming to Nunivak, and it wasn't like I'd come searching for salvation from elders. It's just that I was aware of something that seemed right, a good alignment for me, to be leaving death and disease down below, and coming up to Alaska to spend time with an experienced Eskimo hunter, an elder in his seventies.

And the turn to native elders is, in a way, a search for something that white men have had trouble getting from their own fathers.

But the weather doesn't clear for several days, and I sit in Ed's house, watching the wind and the forbidding skies. Over bits of salmon and seal in brine on the kitchen table, I talk with Ed and his brother Henry for long hours.

Henry is tall and lanky and loquacious. He wears a satiny blue bowling jacket with The Singing Fisherman stitched on it in gold letters. He's a well-known singer, and has traveled widely in Alaska and the Lower Forty-eight. He has an active sense of humor, and when he walks, he bends slightly at the hips, reminding me of Groucho Marx. He is constantly, incorrigibly cheerful.

Ed is the younger brother, serious and respectful of his more performative older brother. Ed has an air about him of quiet thoughtfulness and deep practical wisdom. Ed tells me he has been going to sea for more than fifty years, that he learned to hunt walrus from kayaks.

"We learned by listening to our elders," he says. "We'd sit in the sweat lodge with the men, and we'd listen. That's how we learned to hunt."

"Plus, we learn by going to sea," he continues. "The men give instruction on what to do if you're stuck in an ice floe. Or if a walrus attacks. We learn that you do not hunt by computer. You have to use your eyes and your judgment."

Ed tells another story, too, about his grandfather, that I find almost magical, about this connection between men and animals, a connection that links the people to each other. "I remember when I was a little boy, my grandfather has a .30 Remington rifle. Really old-time rifle, odd-looking rifle that he has. When I was a boy, I opened a walrus. There was brass inside the walrus stomach. Tiny writing: .30 Remington. The walrus was eating brass in the ocean, with the clams on the bottom. It makes me think of my grandfather."

Animals carrying the tokens, the memories, of beloved humans. I find the story deeply eloquent.

Meanwhile, in the background at the house, the TV is on. Bob Barker is playing "The Price Is Right," beamed in via satellite to this island in the Bering Sea. He's tempting contestants with games and the promise of hot tubs and trips to Tahiti. Henry pours some seal oil from the ketchup bottle over a piece of bread. He comments on how delicious walrus flipper is, a real delicacy, a favorite food of the people. He hopes we will get some soon.

6

Modern white hunters have turned, increasingly, to native hunters to help them redefine hunting and themselves as hunters. Ted Kerasote, in *Blood-*

ties, for example, writes for white North American sport hunters, and is an eloquent apologist for a new vision of hunting for white men. His book is a long meditation, really, on the need for a greater intimacy with the earth, and he argues that the meat of the elk moves through him, like stars in the sky. And if he is defensive in the company of Buddhist vegetarian friends, he nevertheless insists that hunting connects him with tangible facts of life, woven in the spirals of his DNA.

This materialist strand in hunters is to me always the least convincing part of their arguments and manifestos, but reflects a powerful sense of physical attachment to the earth. It's a part of the poetics of hunting, that the gene is woven into human DNA, but the notion of man the scavenger suggests that, by this thinking, a scavenging gene is perhaps responsible for our appetites for meat.

Kerasote and other hunters are on stronger ground when they simply follow their spirit. Kerasote believes, for example, that hunting is "the bedrock of our oldest relationship with animals." Tracing a mythological chronology, Kerasote is searching for a spiritual dimension to the hunt. He suggests that hunting became a "holy act" among the first peoples:

> When people evolved a conscience, understanding for the first time that death ran the world, they could no longer be one with all its crea-tures. . . . Call this our first guilt, or our first responsibility. . . . In some societies an ethos of restraint was passed down. From this restraint, this guilt, this self-interest—call it what you will . . . grew the painted cave walls, the shrines of piled bear skulls, and the many worldwide prayers, lofted on smoke and chanted to every animal soul killed for food and clothing . . . prayers for forgiveness and rebirth, prayers offered in sad-ness for the web enfolding us all. It is the recognizance of those sacri-fices made and the respect for those creatures who made them, that became our first accord with animals and that made hunting a holy act.[4]

There is a great deal of primitive mythmaking in this passage, and it is probably best understood as an attempt to reconfigure for modern white hunters the meaning of hunting through a new poetics of "original" peo-ples. It focuses on an "ethos of restraint," which can't disguise the guilt that is the driving motive of the passage—a guilt that has come to define the modern hunter.

I have found very few men for whom hunting is a "holy act," frankly. Most are not Elmer Fudds in oversize hats, driving Broncos and drinking Coors. But they aren't "holy," either. When one hunter talks about the hunt as a place of male bonding, he's located the pretty much typical notions of the hunt: "In fact, when supposedly straight guys go off to hunting lodges together for days at a time, they by and large drink beer, shoot at inoffensive animals, and talk about pussy."[5]

In the way of plain talk, this is what the "male tribe" amounts to in most men's fantasies.

Still, the attempt to find a new spiritual direction in this passage is powerful and an important sign—and its sensitivities are not just for hunters.

Perhaps the most thoughtful recent apologist for the hunt, and the native way of life, is Richard Nelson, the anthropologist who has spent some twenty years learning from native elders in Alaska. In *The Island Within*, Nelson describes a hunter's deepening connection to the animals and the forest, what he calls a "mystical forest" of spirit and powers, which native elders introduced him to: "a spirit forest, a forest that envelops me with shining, consecrated webs and binds me here forever."

In an essay called "The Gifts," Nelson describes two experiences with deer—one a hunt, in which he relives the advice and teachings of the Koyukon elders in how to think like an animal, the other an occasion in which a doe leaves a buck in the wild, and comes up to him. They touch. Both of these are "gifts," spiritual gifts, signs of a deeper bond between the deer and himself:

> But there are vital lessons in the experience of moments such as these, if we live them in the light of wisdom taken from the earth and shaped by generations of elders. Two deer came and gave the choices to me. One deer I took and we will share a single body. The other deer I touched and we will now share that moment. These events could be seen as opposites, but they are in fact identical. Both are founded in the same principles, the same relationship, the same reciprocity. . . . Koyukon elders would explain, in words quite different from my own, that I moved into two moments of grace, or what they call luck. This is the source of success for a hunter or a watcher, not skill, not cleverness, not guile. Something is only given in nature, never taken.[6]

Nelson writes out of respect for the culture and traditions of the natives, and of the wisdom they have to offer us as we seek to redefine our notions of selfhood and intimacy with the earth.

The men's movement has also turned to Native American and tribal traditions for its "mythopoetic" reinterpretation of masculinity, explicitly using the figure of the hunter to help many American men. The men's movement is easily satirized and frequently mocked. Feminists suspect it as a reaction to feminism, with some justification. But the men that I've met in this movement are less interested in backlash than focusing on their own maleness, and their need for models of masculinity that give them a sense of integrity and self-worth. They want to feel both "wild" and strong, yet emotionally vulnerable, especially with other men. There is a profound sense of frustration with the American and capitalistic imperatives of competition and self-control, and a hunger to connect with themselves at some "mythic" level, a level defined by universal archetypes.

The movement powerfully connects psychoanalytic, Jungian themes with patriarchal frameworks. And it's all very cleverly presented in tribal trappings: beating drums and ceremonies of "initiation." The men are looking for mentoring and what I've heard called "remasculinization"—feeding their hunger for nurture without making them feel feminine or weak.

The hunter is one of the archetypes of this movement. Michael Meade often leads workshops or retreats for men, along with Robert Bly, and has his own book called *The Water of Life: Initiation and the Tempering of Men*. In his workshops and in the book, he opens with the story called "The Hunter and His Son."[7] Here's how the story opens:

> Pay heed to this story of the father and son!
> A hunter and his son went to the bush one day to pursue their occupation. They hunted all morning and found nothing to sustain them but one small rat. The father gave the rat to the son to carry. It seemed of no consequence to the son, so he threw the rat into the bush. The rest of the day they saw no other game. At dusk the father built a fire and said, "Bring the rat to roast, son; at least we will have something to eat." When he learned that the son had thrown the rat away, he became very angry. In an outburst of rage, he struck the son with his ax and turned away. He returned home, leaving his son lying on the ground.

The story continues with the son running away, being adopted by another man, but the birth father comes to find him. And through being ordered to kill horses and slave girls, the son learns the hard lessons that violence and the wound from the father are inevitable in life.

Meade writes passionately of the way in which many men feel that they've been struck by the father. Many men can point directly to a place on their bodies where they still feel this wound, he says. The nature of the wound is this: "At one memorable point in my life, the rat was more important to my father than I was."

I understand the focus on the wound given by the father. What I think is profoundly problematic about the men's movement is that it tends to justify the wound and the violence of the father/hunter as the violence is specifically viewed as male. This movement even glorifies violence— Meade's story goes on to justify the killing of horses, the killing of slave girls, the striking of children. The idea of the hunter is used once more as a justification for violence in men: against a whole range of "others."

Kerasote, Nelson, and Meade turn to the native hunter as an image from which white men can learn. The native hunter promises us a kind of wisdom. His is a hunger for personal meaning and a spiritual relationship to nature and the elders. In the very different ways these three writers evoke the spirituality of the native hunt, there is clearly some longing among modern men for new modes of identity, new abilities in intimate relationships. Under the wound is a longing for change and wholeness.

And I wonder, among the stories told by Ed, and the very different views of these three white men, what is the wisdom that we can take in from the traditions of the native hunters?

7

I wake up on the third morning in Mekoryuk after a heavy sleep, in the midst of a dream that the ice is breaking. When I get up, Ed is already checking the weather, looking out over the sea. He doesn't say anything, but all morning he keeps a close eye on the wind.

Something about the trip to Nunivak feels propitious to me. I feel as though it is somehow right for me to be here: after the death of Eric, to come up here, and be with Ed, and to go out after walruses. The world of my dreams, also, is overlapping in strange and meaningful ways for me with the world I wake up to. For many years, I have been going through changes, opening new and, in some cases, painful parts of myself. I have always been emotional, but there is some coldness, some frozen place inside me. The grief over Eric distills that sense of some change happening in me.

It is reflected in the jam-up of the ice on the shore under a stiff north wind. Under brooding skies, I walk out on the dry grass, longing for a shift in the wind, a change in the weather, a movement in the ice.

When the world outside begins to reflect the world inside, I always know that things are coming together, that I'm sliding into a new connection with myself and the world outside me. That's when there is poetry for me, when the two worlds connect and correspond. I feel myself opening up, releasing, breaking up myself. All my words seem to echo way back into my life, and reverberate with memories that are coming dislodged themselves, loosened, moving. Words and memories, each one taking me further into myself, further into a sense of release.

Outside the windows, there's a strong anticipatory wind, swirling to the southwest, and there's a somber grace moving in the dark sky and the white sea.

While Ed checks the weather, he tells me a "funny story." "I remember one man, a really good hunter named Tom Toots. He was really old. He lived up on one side of the mountain in the west. He saw the mountain open once, saw lots of half-people and half-wolves. Only the great ones, they said, only the really lucky lucky people saw those ones. And he always said, too, that people should share as one big family, and that, when he was a young man, he learned from the elders that as people change in their attitudes and the way they live, the weather shares in that."

Ed's wife Esther is talking, hoping we can get out hunting today. She's growing eager for walrus flipper, which, when boiled, is a favorite delicacy. It's the food of a Nunivak spring, sign the winter's ended and summer has come, with the ice breakup and the summer fishing camps throughout the island. I am listening, and there's poetry everywhere this morning. I write down what Esther says, and it turns into a poem even as I write it in my journal.

> The Chupik woman says,
> I think the rain is going to stop.
> The sun is going to come out.
> The walruses will sleep on the ice.
> I hope so
> Because we need
> Some flippers to eat.

Ed has said very little, and the morning moves along. Soon, without a word, he's begun making sandwiches, and I learn we are leaving in an hour in his twenty-foot, open boat to hunt for walruses.

Soon, we're down by the boat. The tide is out in the harbor, in the mouth of the river, and the boat is up in the mud. We drag it down, put on heavy snowsuits, and Ed guides us through the ice floe, heading out past the dark headlands on the east side of the island.

It's dark, almost like nighttime, on the river as we head out. Birds come tilting past us on the wind, dark shapes that are hard to identify. A small flock of low-flying geese catapults past, almost at eye level. I watch them closely: white heads and gray bodies, beautiful emperor geese. They seem to be flung along with the wind, necks taut as ropes and wings beating stiffly, dark blessings to us.

I am accompanied by the spirits of the place, lifting everywhere off the water and taking flight. As we round Etolin Point and head out into Etolin Strait, several tufted puffins slowly come up alongside us, flying faster than the boat. They have fat black bodies and small wings that are beating like crazy in the air, and they have oversize orange beaks that give them a wild, comical look, like they're about to nosedive out of the air in a kamikaze crash into the ice. But they whiz past us, wings like little eggbeaters, dark shapes against a smoky sky.

The sky and the sea and the ice are a watercolor wash of grays and creams and hazy, subtle pewter blues. We head farther out, amid the floating ice in Etolin Strait, and Nunivak becomes a featureless, storm-beaten sheet of low volcanic rock off the starboard, rising in the middle to a modest peak against the oyster sky, the original and extinct volcano that created the island.

We search the drift ice within ten miles of shore all day, Ed frequently pulling us onto ice floes to scan for the sleeping mammals. The bull walruses come up when the ice is breaking, heading from their wintering place on Round Island, to the south, up to the Chukchi Sea in the high Arctic for summer. The cows and the calves come first. The bulls often pull themselves out of the sea to rest on floating ice pans, frequently three or four in a big blubbery pile. "When walrus sleeps on the ice," Ed says, "you can see it a long ways. It looks reddish."

I look into a white icescape, a world of horizontal whites and grays and blues that all seem to drift and melt into each other. I occasionally spot a seal, but no walruses. After eight hours at sea, we give up, and Ed takes us back. He apologizes, unnecessarily. "I tried very hard to find a walrus," he says. "I hope the walrus have not already come through."

But I don't mind. I've seen tufted puffins and horned puffins, crested auklets and Steller's eiders, and the whole wide seascape of ice and dripping sky. I love feeling the sea as the strong current between the island and the mainland breaks and moves the ice. I love being out amid the birds and the seals. I love seeing the parasitic jaegers, tilting with the billow and blow of the wind, with their dark caps and their sharply pointed, angular wings: a fierce predatory beauty. They're really scavengers, or pirates, patrolling the sea, harassing gulls to make them spit up their food. Jaegers are maybe the most beautiful scavengers in the world.

I love being out with Ed and Henry and Ed's son Chuck. As we bounce across the confused chop in the waves, on the long ride home, Ed tells me a story. It is about the experience in which he learned his "biggest lesson as a hunter" in the fifty years he has been hunting at sea.

He had come to this water. He was in a small open boat, like the one we are now in, only smaller. Only sixteen feet long.

"I was seal hunting," Ed says, his words slow and measured. "Bearded seals. We call them *mukluk*. This is before I am married, more than forty years ago. The water was very rough at sea, and the sky very dark. My skiff seemed very little to me, and the waves were breaking all around me. And then my engine died. I could not get my motor to start. I was very far at sea."

It is unusual for Ed to say so much, to speak so long, and I listen carefully. Occasionally he pauses between sentences. I keep looking out over the waters, waiting for him to resume, saying nothing.

"I tried to drag my anchor to keep the boat into the waves. Then my anchor line broke. My father always had told me to respect the animals. I watched the seabirds and the seals. I was in a storm. The shoreline was gone. The boat was dragging and drifting. I looked at the seabirds and seals. I wished I could be one of them. Then I would not have this problem, I thought.

"I spent the night at sea. I did not know how to pray. But that night, I kneel from my head down to my toes, in that little sixteen-foot skiff out in the middle of the ocean, and I pray. That is where I learned who made the earth and the wind and the sea.

"Waves broke around me all night. The next morning, the motor ran on one cylinder, and I got to an island by the mainland. I was strong in body, and strong in mind. I learned to respect the sea, the wind, and the weather. I have hunted all my life, and I know safety is number one. Human beings are very important. We have family and friends. I learned this from my old man."

Ed concludes his story. I look over at him. His face is in shadows under the hood of his snowsuit, bundled against the wind. He keeps his eyes trained on the sea. But his heart is in the shadows of his face. In the gaze of his eyes.

His words fly around on the wind between us, like birds I can almost see, fluttering, not landing. This story is theology, I think. It is about spirit. It is about a man, a hunter, connecting with first things in his world. It is about a man, a hunter, finding his place in the world. This is the hunter as spiritual teacher and guide, told with humor and humility.

At that moment, I feel something new. Spirituality is not a matter of transcendence, though it has everything to do with the ability to reach outside of the self. Somebody I love once told me that spirituality is about the ability to connect. That suddenly makes sense to me. It is about being in the world and linking one's own personal destiny with the destiny of the creatures on the earth. It is the image of Ed in a small boat, amid the seals and seabirds, "kneeling from my head down to my toes."

This kind of spirituality is the ability to connect from the inside out. I feel a certain envy of Ed, who was in a sense born amid the seals and seabirds, the wind and the storm on these very waters. What our hyperactive manhood lacks now is not so much a knowledge of this kind of spirituality, but the experience of it.

8

When Eric died, the end came much more swiftly than I had ever expected. During the month before he died, he'd been sick, but those of us close to him had hoped he'd get better. But then, one night, it began to look very much as if Eric were in his final days.

He had a high fever from pneumonia, plus he had toxoplasmosis, an infection that inflames the skull lining. Eric's brain was on fire. He lay in bed, hallucinating. Talking endlessly. He wasn't incoherent, exactly. It's just that none of us by him could tell what anything he talked about referred to. He was living someplace deep inside himself. He was still deceptively muscular. But he had a distant look on his face, not vacant, but far, far away. His words were coming to us from some deeply private, internal place.

It was as though, in what he said, he was carrying on conversations with figures from his past, as if, perhaps, he was finishing conversations in his life that were incomplete. He obviously still had things to say.

I found his language utterly compelling, utterly profound. Some grand mystery and important process was going on before me, and I wanted to be as present to it as possible. This is one of the great imperatives of life—to be as present in the moment as possible, and to recognize these defining moments, these times when something important is happening. I wanted simply to pay attention, though what Eric was saying was utterly inaccessible to me.

There was something Shakespearean in his language. Once, he pulled himself up by the bar dangling above his bed. He was still very strong. But it was done convulsively, in a sort of throe. He jabbed his long, slightly crooked index finger at the blank wall, and bellowed at no one who was visible:

"The guilt must be heavy on you."

There was a pause. Whom was Eric speaking to? What was this guilt?

"I'm gonna say this one time, so ya' better listen," he said threateningly, still pointing one finger at an imaginary figure.

"The lady can't stand it no mo', and I'm gonna get cha."

Then he fell back down on his pillow, and went quiet again for a while. He went on like this for hours.

I sat transfixed. He was the poet of his own death.

The next morning, he was quiet. He didn't say anything. There was some other, greater peace that had come over him. Perhaps, he'd now said what he had needed to say. He lay in bed, his hair crumpled from the pillow, and I fed him raspberry Jell-O. He stared blankly into the distance.

When I left him, I said, "I love you, Eric." I said it twice. He smiled faintly, so I know he heard. It would have been easy to say nothing. And I'm really glad I told him that I loved him. He died early the next morning, before I could come to see him again. They were my last words to him.

I sat for a while, after he died, in his room. And then, still full of his presence and my grief, I rode three different airplanes to the Bering Sea.

9

We are standing on a small pan of ice, at least twenty miles out to sea. On the ice with us, right next to me in fact, is a huge walrus, sad-eyed and barrel-chested. It must weigh well over a ton, maybe 2,500 pounds, though I can only guess. One of its long, scimitar-shaped tusks, yellowed and precious ivory, stabs the ice like a knife. The other is off the edge and cuts the water. Its skin is like wrinkled leather, with big warts, and, on its neck, a faint and glowing pink. Here, the tobacco brown fur had been worn off in fights, exposing its pink skin underneath.

Chuck and Henry are trying to kill it.

It eyes us as we stand beside it, its eyes slightly bloodshot. They look, I must say, infinitely pained and sorrowful. Ed and Henry are frustrated. The animal is precariously perched on the edge of a small ice floe, and it won't die. We had snuck up on it as it was sleeping with another walrus, and have gotten a couple of fine shots. The partner crashed into the sea as soon as it realized we were there, only five feet away, in a paroxysm of panic. But this one was too wounded.

We rounded it in the boat, coming within a foot or two as it lay on the ice. We pushed the boat onto the pan, which is only about seven feet in diameter, and are trying to decide what to do. I have the distinct awareness of danger, standing so close to this resting giant, at least ten feet long, its rear flippers dangling in the sea off the ice. Its eyes are open and watching us, eerily aware even as its body is completely, massively inert.

We have been hunting again today, all day. It's the second day of hunting. In the morning, we headed north, straight into the Bering Sea. There, the ice had been pristine and beautiful, and while Henry succeeded in shooting a lovely little ringed seal, we hadn't found sight nor sound of walrus. Late in the afternoon, Ed steered the small boat back into the Etolin Strait, and we've skimmed full speed out into the middle of the strait, twenty miles from Nunivak, which lies behind us lost in a dark layer of heavy fog.

That brings us to this spot, with this walrus.

We stand on the ice, beside the walrus, in a bright and glittering sun. It breathes, and the vapor of its own breath clouds its head in the cold air.

Ed pauses to decide what to do. Then, as we watch, the walrus groans in a loud and terrible way. Its body convulses and all of us, instinctively, step backward. The walrus lifts his head off the ice, its yellow tusks curving into the air. At the same time, the walrus lifts its tail flippers off the ice. Its whole body is torqued and contorted and tortured. And for one uncertain second, none of us knows what will happen next.

And then it bellows again, its eyes staring at us from the sides of its head, a groan that comes from the depths of its animal being. It heaves its immense physical bulk, head and tail, up in the air, and it looks like it might do a flip. Ed screams painfully about it heaving itself into the water, and the rest of us stare at each other impotently, horrified. In a final convulsion, it rolls off the ice and splashes into the sea.

It sinks out of sight like a stone.

I step to the edge and watch it go down in the clear water.

In the face of all that animal power, we can only stare at one another, us four men, wordless and deeply disappointed. We can only watch in dumb awe.

As the walrus rose up on the white ice and groaned something that had no meaning to me whatsoever, the image of my friend Eric rose in my mind, as he had risen in his bed and yelled at an invisible figure on the wall, his final outburst of energy on his white sheets. Then he had sunk back into himself and died. A roar, a release, and a letting go. The two images—animal and human—merged into one in my mind, memory and reality, past and present.

It's moments like these, when inner reflects outer worlds, that I know I'm present and located, in a place and moment, fully present. These moments may seem coincidental, even accidental, but they reflect a deeper intent and purpose. They reflect the way the world is organized from the inside. And I'm present in a way that has nothing to do with domination, nothing to do with control. It has nothing to do with reading someone else's script, some historical drama handed down. But it comes from within me, and even though these are both sad experiences, I have all the relief and release of feeling profoundly connected to myself and my experience.

I feel as lucid as sunlight on sea and ice, moving inward and outward in deepening orbits of perception and feeling. On the horizon, the sea and the sky seem to merge, and it's hard to tell, except for floating pieces of ice, where one begins and the other ends, a moody damask of barely distinguishable, subtle shades of blue.

10

Stalking walruses on the floe ice is a complex emotional experience. I have immense sympathy for the walruses, especially the wounded walrus that tumbled off the ice and into the sea. At the same time, I understand the three hunters, whose emotions were also complex, a mix of impotence and regret and disappointment. We all stare at one another for a moment, wordlessly, on the ice. They were simply doing what they have done all their lives, what their ancestors have done for the last thousand years that they and their ancestors have been on Nunivak Island—hunting bull walrus during spring migration.

I have thought carefully about telling—or more precisely, not telling—this story. Native cultures have suffered from enough misunderstanding, and perhaps this story seems to present them in an unflattering light. But I hope I will be excused my honesty, because I think honesty is the only way we can come to the truth, insofar as we're ever able to know the truth. But there are realities in hunting, all hunting, that I can't overlook.

Not for a moment can I begrudge these men their hunt, and I know they do not want to lose a walrus. I completely support their right to maintain the hunt that is part of their culture, part of their native identity, part of their subsistence. But it also is clear to me that, in all hunting, there is wounding and waste. I respect profoundly what the hunt means for Ed, the way it is the vehicle not only for his subsistence, but also for a connection to seals and seabirds, wind and storms. It takes him into nature, and it binds him to a long tradition of his culture.

Few white Americans, though, are subsistence hunters. I don't begrudge hunters the right to get their meat for the table, either. But both literally and symbolically, hunting has inflicted too many wounds, created too much damage. I don't even want to get into weighing the relative merits of different kinds of hunting. At least subsistence hunters, as opposed to sport and trophy hunters, are likely to be in touch with some notion of "first things." Hunting for them is a kind of science, a way of knowing, a spiritual discipline. Richard Nelson calls it "stalking the sacred game."[8]

Somehow, standing on the ice pan, with the stain of blood where the walrus has just been, it is similarly clear that I have followed the hunting metaphor as far as it is going to take me. For me, the metaphor exhausted itself right there. Feminists have come upon the question themselves in their study of other cultures: the issue always is, what lessons do we take for ourselves, and what do we leave?

In the Western tradition, tracing the metaphor of hunting is like doing a natural history of the dead. I respect people who hunt for their food. And perhaps it makes an important statement about the evolution of my attitudes toward hunting to say that, in the course of my research on hunting, I quit eating meat.

Plus, the metaphor itself is too deeply implicated in a symbolic system which, in my view, has exhausted its value. Not its power, as its ongoing usefulness demonstrates. But it forces us into modes of being and relating that inhibit and constrict men's souls. Worse, the image of the hunter can even foster a kind of willful, in-your-face, I'll-shoot-it-if-I-want-to belligerence that only creates more wounds in the national psyche.

I can put it simply, if perhaps a bit too formulaically: After so much dis-membering, men need to learn to re-member themselves and the world.

Western heroes and gods were hunters—Apollo and Dionysus. Jove was less a hunter than an Olympian sexual predator, changing into beasts to steal young women, like Europa or Callisto. The heroic hunt takes us into domination. The erotic hunter takes us some way into our minds and hearts. But perhaps the motif that gives the hunt its greatest psychological depth, and keeps it forever truly fresh and in a sense honest, is the "cursed hunter," either in a perpetual hunt, like Orion in his doomed chase in the sky, or like Actaeon, the hunter who discovers, suddenly, that he's the hunted, ripped by his own dogs, no longer able to say his own name.

We need to invent modes of being that are not based, as they are in Western hunting, on adversarial modes of relationship. It is this assumption, so deep in our psyches, that is no doubt the most difficult to deal with. Every hero requires an enemy, and the attractiveness of violence as a way of solving problems, inherited from our ancient heroes and our frontier hunters, has turned upon us and made us victims of our own myths.

It is my belief that men can be more fully the authors of their own experience. We now make our lives inside a set of ideals that were constructed under different conditions, for different problems. I don't believe that metaphors and myths derive from universals in the human imagination. The hunt is a common metaphor and myth, but not because it states universal and absolute truths. It is arrayed in cultures in widely divergent ways, and reflects not truths of nature, but the values of the culture—from Greek heroics to the country squire, from the extremely elaborate feudal artifice to a frontiersman's rawhide pragmatism. But there is still some sense in which the hunter as an image has condensed in a single, if complexly variable, image, something of our psychological and historical development.

I'm not a utopian, or even an idealist. We live our lives in the space between our ideals and the demands of our daily lives. New metaphors to help us deal with the new circumstances of our lives will be generated out of the dialectic of our hopes and our realities, and will gain currency by their ability to satisfy the emotional needs of changing times. Already, the traditional hunter seems outdated in our popular media, though he is being repackaged in spaceman's clothes for the next frontier. The metaphor serves the function of reducing complexities to a manageable shape, one that can fit in the mind. It is a way of creating identity and even solving problems for us, making sense out of a complex world. There is enough violence and pain in life, already, without seeking it, without creating it, without glorifying it in our national mythologies.

But the hunting metaphor, as we've understood it, is likely to make us misunderstand and mis-take the opportunities we face. It contains and stylizes our experience, reflecting it back to us in simpler terms which, when reality changes, cause us to mistake the world for our fantasies. The world is reduced and subjected, and animals are no longer a threat to our safety, and not a suitable image for domination. Other peoples need to be listened to, not patronized or conquered. And women are not the threat that the hunting metaphor almost always makes them out to be. We are searching for a set of metaphors that will not try to deny parts of our history the costs in death we've inflicted to win our identities.

We move forward with our history. We move forward from inside the consciousness we've created, as men, out of the myth and metaphor of the hunter. We may need a radical change of imagery to overcome the depredations inherent in a hunting culture, but our new images must either come from within, or, if they come from without, they have to be able to take root and grow. Perhaps they'll come from outer space, if you will, but the imagery will have to find a home in our hearts.

For men, the whole constellation of imagery that is condensed in the figure of the hunter has been profoundly useful. It is perhaps the most powerful image through which men were enabled to experience themselves and the world that seemed so vast and large and, on the margins, frightening. Through hunting, men made the world over, tamed it, gave it a face that made them safe. It gave men, each individual man, a sense not only that he could make a mark on the wilderness, but that he participated in a larger human destiny.

For many men, those metaphors remain useful. Language and imagery can be deeply conservative, satisfying deeply felt emotional needs. Images and language tend to change slowly as they are passed on from generation to generation. We are not likely to invent new metaphors, and new modes of masculinity, out of a historical vacuum. We work slowly toward something new, finding our way, experimenting with possibilities. In the process, we slowly change, constructing and reconstructing reality. In the process, we transform our consciousness, sometimes by degrees, sometimes by big steps.

Perhaps this is something of the key to what we need in our ability to imagine ourselves. It is through metaphor and story, myth and narrative, that we make sense of our experience. And it is poets and storytellers and artists who create, out of the material of experience, the images that in turn become the lenses of perception.

Social and psycholinguists have begun to understand how intimate are the relations among images and words, speech and perception, and action. Metaphor is part of our evolutionary equipment, helping us through its inventiveness and flexibility to fit ourselves into the world. Like dreams, they give us new possibilities, moving us between memories of what has been and a desire for something new. It may be that the hunter was never really the hero of culture. It's an ancient debate, prevalent already among the Greeks, between the hero and the artist. Odysseus required Homer. Someone had to sing his heroism. Someone had to create, out of the hunter's deeds, the stuff of legend and myth. The poet, the storyteller, the artist—as surely as the hunter, the creators are also the heroes of culture.

The magic of metaphor is that, as the hunter was the hero once, the poet and storyteller and the artist may be the heroes to lead us forward now.

11

Ed, Henry, Chuck, and I clamber back into the aluminum boat, our spirits depressed after the ordeal with the dying walrus. We prowl slowly through the ice floe again, watching for more walruses. We find several others. Apparently, Ed says, the walruses are farther out on the ice floes than he had taken us yesterday.

Finally, after several tries, we maneuver through the jungle and jumble of ice pans, using oars as pikes to push us quietly close to a huge mass of three deeply sleeping walruses. We work our way through a wilderness of thick ice, pushing our way slowly and silently, until we get close enough for a shot. The hunters fire. Several times. The big walrus in the middle falls onto the ice.

We pull up to the ice, and I watch the walrus expire on the ice. We tie it up so it cannot fall into the sea, and the hunters begin cleaning it. Ed and Henry cut off the flippers.

Chuck is an ivory carver, and he extracts the long, curved, yellowing tusks of ivory. He also takes out, along with the walrus's tusks, the animal's ivory teeth, which are flat as molars for grinding clams.

I help for a while, mostly holding the walrus, which is very precariously dangling off the melting ice, so it does not slip away. Then, I step back.

The two companions of the dead walrus, the ones that had been sleeping with him on this ice, have come back to watch us. I see one of them, its head bobbing in the small space between two drifts of ice. His round head and bulging black eyes and brushy walrus mustache lift and fall, like the ice, in the swell of the sea. The walrus looks very different in the water, smaller, more on a human scale. It's only a head, a floating head. No body. It looks like a man treading water in the sea.

Except for the two long tusks of ivory, like massive buck teeth, that curl over his lower lip and cut into the water.

The walrus's curiosity is a dangerous trait under the circumstances, coming back to watch the hunters who are still working on his dead migration partner. On the ice, the walrus seems all lethargy and weight, corporeal and bestial. In the water, strangely, it is curious and heady, and seems somehow human in its attachments.

I stand on the edge of the pan. I keep my eyes on this one walrus, which ducks and bobs and keeps its eyes on me. The sun is warm in the late afternoon, early evening. The ice on the pan is visibly melting, dripping from the sides of the pan in musical splashes into the sea. I am suddenly aware of the sounds—the splashes are near and intimate, and the thud and scraping of ice pans as they collide is the sound of large natural forces at work. I hear Ed and the others, talking and working, just to my right. The pan is small, no more than fifteen feet across. The swimming walrus is scarcely twenty feet away. We are all drifting in a very strong current, all of us, people and animal, farther out into the strait. It's the choreography of the tides.

I feel a part of large correspondences—respond and co-respond.

Of all the images of hunting that are most compelling to me, it is the ones that express a deep spiritual longing that are most deeply lodged in my imagination. I remember especially the images of the men on the walls of the prehistoric caves in France and Spain. Especially the ones that seem to be half-animal, half-human. I remember the bearded man from the time I got to get into the most famous of prehistoric caves in the world—Lascaux. In what seems to be a strange straight-horned animal, you realize as you look that it has, like other images in the caves, a human and bearded face. I remember the image from the cave on El Castillo, the baroque bull with the face of a man.

And I especially remember an image from the small hidden cave in northern Spain, El Horno de la Peña—oven of the mountain. It is the image of the figure tucked deep in the farthest recess of the cave. It is a man with a bird's beaked face, and the claws apparently of a cave bear. Its hands are full of human expression—held outward, turned upward. Palms amazingly, wonderfully open.

This is the attitude of longing, of spiritual supplication. And he has, also, a large erection.

The images of the hunt that are most profoundly moving, to me, are not simply sexual ones, the ones of explicit sexual desire. They are also the spiritual ones. These link the human spirit with the divine and the animal and the body in the most profound images of desire. Artemis, the Greek goddess of the hunt and chastity, is one such image, with her Cerynian stags with the golden horns, drawing her chariot—the image of chaste desire. Even Venus, huntress of a sort that she is. And Placidas, who becomes Saint Eustace, who is granted the vision of Christ on the horns of the magical deer. Even Tristan, the saint of love, has his own erotic vision, tinged with spiritual longing. And Cernunnos, the Celtic "Lord of the Animals," a male figure with stag horns, surrounded by beasts.

I realize it is this imagery of the connection between animal and spirit, mixed confusedly with a suggestion of sexual desire, that I love the most deeply. And I realize that this imagery is associated less with hunters than with saints, and artists, and what must be the shaman in the caves.

I am drawn back to Etolin Strait. This is where Ed Shavings knelt in his boat from his head to his toes, feeling the power of the wind and the storm and the seals.

I have been on a hunt myself. A hunt among hunters. Perhaps it is this figure, the shaman and the artist, who emerges behind the mask of the hunter-hero. It is a complex time, and a country of strangers like America may be looking for someone who can help us find this new intimacy with ourselves and, I hope, other people. The challenge is to be able to experience ourselves without the intense dichotomies between spirit and sexuality, self and other, men and women, that have characterized our emotional lives for most of men's emotional history.

In *The Way of Animal Powers*, Joseph Campbell writes of the conflict between the mythology of the hunter and the mythology of the shaman.[9] The hunter provides an ethic for world heroes, dominators, rulers, exploiters. The shaman is a mystic, a traveler in consciousness, a saint and a seer. The hunter as man of action in the West has usually defined himself in direct opposition to men of reflection and feeling and mind. Xenophon loathed and attacked the rhetoricians in his "On Hunting." The Renaissance hunting aristocracy spurned the prissy humanists, men like Thomas More and Erasmus, who in turn loathed and satirized their sport as degrading to the sensibilities of a man. And in the early part of our century, Teddy Roosevelt and others abused the men of feeling as "tenderfeet," and sissies. We persist in this unfortunate dichotomy.

Surely, in our current uncertain situations, we are ready, at least, for more of this dimension latent in the metaphor of the hunt to come forward—the quest without the kill. The seeker and the shaman represent one feature of this metaphoric construction we can follow forward. If that smacks a bit uneasily of the mystical and even the heroic, I would ally to it the artist and poet, the intellectual and the musician. Not an ascetic or monkish type, but a man of true feeling. He'd have a combination of spirit and soul, of the ethereal and the bluesy real, of the Buddhist and bluesman. He'd be part psychologist and part naturalist. I picture the man of the future, in my hopeless ideal, as a combination of Leonard Cohen and Van Morrison, Black Elk and B.B. King, Barry Lopez and Michel Foucault.

On the small ice pan, I walk to the very edge. One of the swimming walruses has come within ten feet of me. It's a dangerous thing to do. Ed warns me to be careful of the ice, which is growing very soft in the warm sun. I promise that I will. I love it that the ice is melting, and that I am on a strong current, which is pulling me and the walrus.

We look carefully at each other. I am with hunters, who have brought me to this place and this moment and this intense awareness I now feel. I am aware of Chuck, the son, cutting out the walrus tusks, and I remember that he has come home from traveling in the U.S. military to be a carver of ivory. The family name of the Shavings comes from their tradition as ivory carvers, a translation of the Eskimo word.

The walrus and I look at each other. His eyes are dark, almost invisible in his dark wet body. But they glint with the sun, which lights his face like a floating moon. His whiskers are a soft amber, glistening. His tusks, like huge buck teeth, are just visible above the line of the water. He seems as fascinated in me as I am in him. He stares at me with eyes that are so large they seem to be coming out of his head, bug-eyed. Suddenly, his mannish head reminds me vaguely of the pictures of Theodore Roosevelt, with his round face and bully mustache.

We lift and fall on the tidal heave. I cannot help but wonder what dreams have flitted through the deep sleep of this walrus. I wonder what walrus-dreams swim through his head, and what walrus-knowledge he has of the depths of this sea, digging for clams on the murky bottom. And I wonder, after all the speculations about the way animals are known as either predator or prey by men, what this walrus would have to say for himself, as prey, if he were asked to give an account of his life. And I know that I am a seeker, and that it is my own quest that has brought me to this moment on the ice. I feel anything but a stranger.

I feel vaguely like I'm dreaming, except that I feel so lucid. A lucid, waking dream. I resolve to go with it, as I am riding the ice and current.

By the time that Ed and the others finish with their walrus, we have drifted in the current another five miles out to sea. The ice pan is noticeably smaller. Nunivak Island is small and distant, still lying under a heavy blanket of clouds. I am ready to head back.

For a moment, I am a child with a beast's heart, joyous and alive. The old guides have all vanished. But there are new guides to help us find new ways forward. I turn now to men of vision, the men of heart and soul, artists and poets and even men of healing. I do a little shuffle, a dance of happiness on the melting springtime ice, and look up to see Ed smiling at me. He is standing beside the boat, with his hand on the bow, ready to take us back home.

NOTES

CHAPTER ONE: **Men on Ice**

1. From *Eskimo Poems from Canada and Greenland*, trans. Tom Lowenstein (Pittsburgh: University of Pittsburgh Press, 1973), 38–40; from material originally collected by Knud Rasmussen.

2. This assumption was pervasive amid anthropologists from the early decades of the twentieth century, and continues to inform our perspective on native cultures as "primitive" peoples. For a discussion of the relation in anthropological thinking between modern and prehistoric hunting peoples, see the now-classic statement in the symposium called *Man the Hunter*. The proceedings were published under the same title, eds. Richard B. Lee and Irven DeVore (Chicago: Aldine, 1968). See, for example, Chapter 1: "The time is rapidly approaching when there will be no hunters left to study. Our aim in convening the symposium on the Man the Hunter was to bring together those who had recently done field work among the surviving hunters with other anthropologists, archaeologists, and evolutionists. . . . Therefore, the first half of this book is devoted to the presentation of new data on contemporary hunters, along with discussion and evaluation of current issues. The later chapters consider the relevance of these data to a reconstruction of life in the past" (3–4).

3. See José Ortega y Gasset, *Meditations on Hunting*, trans. Howard B. Wescott (1942; New York: Charles Scribner's Sons, 1972), 44, 48, 66, 116. For some of the most beautiful prose written about "native" hunters, see Laurens Van Der Post, *The Heart of the Hunter: The Customs and Myths of the African Bushman* (New York: William Morrow, 1961); for example, the chapter called "Love, the Aboriginal Tracker," 135–36: "Whatever sets a dreamless heart dreaming again," he writes, "was not to be despised. . . . The mystery we take upon ourselves in order to free our arrested being is that of the first things of life, which our twentieth century civilization puts last, but of which the Bushman gives us so consummate an image, representing the child before whom we are commanded to humble ourselves and to become like if we are to enter the Kingdom."

4. In this definition of metaphor, see Aristotle, *Poetics*, trans. Ingram Bywater (New York: Modern Library, 1954), 1457b: "Metaphor consists in giving the thing a name that belongs to something else; the transference being either from genus to species, or from species to genus, or from species to species, or on grounds of analogy." For the use of metaphor to create knowledge and vividness in our understanding, see *Rhetoric*, trans. W. Rhys Roberts (New York: Modern Library, 1954), 3, 1410b: "We will begin by remarking that we all naturally find it agreeable to get hold of new ideas easily: words express ideas, and therefore words are the most agreeable that enable us to get hold of new ideas. Now strange words simply puzzle us; ordinary words convey only what we know already; it is from metaphor that we can best get hold of something fresh." Metaphor operates someplace between the unknown and the known, and produces fresh knowledge. The famous quote by Shakespeare is from *A Midsummer Night's Dream*, in *The Riverside Shakespeare*, ed. G. Blakemore Evans (Boston: Houghton Mifflin, 1974), 5.1.16–17. All subsequent references to Shakespeare are from this edition.

5. Benjamin Lee Whorf, *Language, Thought, and Reality*, ed. John B. Carroll (1956; reprint, Cambridge, Mass.: M.I.T. Press, 1969); see esp. pp. 156, 158, 252.
6. These statistics come from the United States Fish and Wildlife Service. Since 1955, the USFWS has conducted national surveys every five or so years. United States Fish and Wildlife Service, *1991 National Survey of Fishing, Hunting, and Wildlife-Associated Recreation* (Washington, D.C.: Government Printing Office, 1993). On hunting, men, and motives, see also Stuart A. Marks, *Southern Hunting in Black and White: Nature, History, and Ritual in a Carolina Community* (Princeton: Princeton University Press, 1991), 306; and John Mitchell, *The Hunt* (New York: Knopf, 1980), 19ff.
7. Ortega y Gasset, 48–49; Plato, *Euthydemus*, Loeb Classical Library (1962), 290b, 445: "no art of actual hunting, he replied, covers more than chasing and overcoming. . . ."
8. From Plato, *The Sophist*, Loeb Classical Library (1961), 222c, 287. Aristotle considers hunting in his *Politics*, Loeb Classical Library (1959), 1256b, 23–26.
9. There is a wide range of views on myth. For classical definitions, see Joseph Fontenrose, *Orion: The Myth of the Hunter and the Huntress* (Berkeley: University of California Press, 1981); Walter Burkert, *Greek Religion*, trans. John Raffan (Cambridge: Harvard University Press, 1985); Edmund Lowell, ed., *Approaches to Greek Myth* (Baltimore: Johns Hopkins University Press, 1990); E. O. James, *The Ancient Gods: The History and Diffusion of Religion in the Ancient Near East and Eastern Mediterranean* (New York: Capricorn, 1964); and Theodor Gaster, *Thespis: Ritual, Myth and Drama in the Ancient Near East* (New York: Schuman, 1950). For semiotic and anthropological definitions of myth, a fine overview is provided by Terence Hawkes, *Structuralism and Semiotics* (Berkeley: University of California Press, 1977). Hawkes describes the process of uncovering the central and often unconscious myths of a culture, in an anthropologist like Lévi-Strauss, as itself a hunt: "In fact, the anthropologist's concern lies with the 'unconscious foundations' . . . on which that social life—and that language—rest. His quarry, in short, is the *langue* [underlying linguistic and mental structure] of a whole culture; its systems and its general laws: he stalks through the particular varieties" of its speech (39). See as well Roland Barthes for a definition of his view of myth in everyday bourgeois life as the creation of certain controlling fictions, in *Mythologies*, trans. Annette Lavers (London: Paladin, 1973), 11: "In short, in the account given of our contemporary circumstances, I resent seeing Nature and History confused at every turn, and I wanted to track down, in the decorative display of what goes without saying, the ideological abuse which, in my view, is hidden right there." The locations for anthropological ideas about myth include Claude Lévi-Strauss, *The Savage Mind* (Chicago: University of Chicago Press, 1962), and *Myth and Meaning* (New York: Schocken Books, 1979), and *Totemism*, trans. Rodney Needham (Boston: Beacon Press, 1963); James G. Frazer, *The New Golden Bough*, ed. Theodor Gaster (New York: New American Library, 1959); and A. E. Jensen, *Myth and Cult among Primitive Peoples*, trans. Marianna Tax Choldin and Wolfgang Weissleder (Chicago: University of Chicago Press, 1963). For Jungian interpretations of myth, see Carl Gustav Jung, *Psyche and Symbol: A Selection from the Writings of C. G. Jung*, ed. Violet S. de Laszlo (Garden City, N.Y.: Doubleday, 1958), and *Man and His Symbols* (New York: Dell, 1964); and Joseph Campbell, *The Hero with a Thousand Faces* (Princeton: Princeton University Press, 1949); and *The Masks of God*, 4 vols. (New York: Viking Penguin, 1959–70). See also Thomas Sebeok, ed. *Myth: A Symposium* (Bloomington: University of Indiana Press, 1965).
10. For the unicorn hunt, see Francis Klingender, *Animals in Art and Thought: To the End of the Middle Ages*, eds. Evelyn Antal and John Harthan (Cambridge, Mass.:

M.I.T. Press, 1971), 464–68. Barry Lopez, *Arctic Dreams: Imagination and Desire in a Northern Landscape* (New York: Charles Scribner's Sons, 1986), 107–36, discusses the narwhal beautifully, and its connection in imagination to the unicorn.

11. Rainier Maria Rilke, "This is the Creature," in *The Sonnets to Orpheus*, trans. Stephen Mitchell (New York: Simon and Schuster, 1985), 79.

12. Philip Booth, "Creatures," in *Relations: Selected Poems, 1950–1985* (New York: Viking Penguin, 1986), 248–50.

13. Robert Munsch and Michael Kusugak, *A Promise Is a Promise* (Willowdale, Ontario: Firefly, 1988).

CHAPTER TWO: **A Hunger Deeper Than Memory**

1. Joseph Campbell, *The Way of the Animal Powers*, vol. 1, *Historical Atlas of World Mythology* (San Francisco: Harper and Row, 1983), 47.

2. Paul Shepard, *The Tender Carnivore and the Sacred Game* (New York: Charles Scribner's Sons, 1973), 122–23.

3. Ortega y Gasset, *Meditations*, 116.

4. Sam Keen, *Fire in the Belly: On Being a Man* (New York: Bantam, 1991), 90–91.

5. For an account of the discovery of Dart's famous skull, see Phillip V. Tobias, *Dart, Tuang, and the "Missing Link": An Essay on the Life and Work of Emeritus Professor Raymond Dart* (Johannesburg: Witwatersrand University Press, 1984). The quote is on 27. For an anthropologist's critical review of the theory of the hunter in evolutionary thought with particular reference to modern misanthropy, see Matt Cartmill, *A View to a Death in the Morning: Hunting and Nature Through History* (Cambridge, Mass.: Harvard University Press, 1993), 1–27.

6. Raymond Dart, "The Cultural Status of the South African Man-Apes," *Annual Report of the Board of Regents of the Smithsonian Institution*, Publication 4232 (1955), 320.

7. Raymond Dart, "The Predatory Transition from Ape to Man," *International Anthropological Linguistics Review*, 1 (1953): 206.

8. Dart, "Predatory," 209.

9. Dart, "Predatory," 204.

10. Dart, "Predatory," 207–8.

11. Robert Ardrey, *African Genesis: A Personal Investigation into the Animal Origins and Nature of Man* (New York: Atheneum, 1961), 33. See also Ardrey, *The Hunting Hypothesis: A Personal Conclusion Concerning the Evolutionary Nature of Man* (New York: Atheneum, 1976).

12. William S. Laughlin, "Hunting: An Integrating Biobehavior System and Its Evolutionary Importance," in *Man the Hunter*, eds. Lee and DeVore, 304–20. This volume contains the proceedings of the conference. See also Carleton S. Coon, *The Hunting Peoples* (New York: Little Brown, 1971), i, for an example of the way it was taken as an unchallenged assumption that all men hunted and hunting guided their whole lives: "Ten thousand years ago *all men were hunters*, including the ancestors of everyone reading this book. The span of ten millenia encompasses about four hundred generations, too few to allow any notable changes. Insofar as human behavior, like the behavior of other animal species, depends ultimately on inherited capacities (including the capacity to learn), our natural tendencies cannot have changed very much. *We and our ancestors are the same people.*" (Italics mine.)

13. Sherwood L. Washburn and C. S. Lancaster, "The Evolution of Hunting," in *Man the Hunter*, eds. Lee and DeVore, 293, 303.

14. For overviews of human evolution and the chronology of species and culture, see

Jacquetta Hawkes, *The Atlas of Early Man* (New York: St. Martin's, 1976); Paul Shepard, *Tender Carnivore*, Appendix; Valerius Geist, "Neanderthal the Hunter," *Natural History*, January 1981, 26–36; David A. Pilbeam, "The Descent of Hominoids and Hominids," *Scientific American*, 250 (March 1984), 84–96; Louis Leakey, "Adventures in the Search for Man," *National Geographic*, January 1963, 132–52; Lawrence Guy Straus, *Iberia Before the Iberians: Stone Age Prehistory in Cantabrian Spain* (Albuquerque: University of New Mexico Press, 1992); Philip E. L. Smith, "The Solutrean Culture," *Scientific American*, 211 (August 1964), 86–94.

15. Washburn and Lancaster, "Evolution," 300.

16. Washburn and Lancaster, "Evolution," 296, 301.

17. Washburn and Lancaster, "Evolution," 297.

18. W. C. McGrew, "The Female Chimpanzee as Evolutionary Prototype," in *Woman the Gatherer*, ed. Francis Dahlberg (New Haven: Yale University Press, 1981), 65–66. For other feminist critiques of the hunting paradigm in human evolution, see Nancy Tanner and Adrienne Zihlman, "Women in Evolution. Part I: Innovation and Selection in Human Origins," *Signs*, 1 (1976), 585–608; and Donna J. Haraway, "Remodelling the Human Way of Life: Sherwood Anderson and the New Physical Anthropology, 1950–1980," in *Bones, Bodies, Behavior: Essays on Biological Anthropology*, ed. G. Stocking, (Madison: University of Wisconsin Press, 1988), 206–59.

19. Washburn and Lancaster, "Evolution," 299.

20. Desmond Morris, *The Naked Ape: A Zoologist's Study of the Human Animal* (New York: McGraw-Hill, 1967), 43.

21. Richard B. Lee, "What Do Hunters Do for a Living, or, How to Make Out on Scarce Resources," in *Man the Hunter*, eds. Lee and DeVore, 37. For a detailed chart on the "percentage dependence on" gathering, hunting, and fishing in cultures from Copper Eskimos to Umatilla Native Americans to Yavapai, see page 48.

22. Richard B. Lee, "What Do Hunters Do," 43.

23. C. K. Brain, *The Hunters or the Hunted? An Introduction to African Cave Taphonomy* (Chicago: University of Chicago Press, 1981), 269.

24. Brain, *Hunters or Hunted?*, 273–74.

25. Pat Shipman, "Scavenger Hunt," *Natural History*, April 1984, 27. In the same year, she writes of scavenging, "It is not a flattering image of our early ancestors—how much easier it is to view ourselves as noble hunters or even killer apes." "Early Hominid Lifestyle: The Scavenging Hypothesis," *Anthroquest*, 28 (1984): 9–10. Why hunting should necessarily be considered more flattering is probably its own subject for debate.

26. Lewis R. Binford, "Human Ancestors: Changing Views of Their Behavior," *Anthropological Archaeology*, 4 (1985), 321.

27. Ted Kerasote, *Bloodties: Nature, Culture, and the Hunt* (New York: Random House, 1993), 221, and for the "first accord," see 225.

28. Francis Dahlberg, "Introduction," in *Woman the Gatherer*, 27.

29. Herbert Read, *Icon and Idea: The Function of Art in the Development of Human Consciousness* (Cambridge: Harvard University Press, 1955), 30. His view of this "vitalistic" art is developed in the chapter "The Vital Image," 17–34.

30. Read, *Icon and Image*, 31.

31. For the best summary of the difficulties of interpretation of the cave art of prehistoric Europe, still considered the single best view of the subject, see Peter J. Ucko and Andrée Rosenfeld, *Paleolithic Cave Art*, (New York: McGraw-Hill, 1967). Sympathetic magic, totemism, and fertility theories are discussed on pages 116–49. For example, "For later authors obsessed by the interpretation of sexual magic, the Paleolithic

world was often dominated by the worship of a Mother Goddess to which all Paleolithic art could ultimately be related" (138).
32. Ucko and Rosenfeld, *Cave Art*, 187–88.
33. Shepard, *Tender Carnivore*, 169–70.
34. Shepard, *Tender Carnivore*, 170.
35. Shepard, *Tender Carnivore*, 173.
36. Shepard, *Tender Carnivore*, 174.
37. The most useful overview of Leroi-Gourhan's theoretical views on the caves is "The Religion of the Caves: Magic or Metaphysics," trans. Annette Michelson, *October*, 37 (1986), 7–17. See also his monumental study, *Treasures of Prehistoric Art*, trans. Norbert Guterman (New York: Harry Abrams, 1967).
38. Hawkes, *Structuralism and Semiotics*, 18.
39. Leroi-Gourhan, "Religion of the Caves," 10.
40. Leroi-Gourhan, *Treasures*, 174.
41. Ucko and Rosenfeld, *Cave Art*, 154–55.

CHAPTER THREE: **The Hunter in Mind**

1. Bible, King James Version, ed. C. I. Scofield (New York: Oxford University Press, 1967), 597.
2. Hesiod, "The Astronomy," in *The Homeric Hymns and Homerica*, Loeb Classical Library (1954), 71–73.
3. Xenophon, "On Hunting," in *Scripta Minora*, Loeb Classical Library (1925), 365–457. For biographical material on Xenophon, see J. K. Anderson, *Xenophon* (London: Duckworth, 1974), esp. 98–119, 162–71, 183–84.
4. J. K. Anderson, *Hunting in the Ancient World* (Berkeley: University of California Press, 1985), 29. For general studies on hunting among the ancients, see also Denison Bingham Hull, *Hounds and Hunting in Ancient Greece* (Chicago: University of Chicago Press, 1964); J. M. C. Toynbee, *Animals in Roman Life and Art* (Ithaca, N.Y.: Cornell University Press, 1973); A. J. Butler, *Sport in Classic Times* (London: E. Benn, 1930); and Jacques Aymard, *Essai sur les Chasses Romaines* (Paris: E. de Boccard, 1951).
5. Strabo, *The Geography of Strabo*, Loeb Classical Library (1961), 10.4.20–21, pp. 153–9; on Macedonia, see Anderson, *Hunting*, 29, 80. For a modern French view of hunting in the classical world, see Marcel Detienne, *Dionysius Slain*, trans. Mireille Muellner and Leonard Muellner (Baltimore: Johns Hopkins University Press, 1979), 34. He comments on hunting as one of the myths "long since inscribed in 'the architecture of the spirit' " (1). As Detienne and others notice, there is a parallel in the ritual abduction by boys into the male world of the hunt and a story of a hunter named Melanion, who abjures the society of women to live celibate and alone hunting in the mountains, hunting hare with nets, a misanthrope and misogynist (41). See Chapter Four, note 10, for the reference in Aristophanes. Hunting carves out a territory that is explicitly male, whether ascetic and chaste, or homoerotic: "Choice haunt of the powers of savagery, the domain open to the hunter belongs exclusively to the male sex. . . . It also constitutes a space outside of marriage that welcomes deviant forms of sexuality in those that are simply considered strange by the city-state. Thus a system of relations seems to form between hunting and sex. Out of hatred for women, a young man goes off to track hares in the mountains and never returns" (24–25).
6. Xenophon, "On Hunting," 13.6–9, pp. 451–53: "Many others besides myself blame the sophists of our generation—philosophers I will not call them—because the

wisdom they profess consists of words and not of thoughts. . . . Avoid the behests of the sophists, and despise not the conclusions of the philosophers. . . ."
7. Xenophon, "On Hunting," 1.17–18, p. 373.
8. Xenophon, "On Hunting," 12.1–9, pp. 443–45.
9. See for example John M. MacKenzie, *Empire of Nature: Hunting, Conservation, and British Imperialism* (Manchester: University of Manchester Press, 1988), 10: The progressive restriction on social access to hunting "constitutes the enduring theme of hunting in a wide range of societies. This upward exclusiveness tends to mark a shift from utility to inutility, and often edibility to inedibility. The symbolic and normative content is emphasised. . . . Hunting [for food] usually survives, continuing to perform its humble subsistence role, but it is despised by the elite and their apologists. It fails to exhibit the character-forming, moral attributes."
10. Plato, *Laws*, vol. 2, Loeb Classical Library (1961), 7.822a–24c, pp. 115–21. "None shall hinder these truly sacred hunters," according to Plato's perfect law, "from hunting wheresoever and howsoever they wish." All other forms of hunting would be carefully regulated and restricted, and Plato makes it clear in his references to the philosophic hunter that he spurns the practical dimensions of hunting for use of the booty. See note 30 below. The final quotation on "manlike godliness" is translated by Eric Nelson.
11. See Pierre Vidal-Naquet, "The Black Hunter and the Origin of the Athenian Ephebeia," *Proceedings of the Cambridge Philological Society*, 194 (1968), 60: "It goes without saying that all heroes are hunters and all hunters are heroes."
12. Joseph Fontenrose gives a complete summary of the several strands of the Orion myth, including the cognate myths that relate to it, not only in Greek and Roman myths, but in the mythology of the Near East as well, in *Orion: The Myth of the Hunter and Huntress*. He argues there are three plots in the Orion myth. First, the hunter and huntress are in love, but she is tricked into killing him by a jealous god [Apollo, Zeus], who later makes his own amorous advances. He either rapes her, or she escapes through transformation. Second, the two hunters enjoy each other, and are hunting companions. She is chaste, but his lust makes him try to rape her, and she kills or punishes him. Third, the hunter and huntress love each other, but a goddess seduces the hunter [e.g., Aurora], and the huntress kills him in anger (142–43). In all three, hunting is used as symbolic of sexual relations, focusing especially on jealousy, rape, and revenge. For classical sources, I've drawn from Hesiod, *"The Astronomy"*; and Apollodorus, *The Library*, vol. 1, Loeb Classical Library (1961), 1.4.3–5, pp. 30–33. Xenophon also mentions Orion as a progenitor of hunting, as does Oppian, honorifically, in *Cynegetica, or The Chase*, Loeb Classical Library (1958), 2.29, p. 57: "And snaring by night, the guileful hunting of the dark, crafty Orion first discovered."
13. Homer, *Odyssey*, trans. Robert Fitzgerald (Garden City, N.Y.: Doubleday, 1961), 5.120–23, p. 97.
14. Xenophon, "On Hunting," 1.1, pp. 366–67.
15. Fontenrose, *Orion*, 252: "Hunting is perhaps symbolic in these stories, and not so significant in itself as the passions and deeds. . . . In these myths hunting obviously has a meaning in relation to the passions, aversions, transgressions and violent deeds that are their subject." Nancy Chodorow, in *The Reproduction of Mothering* (Berkeley: University of California Press, 1978), describes Freudian oedipal identity in men as part of object-relations theory, and describes men's sense of self emerging through the oedipal triangle as oppositional, coming from a sense of separateness. See 75ff., and, for example, 207: "The greater length and different nature of their preoedipal experience, and their continuing preoccupation with the issues of this period, mean that

women's sense of self is continuous with others and that they retain capacities for primary identification, both of which enable them to experience the empathy and lack of reality sense needed by a cared-for infant. In men, these qualities have been curtailed, both because they are early treated as an opposite by their mother and because their later attachment to her must be repressed. The relational basis for mothering is thus extended in women, and inhibited in men, who experience themselves as more separate and distinct from others."

16.   Ovid, "Hero to Leander," *Heroides*, Loeb Classical Library (1977), 9.9–16, pp. 260–61.

17.   See for example Butler, *Sport*, 26: "Dido of Carthage was no doubt, like Phaedra, an exception in her time: possibly there may be other exceptions today."

18.   Anderson, *Hunting*, 29.

19.   The story of Eurykleia bathing Odysseus, and the flashback to his boar hunt with his uncles on Mount Parnassus, occurs in the *Odyssey*, 19.380–476, pp. 377–80. All quotes are from these pages.

20.   Chaucer moralizes the hunting of Hercules as an example of how "beastly" lust might be overcome by the hero in his translation of Boetheus's "Consolation of Philosophy," Book V, Metre 7, in *The Complete Works of Geoffrey Chaucer*, ed. Walter W. Skeat (Oxford: Clarendon Press, 1894), 125–26. See any number of summaries of Greek myths. For example, Robert Graves, *The Greek Myths* (Baltimore: Penguin, 1955); H. J. Rose, *Gods and Heroes of the Greeks* (London: Methuen, 1957); H. J. Rose, *A Handbook of Greek Mythology*, (New York: Dutton, n.d.). The passage on Achilles's shield is in the *Iliad*, trans. Robert Fitzgerald (Garden City, N.Y.: Doubleday, 1974), 18.490–94, 577–85, pp. 450–51, 453.

21.   The Bible speaks of great hunters, and uses the metaphor in places. It is the image of the pagan and the hero—see Nimrod, for example. Samson, also, was said to be a great hunter. The Christian tradition, as I'll show, uses the metaphor of the hunt—particularly the demonic hunt of the devil. But it is a metaphor not particularly congenial to the Christian message, and its most powerful expression in association with Christ is when He appears to pagan hunters in the image of a deer with golden horns and a crucifix—when He appears, that is, in the likeness of the prey. See Anne Rooney, *Hunting in Middle English Literature* (Bury St. Edmunds, UK: Boydell, 1993), especially the chapter "The Hunt of the World and the Hunt of Christ," 102–39. See also Marcelle Thiébaux, *The Stag of Love: The Chase in Medieval Literature* (Ithaca, N.Y.: Cornell University Press, 1974), esp. 40–46, "The Iconography of the Stag," and 59–65, "The Sacred Chase." Butler, in *Sport*, remarks, "It is perhaps curious that in the Old Testament there is no mention of horse or hound for use in the chase; nor is there any hint that Nimrod, mighty hunter, depended upon anything but bow and spear and speed" (17).

22.   Joseph Fontenrose, *Python: A Study of Delphic Myth and Its Origins* (Berkeley: University of California Press, 1959), 22: "Often in the following chapters the name of Python [the dragon slain by Apollo] will be used merely as a convenient designation for Apollo's opponent without regard to sex or species." The story of Apollo and Python is derived largely from Fontenrose's methodical study.

23.   "To Pythian Apollo," in *Hesiod and The Homeric Hymns*, Loeb Classical Library (1954), 300ff, pp. 345–51.

24.   "To Pythian Apollo," 364–74, pp. 351.

25.   H. W. Parke and D. E. W. Wormell, *The Delphic Oracle*, vol. 1, *The History* (Oxford: Basil Blackwell, 1956), 7. For a discussion of historical interpretations of the myths of the Delphic oracle, see "Myth as History: The Previous Owners of the Delphic Oracle," Christiane Sourvinou-Inwood, in *Interpretations of Greek Mythology*, ed. Jan Bremmer (Totowa, N.J.: Barnes and Noble, 1986), 215–41. See also Marija Gimbutas, *The Goddesses and Gods of Old Europe: 6500–3500 B.C., Myths and Cult Images* (Berkeley: University of California Press, 1982), 238, for a feminist reading of the conflict of the two cultures, two mythical systems: "Some scholars did in the past classify European prehistory and early history into matriarchal and patriarchal eras respectively. 'The beginning of the psychological-matriarchal ages,' says Neumann, 'is lost in the haze of prehistory, but its end at the dawn of our historical era unfolds magnificently before our eyes.' . . . It is then replaced by the patriarchal world with its different symbolism and different values. . . . Two entirely different sets of mythical images met. Symbols of the masculine group replaced the images of Old Europe. Some of the old elements were fused together as a subsidiary of the new symbolic imagery, thus losing their original meaning. Some images persisted side by side, creating chaos in the former harmony. Through losses and additions new complexes of symbols developed which are best reflected in Greek mythology. One cannot always distinguish the traces of the old since they are transformed or distorted. . . . The earliest European civilization was savagely destroyed by the patriarchal element and it never recovered, but its legacy lingered in the substratum which nourished further European cultural developments. The Old European creations were not lost; transformed, they enormously enriched the European psyche."

26. Sherry B. Ortner, "Is Female to Male as Nature Is to Culture," in *Woman, Culture, and Society*, ed. Michelle Zimbalist Rosaldo and Louise Lamphere (Stanford, Calif.: Stanford University Press, 1974), 75.

27. Claude Lévi-Strauss, *From Honey to Ashes: Introduction to the Science of Mythology*, trans. J. and D. Weightman (New York: Harper and Row, 1973), 473: ". . . it will be agreed that mythic thought transcends itself and, going beyond images retaining some relationship with concrete experience, operates in a world of concepts which have been released from any such obligation. . . . We know, as it happens, that just such a dramatic change took place along the frontiers of Greek thought, when mythology gave way to philosophy and the latter emerged as the necessary pre-condition of scientific thought." The quote from Thomas Henry Huxley on hunting and philosophy is in *Hume* (1879; reprint, New York: Harper and Brothers, 1901), 139.

28. Plato, *Euthydemus*, 290b, c, d, 365–67. Plato uses the idea of the hunter in connection with philosophers in *Sophist* 235b, *Phaedo* 66c, *Laws* 654e, *Parmenides* 128c, *Lysis* 218c, and *Republic* below.

29. Plato, *Republic*, vol. 1, Loeb Classical Library (1963), 4.432b, pp. 365–67.

30. Plato, *Sophist*, 219c, p. 275; "a hunting of man" is from 222c, p. 285.

31. Sophocles, *Oedipus the King*, in *Three Tragedies*, trans. H. D. Kitto (New York: Oxford, 1964), lines 110–11. See also Thiébaux, *Stag*, 50–58, on Oedipus and the metaphors of the philosopher's hunt.

32. Aristophanes, *Clouds*, ed. K. J. Dover (Oxford: Clarendon, 1968), line 358. The translation of this sentence is by Eric Nelson.

33. Cicero, *De Natura Deorum*, Loeb Classical Library (1951), 1:83, pp. 80–81. On Thomas Aquinas, see under *venari* (to hunt) for various uses of the concept, in Ludwig Schütz, *Thomas-Lexikon: Sammlung, Übersetzung und Erklärung der Sämtlichen Werken des h. Thomas von Aquin* (New York: Frederic Ungar, 1957).

34. Ortega y Gasset, *Meditations*, 132.

35. Robert Bly, *Iron John: A Book about Men* (Reading, Mass.: Addison-Wesley, 1990), 4. The parable of the hunter is in the first chapter.

36. Margaret Atwood, "The Female Body," in *The Best American Essays, 1991*, ed. Joyce Carol Oates (New York: Ticknor & Fields, 1991), 11–12.

37. *The Epic of Gilgamesh*, trans. N. K. Sanders (Harmondsworth, UK: Penguin, 1960), 106, 62, 63; *Genesis* 10:8; Anderson, *Hunting*, 4–10; Andrew Sherratt, "The Chase: From Subsistence to Sport," *The Ashmolean*, 10 (Summer 1986): 4–7; Toynbee, *Animals*,—the topic of *venationes* pervades the book; Erich Horbusch, *Fair Game: A History of Hunting, Shooting and Animal Conservation* (New York: Arco, 1980), 31–70; Xenophon, *Cyropaedia*, vol. 1, Loeb Classical Library (1957), esp. 1.2.9–16, pp. 19–23 on hunting as a school for war; and 1.4.1–18, pp. 45–51 on Cyrus the emerging hero-general as hunter.

38. The quotations describing Gilgamesh as hunter and as tyrant/lover are on p. 106 and p. 62, respectively; the description of Humbaba is on p. 71; Enkidu is described on pp. 62ff.

39. Parke and Wormell, *Delphic Oracle*, 9–13.

CHAPTER FOUR: **The Metaphors of Male Desire**

1. Ovid, *Amores*, in *Heroides and Amores*, Loeb Classical Library (1977), 407–9. Unless otherwise indicated, the Latin translations throughout are my own.

2. Tibullus, *The Elegies of Albius Tibullus*, ed. Kirby Flower Smith (Darmstadt: Wissenschaftliche Buchgesellschaft, 1971). Sulpicia writes a short letter in which she makes clear she doesn't want to hunt with Cerinthus, a devoted hunter, but she is willing to join him in the snares of love. Better yet, she invites him to leave hunting and return to her at home.

3. See W. H. D. Rowse, *Shakespeare's Ovid* (Carbondale: Southern Illinois University Press, 1961), n.p. (Publisher's Forward). See also Francis Meres, *Palladis Tamia, Wits Treasury* (1598): "As the soul of Euphorbus was thought to live in Pythagorus, so the witty soule of Ovid lives in mellifluous and honey-tongued Shakespeare. . . ." in *Riverside Shakespeare*, 1844. The *Times*, London, 2 October 1957, Royal Edition. Other powerful "teachers of love" in the ancient world, who also rely on tropes of hunting, include Tibullus, Propertius, and Callimachus.

4. Ovid, *Artis Amatoriae*, Loeb Classical Library (1962). This work is usually referred to as *Ars Amatoria*. References to specific lines are given in the text.

5. Isidore of Seville, "de Vocabularis," in *Etymologiae*, ed. W. M. Lindsay, 2 volumes (Oxford: Clarendon, 1911), 2.x, A.5.

6. The conception of desire as a lack leads almost inevitably to a philosophy of desire that requires metaphors of the hunt, possession, capture, and domination. The post-Freudian psychoanalytic theorist Jacques Lacan is an example. In "The subversion of the subject and the dialectic of desire in the Freudian unconscious," in *Ecrits*, trans. Alan Sheridan (New York: W. W. Norton, 1977), 292–335, he says desire is rooted in language, not instinct. And men desire an object which they lack. Desire a quest or hunt for a thing lacked. In his influential post-Freudian analysis of desire, the erotic hunt is a quest for the Other of the subconscious, but we act out the hunt in our external relations, through both "physical combat or sexual display": "Pretence of this kind is deployed in imaginary capture, and is integrated into the play of approach and rejection that constituted the original dance, in which these two vital situations find their rhythm, and in accordance with which the partners ordered their movements—what I will dare to call their 'dancity' (*dansité*). Indeed, animals, too, show that they are capable of such behaviour when they are hunted; they manage to put their pursuers off the scent by making a false start. This can go so far as to suggest on the part of the game animal the nobility of honoring the element of display to be found in the hunt" (305). See also

Peter Brooks, *Reading for the Plot* (New York: Knopf, 1984), and Roland Barthes, *The Pleasure of the Text*, trans. R. Miller (New York: Farrar Straus & Giroux, 1975), for additional discussions of desire as lack (and chase and hunt).

7. Michel Foucault, *The Use of Pleasure: The History of Sexuality*, Volume 2, trans. Robert Hurley (New York: Vintage, 1985). Foucault says that it is his purpose, in writing a history of sexuality, to see "how an 'experience' came to be constituted in western societies, an experience that caused individuals to recognize themselves as subjects of a 'sexuality,' which was accessible to very diverse fields of knowledge [e.g., biology, theology, psychology] and linked to a system of rules and constraints." Sexuality amounted to a study of power relations, and they are not simply studies in domination and subordination. It is the study of complex strategies, in which power shifts and sways between parties—much the way power shifts between the pursuer and the pursued in love: "And the analysis of power relations and their technologies made it possible to view them as open strategies, while escaping the alternative of a power conceived of as domination or exposed as a simulacrum" (4–5). That is, power is transgressive and subversive as well as repressive, it is erotic as well as punitive, productive as well as destructive. Sexual power is complex and constantly in flux.

8. I use the Latin edition of the *Metamorphoses*, Loeb Classical Library (1951). The Apollo and Daphne story occurs in lines 452–567, pp. 32–43, and I'll indicate subsequent line numbers in parentheses in the text.

9. The Amazons likewise challenge male expectations, taking on the attributes of men, one of the most important of which was that of hunter. See William Blake Tyrell, *Amazons: A Study in Athenian Mythmaking* (Baltimore: Johns Hopkins Press, 1984), 83: "The Amazon's likeness to men defines them in the Greek mentality as rivals of men; that is, they are viewed as opposed or antithetical to the male as father. This antithesis takes the form of their refusal to grant men their reproductivity. Again, all Amazons refuse patriarchal marriage and restrictions on sex. On the one hand, they do so actively by usurping men's roles and using their reproductivity for their own purposes. On the other hand, they remain extrapolations of the boy who refuses to grow up, and their threat is passive: they run away. Figures representing this plane of the myth's structure [Amazonian myth] flee patriarchal society and its marriage and for the wilds and the life of the hunter."

10. Callimachus, "To Artemis," Hymn 3 in *Hymns and Epigrams*, Loeb Classical Library (1960), lines 6–19, pp. 60–83. For the reference to Agamemnon and the stags of Artemis, see "Electra," in *Sophocles*, eds. David Green and Richmond Lattimore, trans. David Green (Chicago: University of Chicago Press, 1959), line 566ff. The reference to Melanion, the "Black Hunter," is in Aristophanes, *Lysistrata*, Loeb Classical Library (1955), lines 785–96, pp. 78–81: "All to shun the nuptial bed, / From his home Melanion fled." In the forests he kept his dog and trapped his hares: "He detested women so." For discussions of solitary huntresses among the Norse, Irish, Germanic, as well as Indo-European proto-Artemis figures, see H. R. E. Davidson, *Gods and Myths of Northern Europe* (Harmondsworth, UK: Penguin, 1964), 123ff. Jensen, *Myth and Cult among Primitive Peoples*, 37ff., discusses the "master of animals." See also Gimutas, *Goddesses and Gods of Old Europe*, on the bear goddess and Diana as images of a free and untamed nature as well as protectress of weaklings, 190ff. W. F. Otto, in *Dionysius: Myth and Cult* (Bloomington: University of Indiana Press, 1965), called Diana/Artemis the feminine in nature.

11. See Fontenrose, *Orion*, 33–47. He gives exhaustive sources for the myth. For other versions, see esp. Callimachus, "On the Bath of Pallas," Hymn 5, lines 107–16, p. 121; Apollodorus, 3.4.4, pp. 323–25; and Nonnos, *Dionysiaca*, Loeb Classical Library

(1940), 5.287–555, pp. 189–207. Nonnos gives a very different version of the story of Actaeon, describing him as "gazing greedily" at the naked goddess, emphasizing his relation to his father, and describing Actaeon as a man who obeyed the call of Dionysus and followed in his train, 13.54.

12. See Michel Foucault, *The History of Sexuality. Volume I: An Introduction*, trans. Robert Hurley (New York: Vintage, 1980), 11. He asks how power is distributed in Eros: Who has power? Who is subservient? How is power maintained and subverted? Foucault calls these the "polymorphous techniques of power," echoing Freud's concept of the "polymorphous perverse" in sexuality.

13. Euripedes, *The Bacchae*, in *The Complete Greek Tragedies*, vol. 4, eds. David Green and Richmond Lattimore (Chicago: University of Chicago Press, 1958), 135–37.

14. Quoted from Don Cameron Allen, *Image and Meaning: Metaphoric Traditions in Renaissance Poetry* (Baltimore: Johns Hopkins University Press, 1960), 2.

15. Edmund Spenser, "March," in "The Shepeardes Calendar," in *Spenser: Poetical Works*, eds. J. C. Smith and E. De Selincourt (London: Oxford University Press, 1912), 428–30. Shakespeare, *Much Ado about Nothing*, 3.1.106.

16. Plato, *Symposium*, Loeb Classical Library (1925), 202c–d, p. 117.

17. Plato, *The Sophist*, 222e, p. 287.

18. Michel Foucault, "Nietzsche, Genealogy, History," in *Language, Counter-Memory, Practice: Selected Essays and Interviews*, ed. Donald F. Bouchard, trans. Donald F. Bouchard and Sherry Simon (Ithaca, N.Y.: Cornell University Press, 1977), 144–45. The full quotation is as follows: "A genealogy of values, morality, asceticism, and knowledge will never confuse itself with a quest for their 'origins,' will never neglect as inaccessible the vicissitudes of history. On the contrary, it will cultivate the details and accidents that accompany every beginning; it will be scrupulously attentive to their petty malice; it will await their emergence, once unmasked, as the face of the other. Wherever it is made to go, it will not be reticent—in 'excavating the depths,' in allowing time for these elements to escape from a labyrinth where no truth had ever detained them. The genealogist needs history to dispel the chimeras of their origin, somewhat in the manner of the pious philosopher who needs a doctor to exorcise the shadow of his soul. He must be able to recognize the events of history, its jolts, its surprises, its unsteady victories and unpalatable defeats—the basis of all beginnings, atavisms, and heredities. Similarly, he must be able to diagnose the illnesses of the body, its conditions of weakness and strength, its breakdown and resistances, to be in a position to judge philosophical discourse. History is the concrete body of a development, with its moments of intensity, its lapses, its extended periods of feverish agitation, its fainting spells; and only a metaphysician would seek its soul in the distant ideality of the origin."

19. Virgil, *The Aeneid of Virgil*, ed. T. E. Page (New York: St. Martin's, 1967). All references to the *Aeneid* are from this edition, and references to specific lines will be given in parentheses in the text. Venus *venatrix*, with her "*virginis arma*," occurs in 1.318; Dido is sticken by arrows and wounded, "*infelix Dido*," in 4.68–79.

20. The hare was famous as a favorite victim of Venus. Shakespeare's Venus begs Adonis to chase "the timorous flying hare," not the more manly boar, in "Venus and Adonis," 613–708. See also Marcel Detienne, *Dionysius Slain*, 48: ". . . the hare plays a complex role in his relations with the divinities of sexuality. His amorous temperament qualifies him as an effective gift between male lovers for whom intrigue cannot be divorced from hunting. In addition, his timidity and fearful nature predispose his serving as an emblem for the shy object of lust." For a discussion of the conflict between Venus and Diana as huntresses, see Michael B. Allen, "The Chase: The Development of a Renaissance Theme," *Comparative Literature*, 20 (1968): 301–12. Like so many apparent opposites, the two goddesses are implicated in each other.

21. Thiébaux, *Stag*, 93, discusses the hunting scene in the *Aeneid* as a glimpse of actual eastern hunting traditions.

22. For a discussion of Aeneas as hunter, see Thiébaux, *Stag*, 95, and M. C. J. Putnam, *The Poetry of the Aeneid: Four Studies in Imaginative Unity and Design* (Cambridge, Mass.: Harvard University Press, 1965), 154–57, 171–72, 187–88.

23. *Remedia Amoris, in The Art of Love, and Other Poems*, Loeb Classical Library (1929), lines 199–206, pp. 190–93.

24. Richard Wilbur, *Ceremony and Other Poems* (New York: Harcourt, Brace, 1948), 10–12.

25. Grace Hart Seely, *Diane the Huntress: The Life and Times of Diane of Poitiers* (New York: Appleton-Century, 1936).

CHAPTER FIVE: **The Gentles Are at Their Game**

1. *The Canterbury Tales*, "The Knight's Tale," 815–24, in *Chaucer's Poetry: An Anthology for the Modern Reader*, ed. E. T. Donaldson (New York: Ronald, 1958).

2. Thomas More, in "Pageant Verses." This set of "verses" or poems, including the one on Manhood, were written by More (1477–1535) "in hys youth" to explain nine images of the pageant of life on a tapestry in his father's house in London, according to the introduction he wrote to accompany the poem. In *The Anchor Anthology of Sixteenth-Century Verse*, ed. Richard S. Sylvester (Gloucester, Mass.: Peter Smith, 1983), lines 25–29, p. 120.

3. George Gascoigne, "In the commendation of the noble Arte of Venerie," in George Turberville, *The Noble Art of Venerie or Hunting*, (London: Thomas Purfoot, 1611; reprint, Tudor and Stuart Library, 1908). The original edition of this very popular Elizabethan treatise on hunting, by the poet Turberville, was published in 1575. The ascription of the poem is controversial, but it is generally considered to belong to Gascoigne.

4. See Thiébaux, *Stag*, 65. See also Horbusch, *Fair Game*, 75–76. Visual representations of the legend of Saint Hubert may be seen in the National Gallery in London. The Master of the Life of the Virgin painted a "Conversion of St. Hubert" between 1480 and 1485, used at the altar of the Benedictine Abbey at Werden, near Cologne. A twelve-point stag with a pale Christ between his horns is chased by hounds across verdant hills. The same painter did a companion piece, "Mass of St. Hubert," as well. Pisanello (b. 1395) painted an exquisite image of the conversion, called "The Vision of St. Eustace" (an original name for the saint). The painting exhibits an exhilarating abundance of animals—hounds, hare, various species of deer, bear, and many exquisite birds.

5. See Edward Plantagenet, Second Duke of York, *The Master of Game*, 1407; eds. W. and A. Baillie-Grohman (London: Chatto and Windus, 1909), 235; see also Marcell Thiébaux, "The Medieval Chase," *Speculum*, 42 (1967): 265.

6. Horbusch, *Fair Game*, 7.

7. Einhard and Notker the Stammerer, *Two Lives of Charlemagne*, trans. Lewis Thorpe (Harmondsworth, UK: Penguin, 1969), 148. For a description of boar hunting in the "great park attached to Aachen," as well as other royal hunts, see Richard Winston, *Charlemagne: From the Hammer to the Cross* (Indianapolis: Bobbs-Merrill, 1954), 237–39.

8. The story is told in Einhard and Notker, *Two Lives*, 160.

9. *The Anglo-Saxon Chronicle*, trans. Dorothy Whitelock (Westport, Conn.: Greenwood, 1961), 164–65. John Manwood, *A Treatise of the Lawes of the Forest*, 3rd ed.,

(1598; facsimile reprint, Amsterdam: Theatrum Orbis Terrarum, 1976), preface and "What a Forest Is"; J. Charles Cox, *The Royal Forests of England* (London: Methuen, 1905), 1–40; G. J. Turner, *Select Pleas of the Forest* (London: Seldon Society, 1901), x–xiii; and John M. Gilbert, *Hunting and Hunting Reserves in Medieval Scotland* (Edinburgh: John Donald, 1979), 5–48. For other examinations of the role of hunting in establishing the power of the monarchy, see Charles Chenevix-Trench, *The Poacher and the Squire: A History of Poaching and Game Preservation in England* (London: Longmans, 1967), 16, 22; Claus Uhlig, " 'The Sobbing Deer': *As You Like It*, II.i.21–66 and the Historical Context," in *Renaissance Drama*, ed. S. Schoenbaum (Evanston, Ill.: Northwestern University Press, 1970), 91; Albert S. Barrow, *Monarchy and the Chase* (London: Eyre and Spottiswoode, 1948), 12–13; Michael Brander, *The Hunting Instinct: The Development of Field Sports over the Ages* (Edinburgh: Oliver and Boyd, 1964), 30; and P. B. Munsche, *Gentlemen and Poachers: The English Game Laws 1671–1831* (Cambridge: Cambridge University Press, 1980), 9. On Gaston's 1600 hounds, see Jean Froissart, *Chronicles of England, France, Spain and the Adjoining Countries, from the Latter Part of the Reign of Edward II to the Coronation of Henry IV*, vol. 1, trans. Thomas Johnes (New York: Colonial, 1901), 78.

10. Munsche, *Gentlemen*, 11.

11. The precise meaning categories of beasts of venery, chase, and warren varied widely through the centuries, but the general principle of categorizing types of hunt was universally observed in the manuals. See Dame Juliana Berner, *The Craft of Venery*, printed at St. Albans, 1486; reprint in *Cynegetica 11*, ed. G. Tilander (Karlshamn, 1964), 1. On the boar, or *sanglier*, see also Gaston Phébus, *La Livre de Chasse*, chapters 42–43, 1391; reprint, *Cynegetica XVIII*, ed. G. Tilander (Karlshamn, 1971), 184–88.

12. Barrow, *Monarchy*, 66–67.

13. The quote from King James is from the Folger Library, Folger MS. 1027.2, p. 6, quoted in G. P. V. Akrigg, *Jacobean Pageant, or Court Life* (Cambridge, Mass.: Harvard University Press, 1962), 159–60. For an example of complaints about the king's excessive hunting, see N. E. McClure, ed. *The Letters of John Chamberlain*, 2 vols. (Philadelphia: American Philosophical Society, 1939), 1.610.

14. Quoted from Anthony Vandervell and Charles Coles, *Game and the English Landscape: The Influence of the Chase on Sporting Art and Scenery* (New York: Viking, 1980), 15.

15. Hector LaFerrier, *Les Chasses de François Premier*, racontées par Louis de Brézé précédées *La Chasse sous les Valois* par la compte Hector de la Ferrière (Paris, 1869), 23–24. Translated by Roberta Brown.

16. Edward, Second Duke of York, *Master*, 223; Thiébaux, "Medieval Chase," *Speculum*, 269.

17. This quotation on "skillful Trystram" is from George Turberville, *Venerie*, 40. The extended quotation from Sir Thomas Malory is in Book 8, Chapter 3—"Sir Tristram de Lyones," in *Le Morte Darthur*, ed. Edward Strachey (London: Macmillan, 1904), 163.

18. *Tristan and Isolde*, trans. A. T. Hatto (London: Penguin, 1960), 78–86. The story of Tristan "breaking up" the stag is told in chapter 4, "The Hunt," and all quotations in this section are from these pages.

19. See Baillie-Grohman, in Edward, Second Duke of York, *Master*, endnotes on "Numbles," 244.

20. Jean Froissart, *Chronicles*, 312–32. See Gaston Phébus, *Livre de Chasse*, ed. Gunnar Tilander, *Cynegetica 18* (Karlshamn, 1971). The title is given in various ways. The manuscript is Gaston Phébus, *Le Livre de la Chasse*, Manuscrit Français 616, Bibliothèque Nationale, Paris, ca. 1400. It is available in a modern edition, Gaston Phoe-bus, *Le Livre de la Chasse*, Manuscrit Français de la Bibliothèque Nationale, Paris. Introduction et commentaires, Marcel Thomas, François Avril, Duc de Bris-sac; traduction en français moderne, Robert et Andrè Bossuat (Paris: Club du Livre, 1976). This modern edition contains a biography of Gaston. The English version of this hunting manual is contained in several manuscripts. I looked at Edward of Norwich, Second Duke of York, "The BOOKE of Hunting called The Maister of the Game, ded-icated to Henrie the Fifth, then Prince of Wales," Royal Collection 17 A.LV, British Library. For the history of Gaston and the manuscripts of his book, see William A. Baillie-Grohman, *Sport in Art: From the Fifteenth to the Eighteenth Century* (New York and London: Benjamin Blom, 1925), 5–35; D. H. Madden, *A Chapter of Me-dieval History: The Fathers of the Literature of Field Sport and Horses* (Port Washing-ton, N.Y.: Kennikat, 1924; reprint, 1969), 105–77. See also Thiébaux, *Stag of Love*, 21–40, and Rooney, *Hunting in Middle English*, 7–12. Each of these titles treats the history of the genre of medieval hunting manuals. For the most important and influen-tial Spanish document on hunting, see *El Libro de la Monteria del Rey Alfonso XI*, ca. 1350, ed. José Gutierrez de la Vega (1877), which describes hunting for deer as the perfect training for *un caballero*, a soldier on horse, the modern knight.

21. Chaucer, *Canterbury Tales*, "The General Prologue." The full description of his love of venery, horses, and his greyhound is in lines 165–93. It defines his worldliness.

22. Juliana Berners, *The Boke of St. Albans*, 1486; reprint, Harding and Wright, pub-lishers, for White, Cochrane, and R. Trithook, 1810; reprint, *The Book of Saint Albans* (New York: Abercrombie and Fitch, 1966), no page numbers.

23. Gilbert, *Hunting Reserves*, 74.

24. Joseph B. Pike, *Frivolities of Courtiers and Footprints of Philosophers: Being a Translation of the First, Second, and Third Books and Selections from the Seventh and Eighth Books of the "Policraticus" of John of Salisbury* (Minneapolis: University of Minnesota Press, 1938), 16. For a history of the humanist objections to hunting, see Uh-lig, "The Sobbing Deer," who describes John of Salisbury as the "spiritual authorities of the high Middle Ages" and the "*locus classicus* of humanistic criticism of hunting" (90).

25. For humanist complaints about excessive aristocratic interest in hunting, see J. H. Hexter, "The Education of the Aristocracy in the Renaissance," *Reappraisals in History: New Views on History and Society in Early Modern Europe* (New York: Harper and Row, 1963), 45–70; and Lawrence Stone, *The Crisis in the Aristocracy, 1558–1641* (London: Oxford University Press, 1967), 672ff. Gervaise Markham, *The Gentlemans Academie* (London: H. Lownes, 1595).

26. Ben Jonson, *Every Man in His Humor*, in *The Complete Plays of Ben Jonson*, vol. 1, ed. G. A. Wilkes (Oxford: Clarendon, 1981), 1.1.36–40.

27. See also Madden, *Chapter*, 217.

28. Richard Blome, *The Gentleman's Recreation*, 2nd ed. (London, 1710), part 2, 141.

29. Hugo of St. Victor, *Patriologiae Latina Cursus Completus, series latina*, ed. J.-P. Migne (Paris, 1844–64), 177:575A. My translation. See also Thiébaux, "The Medieval Chase," *Speculum*, 42 (1967): 4; and Horbusch, *Fair Game*, 74.

30. *Les Livres du Roy Modus et de la Royne Ratio*, ed. Gunnar Tilander (Paris: So-ciété des Anciens Textes Français, 1932), 140ff. See also Marcell Thiébaux, "The Mouth of the Boar as a Symbol in Medieval Literature," *Romance Philology*, 22 (1968): 281–99.

31. See Allen, *Image and Meaning*, 93–114, for a detailed analysis of the spiritual sig-nificance of the deer as background to Andrew Marvell's "The Nymph Complaining on the Death of her Faun." See also Uhlig, "Sobbing Deer," 87; Turberville, *Venerie*, 41–44.

32. The story of the mystical white hart appearing and speaking for Jesus occurs in Book 17, Chapter 9, which is the book of Sir Galahad. The quotation of Thomas Malory is *Le Morte Darthur*, 399.

33. See Thiébaux, *Stag*, 59–66. See also Allen, *Image and Meaning*, 100–1 for a Latin poem on Saint Eustace. Jacobus de Voraigne, *The Golden Legend*, trans. Granger Ryan and Helmut Ripperger (New York: Arno, 1969), 555–61.

34. For the historical material concerning the forest laws in England and on the Continent, see Chester and Ethyn Kirby, "The Stuart Game Prerogative," *English Historical Review*, 46 (1931): 239–46; and Charles Chenevix-Trench, *The Poacher and the Squire: A History of Poaching and Game Preservation in England* (London: Longmans, 1967), 21–33. See also, Cox, *Royal Forests*, 10–24; Horbusch, *Fair Game*, 72–73, 116–18; Thiébaux, *Stag*, 22; Barrow, *Monarchy*, 11–25; Brander, *Hunting Instinct*, 26–43; Munsche, *Gentlemen*, 8–14.

35. Gaston Phèbus, *Le Livre de la Chasse*, 250; for similar sentiments, see *Roy Modus*, 12.

36. Maurice Keen, *The Outlaws of Medieval Legend* (London: Routledge and Kegan Paul, 1961), 95–173, provides a history of the outlaw and of the Robin Hood legend. For other poaching narratives, see *The Parlement of the Thre Ages*, ed. I. Gollancz (London: Oxford University Press, 1915) and "The Tale of Gamelyn," in *Middle English Metrical Romances*, ed. Walter Hoyt French and Charles Brockway Hale (New York: Russell and Russell, 1964), 209–35.

37. See Keen, *Outlaws*, 100ff.

38. For the history and meaning of Cernunnos in Celtic mythology, from which my discussion is derived, see Anne Ross, *Pagan Celtic Britain: Studies in Iconography and Tradition* (London: Routledge and Kegan Paul, 1967), 127–51; and Proinsias MacCana, *Celtic Mythology* (London: Hamlyn, 1970), 38, 43, 44–48.

39. Cervantes, *Don Quixote*, 2.30; Seeley, *Diane*, 32, 102, 176. For Lyly, see below, p. 334, n. 21.

40. La Ferrière, *Chasses de François*, 26.

CHAPTER SIX: **The Shot and Danger of Desire**

1. The classic discussion of the new idealization of women as originating in the cult of the Virgin Mary is in C. S. Lewis, *The Allegory of Love: A Study in Medieval Tradition* (London: Oxford University Press, 1977). For a study of the complex history and permutations of the idealization of love, see Roger Boase, *The Origin and Meaning of Courtly Love: A Critical Study of European Scholarship* (Manchester: University of Manchester Press, 1977). The quote from *Hamlet* is 1.3.35.

2. Foucault, *Use of Pleasure*, 92.

3. Rooney, *Hunting in Middle English*, 50–51, makes this point explicitly, but it can be seen in the way the creative energy transfers from narratives of the heroic to narratives of the erotic hunt.

4. Gottfried von Strassburg, *Tristan*, 198ff., the chapter of "The Avowal." The next quotation is also from this chapter.

5. Gottfried von Strassburg, 261.

6. Gottfried von Strassburg, 266.

7. Many report the sexual magic, both fecundity and dual sexuality, of the hare. See Beryl Rowland, *Animals with Human Faces: A Guide to Animal Symbolism* (Knoxville: University of Tennessee Press, 1973), 88–93. Figured with Venus on vases, given by youths as a gauge of love to their lovers, the hare became a symbol of Lust and Luxuria, or sensual pleasure.

8. *Riverside Shakespeare.* Line numbers are given in parentheses after the quotations.
9. Coppélia Kahn, "Self and Eros in *Venus and Adonis,*" in *Man's Estate: Mascu-line Identity in Shakespeare* (Berkeley: University of California Press, 1981), 21–46. She argues that Adonis takes a rite of passage in reverse in the poem. His problem is narcissism, and he uses "hunting as a defense of his masculine self" against love. I'm not sure narcissism accounts for Adonis, though. The boar as a "manly" prey is a standard motif in classic heroes like Odysseus and Hercules and Meleager, as well as Renaissance lore. For the boar as Shakespeare understood it, see A. T. Hatto, " 'Venus and Adonis'—and the Boar," *Modern Language Review,* 41, 4 (1946), 353–61; and Thiébaux, "Mouth of the Boar," 281–99.
10. Jeanne Addison Roberts, in *The Shakespearean Wild: Geography, Genus, and Gender* (Lincoln: University of Nebraska Press, 1990), 35–37, describes "Venus and Adonis" as laying "out many of the central themes" of the conflict between male wilderness and female wilderness in Shakespeare. In the end, the poem "suggest[s] the victory of male principles over female. As a hunter of animals, Adonis has chosen the known perils of the male Wild over the perilous pleasures of the female forest. One might even argue that the boar is the specter of the vengeful father that has forced his son back to infantile regression to the mother, a kind of death. Male rivalry is stronger than heterosexual eroticism." But these analytic categories seem to leave out much of the male erotics in the poem.
11. Northrup Frye, *A Natural Perspective* (New York: Columbia University Press, 1965), 117.
12. See Mary Beth Rose, "Conceptions of Sexual Love in Elizabethan Comedy," in *The Expense of Spirit: Love and Sexuality in English Renaissance Drama,* ed. Mary Beth Rose (Ithaca, N.Y.: Cornell University Press, 1988), 12–42.
13. See the introduction by Theodor E. Mommsen to Petrarch, *Songs and Sonnets,* Italian-English Edition, trans. Anna Maria Armi (New York: Grosset and Dunlap, 1968), xxxi–xlii. All translations from Petrarch are from this edition.
14. *Rime* L, in Petrarch, *Songs and Sonnets,* 39–40.
15. See Don Cameron Allen, *Image and Meaning: Metaphoric Traditions in Renais-sance Poetry* (Baltimore: Johns Hopkins University Press, 1960), 96ff.
16. See for example Mark Breitenberg, "The Anatomy of Masculine Desire in *Love's Labor's Lost,*" *Shakespeare Quarterly,* 43 (Winter 1992), 436: The Petrarchan lyric, with its split between the impossible ideal and the suffering lover who is perpetually in a pursuit he cannot gratify actually "*produces* masculine desire. . . . This posture sus-tains men in the active position of pursuit, and the constant deferral of gratification, along with its frustration, enables men to continue desiring, and continue a mode of be-ing. Petrarch, in other words, invented not simply a poetry of masculine desire, but a way in which men could, through the power of their words and feeling, constitute themselves as *being.* But women had to be the inaccessible Other for this formula, this dynamic of desire, to enable men to continue in the role that fueled them with passion and a sense of being." See also Giuseppe Mazzotta, "The Canzioniere and the Lan-guage of the Self," *Studies in Philology,* 75 (1978), 271–96; and Nancy Vickers, "Di-ana Described: Scattered Woman and Scattered Rhyme," *Critical Inquiry,* 8 (1981), 265–79.
17. Sir Thomas Wyatt, Sonnet 37, in *Collected Poems of Sir Thomas Wyatt,* ed. Ken-neth Muir (Cambridge, Mass.: Harvard University Press, 1950), 28. The spelling has been modernized.
18. For a number of studies on women and sexuality in the period, see *Women in the Middle Ages and the Renaissance: Literary and Historical Perspectives,* ed. Mary Beth

Rose (Syracuse, N.Y.: Syracuse University Press, 1986). See particularly "The Heroics of Virginity: Brides of Christ and Sacrificial Mutilation," by Jane Tibbetts Schulenburg, 29–72. Among the voluminous literature on women and desire in the Renaissance, see Linda Woodbridge, *Women and the English Renaissance: Literature and the Nature of Womankind, 1540–1620* (Urbana: University of Illinois Press, 1984); Valerie Wayne, *The Matter of Difference: Materialist Feminist Criticism of Shakespeare* (New York: Harvester Wheatsheaf, 1991); Juliet Dusinberre, *Shakespeare and the Nature of Women* (New York: Barnes and Noble, 1975); Karen Newman, *Fashioning Feminity in English Renaissance Drama* (Chicago: University of Chicago Press, 1991); and Katharine M. Rogers, *The Troublesome Helpmate: A History of Misogyny in Literature* (Seattle: University of Washington Press, 1966). See also Leonard Forster, *The Icy Fire: Five Studies in European Petrarchism* (Cambridge: Cambridge University Press, 1969).

19. Mary Beth Rose, *Expense of Spirit*, 14, for example, writes that "drama not only articulates and represents cultural change, but also participates in it; seeks not only to define, but actively to generate, and in some cases contain, cultural conflict. Far from acting as a fictional reflection of an imagined external reality that can somehow be grasped as true, the drama is a constituent of that reality and inseparable from it" (1–2). In tracing an erotic evolution in Elizabethan playwrights, she argues that Shakespeare brought a new conception of eros and marriage to "fruition with *As You Like It* and *Twelfth Night*, dramatizing more complex representations, in which sexual love and marriage have acquired greater centrality and prestige" than in earlier writers.

20. In *As You Like It*, Shakespeare locates his lovers in the Forest of Arden, where they hunt for deer and hare and each other. The love-sick hero, Orlando, wanders the woods tacking limp poems proclaiming his love onto tree trunks: "If a hart do love a hind," begins one heavily ridiculed and hopelessly idealistic poem, "Let him seek out Rosalind" (3.2.101–2). C. L. Barber and Richard P. Wheeler write of the men in *Love's Labor's Lost*: "a group of men bind themselves together, first to repudiate women, then to conquer them, only to have their amorous quest miscarry when the women take control. Love's labor is lost because the Princess and her ladies are not bamboozled by Navarre [the king] and his company, not even by Berowne, who in his game of running with the hare and hunting with the hounds anticipates later predominating heroines." In *The Whole Journey: Shakespeare's Power of Development* (Berkeley: University of California Press, 1988), 5.

21. The description of the "entertainment" of the queen can be found in *The Complete Works of John Lyly*, vol. 1, ed. R. W. Bond (Oxford: Oxford University Press, 1902), 422–30, under the title "The Honorable Entertainment given to the Queenes Maiestie in Progresse, at Cowdray in Sussex, by the right Honorable the Lord Montacute Anno 1591."

22. Philippa Berry, *Of Chastity and Power: Elizabethan Literature and the Unmarried Queen* (London: Routledge, 1989), 9, traces the complex psychological demands of an idealized love for a chaste woman with political power (the classic situation of the courtly lover) in medieval courtly poetry to "a theological source": the Virgin Mary. She analyzes the contradictions that were created by a man according such power to a "chaste female beloved" in post-structuralist psychological terms. See also Breitenberg, 445–46.

23. See "Falstaff as Actaeon: A Dramatic Emblem," John M. Steadman, *Shakespeare Quarterly*, 24 (Summer 1963), 230–44. See also "Falstaff in Windsor Forest: Villain or Victim?" Jeanne Addison Roberts, *Shakespeare Quarterly*, 26 (Winter 1975), 8–15. Shakespeare refers explicitly to Actaeon only three times (twice in *Merry Wives*, once in *Titus Andronicus*), and all three times the horns are explicitly associated with cuckoldry. The image of the cuckold has received significant historical and interpretive attention lately: Kahn, *Man's Estate*, esp. the chapter "The Savage Yoke: Cuckoldry and Marriage," 119–50; Breitenberg, "Anatomy of Masculine Desire"; Joel Fineman, "Fratricide and Cuckoldry: Shakespeare and His Sense of Difference," *Psychoanalytic Review*, 64 (Fall 1977), 409–53; and Katherine Eisaman Maus, "Horns of Dilemma: Jealousy, Gender, and Spectatorship in English Renaissance Drama, *English Literary History*, 54 (1987), 561–84. Finally, an important foundational article is by Keith Thomas, "The Double Standard," *Journal of the History of Ideas*, 20 (1959), 195–216. Thomas suggests that the double sexual standard derives from men's middle-class interest in women as property; Kahn finds the double standard the result of anxiety concerning male identity.

24. New York: Harper and Row, 1977.

25. See C. L. Barber, "The Family in Shakespeare's Development: Tragedy and Sacredness," in *Representing Shakespeare*, eds. Murray M. Schwarz and Coppélia Kahn (Baltimore: Johns Hopkins University Press, 1980), 188–202. He argues that Shakespeare's focus on domestic emotional life and "the problematic stresses of the family constellation" are one of the reasons for his importance as a poet. He's also concerned with relationships across gender and generations. Helen Gardner, "*As You Like It*," in *Modern Shakespearean Criticism: Essays on Style, Dramaturgy, and the Major Plays*, ed. Alvin B. Kernan (New York: Harcourt, Brace & World, 1970), 193: "the great symbol of pure comedy is marriage. . . ."

26. Kahn, *Man's Estate*, 12.

27. Lynda E. Boose, "Scolding Brides and Bridling Scolds: Taming the Woman's Unruly Member," *Shakespeare Quarterly*, 42 (Summer 1991), 179–213, esp. 195. She notes an interesting connection with the "cucking stool"—a seat on which shrews or "coqueens" were seated and dropped into water.

28. Michel de Montaigne, "Upon Some Verses of Virgil," in *The Essayes of Montaigne*, trans. John Florio (New York: Modern Library, 1933), 784.

29. See Eric Partridge, *A Dictionary of Slang and Unconventional English* (New York: Macmillan, 1937), under "horn": "the physical sign of sexual excitement in the male."

30. See Edward A. Snow, "Sexual Anxiety and the Male Order of Things in *Othello*," *English Literary Renaissance*, 10 (1980), 384–412.

31. Montaigne, "Some Verses," 786.

32. *Inquisition: A Bilingual Guide to the Exhibition of Torture Instruments from the Middle Ages to the Industrial Era, Presented in Various European Cities in 1983–1992* (Florence, Italy: n.p., n.d.), is the source of the quotations.

33. *The Book of Beasts: Being a Translation from a Latin Bestiary of the Twelfth Century*, trans. T. H. White (New York: G. P. Putnam's Sons, 1954), 132.

CHAPTER SEVEN: **"That Master Creation . . . Independent Manhood"**

1. William Cornwallis Harris, *The Wild Sports of Southern Africa; Being the Narrative of a Hunting Expedition from the Cape of Good Hope, through the Territories of the Chief Moselekatse, to the Tropic of Capricorn*, 5th ed. (1839; London: Henry G. Bohn, 1852), xviii.

2. Ernest Hemingway, "The Short Happy Life of Francis Macomber," in *The Snows of Kilimanjaro* (1927; reprint, New York: Charles Scribner's Sons, 1964), 150.

3. Henry Fielding, *Tom Jones*, ed. Fredson Bowers (New York: Modern Library, 1975), 4.5 (p. 167), 4.12 (p. 199). This classic novel gives a sweeping panorama of

England in the mid-eighteenth century. Comments on hunting are ubiquitous, and the metaphor of hunting is built into its conceptual core by Squire Western and the multiple chases of Sophia by Tom and the couple by Squire Western. For a few examples, see 3.10 (p. 147), 5.6 (p. 234) about hunting itself, and then numerous metaphors of hunting to men's views of women as prey in 5.12 (p. 267) and 6.10 (p. 305) which both liken "puss" or the hare to a wench. This suggests that "pussy" as a sexual reference may derive from "hare" and not the cat. "Puss" as hare was common in the Renaissance as well. See also 9.7 (p. 551) for the wife as a hunted hare; 10.9 (p. 565) for tracking Sophia as a partridge; 17.5 (p. 887) for women as does to be hunted. R. S. Surtees was the second great sporting journalist in England, writing for *The Sporting Magazine*, and he uses hunting as a lens for surveying and satirizing the whole of English nineteenth-century society. This quotation is from *Handley Cross* (1843; reprint, London: The Folio Society, 1951), 1. The first and perhaps most famous sporting journalist was C. J. Apperley (called "Nimrod"). His *The Chace, the Turf, and the Road* (n.p., 1837), offers classic descriptions of hunting of the time, and the theme of England's greatness, reflected in hunting establishments like Quorn, is prominent: "The *style* of your Meltonian fox-hunter has long distinguished him above his brethren of what he calls the *provincial* chace. When turned out at the hands of his valet, he presents the very *beau-ideal* of his *caste*" (20). Two other important works by Nimrod are *My Life and Times*, ed. E. D. Cuming (1842; reprint, London: William Blackwood and Sons, 1927) and *Nimrod Abroad*, 2 vols. (London: Henry Colburn, 1843); Anthony Trollope "sketched" his own elegant view of upper-class British hunting manners in *Hunting Sketches* (London: Chapman and Hall, 1866). David C. Itzkowitz, *Peculiar Privilege: A Social History of Foxhunting, 1735–1885* (Hassocks, UK: Harvester, 1977), esp. 21–22, "Myth and Ideal," gives an analysis of manliness and foxhunting. For the history of foxhunting and its relations with English patriotism and breeding true men, see also Roger Longrigg, *The History of Foxhunting* (New York: Clarkson N. Potter, 1975), esp. 57, 70, 90–93, 198; also, by Longrigg, *The English Squire and His Sport* (New York: St. Martin's, 1977); Anthony Vandervell and Charles Coles, *Game and the English Landscape: The Influence of the Chase on Sporting Art and Scenery* (New York: Viking, 1980); and Joseph B. Thomas, *Hounds and Hunting through the Ages* (Garden City, N.Y.: Garden City Publishing, 1937). For contemporary journalistic accounts of English foxhunting, see *Hounds and Hunting in the Morning: Sundry Sports of Merry England, Selections from The Sporting Magazine, 1792–1836*, ed. Carl B. Cone (Lexington: University of Kentucky Press, 1981).

4.   Thomas Henricks, "The Democratization of Sport in Eighteenth-Century England," *Journal of Popular Culture*, 18 (1984), 17. Munsche, *Gentlemen*, esp. 76–131; Charles Chevenix-Trench, *The Poacher and the Squire: A History of Poaching and Game Preservation in England* (London: Longmans, 1967), 122ff.; E. P. Thompson, *Whigs and Hunters: The Origins of the Black Act, 1723* (New York: Pantheon, 1975); and Douglas Hay, Peter Linebaugh, John G. Rule, E. P. Thompson, and Cal Winslow, *Albion's Fatal Tree: Crime and Society in Eighteenth Century England* (New York: Pantheon, 1975), 189–253. Squire Western has quite a bit to say about the game laws and social class in *Tom Jones*; for example 7.9 (p. 357).

5.   Robert Baden-Powell, *Scouting for Boys* (1908; reprint, London: Pearson, 1915; facsimile reprint, 1990), 5.

6.   Baden-Powell, *Scouting*, 56.

7.   Baden-Powell, *Scouting*, 19; Ernest Thompson Seton, *Boy Scouts of America: A Handbook of Woodcraft, Scouting, and Life-craft* (New York: Doubleday, Page, 1910). Excerpted in *The Call of the Wild*, ed. Roderick Nash (New York: George

Braziller, 1970), 23. See also David I. Macleod, *Building Character in the American Boy: The Boy Scouts, YMCA, and Their Forerunners, 1870–1920* (Madison: University of Wisconsin Press, 1983); Jeoffrey P. Hantover, "The Boy Scouts and the Validation of Masculinity," in *The American Man*, eds. Elizabeth H. Pleck and Joseph H. Pleck (Englewood Cliffs, N.J.: Prentice-Hall, 1980); and Peter Gabriel Filene, *Him/Her Self: Sex Roles in Modern America* (New York: Harcourt Brace Jovanovich, 1975), 106–7. For the relations between the American frontier and European notions of the hunter, see Ray Allen Billington, *Land of Savagery, Land of Promise: The European Image of the American Frontier in the Nineteenth Century* (New York: W. W. Norton, 1981).

8.   Thorton W. Burgess, "Making Men of Them," *Good Housekeeping Magazine*, 59 (1914), 12.

9.   The statistics come from Hantover, "Boy Scouts," 290. Frederick Jackson Turner's obituary on the frontier was written for the American Historical Association in 1893, and collected in *The Frontier in American History* (1920; reprint, New York: Holt, Rinehart & Winston, 1962).

10.   This analysis of the pressures on and changes in the ideals of manhood derives from E. Anthony Rotundo, *American Manhood: Transformations in Masculinity from the Revolution to the Modern Era* (New York: HarperCollins, 1993), esp. 222–74; Rotundo, "Learning about Manhood: Gender Ideals and the Middle-Class Family in Nineteenth-Century America," in *Manliness and Morality: Middle-Class Masculinity in Britain and America, 1800–1940*, eds. J. A. Mangan and James Walvin (New York: St. Martin's, 1987), 35–52; Rotundo, "Body and Soul: Changing Ideas of American Manhood," *Journal of Social History*, 16 (1983), 23–38; Joe L. Dubbert, "Progressivism and the Masculinity Crisis," in *The American Man*, eds. Elizabeth H. Pleck and Joseph H. Pleck (Englewood Cliffs, N.J.: Prentice-Hall, 1980), 303–20; Joseph F. Kett, *Rites of Passage: Adolescence in America, 1790 to the Present* (New York: Basic Books, 1977), esp. "Dead-End Jobs and Careers," pp. 144–72, and "The Invention of Adolescence," 215ff.; and James R. McGovern, "David Graham Phillips and the Virility Impulse of the Progressives," *New England Quarterly*, 39 (1966): 334–55. On the social forces shaping fears of emasculation and ideals of manliness, see Filene, *Him/Her Self*, esp. "Men and Manliness," 72–104, particularly 72–74 on the changes in work and middle-class conceptions of manhood. Among the many fears of the influence of women, men put female teachers high on the list. See G. Stanley Hall, "Feminization in the School and Home: The Undue Influence of Women Teachers—The Need of Different Training for the Sexes," *World's Work*, 16 (1908): 10237–44. The best major study on this topic is Ann Douglas, *The Feminization of American Culture* (New York: Knopf, 1977).

11.   Henry James, *The Bostonians* (New York: Macmillan, 1886), 333–34.

12.   Theodore Roosevelt, *Ranch-Life and the Hunting Trail* (New York: Century, 1899; reprint, Ann Arbor, Mich.: University Microfilms, 1966), 55–56.

13.   Roosevelt's famous speech, "The Strenuous Life," was delivered before the Hamilton Club in Chicago, April 10, 1899. It is contained in Theodore Roosevelt, *The Strenuous Life: Essays and Addresses* (New York: Century, 1902), 1. On "sissyism," see James West, "The Real Boy Scout," *Leslie's Illustrated Weekly Newspaper* (1912), 448: "The real Boy Scout is not a 'sissy,' " the article begins. See also Rafford Pyke, "What Men Like in Men," *Cosmopolitan*, 33 (1902), 404–5, on "sissyism." On Roosevelt and masculinity, see also Rotundo, *American Manhood*, 274.

14.   Baden-Powell, *Scouting*, 3.

15.   Roualeyn Gordon Cumming, *Five Years in a Hunter's Life in the Far Interior of*

South Africa, with Notices of the Native Tribes, and Anecdotes of the Chase of the Lion, Elephant, Hippopotamus, Giraffe, Rhinoceros, etc., vol. 1 (New York: Harper & Brothers, 1850), 54.

16.   A common observation among historians of the time. See for example MacKenzie, *Empire*, 37; John M. MacKenzie, "The Imperial Pioneer and Hunter and the British Masculine Stereotype in Late Victorian and Edwardian Times," in *Manliness and Morality*, eds. Mangan and James, 193; and Filene, *Him/Her Self*, 85.

17.   H. A. Bryden, "The Extermination of Game in South Africa," *Fortnightly Review*, 62 (1894), 543.

18.   See Harriet Ritvo, *The Animal Estate: The English and Other Creatures in the Victorian Age* (Cambridge, Mass.: Harvard University Press, 1987), esp. the chapter on "The Thrill of the Chase," 243–88; and MacKenzie, *Empire*, esp. the chapter on "Hunting and Settlement in Southern Africa," 85–119.

19.   Cumming, *Five Years*, viii, ix.

20.   Cumming, *Five Years*, 114.

21.   Cumming, *Five Years*, 67, 93.

22.   Cumming, *Five Years*, 177.

23.   Cumming tells the story in *Five Years*, 181–83.

24.   Cumming, *Five Years*, 183.

25.   Cumming, *Five Years*, 183–84.

26.   Ritvo, 265. For an extended analysis of the narrative structure of the hunting literature, see 259–69.

27.   J. G. Millais, *Life of Frederick Courteney Selous, D.S.O., Capt. 25th Royal Fusiliers* (London: Longmans, Green, 1919), 363.

28.   Letter to Millais, quoted in *Life*, 375.

29.   J. G. Millais, *Life*, 112. See also MacKenzie, *Empire*, 128.

30.   *Travel and Adventure in South-East Africa* (1893; reprint, New York: Arno, 1967), 223. The other major works by Selous are *A Hunter's Wanderings in Africa; Being a Narrative of Nine Years Spent among the Game of the Far Interior of South Africa* (1881; reprint, London: Macmillan, 1907); *African Nature Notes and Reminiscences* (1908; reprint, Salisbury, Rhodesia: Pioneer Head, 1969); and Frederick Courteney Selous, J. C. Millais, and Abel Chapman, *The Big Game of Africa and Europe* (London: London and Counties, 1914).

31.   The story is told in Selous, *Travel and Adventure*, 412–25.

32.   Selous, *Travel and Adventure*, 286.

33.   The quotation from Selous is in *Travel and Adventure*, 420. See Agnes Herbert, *Two Dianas in Somaliland: The Record of a Shooting Trip by Agnes Herbert* (London: John Lane, 1908), 53ff., for a humorous account of women hunting and making fun of the manly conventions of lion hunting. One nearly faints in her encounter with a lion, and calls to mind Bottom's line—and lion—from Shakespeare's *A Midsummer Night's Dream*: "a lion among ladies, is a most dreadful thing. . . ." (3.1.30).

34.   Selous, *Travel and Adventure*, 423.

35.   Selous, *Travel and Adventure*, 383–84; the comment on the "effeminate" Portuguese is on 286.

36.   MacKenzie, *Empire*, 36. On the ambivalence to animals as well as its relation to Darwinian ideas, see James Turner, *Reckoning with the Beast: Animals, Pain, and Humanity in the Victorian Mind* (Baltimore: Johns Hopkins University Press, 1980); and Michael Ruse, *The Darwinian Revolution* (Chicago: University of Chicago Press, 1979).

37.   MacKenzie, *Empire*, 31.

38.   Stuart A. Marks, *Southern Hunting*, 160–61. For a feminist deconstruction of the relations between science, hunting, museums, and gender in the early twentieth century, see also Donna Haraway's chapter, "Teddy Bear Patriarchy," in *Primate Visions: Gender, Race, and Nature in the World of Modern Science* (New York: Routledge, 1989), 26–57ff.

39. Marks, *Southern Hunting*, 161.

40. Jack London, *The Sea-Wolf* (New York: Macmillan, 1904), 129. The effete, belletristic narrator (a writer) named Van Weyden argues frequently with Wolf Larsen, the super-male commander of the boat: " 'You have read Darwin,' I said. 'But you read him misunderstandingly when you conclude that the struggle for existence sanctions your wanton destruction of life' " (69). Van Weyden, however, succumbs to Wolf, his captain, finding in his "forbidding philosophy a more adequate explanation of life than I found in my own" (121).

41. R. S. S. Baden-Powell, *Sport in War* (London: William Heinemann, 1900), 83–119.

42. Baden-Powell, *Sport*, 18, 21–22.

43. Baden-Powell, *Sport*, 117–18.

44. W. H. Auden, *The English Auden: Poems, Essays, and Dramatic Writings, 1927–1939*, ed. Edward Mendelson (New York: Random House, 1977), 217.

45. Roy Blount, Jr., "Prime Time," *Men's Journal*, June–July 1994, 31–32.

46. Cumming, *Five Years*, x; Theodore Roosevelt, *Ranch-Life*, 82–83.

47. Edward Abbey, *The Monkey-Wrench Gang* (New York: Avon, 1975).

48. Ortega y Gasset, *Meditations*, 77–78.

49. Rotundo, *American Manhood*, esp. Chapter 10, "Passionate Manhood: A Changing Standard of Masculinity," 231: "Talk of man's 'bestiality' was largely a figurative language to discuss the passions that were ascribed to him."

50. Cumming, *Five Years*, 97.

51. Selous, *A Hunter's Wanderings*, 239.

CHAPTER EIGHT: **The Long Hunt**

1. James Fenimore Cooper, *The Pioneers; or The Sources of The Susquehanna*, ed. James D. Wallace (Oxford: Oxford University Press, 1991), 189.

2. John Mitchell, *The Hunt*, 122.

3. See Constance J. Poten, "A Shameful Harvest," *National Geographic*, 180, September 1991, 106–32.

4. These statistics come from the U.S. Fish and Wildlife Service, *1991 National Survey of Fishing, Hunting, and Wildlife-Associated Recreation* (Washington, D.C.: Government Printing Office, 1993); *1995 World Almanac and Book of Facts* (Mahwah, N.J.: World Almanac, 1995); and Stephen R. Kellert, "Attitudes and Characteristics of Hunters and Antihunters," *Transactions of the North American Wildlife Natural Resources Conference*, 43 (1978), 412–23. See also Alan Farnham, "A Bang That's Worth a Thousand Bucks," *Fortune*, March 9, 1992, 80–86.

5. Pam Houston, introduction to *Women on Hunting* (Hopewell, N.J.: Ecco, 1995), xi.

6. "A Narrative of the Life of David Crockett, of the State of Tennessee (1834)," in *The Autobiography of David Crockett* (New York: Charles Scribner's Sons, 1923), 120–25.

7. See Carroll Smith-Rosenberg, "Sex as Symbol in Victorian Purity: An Ethnohistorical Analysis of Jacksonian America," in *Turning Points: Historical and Sociological Essays on the Family*, eds. John Demos and Sarane Spence Boocock, a supplement

of the *American Journal of Sociology*, 84, 1978 (Chicago: University of Chicago Press, 1978), S239–S240.
8.   Mitchell, *Hunt*, 93.
9.   Mitchell, *Hunt*, 3–6. These quotations are all from the opening pages of the book.
10.   Norman Mailer, *Why Are We in Vietnam?* (New York: Henry Holt, 1967), 3–4; 157. The copyright on the Preface is 1977.
11.   For the interpretations in this section, I draw upon Henry Nash Smith, *Virgin Land: The American West as Symbol and Myth* (1950; Cambridge, Mass.: Harvard University Press, 1970); Annette Kolodny, *The Lay of the Land* (Chapel Hill: University of North Carolina Press, 1975); Richard Slotkin, *Regeneration through Violence: The Mythology of the American Frontier, 1600–1860* (Middletown, Conn.: Wesleyan University Press, 1973); Richard Slotkin, *The Fatal Environment: The Myth of the Frontier in the Age of Industrialization 1800–1890* (New York: Atheneum, 1985); Jane Thompkins, *Sensational Designs: The Cultural Work of American Fiction 1790–1860* (New York: Oxford University Press, 1985), Chapter 4, "No Apologies for the Iroquois"; David Leverenz, *Manhood and the American Renaissance* (Ithaca, N.Y.: Cornell University Press, 1989); David Leverenz, "The Last Real Man in America: From Natty Bumppo to Batman," in *Fictions of Masculinity: Crossing Cultures, Crossing Sexualities*, ed. Peter Murphy (New York: New York University Press, 1994), 21–53; Walter Benn Michaels, "The Vanishing American," *American Literary History*, 2 (Summer 1990), 220–41; and Lora Romero, "Vanishing Americans: Gender, Empire, and New Historicism," *American Literature*, 63 (September 1991), 385–404. For the hunter as a myth of American identity, see Slotkin, *Regeneration, passim*; for more general concerns of Americans with landscape and identity, see Kolodny, *Lay*, 71; and Smith, *Virgin Land*, 3–12. Kolodny writes, "A conscious and determined struggle to formulate the meaning of their landscape characterizes the writing of nineteenth-century Americans." Smith writes, "What is an American? asked St. John de Crève-coeur before the Revolution, and the question has been repeated by every generation from his time to ours." And Slotkin asserts, "The belief that a new nationality had been created in America, a new and better race of men, characterized the nationalistic fervors of the post-revolutionary and Jacksonian generations. . . . The great emphasis on the theme of individual initiation into the life of the New World has at its roots the same dream of the re-creation of the self in a new image. This conversion, or self-creation, or initiation, is essential a personal process . . . But in American society the experience of acculturation and of nation building made this individual experience a social one as well. All men, individually and collectively, were engaged in becoming Americans" (*Regeneration*, 473).
12.   Cooper, *Pioneers*, 20–21.
13.   Cooper, *Pioneers*, 135.
14.   Cooper, *Pioneers*, 112. On the history of the ownership of wildlife, see James A. Tober, *Who Owns the Wildlife? The Political Economy of Conservation in Nineteenth-Century America* (Westport, Conn.: Greenwood, 1981).
15.   Cooper, *Pioneers*, 246.
16.   See Geerat J. Vermeij, "The Biology of Human-Caused Extinction," in *The Preservation of Species*, ed. Bryan G. Norton (Princeton: Princeton University Press, 1986), 31; and W. B. King (compiler), "Endangered Birds of the World," in *ICBP Bird Red Data Book* (Washington, D.C.: Smithsonian Institution Press, 1981).
17.   James Fenimore Cooper, *The Deerslayer; or The First Warpath* (New York: New American Library, 1963), 13.
18.   Cooper, *Deerslayer*, 48.

19. Cooper, *Deerslayer*, 77, 111–14.
20. Cooper, *Deerslayer*, 374–77, 12, 13. The quote on the rifle as companion is from *Pioneers*, 153.
21. Cooper, *Deerslayer*, 431–33.
22. On the popularity of hunting for manly exercise and recreation, see Elizabeth Johns, *American Genre Painting: The Politics of Everyday Life* (New Haven: Yale University Press, 1991), Chapter Three, "From the Outer Verge of Our Civilization," 60–99; Thomas L. Altherr, "The American Hunter-Naturalist and the Development of the Code of Sportsmanship," *Journal of Sport History*, 5 (Spring 1978), esp. 10–13; and John Richards Betts, *America's Sporting Heritage: 1850–1950* (Reading, Mass.: Addison-Wesley, 1974), 232–43. Byrd is quoted from James Oliver Robertson, *American Myth, American Reality* (New York: Hill and Wang, 1980), 137–39.
23. The historical material on Daniel Boone comes from John Bakeless, *Daniel Boone: Master of the Wilderness* (1939; reprint, Lincoln: University of Nebraska Press, 1989); John Filson, *The Discovery, Settlement, and Present State of Kentucke: and an Essay Towards the Topography, and Natural History of that Important Country: To which is added, an Appendix, Containing, I. The Adventures of Col. Daniel Boon, One of the First Settlers, Comprehending Every Important Occurrence in the Political History of that Province; II. The Minutes of the Piankashaw Council, Held at Post St. Vincents, April 15, 1784; III. An Account of the Indian Nations Inhabiting within the Limits of the Thirteen United States, Their Manners and Customs, and Reflections on Their Origin; IV. The Stages and Distances between Philadelphia and the Falls of the Ohio; from Pittsburgh to Pensacola and Several Other Places: The Whole Illustrated by a New and Accurate Map of Kentucke and the Country Adjoining. Drawn from Actual Surveys*, 1784, reprinted in *The Discovery of Kentucke and the Adventures of Daniel Boon*, The Garland Library of Narratives of North American Indian Captivities, vol. 14, arranged and selected by Wilcomb E. Washburn (New York: Garland, 1978); and Timothy Flint, *Biographical Memoir of Daniel Boone, The First Settler of Kentucky, Interspersed with Incidents in the Early Annals of the Country*, ed. James K. Folsom (1833; reprint, New Haven, Conn.: College and University Press, 1967).
24. Filson, *Kentucke*, 54.
25. Bakeless, *Boone*, 63.
26. Filson, *Kentucke*, 64–65.
27. The narrative is given in Bakeless, *Boone*, 124–40.
28. For this distinction and dual imperative in the American response to nature, see Slotkin, *Regeneration*, 155. Slotkin views the "autobiography" of Daniel Boone, written by John Filson, as an appendix to Filson's promotional land sale advertisement of Kentucky in 1784, and the first full realization of the frontier myth and the hunter hero in the American psyche. See "Narrative into Myth," 268–312.
29. Theodore Roosevelt, *The Wilderness Hunter: An Account of the Big Game of the United States and Its Chase with Horse, Hound, and Rifle* (New York: G. P. Putnam's Sons, 1893), 6, 8.
30. The phrase is from Roosevelt's "Foreword to the First Edition" of *The Master of Game*, ed. William Baillie-Grohman (London: Chatto and Windus, 1909), xxiii, where he also scorns the "debased sport" and "luxurious and effeminate artificiality" of old lords who hunted by batteau and drive, and kept track of their huge numbers of killings.
31. See Thomas L. Altherrer, "The American Hunter-Naturalist and the Development of the Code of Sportsmanship," *Journal of Sport History*, 5 (Spring, 1978), 7–22. See also John F. Reiger, *American Sportsman and the Origins of Conservation*

(New York: Winchester, 1975). For an honorific view of conservation and the sportsman, see *Governor's Symposium on North America's Hunting Heritage: Proceedings* (Minnetonka, Minn.: North American Hunting Club and Wildlife Forever, June 16–18, 1992). In Europe, the protests against hunting came from reformed hunters, as it did also in the United States with Ernest Thompson Seton. One of the most notable was W. H. Bryden, who documented the destruction by sport hunters in Africa in a work referred to in the last chapter, "The Extermination of Great Game in South Africa"; Florence Dixie, "The Horrors of Sport," *Westminster Review*, 137 (1892), 49–52; and *Killing for Sport: Essays by Various Authors*, ed. Henry Salt (London: G. Bell and Sons, 1914), with its introduction by George Bernard Shaw. On his fight with eco-fakers, see Theodore Roosevelt, "Nature Fakers," *Everybody's Magazine*, 17 (September 1907); reprinted in Roosevelt, *Works*, 5, 375–83. See also Paul R. Cutright, *Theodore Roosevelt, The Naturalist* (New York: Harper and Brothers, 1956), and R. L. Wilson, *Theodore Roosevelt, Outdoorsman* (New York: Winchester, 1971).

32.   Annie Dillard, *Pilgrim at Tinker Creek* (New York: Harper's Magazine Press, 1974), 12.

33.   D. H. Lawrence, *Studies in Classic American Literature* (1923; reprint, Garden City, N.Y.: Doubleday, 1951), 72–73.

34.   William Faulkner, "Delta Autumn," in *The Portable Faulkner*, ed. Malcolm Cowley (New York: Viking, 1946), 718–19.

35.   James Dickey, *Deliverance* (New York: Houghton-Mifflin, 1970), 149–59.

36.   "Predatory," in *The Compact Edition of the Oxford English Dictionary* (Oxford: Oxford University Press, 1971), 2273.

37.   James W. Messerschmidt, *Masculinities and Crime: Critique and Reconceptualization of Theory* (Lanham, Md.: Rowman and Littlefield, 1993), 1; Winifred Gallagher, "How We Become What We Are," *Atlantic Monthly*, September 1994, 48.

38.   Elliot Leyton, *Compulsive Killers: The Story of Modern Multiple Murder* (New York: New York University Press, 1986), 31; reprinted in paperback as *Hunting Humans*.

39.   Leyton, *Killers*, 15.

40.   Leyton, *Killers*, 265.

41.   Leyton, *Killers*, 16.

42.   Kemperer's story is told in Leyton, *Killers*, 36–72.

43.   Quoted from Leyton, *Killers*, 95.

44.   Leyton, *Killers*, 81.

45.   Quoted from the journals of Carl Panzram, as put together in Thomas E. Gaddis and James O. Long, *Killer: A Journal of Murder* (New York: Macmillan, 1970), 12.

46.   Leyton, *Killers*, 262; he is quoting sociologist Philip Abrams, *Historical Sociology* (Ithaca, N.Y.: Cornell University Press, 1982).

47.   Susan Griffin, *Woman and Nature: The Roaring Inside Her* (New York: Harper and Row, 1978), 103–104. She wrote an early article on rape in 1971, in *Ramparts*, called "Rape—The All-American Culture," 10 (September 1971), 26–35.

48.   Andrée Collard, *The Rape of Nature* (Bloomington: Indiana University Press, 1989), 46. See also Merrit Clifton, "Killing the Female," *The Animals' Agenda*, 5 (September 1990), 28, who argues that "in symbolic lieu of raping and killing women, much of hunting is killing the feminine in the hunter's own self." A classic feminist statement on rape is Susan Brownmiller, *Against Our Will* (New York: Simon and Schuster, 1975), 26, where she says that rape is "a conscious process of intimidation by which *all* men keep *all* women in a state of fear." See also Andrea Dworkin, *Inter-*

course (New York: Free Press, 1987). For other studies of sexual violence and power, see Diana Scully, *Understanding Sexual Violence: A Study of Convicted Rapists* (Boston: Unwin Hyman, 1990), esp. 128–29, in which rapists' behavior is guided by "cultural stereotypes," as of a dangerous and violent animal; Lloyd Vogelman, *The Sexual Face of Violence* (Johannesburg: Raven, 1989), esp. 33, focusing on "stereotypical notions of masculinity" concerning power and submissiveness; Carolyn J. Hursch, *The Trouble with Rape* (Chicago: Nelson-Hall, 1977); and Diana E. H. Russell, *The Politics of Rape: The Victim's Perspective* (New York: Stein and Day, 1979), esp. 256, "Rape is then the logical expression of the stereotypical male. Obviously, solutions to what is not yet seen as a problem must go beyond therapy, imprisonment, or castration, and attack the cultural acceptance of male supremacy where aggressive, depersonalized power ploys are hallmarks of masculinity."

49. Mitchell, *Hunt*, 140.
50. Leyton, *Compulsive Killers*, 269, 277, 287.
51. R. G. Sipes, "War, Sports and Aggression, *American Anthropologist*, 75 (1973): 64–86.

CHAPTER NINE: **That Stranger Man**

1. *Eskimo Poems*, xxii.
2. Ortega y Gasset, *Meditations*, all quotes on pp. 49, 50.
3. William Carlos Williams, *In the American Grain* (1925; reprint, New York: New Directions, 1953), 213.
4. Kerasote, *Bloodties*, 225.
5. Roy Blount, Jr., *Crackers: This Whole Many-Angled Thing of Jimmy, More Carters, Ominous Little Animals, Sad-Singing Women, My Daddy and Me* (New York: Knopf, 1980), 207.
6. The first quote is from Richard Nelson, *The Island Within* (San Francisco: North Point, 1989), 60; the second is from "The Gifts," in *On Nature: Nature, Landscape, and Natural History*, ed. Daniel Halpern (San Francisco: North Point, 1987), 130.
7. The story appears in Michael Meade, *Men and the Water of Life: Initiation and the Tempering of Men* (San Francisco: HarperSanFrancisco, 1993), 23–26. Pages 27–82 are essentially explications and meditations on the themes in the story.
8. Richard Nelson, "Stalking the Sacred Game," in *Governor's Symposium on North America's Hunting Heritage, Proceedings*, 22–32.
9. Joseph Campbell, *The Way of the Animal Powers*, vol. 1, *Historical Atlas of World Mythology* (San Francisco: Harper and Row, 1983), 65, 73–79.

INDEX

Abbey, Edward, 235
Achilles, 83
Actaeon, 111, 112, 115–19, 120, 123, 192, 294, 311, 328–29n11, 335–36n23
Adonis, 111, 125, 181–84, 334n9
Adversary, 72–73, 293, 311
Aeneas, 80, 101, 123–28, 177
Aeneid (Virgil), 123–28
African Genesis (Ardrey), 39
"African myth," 218–27
African Nature Notes and Reminiscences (Selous), 222
Agamemnon, 114–15
Agesilaus, King of Sparta, 67
Aggression
    as "instinct," 275
    and "killer ape," 39–40, 41
    linked with hunting, 46, 52
    and predatory desire, 105
    trophy as mask of, 228, 229
Ahab, Captain, 268
AIDS, 199, 295–96
Alferic, Saint, 157
Alfred, Prince of England, 217–18
Altamira cave, 54–55, 62, 65
Amazons, 119, 328n9
American frontier, 242–88, 341n11
Amor, derivation of, 105
Anderson, J. K., 68, 80
Animal Estate, The (Ritvo), 218
Animal(s)
    in cave art, 60–61, 64–66
    demonization of, 90
    extinction of, 254, 267, 343n31
    and frontier hunter, 266
    and identity, 238–40
    killing or controlling, 292–93
    listening to, 98
    loving and killing, 172
    and native hunters, 300–1
    puns in England, 178, 190

and spirit, 167, 315
as spiritual messenger, 158–59
and trophies, 227–28
Anne of Brittany, 22
"Anthropomorph" figure, 35
Antichrist, 154–55
Apollo, 18, 73, 77–78, 118, 120, 291, 311
    and Daphne, 107–12, 119, 122, 123
    and Hyacinth, 111
    and modern male, 94
    and Python, 86–88, 119, 122, 325n22
    as "rational" god, 90–92, 97–98
Apollodorus, 77
Apperley, C. J. ("Nimrod"), 337n3
Aquinas, Saint Thomas, 92
Archetype, 57
Ardrey, Robert, 39–40, 46, 275
Arethusa, 111
Aristocracy, 71, 136, 151–53, 162, 168, 316
Aristophanes, 92, 113
Aristotle, 17, 56
Artemis, 16, 18–19, 76–78, 80, 83, 86, 112–19, 158, 174, 315
Ars Amatoria (Art of Love) (Ovid), 103–6, 123
Art of Courtly Love, The (Capellanus), 189
Ascanius, 125
As You Like It (Shakespeare), 164, 178, 180, 195, 335nn19–20
Atalanta, 109–10, 112
Atwood, Margaret, 94
Auden, W. H., 233
Avril, François, 149
Aurora, 111
Australopithecus africanus, 36–42

Baboon skull holes, 36–39, 49–50
Baccae, The (Euripedes), 118

Bacchus, 101, 111
Bacon, Sir Francis, 141
Baden-Powell, R. S. S, 211, 212, 215, 230–33, 292
Barber, C. L., 335n20, 336n25
Barnes, Dame Juliana, 150, 152
Barthes, Roland, 320n9
Bear, 113, 154, 235, 244, 249–50, 255–56, 263, 287, 288
"Bear, The " (Faulkner), 270–71
Beast
  of chase, warren and venery, 140, 330n11
  in Christian allegory, 153–59
  and courtly love, 189
  emotions displaced onto, 198–99
  and Greek heroes, 83
  killing, vs. taming, 291–92
  and loss, 122, 123
  and male identity, 238–39
  myth, 19
  overcoming, by male, 86–87
  and poaching, 161–66
  and sexual predators, 274
  solitary encounter with, 221
  as spiritual symbol, 153
  superiority to, 225, 227
  sweet vs. stinking, 154
  trophys and guilt, 253–54
Bellerophon, 83
Beowulf, 154
Berkowitz, David, 275
Bernini, 109, 110
Berry, Philippa, 335n22
Bêtes noires, 154
Bible, 153, 155, 325n21
Big-game hunters, 71, 208, 209–41, 343n31
Binford, Lewis, 51
Bion, 120
Bison/auroch, 60, 61, 62–63
Black Elk, 316
Blackfish, Chief, 264
"Blading," 136, 159
Blome, Richard, 152
Blood
  brothers, 30
  and intimacy, 293
Bloodties (Kerasote), 299–300

Blount, Roy, Jr., 233, 234
Bly, Robert, 6, 93–94, 302
Board, 69, 83, 98, 168, 330n7, 334n9
  in England, 140
  and François I, 142–43
  modern hunt, 84–88
  in Shakespeare, 182–85
  as stinking beast, 154–55
Boke of St. Albans, The (Barnes), 150–51
Book of Howlett, 151
Boone, Daniel, 263–67, 292, 342n28
Boone, Jemima, 264–65
Boone and Crockett Club, 246, 267
Booth, Philip, 23
Bostonians, The (James), 213–14
Boundaries
  animal/human, 167, 266
  in erotic hunt, 198–99
  and poaching, 164–66
  rising past, 202–3
  sex/emotions, 186–87
Boys, education of
  in Greece, 68–73, 80, 323n5
  and industrialization, 213, 221–22, 337n10
  and scouting, 211–13, 292
  and trophies, 228
Boy Scouts, 211–13, 215, 230, 276, 337n13
Brain, C. K., 42–43, 50
Breitenberg, Mark, 334n16
Bridges of Madison County, The (film), 273
British Empire, 208, 209, 220–26
Brownmiller, Susan, 343n48
Bryden, W. H., 343n31
Buck, 140, 229
Buddhism, 158
Buffalo, 267, 293
Bull, 31–32, 35, 83
Bumppo, Nathaniel, 257, 258–62
Bundy, Ted, 275, 276–77
Burroughs, Edgar Rice, 6, 215
Byrd, William, 263
Byron, Lord, 210

Cacus, 83
Caesar, Julius, 95, 111, 156

Callaway, Betsey, 265
Callaway, Fanny, 265
Callimachus, 113
Callisto, 111–13, 311
Call of the Wild, The (London), 215
Calydonian boar, 83, 109–10, 111
Campbell, Charles, 100
Campbell, Joseph, 28, 30, 52, 316
Canterbury Tales, The (Chaucer), 133, 150, 178
Capellanus, Andreas, 189
Capitalism, 273, 277
Carlyle, Thomas, 208
Carson, Kit, 266
Catholic church, 133
"Cave of Lovers," 177–78
Cave paintings, 31–36, 210, 322–23*n*31
    human images in, 62–66, 315
    and sexuality, 54–62
Ceballo, José Maria (Chema), 32
Celts, 166–67
Cephalus, 111, 112
Cerinthus, 101, 106, 327*n*2
Cernunnos ("Horned One," lord of animals), 139, 166–67, 315
Cernyneian stag, 83, 114
Charlemagne, King of Franks, 138, 291
Charles, Prince of England, 206
Charles VI, King of France, 156
Charles VII, King of France, 149
Charles X, King of France, 142
Chasse Royale, La (Charles X), 142
Chaste/chased pun, 178
Chastity, 107, 335*n*22
    and courtly love, 189–90
    and Diana, 112–15
    and Queen Elizabeth, 168
Chaucer, Geoffrey, 83, 132, 133, 140, 150, 153, 178, 325*n*20
Cherokees, 265
Chimera, 83
Chiron, 83
Chivalric spirit, 174, 189
Chodorow, Nancy, 324*n*15
Christ, as stag, 155–56
Christianity, 23, 86, 153–59, 175, 325*n*21
Chupik Eskimos, 295, 297–98
Cicero, 92

Circe, 93, 111
Cleopatra, 124
Clifton, Merrit, 343*n*48
Clinton, Bill, 101
Clouds (Aristophanes), 92
Cobbett, William, 208
Cody, Buffalo Bill, 213, 214, 221, 266
Cohen, Leonard, 316
Cola del Caballo, 54–56, 62–63, 65
Collard, Andrée, 279
Comedy of Errors, The (Shakespeare), 197
Compulsive Killers (Leyton), 275
Conkey, Margaret, 61
Control, 198, 292–93
Cooper, James Fenimore, 242, 257–63, 265
Council of Agde (506), 153
Courtly love, 187, 189–92
Crete, 68
Crockett, Davey, 249–51, 254, 256, 260, 266–68, 274, 288, 291
Cro-Magnons, 42, 62, 64
Cross, Harry, 206
Cuckold, 192–98, 336*n*23
Cuckoo bird, 194
Cumming, Roualeyn Gordon, 215, 218–21, 239, 291
Cupid (Eros), 108, 119–20, 122, 123, 125, 179
"Curée," 147, 150
"Cursed hunter," 311
Custer, General, 254
"Cut marks," 51
Cymbeline (Shakespeare), 136, 164
Cyparissus, 111
Cyrus the Younger, 67

Dahlberg, Francis, 52–53
Dahmer, Jeffrey, 274, 275
Daphne, 107–11, 112, 123
Dart, Raymond, 36–41, 49–50, 321*n*5
Deer, 240–41, 245, 246, 256–59
    and love, 178, 188, 191, 202
Deerslayer, The (Cooper), 260–62, 271, 292
Deliverance (Dickey), 271
Delphi Oracle, 87–89, 97–98, 325–26*n*25

"Delta Autumn" (Faulkner), 270–71
Desire
    and biology of sex, 44–45
    and Greeks and Romans, 99–131
    as hunger of hunter, 30
    as lack, 129–31, 327n6
    vs. love, 106
    and opposition and conflict, 78
    in Middle Ages and Renaissance, 173–203
    as transformation, 62
Detienne, Marcel, 323n5, 329n20
Diana, 16, 104, 107, 109, 111, 121, 127, 158, 164
    and Acteon, 112, 115–19, 123, 192
    vs. Venus, 125, 329n20
Diana and the Stag (statue), 168
Diane de Poitiers, 16, 129, 168
Dickey, James, 271
Diderot, 37
Dido of Carthage, 79–80, 101, 123–28, 177
Dillard, Annie, 268
Dionysus, 107, 111, 118–19, 121, 125, 174, 192, 311
Diotima, 120
Distance
    emotional, 186–87, 197–98
    from self, 293–94
Division of labor, 43–44
Divorce, 185–86, 199
Dodd, Wesley Allen, 275
Doe, 113, 140
    white, 188
Domination
    and American wilderness, 266
    erotic, and Orion myth, 76–77
    and overt power, 291
    and sex and cave art, 58–59
    and sexual hunt, 102, 110, 112, 117, 185
    and Tristan, 177–78
Don Quixote (Cervantes), 168
Dragon, 87–88, 97, 189
Du Bellay, 190

Eagleton, Terence, 61
Echo, 111

Education
    attack on hunting as, 151–52
    in Greece, 68–73
    sexual, in courtly love, 190–92
    See also Boys, education of
Edward, second duke of York, 150
Edward II, King of England, 141
Effeminacy, 215, 226
Elephant hunting, 222, 239
Elizabeth I, Queen of England, 16, 141, 168, 191–92
Elk, 245, 246, 247
Emotions
    and big-game hunter, 240
    and courtly love, 189–92
    displaced onto others, 198–200
    escape from, 172–73
    finding, 294–95
    and hunting and sex images, 57–58
    inability to talk about, 294
    reclaiming, 202–3
    vs. sex, 186–87
Empire of Nature, The (MacKenzie), 218
"Enemy," 78, 102, 311
    and Apollo, 88, 90
    and intimacy, 293
Enkidu, 95–97
Enoogoo, Willy, 3–6, 11–16, 21–22
Eos, 76–77
Epic hunt. *See* Heroic hunt
Epic of Gilgamesh, The, 95–97
Erasmus, 316
Erastes, 68
Eromenos, 68
Erotic or sexual hunt, 311
    in ancient Greece and Rome, 99–131
    vs. epic hunt, 124–28, 174, 176, 178, 181–82
    hero victimized by, 118
    and hunter becoming hunted, 122–23
    and love, 120–21
    metaphors of, in language, 9–10
    in Middle Ages and Renaissance, 174–203
    predation as culmination of, 273
    subordinated to heroic hunt, 127
    psychology of, 327n6

and wounding of female, 35
See also Sexual predator.
Erymanthus, 83
Eskimos, 46. *See* Chupik Eskimos;
    Inuit
Estrus, loss of, 44–45
Eugenics, 227
Euripedes, 118
Europa, 311
Eustace, Saint (Placidus), 157–59, 160,
    315
Euthydemus (Plato), 90
Evolution
    hunting and, 29–30, 41–47, 320–21*nn*
    scavenging and, 49–54

Falconry, 161, 168, 169
Falstaff (character), 164–67, 192
Family, 44
Family, Sex and Marriage in England,
    1500–1800, The (Stone), 193
Fatal Attraction (film), 273
Father, 291–92
    learning hunting from, 25–26
    men haunted by victims of, 253–54
    wound from, 302–3
Faulkner, William, 270–71
Fear of female, and trophies, 228
Fear of sexuality, 181–84
    and cuckold, 192–98
Female
    body, as habitat of sex, 183
    in cave art, 56, 59, 60–61
    as erotic hunter, in Ovid, 174
    as "other," 122–23
    power of, and Diana, 114
    role, and erotic hunt, 110–11
    unconscious hostility to desired, 233
    See also "Other"; Women
Feminists, 273, 278, 311
    on Greek myths, 89, 326*n*25
    on hunting, 246, 322*n*18
    and men's movement, 301–2
    and prehistorians, 52
Feminization of culture, 213–15, 229
Feminized landscape, 268
Ferdinand of Aragon, 149
Fielding, Henry, 207, 336–37*n*3

Filson, John, 264, 266, 342*n*28
Fire in the Belly (Keen), 34
Five Years in a Hunter's Life in the In-
    terior of South Africa (Cumming),
    218
Flint, Timothy, 266
Fonda, Jane, 16
Fontenrose, Joseph, 87, 324–25*nn*12–13,
    325*n*22
"Forester," 136–37
Forester, Frank (Henry William Her-
    bert), 262
Forest Laws, English, 140, 161–66
Foster, Jody, 274
Foucault, Michel, 107, 122, 175, 316,
    328*n*7, 329*nn*12,18
Foullioux, Jacques de, 142
"Fourchie," 146–47
Fox, 140, 154, 205–9, 337*n*3
François I, King of France, 19, 129,
    142–43, 149
Freeman, Dr. Leslie, 47–48, 49, 53,
    55–56, 62, 63, 64
Freud, Sigmund, 122, 182, 227, 233,
    324*n*15
Froissart, Jean, 149
Frontier and frontiersman
    American hunter myth, 250–70,
    341*n*11
    clown, 261
    "last," 269–71, 285
    vanishing, 213, 215
Frye, Northrop, 185
"Fumes," 137

Gaea, 19, 75, 77, 87–89, 97, 122
Galatea, 111
Game, hierarchies of, 151, 152. *See*
    also specific animals
Game law, English, 139–40, 161–66,
    207–8
Ganymede, 111
Gascoigne, George, 132
Gatherers, 53
Gawain, 175
Gender roles, 214
    and Atalanta, 109–10
    and crime, 273

Gender roles *(cont.)*
  and trophies, 229–30
  trumped by class, 168
"Genealogy of values," 122
Genetics, 227, 275
Gentleman's Academy, The, 151–52
Gentlemen hunters, 145–48, 151–52
George, Saint, 19, 189
George V, King of England, 212
"Gifts, The" (Nelson), 301
Gilgamesh, 95–97
Gonzalez, José Luis, 84–86
Good citizen-hunter ideal, 72
Gottfried von Strassburg, 145, 146, 148, 176, 177
Goujon, Jean, 168
Grande chasse à courze de cerf, 133–37, 149, 158–61, 167–72
"Great White hunter," 215–16, 218–19, 222–23, 239
Greek myths, 16, 18, 107, 153
  of hunter, 72–79
  of hunter overcoming beast, 86–89
  and Iron John, 93–94
  and philosopher-hunter, 90–92, 97–98
Greeks, 67–92, 153, 174
  and hunting as education, 68–72
  and erotic hunt, 175
Green River Killer, 282
Griffin, Susan, 278–79
Guilt, 300, 307
  and American hero, 269
  for killing beast, 253–54
Gundestrup cauldron, 166

Hadrian, Emperor of Rome, 158
Haggard, H. Rider, 221
Hamlet (Shakespeare), 174, 195, 200
Hare, 140, 152, 154, 329*n*20, 333*n*7
  puns on, 178
Harriers, 144–45
Harris, William Cornwallis, 204
Hart, 140, 146, 155–56
  and heart, 178
Hawkes, Terence, 59, 320*n*9
Hawks, 151
Heart of the Hunter, The (Van Der Post), 318*n*3

Helios, 75, 87–88
Hemingway, Ernest, 204, 211, 230
Henri II, King of France, 129
Henry I, King of England, 162
Henry IV, part 1 (Shakespeare), 164
Henry V, King of England, 150
Henry VIII, King of England, 142
Hera, 75
Hercules, 74, 83, 102, 114, 119, 325*n*20
Hermaphroditus, 111
Hermes, 75
Herne the Hunter, 165–67
Hero
  artists as, 313, 315–16
  ethic of, defined, 72–73, 80–84
  and identity, 101–2
Heroic or epic hunter
  of American frontier, 250–51, 268
  and domination, 311
  vs. erotic hunter, 118, 124–28, 174, 176, 178, 181–82
  and evolution, 42–47
  and Greeks, 72–73, 79–89, 324*n*11
  and identity, 101–2
Heroides (Ovid), 79
Hero (mythical lover), 79
Hesiod, 67, 77
Hind, 140
Hippolytus, 111, 119, 125, 182
History of Sexuality (Foucault), 175
Homer, 74, 76, 80–81
Homeric Hymns, 87
Hominids, 37–40, 42, 44, 51–52, 53
Homoerotic pleasures, 184
Homo sapiens, 42, 64
Hoopoe (bird), 201–2, 203
Hopkins, Anthony, 273, 274
Horns, 194–95
Horse, 60, 61
Houston, Sam, 298
Hubert, Saint, 133, 135, 136, 153, 156–57, 158, 160, 330*n*4
Humans
  hunted by predatory criminals, 272, 275, 276
  native, hunted by imperialists, 230–31
Humbaba, 95–96
"Humble pie," 147

Hume, David, 90
Hunt, The (Mitchell), 251, 288
Hunted
  Dido as, 125
  as inferior, 17–18
  mutual dependency of hunter and, in Christianity, 159
  transition to hunter from, 50–51
Hunters and hunting
  and American frontier, 235, 236, 242–88
  ancient Greek and Roman, 67–92, 99–131, 153, 174
  becomes hunted, 112, 115–23, 176, 181, 294
  big-game, 71, 208, 209–41
  codes and manuals, 145–53
  and culture, 11, 43, 89, 101, 111, 121, 257, 289–90
  damage of, 310–11
  declining number of, 245
  defensiveness of modern, 251–52
  epic or heroic, 67–92, 124–28, 174, 176, 178, 181–82
  erotic or sexual, 9–10, 35, 55–62, 75, 76–78, 99–131, 174–203, 311
  as ethos, 290–92
  and Gilgamesh story, 95–97
  as male identity, 6–7, 16, 93–94 (*see also* Identity; Masculinity)
  metaphor exhausted, 311–13
  metaphors of, 8–11, 186–87, 327*n*6
  in Middle Ages, 132–72
  native, 2–4, 11–16, 19, 24–27, 299–303, 310–11
  as "natural" man, 33–34
  philosopher, 90–92, 94
  prehistoric, 7–8, 28–66
  as rape, 279, 343–44*n*48
  in Renaissance, 135, 142, 148, 151, 154–56, 164, 168, 173–203
  rights, 161–66, 168–69
  vs. scavenging, 51–52
  as sexual predator, 272–84
  vs. shaman, 315–16
  as superior, 17–18
  as stranger, 293–94

  women as, 16, 77, 79–80, 167–68, 245, 246
  See also specific societies, myths, and types of hunters and hunting
Hunters or the Hunted, The (Vrba), 50
Hunter's Wanderings in Africa, A (Selous), 222
Hurry Harry, 260, 261–62
Huxley, Thomas Henry, 90
Hyacinth, 111

Identity
  and battle or conflict, 18, 72–73, 78–79, 88–89, 93–94, 122–23
  and beast, 238–39
  and cave painting, 33
  in courtly love, 189
  and cuckold anxiety, 195, 197–98
  and desire, 101–2, 173–74, 176
  and hunting as male obsession, 34
  and industrialization, 213–14
  in Leatherstocking tales, 261
  marked by hunting in ancient world, 79–84, 323*n*5
  and marriage, 193
  and mass killers, 277–78
  new images of, 95–97
  and philosopher-hunters, 91 92
  and poaching, 165–66
  and power of hunting, 292–93
  and sexuality, 175, 176, 182, 185
Iliad, 83
Imperialism and empire, 211, 220, 221, 223–27, 230, 233–34
India, ancient, 95, 158, 166
Indians, American, 261, 264–65, 266, 298
Inferior species, 17–18, 292–93
  and identity, 78–79
Intimacy
  adversarial model for, 293
  and frontiersman, 266
  as price for strength, 293
  rediscovering, 201–2
  transition to emotional, 187
  women as teachers of, 197
Inuit (Eskimo), 2–4, 11–16, 19, 24–27, 46. *See also* Chupik Eskimos

Iphigenia, 114
Iron John (Bly), 6, 93–94
Isard hunt, 209–11, 216–17
Isidore of Seville, 105
Island Within, The (Nelson), 301
"Is Man to Culture as Woman Is to Nature?" (Ortner), 89
Isolde, 148, 176–77
Ivory, 222

Jack the Ripper, 275
James I, King of England, 141
James II, King of England, 207
James, Henry, 213–14
Johan Georg I, Elector of Saxony, 138
John, King of England, 161
John of Salisbury, 151
John of the Cross, Saint, 155
Jonson, Ben, 152
Jove, 107, 111–13, 311
Jung, Carl, 57, 302, 320*n*9
Juno, 126, 130
Jupiter, 166

Kadloo, Elijah, 3, 11–15, 22, 24
Kadloo, Lamechi, 2, 3–4, 11–15, 24–27
Kadloo, Tony, 3, 11–15
Kahn, Coppélia, 193, 334*n*9
Kedalion, 75
Keen, Sam, 34–35, 36
Kemperer, Edwin, 276
Kennedy, John F., 252
Kerasote, Ted, 52, 299–300, 303
Killdeer (rifle), 261–62
"Killer ape," 36–41, 47
Killing
   and big-game hunting, 217–19, 221, 222–24, 236, 239–40
   biological bases for, 43
   contradiction of, 172
   and control of "other," 292–93
   eroticized, in Orion myth, 76
   and frontiersmen, 268, 271
   love of, and frontier, 247–48
   of men, vs. animals, 251–53
   and modern predator, 274, 275
   as mystery, 217
   and natural history, 226

pleasure in, 45–46
psychology of, as true hunting, 237–41
quest without, 316
of something in self, 98
King, B.B., 316
Kipling, Rudyard, 212
Knight-errant, 189
Kolodny, Annette, 268, 341*n*11
Kubrick, Stanley, 40
!Kung Bushmen, 48–49

Lacan, Jacques, 327*n*6
Lancaster, C. S., 41–46
Landseer, Edwin, 224, 228
Language
   and boundaries between hunter and hunted, 198–99
   of hunt culture, 289–90
   of hunting manuals, 152
   hunting metaphors in, 8–11, 319*n*4
   loss of, 116, 117
   and love, 130
   of predation, and sexuality, 100–1
   and puns on hunting and sex, 178, 190, 191
   and sexual predator, 280
   slowness to change, 313
   as weapon, in erotic hunt, 128–29
Lardos, Jean Paul, 168, 169–70, 171
Lascaux caves, 7, 315
Last of the Mohicans, The (Cooper), 265
Laughlin, William S., 41
Laura, 187–92
Lawrence, D. H., 268
Laws (Plato), 71
Lay of the Land, The (Kolodny), 268
Leander, 79, 83
Leatherstocking tales, 256–63, 268–69, 270
Lee, R. B., 48, 49
Leicester, Earl of, 141
Lernean hydra, 83
Leroi-Gourhan, Andre, 59–61, 62
Leto, 86
Leverenz, David, 268
Lévi-Strauss, Claude, 45, 90, 320*n*9, 326*n*27
Leyton, Elliot, 275, 277–78

Lion Hunter in Africa, The (Cumming), 218–21

Lion hunting, 83, 219–25, 227, 339*n*33

"Littel Geste of Robyn Hood and his Meiny" (ballad), 163

Livre de la Chasse, Le (Book of the Hunt) (Phèbus), 148–50, 152

Livres du Roy Modus et de la Royne Ration, Les (The Books of King Method and Queen Reason), 153–54

London, Jack, 6, 215, 229–30, 291, 340*n*40

Loner in woods, 263–64, 268

Lorenz, Konrad, 275

Loss, 110–11, 122–23

Louis XII, King of France, 22

Love
    vs. desire, 129–31, 176–78, 187–92, 199
    and hunt, 61, 102–6, 109, 120–21, 178–79
    learning to experience, 202–3
    in Ovid vs. Shakespeare, 185
    See also Courtly love; Romantic love

Love's Labor's Lost (Shakespeare), 134, 190–91, 194, 335*n*20

Lucy, Sir Thomas, 164

Lysistrata (Aristophanes), 113

Machismo, 33, 86

MacKenzie, John, 218, 226, 228, 324*n*9

Maenads, 111, 118, 123

Magic, primitive, 56–57, 59

Magna Carta, 161, 162

Mailer, Norman, 255–56

Male anxiety, 6, 176

Male bonding, 43, 300–1

Male identity. *See* Identity; Masculinity

Malory, Sir Thomas, 145, 156

Man the Hunter (Lee and DeVore), 319*n*2, 321*n*12

Mark, King, 146–48, 176–78

Market hunger, 267

Marks, Stuart, 229

Marriage, 106, 107, 192–98

Mars, 111, 130–31

Marten, 140

Marvell, Andrew, 175, 190

Mary Queen of Scots, 16

"Masculine mystique," 229

Masculinities and Crime (Messerschmidt), 273

Masculinity (maleness, manhood)
    American frontier myth, 251–56, 259–61, 266
    and American hunter-hero, 268, 337*n*10
    and American violence, 251–52, 277–78
    and animal totem, 34
    and beast as metaphor, 238–39
    and big-game hunting, 210–11, 215–16, 217, 218, 221–41
    and cuckold's horns, 194–95
    and desire, 173, 175–76, 178
    and ethos and power of hunting metaphor, 290–95
    and evolutionary legacy of hunting, 29–30, 36, 41–47, 52, 320–21*nn*
    feudal, and books of hunt, 150
    and foxhunting, 207
    and Gilgamesh story, 96–97
    and Greeks, 68–69, 72–73
    hunter as idealized model of, 34
    and hunting in Greece, 68–73
    and men's movement, 93–94, 302
    and metaphor of hunter, 8–11
    and nationality, 208
    and native cultures, 301–2
    new paths for, 294–95
    and Orion, 20–21, 76, 79
    in Petrarch's love, 189
    and prehistoric archetypes, 34, 48–49, 57
    redefinition of, in American culture, 6
    and scouting, 211–13
    and sexual predator, 279–80
    as shaping of life, 236–37
    and trophies, 227–30

Mass murderers, 273, 275–76

Master of Game, The (manual), 150

Meade, Michael, 302, 303

Meditations on Hunting (Ortega y Gasset), 33

Medusa, 83

Melanion, the "Black Hunter," 113, 328*n*10

Meleager, 83, 110–12
Melville, Herman, 230, 268
Men of feeling vs. men of action, 316
Ménoni, Emmanuel, 133–37, 144, 158–60, 167–72
Men's Journal, 234
Men's movement, 6, 34, 57, 93–94, 213, 301–3
Menstrual blood, 58
Merchant of Venice, The (Shakespeare), 197
Merope, Princess of Chios, 75
Merry Wives of Windsor, The (Shakespeare), 164–65, 192, 197
Messerschmidt, James, 273
Metamorphoses (Ovid), 107, 111, 112, 115, 130
Metaphor, defined, 10, 319*n*4
Meynell, Hugo, 205
Middle Ages, 206
    desire in, 173–203
    social order in, 132–72
Millais, J. G., 221
Miller, Eric, 295–97, 303, 307–9
"Missing link," 37
Mitchell, John, 242, 251–54, 256, 288
Mohnejodaro, 166
Monarchs, 137–44
Monogamous sex, 45
Montaigne, Michel de, 193–94, 197
More, Sir Thomas, 132, 316, 330*n*2
Morris, Desmond, 46
Morrison, Van, 316
Morte Darthur, Le (Malory), 145, 156
Mourning doves, 245
Much Ado about Nothing (Shakespeare), 195, 197
"My Breath" (poem), 1, 5
Myth
    as cultural response, 94–95
    defined, 19–20, 320*n*9
    enduring nature of, 119

Naked Ape, The (Morris), 46
Narcissus, 101, 111
Narwhal hunt, 2–4, 11–16, 21–27
Nationalism, 207, 211, 215, 220
National Rifle Association (NRA), 276

Native hunters, 299–303, 310–11, 318*nn.*
    See also specific groups
Natural history, 226
"Natural" man, 33–34
Nature, 7
    American response to, 342*n*28
    asserting superiority over, 88–90
    control of, and empire, 226–27
    -culture link, 11, 20
    good vs. bad, 154
    and prehistoric hunter, 33
    recovering closeness with, 201
    and sexual hunt, 179–81, 190
    and Social Darwinism, 223–24
    woman and, 110–11, 117, 122–23
Neanderthals, 42
Nelson, Richard, 301, 303, 311
Nemean lion, 83
Nets, 71, 104, 130–31
Nibelungenlied, 154
Nimrod, 95, 153, 325*n*21
Nobility, 141–42, 162, 164
Noble savage, 37
Nocturnal hunting, 74–75
Nonnos, 328–29*n*11
Notker the Stammerer, 138, 139
"Numbles," 147

Odysseus, 19, 80–83, 86, 93, 98, 102, 325*n*19
Odyssey (Homer), 74, 76, 81, 93
Oedipus, 91–92
Oinopion, King of Chios, 75
Old Testament, 95, 156
Olduvai Gorge bones, 51
"On Hunting" (Xenophon), 67–70, 86, 103, 316, 323–24*n*6
"Ordeal of the Spear, The" (Baden-Powell), 230–33
Orion, 18–21, 73–79, 83, 86, 102, 174, 291, 324–25*nn*
    and Artemis, 76–78, 112
    birth of, 75
    blindness of, 76, 98
    and Maenads, 111
    and modern male, 94
    and Pleiades, 78–79
    and sexual violence, 75–76, 272

Orpingalik (poet), 5, 289
Ortega y Gasset, José, 7, 17, 33–34, 92, 237, 292
Ortner, Sherry B., 89
Oryx, 239
Oswald, Lee Harvey, 252
Othello (Shakespeare), 195–97
"Other," 334*n*16
    closeness with, 201–3
    creation of, and hunter vs. hunted, 198–99
    and hunting as desire, 121–23
    identity through conflict with, 18, 88–89, 93–94, 292–93
    and men's movement, 303
    as victim, 238
Otter, 154
"Outlaws," 163–64
Ovid, 77, 79, 99, 101–19, 123–25, 127, 130, 174, 181
    vs. Shakespeare, 184, 185

Packwood, Robert, 101, 274
Paleolithic culture, 42
    and bulls, 32, 33, 35
    and magic, 57, 59–60
    role of hunting in, 47–54
Pan, 111
Panzram, Carl, 277
Parke, H. W., 88
Partridge, 140
Pashupati, 166
Passenger pigeon, 260, 267
Passerat, Jean, 190
Patriarchy, 302
Peneus, 109
Penia, 120
Penis, and cave art, 32, 35
Pentheus, 111, 118, 119, 123, 182, 192, 291
Pepin, King of Franks, 138–39
Perseus, 19, 74, 83
Persians, 71, 95
Personal myth, 278
Petrarch, Francis, 187–89, 192, 334*n*16
Phaedra, 80
Pheasant, 140, 205

Phèbus, Gaston, 140–41, 148–49, 150, 152, 154, 156, 162, 331–32*n*20
Philip the Bold, 149
Philosopher-hunter, 90–92, 94, 324*n*10
Phoebe (goddess), 109
Picus, 111
Pig-sticking, 231–33
Pioneers, The (Cooper), 257–58
Plato, 17, 71–74, 90–92, 96, 119, 120–21, 324*n*10
Pleiades, 20, 21, 78
Poaching, 161–66, 208, 244–48
Policraticus (John of Salisbury), 151
Political power
    and medieval hunt, 137–44
    and spiritual longing, 156–57
Politicians, 69
Polyphemus, 111
Poros, 120
Poseidon, 75
Power
    and American frontier, 256
    created by hunt, 17–18
    and desire, 185, 191–92, 328*n*7
    distribution of, in Middle Ages, 146–48
    of flung spear, and sex, 34–35
    hunting as justification for male, 52
    and love, 120–21
    of nature, 241
    and Orion's blindness, 76
    overt vs. covert, 291–94
    and prostitution, 281
    and rape, 279
    vs. sensitivity, 16–17
    between sexes, 45
    and sexual hunt, 102–3, 106–13, 117–19
    and weapons, 93–94
Praeda, 103
Predatory sex, 35, 100–31
    modern criminal, 272–84, 311
    in Ovid, 102–6
Prehistoric hunters, 28–66, 321–22*nn*
Prey
    control of, 293
    preferred, of Greek heroes, 83
    See also Women, as prey
Procris, 111, 112

Promise Is a Promise, A (Inuit story), 26
Propertius, 120
Prostitution, 280–84
Pulp Fiction (film), 274
Python, 87–88, 97–98, 108, 119
Python (Fontenrose), 87

Quail, 245
"Quarry," 147, 150
Quorn hounds, 205, 337n3

Racism, 215–16, 221, 225–26, 229
Raleigh, Sir Walter, 212
Rape
    and American hero, 268, 271
    and Apollo and Daphne, 110
    hunting as, 279, 343–44n48
    and hunt metaphor, 101, 107
    and masculine self-definition, 278–79, 284
    and Orion, 75–78
    and serial killers, 275–80
    and sexual predator, 272
    victims of, 281–84
"Rape of Lucrece, The" (Shakespeare), 272
Rasmussen, Knud, 5
Rationality, 90–92, 95, 97–98
Read, Herbert, 56–57
Red deer, 48, 170. *See also* Stag
Reindeer, 57
Relationship
    vs. desire, 129–31
    vs. opposition model, 78–79
    and reclaiming emotions, 199–203
"Remasculinization," 302
Renaissance, 22, 71, 316
    desire in, 173–203
    social class in, 135, 142, 148, 151, 154–56, 164, 168
    women hunters in, 16
Republic (Plato), 91
Richard Coeur de Lion, 212
Richard III (Shakespeare), 155
Rifle, 261–62
Rilke, Rainer Maria, 23
Rime (Petrarch), 187

Ritvo, Harriet, 218, 221
Roberts, Janne Addison, 334n10
Robin hood, 162, 163, 167
Roe deer, 140, 154
Roethke, Theodore, 199
Romans, 16, 79, 92, 95, 102–7, 120, 124, 174
Romantic love
    vs. erotic hunt, 106
    in Renaissance, 190–91
Romeo and Juliet (Shakespeare), 178, 187–88
Ronsard, Jean, 190
Roosevelt, Theodore, 213–15, 222, 235, 251, 266–67, 291, 292, 316, 342n30
Rose, Mary Beth, 335n19
Rothschild, Baron Lionel, 222
Rousseau, Jean-Jacques, 37

Sade, Marquis de, 275
Salamacis story, 111
Salmons, Josephine, 36, 37
Samson, 75
Sandie (performance artist), 99–100, 106
"Scavenging hypothesis," 51, 322n25
Science
    and big game hunting, 233–34
    and hunting/maleness link, 28–30, 340n38
Scouting for Boys (Seton), 211–12
Sea-Wolf, The (London), 229–30, 340n40
Self
    definition of, and hunting, 5, 7
    discovery of, through love and desire, 175, 178–79, 181–85
    as price for power, 293–95
    as set of relationships, 65
Selous, Frederick Courtenay, 212, 218, 221–28, 239–40, 292
Selous Scouts, 212
Serial killers, 273, 275–76, 282, 284
Serpent, 155–56
Seton, Ernest Thompson, 211–13, 343n31
Settler vs. hunter, 254, 259–60, 262, 266–67
Sex and sexuality

and death, 184–85
and harassment, 101, 273
and language of hunt, 128–29
male aggression in, 52
and Orion, 75–78
and poaching, 164–65, 167
and power, 328n7
and prehistoric culture, 32–35, 44–45, 54–62
in Shakespeare, 181–82
and violence, 61, 75, 100, 272–84
as wounding of female, 35, 58–59, 61
See also Desire; Erotic hunt; Predatory sex
Shakespeare, 103, 120, 125, 134–36, 155, 164, 173, 174, 178–85, 187, 190–97, 272, 335–36nn
Shaman, 26, 315–16
Shavings, Ed, 295, 297–99, 303–10, 313–14, 316, 317
Shawnee Indians, 264, 265
Shellfish gathering, 49, 53
Shepard, Paul, 28, 29, 57–58
Shipman, Pat, 51
Shiva, 166
"Short Happy Life of Francis Macomber, The" (Hemingway), 230
Side, 75
Silence of the Lambs (film), 273, 274
Simpson, O.J., 100–1, 197, 274
Skorpion, 78
Slotkin, Richard, 265–66, 268, 341n11, 342n28
Smith, Henry Nash, 341n11
Snipes, R. G., 288
Social class or order, 71, 324n9
  in ancient world, 70–71, 79–84, 91
  and Celtic "horned one", 166–67
  and forest laws, 139–40, 161–66
  and foxhunting, 207
  and gender, 168
  and hawks for each class, 151
  and Middle Ages, 136, 137, 139–48
  and modern Europe, 168–69
  and poaching, 164–66
  and spiritual symbolism, 154
  and styles of hunting, 229

and types of game, 151–52, 154–55
Social Darwinism, 215, 222–25, 227, 229, 233, 238, 239–40, 277
Socrates, 67, 91, 120, 121, 281
Somerville, William, 141
"Songs of the Snow-Hut" (poems), 5
Sophist, The (Plato), 120–21
Sophists, 69, 70
Sophocles, 91, 92
Southern Hunting in Black and White (Marks), 229
Spenser, Edmund, 120, 190
Spirituality, 23–24, 153–59, 300–2, 306–7, 315–16
Sport in War (Baden-Powell), 230
Springboks, 219
Squirrels, 245
Stag *(cerf)*
  breakup or "undoing" of, 146–48
  and Cernunnos, 166–67
  and Christianity, 133, 154–58
  and hierarchy of game, 152, 154
  and Medieval hunt, 133–37, 144–45, 159–61
  and modern hunt, 168–72
Stag of love (*le cerf d'amour*), 177
Stone, Lawrence, 193
Strabo, 68, 323n5
"Strenuous Life, The" (Roosevelt), 214
Structuralists, 59–61
Subsistence hunters, 310–11
Sulpicia, 101, 106, 327n2
Surtees, R. S., 207, 337n3
Symposium (Plato), 120
Syrinx, 111

Taurus, 20, 21, 73, 74, 78
Ten Commandments, 155
Tender Carnivore and the Sacred Game, The (Shepard), 57
Testicles, as trophy, 171, 217
Themis, 88
Thereutes, 90
Theseus, 74
Thoreau, Henry David, 268
Tibullus, 99, 101, 120
Tom Jones (Fielding), 207, 336–37n3
"To Pythian Apollo," 87

Trajan, Emperor of Rome, 157
Travel and Adventure in South-East Africa (Selous), 222
Treasures of Prehistoric Art (Leroi-Gourham), 60–61
Tristan, 315
  and code of hunt, 145–48, 162
  and erotic hunt, 176–78, 292
Tristan and Isolde (Gottfried von Strassburg), 145–48
Troilus and Cressida (Shakespeare), 135–36, 178
Trophies, 227–29, 232–34, 239, 247, 253–54
  and serial killers, 276
"Trysting" place, 150
Turberville, George, 155–56, 330*n*3
Turner, Frederick Jackson, 213
Turnus, 126
2001: A Space Odyssey (film), 40
Tyrell, William Blake, 328*n*9

Unicorn, 21, 22, 23–24
United States, 16, 244–45. *See also* American frontier

Van Der Post, Laurens, 7, 319*n*3
Venus, 111, 119, 124–27, 130–31, 174, 178, 315
"Venus and Adonis" (Shakespeare), 181–85, 329*n*20, 334*nn*
Vermin, 154
Victorians, 218–27, 238
Vietnam war, 255–56
Violence
  and American hero-hunters, 251–53, 255–56, 260, 269–70
  attractiveness of, 311
  and big-game hunting, 218, 221, 222–24, 227, 233–34
  as discipline for boys, 215
  and erotic hunt, 107, 279
  of father, 302–3
  glorification of, 277–78, 288
  and hunting, 40, 46, 52
  and Iron John, 94
  men's pleasure in, 45–46
  as natural, 290

rationalization of, 92, 97–98
sexual, and Orion, 75, 76–77
urban sexual, 274–80
Virgil, 101, 123–28
Virginian, The (Wister), 215
Vrba, Elisabeth, 50
Vulcan, 130

Wallace, A. R., 223
Walrus hunt, 295, 297–99, 304–10, 313–14, 316–17
War, 17, 38, 39, 46
Washburn, Sherwood L., 41–42, 43–46
Water of Life, The (Meade), 302
Wayne, John, 276
Way of Animal Powers, The (Campbell), 316
Weapons
  and the hunter, 293–94
  inventing, and evolution, 43
  love of, 247
  power through, 93–94
Wheeler, Richard P., 335*n*20
White, T. H., 201
White man, and native cultures, 298–300, 303
Whorf, Benjamin, 10
Why Are We in Vietnam (Mailer), 255
Wilbur, Richard, 129
Wilderness Hunter, The (Roosevelt), 266
Wilderness myth, 266, 269
Wild man, 93–94
Williams, Jeff, 243–44, 247–48
Williams, William Carlos, 298
William the Conqueror, 139–40, 161, 162
Wilson, Edward O., 275
Winter's Tale, The (Shakespeare), 178, 197
Wister, Owen, 215
Wolf, 140, 154, 284–86
Wolverine, 286–88
Woman and Nature (Griffin), 278
Woman the Gatherer (Dahlberg), 52–53
Woman within, 214–15

Women
and big-game hunting, 225, 230, 231–33
and Christian desire, 175–76
"continuous receptivity" of, 44–45
desire to be captured, 104–5
and division of labor, 43–44
domination of, 117–19
as "enemy," 78
hunting by, 16, 79–80, 167–68, 245, 246, 339n33
men's emotions displaced onto, 198–99
men's fears about, 192–98, 323n5
as other, 123
power of, in courtly love, 191–92
as prey, 58–59, 61, 100, 102–6, 108–11, 277–79, 276–79, 337n3
rising strength of, 213–14

as sexual hunters, 101
and trophies, 228, 230–33
Wound
and Bly, 94
in cave art, 57, 60–61
cultural, in men's psyches, 98
and father, 302–3
and hero, 81–82
and the hunter, 293–94
and menstrual blood, 58
and waste, 310–11
Wyatt, Sir Thomas, 189–90

Xenophon, 67–73, 77, 83, 86, 95, 96, 103, 119, 292, 316, 323–24nn

Zeus, 73, 75, 77, 78, 86